SLUM LIFE RISING

How to Enflesh Hope within a New Urban World

ASH BARKER

Urban Shalom Publishing
The Gospel and the Future of Cities

Urban Shalom Publishing
Newbigin House
28 Handsworth New Road
Winson Green
Birmingham
B18 4PT
United Kingdom

Unless otherwise stated., the Scripture quotations contained herein are from the New Revised Standard Version of the Bible, Anglicized Edition, © 1989, 1995 by the division of Christian Education of the National Council of the Churches of Christ in the United States of America, and are used by permission. All rights reserved.

Copyright © 2012 by Ash Barker

Urban Shalom Publishing

All rights reserved. No part of this publication may be reproduced, stored in a retrieval system, or transmitted in any form or by any means - electronic, mechanical, photocopy, recording, or any other - except for brief quotations in printed review, without prior permission of the publisher.

Editor: Craig Brown
Design: Les Colston   les@urbanzeal.com.au
Cover photos: *Boy* - Jackie Rado   www.jackieradophotography.com;
Klong Toey rooftops - Rod Sheard

This important book wrestles with one of the most urgent tasks for contemporary Christian mission. It combines solid biblical/theological reflection with gut-wrenching practical experience. Barker lives what he preaches.

Ronald J. Sider, President,
Evangelicals for Social Action & Professor of Theology,
Public Policy & Holistic Ministry at Palmer Seminary at Eastern University

Ash Barker is now regarded as one of the foremost theological and missional thinkers regarding the transformation of slum communities in the Majority world. This book is the product of careful scholarship and long-term practical engagement. This hopeful book will become a standard text book for all involved in Third world urban mission.

Emeritus Prof. Charles Ringma,
Regent College, Vancouver; Asian Theological Seminary, Manila;
and The University of Queensland, Brisbane

Anyone who takes seriously Christ's call to love our neighbors as ourselves has reason to care about slums because a larger and larger percentage of our neighbors live there. This is the book I wish I had read before my first visit to a slum - and this is the book that will serve as indispensable background to all future engagement. Nobody could ask for a better guide than Ash Barker. With his guidance, more and more of us can love our neighbors more wisely and well, following the One whose incarnation makes the slums a place to love, not shun.

Brian McLaren,
Author, speaker (brianmclaren.net)

This timely publication by Ash Barker on the current issues and challenges of the rising crisis of the slums and squatter settlements of the twenty-first century is meticulously researched; yet is riveted in over twenty years of living and serving Christ among the urban poor.

Through the compassionate eyes of this urban missionary, the reader is presented with an incarnational missional model of enfleshing hope that serves as a vehicle of transformation to the fringe-dwellers living in the heaving cities of the majority world: removing social inertias to change living conditions, bringing people to a living faith in Christ, and alleviating the crippling cycle of injustice and poverty.

This book should be compulsory reading for any scholar, student, or practitioner committed to living faithfully and missionally to the urban marginalized and powerless.

Robert L. Gallagher, Ph.D.
Associate Professor and Chair of Intercultural Studies
Wheaton College Graduate School
Wheaton, Illinois

This book gains its strength from Ash Barker's actual involvement in the Klong Toey slums over many years and his personal knowledge provides gravitas to the excellent theoretical discussions of serious issues relating to slum and squatter neighbourhoods. It includes an original contribution to the theory of incarnational mission and, altogether, it is a distinctive contribution to an important field by a well-read, articulate and thoughtful practitioner.

Brian Edgar, Professor of Theological Studies,
Asbury Theological Seminary http://brian-edgar.com/

From his own vocational calling living among slum-dwellers, Barker offers a compelling apologia for incarnational ministry in the slums of the world's cities--an enormous demographic challenge and unfinished business for Christian mission in the 21st century.

Todd M. Johnson, Associate Professor in Global Christianity,
Gordon-Conwell Theological Seminary, South Hamilton, Massachusetts

In this careful but passionate study of how Christians can engage with urban slums Ash Barker grounds the idea of incarnational mission with a punch. He speaks out of the slums, where he is exploring the meaning of Christ's presence and Good News. Slum Life Rising is the wonderful fruit of reflective practice. I'm so glad Ash made time, in the midst of rolling up his sleeves, to ask what is happening and why, and to suggest what could happen and how. I trust many will read it and be deeply challenged to enflesh hope amongst the world's urban poor.

Dr Ross Langmead is Professor of Missiology at Whitley College in the MCD University of Divinity, Melbourne, Australia.

Slum Life Rising is a gift to us all. It is incredibly rare that an author is a scholar, practitioner, theologian and an engaging writer and Ash Barker is all of those things. He is the real deal! This book should put to rest once and for all any debate or concern over the legitimacy of the incarnational model of ministry. I am thrilled to be part of a new partnership that is sending undergrad students to learn, live and work in the slums with Ash and UNOH where they learn first hand this "enfleshing hope".

Kendi Howells Douglas,
Professor of Cross Cultural Ministry,
Great Lakes Christian College - Lansing Michigan, USA

In 2009, the world's population shifted from being primarily rural to primarily urban. Building upon a decade of life and reflection in Bangkok's Klong Toey slum, Ash Barker's *Slum Life Rising* is a helpful guide for Christians wanting to understand the meaning of their faith in an urban world, and particularly in the rapidly growing slums and squatter neighborhoods. Barker has a deep theological mooring and is a perfect guide for reflection on the urban realities of our times. This is the book to read if you as a Christian want to understand what slums and squatter neighborhoods are and to imagine what it might look like for Christ to be incarnated in these emerging urban places.'

C. Christopher Smith,
The Englewood Review of Books,
Indianapolis, IN

Christians have always been on the side of the poor but often Christians in the west have little practical experience of what that might mean. Ash Barker and his family offer a living demonstration of what a practical involvement might look like. More importantly their pioneering work has created a framework to allow others to join them on this key mission frontier. Creativity, passion, commitment, the crossing of boundaries, all these and more are present in abundance in the Barker's inspiring story.

Martin Robinson,
National Director of Together in Mission

In the late 1970's Ron Sider's book *Rich Christians in an Age of Hunger* helped to awaken a sleeping Evangelical community to God's heart for those living in poverty. *Slum Life Rising* is a 21st century manifestation of *Rich Christians in an age of Hunger*. In these pages Ash Barker carefully explores the explosive growth of slum communities in the Majority World and the sluggish response of churches, governments and NGO's to this alarming demographic. But far from an ivory tower analysis written from a clinical distance, Ash punctuates his writing with stories of his friends and neighbors in Klong Toey, one of Bangkok's largest slums, where he and his family live. As *Rich Christians* sounded an alarm to a previous generation, this work will awaken the next generation to the realities faced by our neighbors living in slum communities in the Majority World.

Scott Bessenecker,
Associate Director of Missions for InterVarsity/USA and author of The New Friars

Karl Barth famously said that we need to take our Bible and our newspaper and read both, interpreting the newspaper from the Bible. How can we begin to grasp the reality of one million slum dwellers, and rising, interpreting this reality through the Good News.? Ash helps us do just this in *Slum Life Rising*. If you want to grapple with the meaning of the Good News among the world's urban poor (and for all of us who are neighbors with them), this book is for you. Looking through the lens of his family's experience in the Klong Toey,, but drawing also from his research and the disciplines of missiology and practical theology, Ash guides us through the terrain of slum life rising. The reality is upon us -- we can put our heads in the sand, or ask God what he requires of us.'

Jude Tiersma Watson, member of InnerChange: A Christian Order Among the Poor
Associate Professor of Urban Mission School of Intercultural Studies,
Fuller Theological Seminary, Pasadena, CA 91182

Slum Life Rising is the most challenging book I have read for a long time. Ash Barker explores the demographic, development, theological, personal and teamwork challenges of responding to the appalling 'perfect storm' of poverty found in urban slum and squatter settlements. I will be steering my church leaders and mission students to read and digest it, and ask of one another, 'what are we going to do about it?' Jesus stood in the gap for those on the margins who needed healing and respect, and I love that about Jesus. Ash Barker is standing in the gap to advocate for and humanise a largely ignored group of people and neighbourhoods, and I love that about him and his recent and most significant book.

Darren Cronshaw,
Pastor, Auburn Baptist Church and Baptist Union of Victoria
Honorary Research Associate, Whitley College (MCD University of Divinity)
Associate Professor of Missiology, Australian College of Ministries (SCD)

The rapid rise of urban slums is one of the great challenges of our time. Ash Barker and the UNOH revolution invite us to hear, smell, and touch Jesus in his most distressing disguises in these most abandoned places of empire. By finding and enfleshing hope here, we can see a better world emerge.

Shane Claiborne,
The Simple Way, Philadelphia

Contents

Forewords ... 9

Preface ... 13

Introduction ... 19

Urban Encounters: Stories and questions for preparation ... 31

Part A:
WHAT IS HAPPENING WITH URBAN SLUM AND SQUATTER NEIGHBOURHOODS? THEIR NATURE, SUDDEN RISE, CHALLENGES AND CHRISTIAN IMPACT.

Chapter 1:
Introducing Urban Slum and Squatter Neighbourhoods Through Klong Toey ... 37

Chapter 2:
The Nature of Urban Slum and Squatter Neighbourhoods in the Twenty-first Century ... 57

Chapter 3:
What Are Christians Doing? The Current State of Christian Response to the Rise of Urban Slum and Squatter Neighbourhoods ... 77

Urban Encounters: Stories and questions to engage Part A ... 101

Part B:
WHY ARE URBAN SLUM AND SQUATTER NEIGHBOURHOODS SUCH A CHALLENGE TO CHRISTIAN FAITH AND MISSION?

Chapter 4:
Klong Toey and Barriers to Transformation in Urban Slum and Squatter Neighbourhoods ... 107

Chapter 5:
Unenfleshed: Rejections of incarnational approaches to mission ... 129

Chapter 6:
More Literally Incarnational: A specific missional methodology or model to emulate ... 139

Chapter 7:
Too Figuratively Incarnational: One value among many in Christian mission ... 159

Urban Encounters: Stories and questions to engage Part B ... 167

Part C:
WHAT OUGHT TO HAPPEN? TOWARD A TRINITARIAN INCARNATIONAL THEOLOGY OF URBAN SLUM AND SQUATTER NEIGHBOURHOOD TRANSFORMATION

Chapter 8:
The Creator Incarnates: Joining God's invitation to make real creation's promise   173

Chapter 9:
The Redeemer Incarnates: Following the risen Jesus into the hidden life of urban slums   183

Chapter 10:
The Advocate Incarnates: Participating with the Spirit's transformative presence in slums   195

Urban Encounters: Stories and questions to engage Part C   211

Part D:
TOWARD ENFLESHED HOPE IN URBAN SLUM AND SQUATTER NEIGHBOURHOODS

Chapter 11:
An Incarnational Approach to Teams Based in Slum and Squatter Neighbourhoods   219

Chapter 12:
An Incarnational Approach to Local and Relational 'Place-Sharing'   233

Chapter 13:
An Incarnational Approach to Urban Poverty Alleviation   247

Urban Encounters: Stories and questions to engage Part D   279

Conclusion: 285

Notes: 289

Bibliography: 315

Foreword

Many of us are acquainted with the translation of John 1:14 in Eugene Peterson's version of the Bible that reads: "The Word became flesh and blood and moved into the neighborhood." The Barkers are a family that has imitated Jesus and has done just that. That have moved into Klong Toey—the largest slum in Bangkok. There they have chosen to live out the Gospel in remarkable ways, and this book will give you some insights as to how they have done this. Not too long ago, I saw a television show about the Barkers that was shown nationwide on the Australian Broadcasting Corporation network, and I was amazed at how this attractive couple, along with their children, chose to commit their lives to dwelling in the midst of this crowded slum in Thailand.

This book, however, is much more than an inspiring story of a heroic family. It is also a description of how Christians can be instruments of social change, making significant differences in the lives of those who become their neighbors in Klong Toey. As you read through this book, you will learn how a missionary couple not only lived out the Gospel in word, but also did so in ways that attacked some of the root causes of poverty.

Poverty is much more than simply a failure to have enough money to adequately provide for the necessities of everyday living. It is a social-psychological condition that emerges out of a subculture. The controversial anthropologist, Oscar Lewis, provided a description of that subculture and outlined the characteristics of the consciousness of those who are socialised into what he called "The Culture of Poverty." Those who have been socialised into this subculture exhibit an array of characteristics that fight against their ability to surmount the social and psychological hindrances to achieving economic success and emotional well being. These include a negative self concept and lack of confidence that they can make their lives better.

The culture of poverty is marked by illiteracy, which in turn, creates a self-concept of inadequacy and generates anger among the illiterate toward those who have information power over them. Lack of literacy closes many people out of a job market that usually requires that applicants know how to read and write.

Those who work among the poor soon come to realise that it is easier to eliminate poverty than it is to eliminate the culture of poverty. The latter requires the creation of a whole new *weltenschaung* (world view). Eliminating the culture of poverty requires a conscious change so profound that some would claim that making this happen would require something akin to a miracle. But such a miracle is exactly what many of us believe is possible through religious conversion and spiritual nurture.

Religious conversion can meet this need. I believe that with God's help, it is possible to overcome the feelings of personal inadequacy and inferiority characteristic of those who have been socialised into the culture of poverty. Through personal conversion, a person can come to affirm God as the most important significant other in his or her life. Such an individual is likely to develop a positive self-image. In conversion, the person can embrace a whole new definition of self by coming to believe the good things he or she thinks that God thinks of him or her.

I believe it is fair to conclude that, when someone comes into a relationship with God whereby a new and positive self-concept is gained, such an individual will experience enhanced possibilities for success in all areas of life. The convert subsequently will become psychologically prepared for successful ventures in his or her economic endeavors. For instance, conversion can be an important factor in generating the desire and confidence necessary to become literate.

To those who are illiterate, reading seems like an awesome ability that is beyond them. Overcoming the sense that they lack the intelligence that reading requires can be a side effect of conversion. Being related to Christ through faith is one of the best confidence builders imaginable. Converts are convinced that "with God, all things are possible!" (Matthew 19:26). By becoming part of a church, they gain a fellowship with other Christians who can be there to encourage them and even to help them along in their lessons.

The Barkers have no illusions that simply getting poor people converted to Christ is all that is necessary to transform a community like Klong Toey into a societal system that evidences the signs of the Kingdom of God (i.e., a glimpse of what that Kingdom might look like can be found in Isaiah 65:17-25 and Zachariah 8:4-5; 20-23). They know that there must be changes in the political and economic structures of the societal system, in this case Thailand, which will have effects that will impact what happens in Klong Toey. Wrestling against those "principalities and powers" (Ephesians 6:12) so that something of God's social justice becomes a reality for those who live in this slum is an absolute necessity. Encouraging those who work for social justice on the macro level of Thailand's society is very much a part of their ministry, but they themselves have heeded the call of Christ to work for change on the micro level. With engagement in the everyday struggles of those who are their neighbors in Klong Toey; through literacy programs with children; through sharing Christ all day long in an ongoing ministry, in which they sometimes use words; they have chosen to be the "leaven" that can permeate their slum community (Matthew 13:33) and be godly instruments for social change. As crucial as are the efforts that address the structural evils that create slums, they see themselves as taking on Christ's challenge to be the "salt" (Matthew 5:13) that alters the flavor of Klong Toey, hoping to enable persons transformed by Christ's love to become participants with Christ in transforming the society in which they live. They know the words of an old hymn that goes:

> *For not with swords loud clashing,*
> *nor roll of stirring drums;*
> *with deeds of love and mercy*
> *the heavenly kingdom comes.*

Tony Campolo
Eastern University
St. Davids, Pennsylvania, USA

Foreword

Slums are the festering wounds of the big family of human beings spread across the world. Slums in Asia, in Africa, and in Latin America have a population of over one billion people and are increasing daily by nearly 100,000 people. Slums are places of extreme material and cultural poverty. They are places of discouragement and of despair. The basic family unit is hurt, many children do not know their fathers, drugs and alcohol are rampant; they bring some relief to the anguish and loss of identity. Many slums are controlled by Mafia groups who prevent humanisation.

Slums can appear impenetrable to Christians who wish to announce the good news of Jesus. Compared to the number of churches in rich areas, there are extremely few in slum areas. Some churches or groups preach a conversion to the Lord as source of eternal salvation but they do not seek to humanise these areas.

With this study we have at last, a vision based on the Word made flesh, Jesus both divine and human. How to share Jesus in slums? How to humanize horrible situations? Ashley Barker is not just a theoretician, a theologian, a philosopher or a social worker; he is a man of experience inspired by a deep Christian faith. He and his family have lived in Klong Toey, the largest slum in Bangkok. He knows what he is writing about. His spiritual and human vision for bringing hope to slum areas contained in this excellent and well documented work should be essential reading for all Christians concerned with the message of Jesus. We cannot continue to ignore the terrible poverty and misery of the poor and hide in comfortable and secure situations. Christians from all churches must work together. Jesus is calling his followers to announce really good news to the poor. This book of Ash's gives hope and a way forward. It is good news.

Jean Vanier
L'Arche
Paris, France

Preface

Theology is never done in a vacuum and this theological endeavour is no exception. The passion for this research is rooted in personal experiences and reflections over two decades of serving as a full-time Christian worker in urban poverty contexts in both Melbourne and Bangkok. However, the specific catalyst for a deeper, more disciplined study came together as a crisis in personal experience at the Lausanne Movement's 2004 Forum for World Evangelisation from September 29th to October 5th in Pattaya, Thailand. The Forum had brought together more than 1,500 Christian leaders from one hundred and thirty countries to focus specifically on the task of evangelism. Lausanne, through a world-wide survey, had identified various 'roadblocks to evangelism.'[1] The aim of this Forum was to find responses that could be published as various Lausanne Occasional Papers.[2] One of these 'road blocks' initially identified was the rise of urban slums. This Forum was hosted not far from the Bangkok slum where my family had relocated from Australia in April 2002 as part of Urban Neighbours Of Hope (UNOH).[3] So not only was this nearby, but since I was also a keen reader of material from the previous Lausanne congresses, I put myself forward to discuss the rise of urban slums with others around the world. The idea was to work with others to help create a Lausanne Occasional Paper (LOP) with an action plan for response.

I arrived in Pattaya with my heavy duffel bag slung over one shoulder, stuffed full of as much slum research as I could carry and a few clothes. My shirt was drenched in sweat and my cracked feet still darkened with light brown slum dirt, as I took the first steps into the ice-cool foyer of the five-star Royal Cliff Resort, Pattaya. It felt as if I stepped into a fantasy world. Literally built on a cliff overlooking the beach and turquoise sea of the Thailand Gulf, the size and grandeur of the resort, complete with multiple swimming pools, air-conditioned spacious lobbies with crystal chandeliers, could not have contrasted more with our slum home that was not much bigger than the size of four double beds. Our hotel room bathroom was larger than our whole family home! A quote from Robert MacAfee Brown came to mind.

> Who we listen to determines what we hear.
> Where we stand determines what we see.
> What we do determines who we are.[4]

I worried, even from those first moments, that we would not 'hear' or 'see' many of the concerns I had come with. Finding meaningful Christian responses that would help find actions to determine 'who' we as Christians could become in this 'first urban century'[5] seemed a very remote possibility.

Though the rise of slums was identified as a key 'road-block issue' and the Forum program itself noted David Barrett's estimate that '50,000 new people are moving to slums each day',[6] in the end only five participants had come like me to devote time to this area. This was deemed too few participants to be considered one of the final thirty-one issue groups. The five of us then were adopted into the 'Transforming Cities' issue group with around forty other people. This issue group was quickly broken up into four sections, with none of these relating specifically to slums.[7] So outside of the main meeting the five original slum-focused participants met, talked and ended up writing a draft section about this issue to be considered for inclusion by the rest of the issue group. We especially noted the recent United Nations report *The Challenge of Slums*[8] and gave an impassioned plea that the Body of Christ needs to spend some of our best time, energy and imagination to discover how we can respond to this crisis before it is too late. After much discussion it was eventually accepted as part of the '*Towards the transformation of cities/regions*' Lausanne Occasional Paper as a section entitled, '*Transforming slums: Will we hear the cries of two billion people before it is too late?*'[9]

My experience at the Lausanne Forum helped crystallise three factors for me that can be considered the genesis of this book.

First, significant work is required to even create awareness of the plight of slum dwellers. The size, scope and complexities of urban poverty issues and evangelism can be overwhelming. The crisis of slums is more like a slow-moving, inevitable rise of a human river over years, rather than one dramatic tidal-wave moment. What is happening is not widely known in Christian circles and finding meaningful responses is not often on the agenda. More pressing and manageable issues for Christian leaders seem constantly on the radar. For example, while only five participants came to the Forum to find responses to slums, around seventy came to find responses to 'future leadership'.[10] Maybe I should not have been surprised by the lack of interest in slums, nor that few other Christian slum activists would want to come to Lausanne to help find answers, but there was something more than just surprise for me. Few Christians seemed willing or able to take notice or even conceive of a world where two billion slum dwellers could live by 2030. Fewer still are taking seriously the implications of this dramatic rise for all humanity, including Christians. Connection between this phenomenon and what Christians had to offer was not being made in any meaningful way. It would stay off the radar unless some new kind of movement, armed with accurate, careful and thoughtful understandings and responses, gave Christians compelling reasons to take notice.

Second, I was overwhelmed by the scale of complexity of the crisis of slums and squatter settlements. This often happened to me in the slum itself: a colliding of the human misery of neighbours would break my heart and confound my mind in terms of what to do, often leaving the bitter taste of futility and powerlessness in my mouth. What the Lausanne Forum gave me was a time away from the coal-face, and space to step back to see the bigger picture: neighbourhoods similar to mine happening for over a billion people now and billions more in my lifetime. Of course, the crisis was even more impossible to grasp when multiplied with figures like this. Yet, if someone like me, already committed to the cause enough to live in a slum, had trouble even conceiving what was happening, then how much more difficult was this for those who were not yet convinced? There was a kind of culture-shock in attending such a Forum, but actually talking over issues with others in this very different setting highlighted for me the urgency and importance of the task.

Third, I also realised that the challenges faced in slums are fundamentally different to the ones I experienced in over a decade of serving the urban poor in Melbourne. Rather than just being another kind of neighbourhood facing poverty, slums were like a 'perfect storm' of poverty. The various 'fronts' of poverty kept thundering together, causing misery to multitudes: evictions, fires, floods, urbanisation, vulnerable employment conditions, dangerous housing materials, sewerage inadequacies, superstitions I didn't understand, corrupt officials, language barriers, sanitation problems, AIDS and other preventable infectious diseases, premature deaths of children, the disabled and the elderly, and often no meaningful connections with Christians. As I did some initial study, trying to make sense of all this, I came across research by a Christian philanthropic trust in an Indian context. It found that 'Christian evangelism and social concern actually hinders the development of poor people'.[11] As a Christian who had relocated into a Bangkok slum not unlike those in India I was rattled by such a statement. Did my faith really have any Good News to offer my neighbours after all?

I was farewelled in Klong Toey to go to the Forum by a young boy called 'Om' whom I coached in football each afternoon at the community centre there. As I looked into his eyes, I knew I had to find something more to offer him before it was too late. Om was one of those kids impossible not to love with his big eyes and mischievous grin. He was quite a footballer too. As a six year old when I first met him, Om scored a freaky goal on our concrete five-a-side futsal ground to great applause, only to celebrate by simulating sex acts in front of the opposition team bench and to be promptly sent off. Somehow he (illegally) charmed his way back onto the ground before the final whistle and scored the winning goal to the uproar of the crowd. I soon found out that Om had lost his mother to AIDS, did not have contact with his father and for all intents and purposes left school at six. I would visit Om, who lived with his elderly grandmother and her hordes of other grandchildren in a small shack that was due to be demolished, and would wonder how they survived. As he started to grow up Om would be confronted with choices no child his age should have to face. Not least would be the choice of how to respond to the organised crime syndicates circling him like sharks, looking for fresh meat to devour. Their grooming of young people for their various mafia enterprises—both legal and outside of the law—was legendary. Of course, not all of Om's choices would be between bad options. The urban allure is due at least partly to increased opportunities not possible in rural villages or farms. For example, Om was offered a scholarship to play for the juniors in the Thai Premier League club, Thai Port FC. However in his chaotic life, even getting to school consistently in the slum was difficult. Getting transport to training outside the slum regularly enough to grasp this opportunity was almost impossible. Om did start training, but was eventually dismissed for not attending training regularly enough. Om, like so many young people in Klong Toey, was caught in the chaos of slum poverty. Every part of his life seemed vulnerable, with nothing stable and everything moving, much of it outside of his control.

As I kept the bigger picture in mind at the Forum, a question began to haunt me: what Good News did I, as a Christian, really have to offer Om and our other 80,000 mostly Buddhist neighbours? In the midst of tremendous hardships we were meeting some of the most generous and courageous people we knew, but they lived lives punctuated by chaos and misery. Would we too, as was reported in India, cause more problems for Om and his neighbours, who were already facing more than their fair share of life challenges? I was determined to find positive answers.

Third, I realised that I needed to spend some of my own best time, energy and imagination in finding Christian responses to slums. It was not enough to whine, 'Someone should really do something about this!' One of my advantages compared to my neighbours was my access to information and ideas, and my ability to speak to the wider world. One of my advantages compared to many scholars was that where I lived was rooted in the reality of slum life; this could help inform what was really happening in our kinds of neighbourhoods. I began by researching what the Bible had to offer a world facing poverty, surveying the different kinds of biblical literature and connecting my findings to my experiences of poverty in Melbourne and Bangkok. The biblical concern for the oppression and poverty faced by my neighbours inspired and strengthened my resolve no end. The book *Make Poverty Personal: The Bible's call to end oppression* resulted from these reflections.[12] This initial study gave me a taste of what was possible, but I was hungry to find Good News specifically for slum dwellers and needed a closer and more disciplined examination. I needed to engage more deeply with the most recent thinking and research relating to slums, and with contemporary Christian theological insights. This was not something I had the resources to do on my own as a writer-activist living in Klong Toey.

It was on the bus-ride home to Klong Toey from the Lausanne Forum that I talked with Simon Holt, then lecturer at Whitley College, about further formal study on slums. He suggested I contact Ross Langmead. In an Irish pub in Pattaya each night after the Forum's sessions, Ross Clifford, principal of Morling College, and John Bond, a pastor at South Perth, also encouraged me to take up this research as a way of putting into practice the impassioned plea to respond to slums that I had worked so hard to get into the Lausanne Occasional Paper. Other people I met at Lausanne like Scott Bessenecker, Doug Priest, Chris and Phileena Hertz and David Kupp also became important conversation partners in this research. I am grateful for their encouragement to pursue this.

While Ross Langmead has long been a friend to colleagues in Urban Neighbours of Hope and myself, he had also written one of the books—*The Word Made Flesh*—that I found especially helpful in my initial biblical reflections.[13] While the incarnational approach was a central motivation for our living in a slum neighbourhood, this study of incarnational mission in various Christian traditions helped me to realise, perhaps for the first time, just why this stance was so crucial to Christian mission in general. I was eager to research specifically what an incarnational approach could offer my neighbours and other slum neighbourhoods. Many discussions and application forms later, the opportunity for Dr Langmead to supervise me personally in this venture was one I was eager to take up. I am grateful for his thoughtful guidance and for his passion for the poor and for this project. Very few supervisors would have the patience that Ross has needed to have with me to see the thesis through. We had many Skype meetings and constant emails, and we were often only able to grab a few face to face hours together when I travelled to Australia—all of this was difficult. Six years of Ross taming my wild rough drafts with re-drafting and guidance are now over. Ross helped to find the scholar buried deep within me and helped focus my passions and thoughts. I am so grateful for Ross's gentle but firm spirit and for the amazing support from all at Whitley College and the MCD University of Divinity. I hope this thesis and now book does you all proud. I am also grateful to others who joined the team to help see this venture completed. These especially include encouragement, advice and support from Tabor College's Les Henson, Concern Australia's John Smith and Alongsiders' Mick Duncan. Helping to find much-needed hard data on the impact of Christianity in slums were World Vision's David Kupp, Darren Stirling and Tim Costello; Atlas of Global Christianity's Todd Johnson;

Christian slum advocates Viv Grigg and Scott Bessenecker; Doug Priest with the mission agencies of Christian Churches USA; and Mick Pilbrow with AusAid statistical help. I also needed a lot of help with proofreading and formatting. As well as Ross, friends Rowland Croucher, Craig Brown and Heather Oulton spent many hours to help make this thesis presentable. Colleagues, Reference Group members and supporters in UNOH, as well as my neighbours and co-workers in Klong Toey, give so much of themselves in ministry but also helped make space for this project to be possible. I especially want to thank Chris and Jodie MacCartney, Rod Sheard and Francis who shared an office with me where I was often stressing out; they also helped with statistics and charts. My wife, Anji, and children, Amy and Aiden, often had to put up with an absent-minded husband and father as I pursued this dream. I am so grateful for their constant love, understanding and support. I hope I can help support more of their dreams coming true too as the years unfold. I also want to thank my mother and father who, though some of brightest people I know, never got the educational opportunities they deserved. I hope they can see my pursuit of this doctorate as a small part of their legacy in the world.

Translating a PhD thesis into a book that is accessible to others was not an easy task. I am grateful to Craig Brown and Les Colston whose creativity and hard work makes this book a partnership in story telling that can include far more than the academy. The stories and exercises were not in the original research, but aim to help humanise and make this research less daunting.

In a world where slums grow at an unprecedented and alarming rate—many in cities that have very few Christians—what can Christians really offer that will not cause harm, but will instead help the growth and the well-being of those living in slums? This is a personal, social and in some sense pragmatic question. It is also a question that can only be answered in committed theological reflection and action. It is hoped therefore that such personal investment in the outcome of this research will not cloud the issues, but will help fuel a determined passion toward finding real Christian responses to the rise of urban slum and squatter neighbourhoods.

Introduction

During this research two anonymous people tipped the balance of human history. The first person was either born or moved into an urban area in 2009. At that moment, people living in urban areas (3.42 billion) surpassed the number of people living in rural areas (3.41 billion) for the first time.[1] What is clear is that this event is unlikely to be reversed,[2] considering that only three per cent of humans lived in urban areas in 1800, only 14% by 1900 and 30% by 1950.[3] As chart 1 below demonstrates, now that the scales have been tipped it is projected that most population growth will occur in urban areas. It is no exaggeration therefore to describe the twenty-first century—in the words of Jo Beall and Sean Fox—as our planet's 'first urban century.'[4]

Chart 1: Rural and urban population of the world, 1950-2050

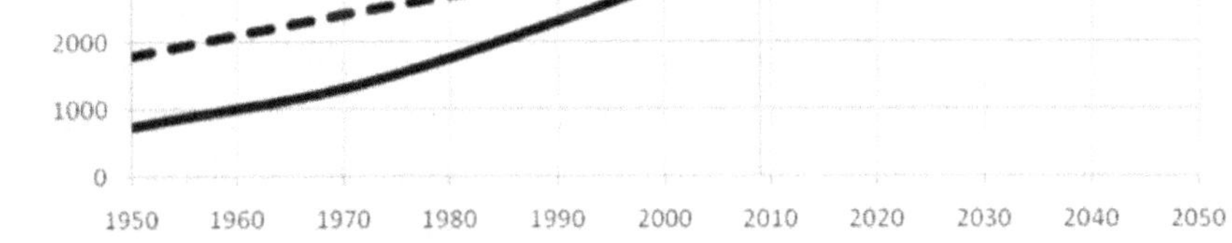

Source: World Urbanisation Prospects—The 2009 revision[5]

The world has changed irreversibly, not least because the majority of new population growth will now be centralised in the urban areas of the Two-thirds World. A 2009 United Nations report projected that the world population will increase 2.3 billion by 2050, but that at the same time the urban population will gain 2.9 billion and rural population will decrease by 0.5 billion. Asia's urban population alone is expected to increase by 1.7 billion by 2050 and that 'most of the population growth expected in urban areas will be concentrated in the cities and towns of the less developed regions. Population growth is therefore becoming largely an urban phenomenon concentrated in the developing world.[6] Unprepared for nearly three billion new urban residents between 2009 and 2050, Majority World countries especially will continue to experience the rise of urban slum and squatter neighbourhoods, as they have since the 1950s.

And this was exactly what our second anonymous person did to tip the scales of human history. This person was born or moved into an urban slum and squatter neighbourhood sometime during 2005 to become the one billionth person to live in a slum.[7] Chart 2 below shows this rapid rise, especially after the 1950s.

Chart 2: The rapid rise of slum and squatter neighbourhoods, 1800-2025

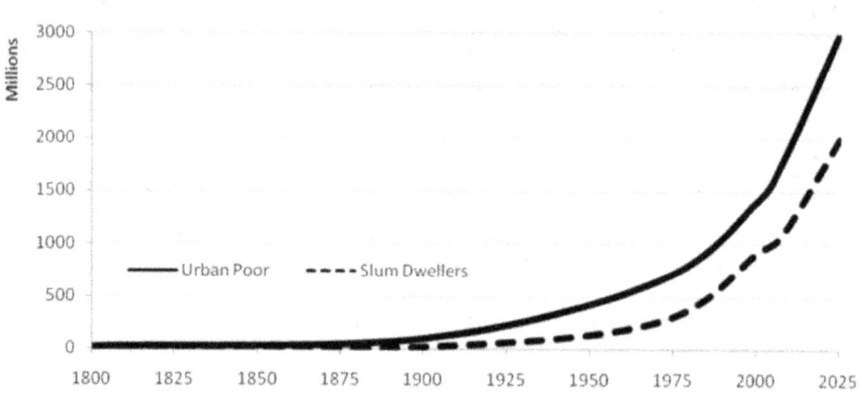

Source: UN-Habitat 2003 and David Barrett[8]

To put this into context, consider that when Christians were first called to go out into 'all the world', that world contained fewer than 200 million people and it took humanity until 1804 to reach one billion.[9] That one unknown slum resident made the ratio one in every six humans living in slums.[10] While difficult to predict, that number could double within twenty years, leading to one in five people (or two billion people) living in urban slums by 2030,[11] the entire world population of 1930.[12] By 2050, the The United Nations Human Settlements Program (also known as UN-Habitat) warns that 'if left unchecked' slum residents could well reach three billion people.[13]

Long-term population growth in general is notoriously difficult to predict, with so many variables, not least infectious diseases and new technologies yet unknown. The fact that over a billion people live in urban slums today and that some in the UN estimate that nearly half the world could live in urban slums by 2050, however, should get the world's best attention, not least Christianity's attention.[14]

1.0 Preliminary Definition of Terms

This study explores what the Christian faith can offer to the transformation process of urban slum and squatter neighbourhoods in the twenty-first century. Some provisional definitions of terms are outlined at this point to help introduce and provide limits for what this research aims to do.

Urban slum and squatter neighbourhoods: According to the UN, in 2005 more than one billion people lived in urban areas:

> that combined, to various extents, the following characteristics (restricted to the physical and legal characteristics of settlements, and excluding the more difficult social dimensions): inadequate access to water, inadequate access to sanitation and other infrastructure, poor structural quality of housing, overcrowding and insecure residential status.[15]

This definition was also used in the Millennium Development Goals, where target 7(d) is 'to significantly improve the lives of 100 million slum dwellers'.[16] The unprecedented growth of these kinds of neighbourhoods, especially since the 1950s, raises many challenges for the global community in general and the Christian community in particular. While general poverty is a significant global issue, this research focuses on the life of those rapidly growing neighbourhoods in urban areas of the Two-thirds World that meet the UN definition of slums.

This book will also propose and define a four part term—'urban slum and squatter neighbourhoods'—to move away from unhelpful labelling and to give precision to the study. 'Urban' describes the density, diversity and 'way of life' of residents' habitat. 'Slum' describes the living conditions residents face. 'Squatter' describes the legal conditions residents face. 'Neighbourhoods' describes the spatial relationship residents have together with the broader city. While this term will be developed in chapter one, shorter terms used by the UN and other scholars, such as 'slum' and 'slum resident', will also be used.

Transformation is a term used in various ways in the contemporary world, but in Christian mission it has a more technical use. J. C. Carrasco, in the *Dictionary of Mission Theology*, explains that transformation is now used in a way that describes, 'the radical and permanent change which the gospel envisages for every dimension of life. As such it is personal, corporate and universal, and speaks of hope of a new created order in conformity to the kingdom of God.'[17] In this book, drawing on key phrases in the Lord's prayer and Paul's use of *metanoia* (change, renewal, turning around) in passages like Romans 12:1-2, a transformative response from a Christian perspective is seen as an ongoing and dynamic process of people, groups and systems living and working together as God intends in a fallen world. Seeking transformation in slums therefore is about the struggles, breakthroughs and gifts of God's will being done on earth as it is in heaven.

The idea of *'enfleshing'* or *'incarnating'* has also been used in many different ways recently. The term comes from the Latin *incarnatus* and literally means a 'fleshing out', used as a metaphor for making real or effective.[18] In Christian theology Jesus is understood as the Incarnate One who, as the Word, 'became flesh' and lived among us (John 1:14). Yet, as will be discussed, the metaphor of enfleshing has more meanings than simply the Divine becoming human in Jesus Christ. What it is possible for Christians to enflesh in slums is an important issue in this study.

Ross Langmead, in surveying different Christian traditions, identified three main uses of the term 'incarnational' in mission and this definition is a starting point. These are:

> (1) following Jesus as the pattern for mission, (2) participating in Christ's risen presence as the power for mission, and (3) joining God's cosmic mission of enfleshment in which God's self-embodying dynamic is evident from the beginning of creation.[19]

This book will explore the various meanings of these three dimensions of incarnational mission as identified by Langmead in relation to urban slum and squatter neighbourhoods. It will also outline and critique a spectrum of ways in which incarnational approaches to slum transformation are currently understood.

Enfleshing hope is a theological motif that builds on Langmead's definition and uses contemporary theological scholarship on the centrality of hope as anticipating and beginning to experience the promises of God. This helps explore a central question: what can a motif of 'hope enfleshed' offer to inspire, invite and inform Christian attempts to transform their slum and squatter neighbourhoods? More practically, can this incarnational motif help Christian responses to poverty to be more holistic, transformative and distinctively Christian in the context of slum and squatter neighbourhoods?

2.0 The Potential Importance of This Research

The kinds of questions raised by the terms described above are of critical significance at this time for the world and for Christians in particular, for the following four reasons.

2.1 The size and rapid growth of urban slum and squatter neighbourhoods

The numbers of those living in slums are as impossible to conceive of as their living conditions, but this does underscore their critical importance. As we have noted, in 2005 there were one billion urban people living in conditions characterised by inadequate shelter, sanitation, drinking water, living areas and security of tenure.[20] At that time, one in three of the people who lived in cities lived in slums. One in every six humans lived in slums. The explosive growth of these neighbourhoods continues, with the UN projecting over two billion people living in such conditions by 2030[21] and as many as three billion by 2050.[22] One UN report explains that

> urban poverty and its attendant human cost is perhaps the single greatest challenge of our time. The future of our towns and cities, which is where most of humanity will live in the next century, hinges on our tackling it successfully.[23]

This century faces unprecedented challenges in the form of urban poverty in general and urban slum and squatter settlements specifically. What Christian faith has to offer such a large segment of the human population is of critical importance, if for no other reason than that few human lives will be left unaffected by the crisis of slums.

2.2 The lack of adequate responses to the problem of slum and squatter neighbourhoods

Many governments around the world are seriously concerned about how to respond to rapid urbanisation. For example, the UN reported a 2009 survey that found '83 percent of Governments expressed concern about their pattern of population distribution, down from 89 percent in the 1970s. Among developing countries, 58 percent expressed the desire to modify in a major way the spatial distribution of their populations, whereas 28 percent wanted to effect only minor changes.'[24] Though few can ignore the problem there seems to be a resignation by the international community about the inevitable rise and misery of those living in urban slum and squatter neighbourhoods. For example, the UN's much publicised Millennium Development Goals aimed only to 'significantly improve the lives of at least 100 million slum dwellers by 2020'.[25] Given the UN projection that around 1.4 billion people will be living in slums by 2020,[26] this Millennium Development Goal, even if achieved, leaves 1.3 billion people falling through the cracks. (It should also be noted that within three years of the goals being announced, the UN recognised that slum residents actually grew in number by seventy-five million.[27]) What does this say about the right to secure shelter and adequate living conditions for those who could number a quarter of the world's population? There have been significant efforts in recent years, especially via the UN's Human Settlements Programme, commonly known as UN-Habitat, to identify and promote 'best practices' in relation to slum responses. Yet, the very city where UN-Habitat is based—Nairobi, Kenya—has the Kibera slum of over 800,000 residents, living in some of the world's worst urban conditions.[28] These 'best practices' have made minimal difference even on its headquarters' doorstep.[29] New (and more engaged) responses and interventions are required by all sections of humanity if there is to be a 'world without slums'.[30] This includes the Christian community.

2.3 The role Christian theology and praxis can play in finding meaningful responses to social problems

Historically, Christian faith and practice has come alive when faced with various social challenges and oppression. Examples include the early church fathers and mothers facing the Roman Empire, William Wilberforce facing slavery, William Booth facing Victorian-era slums and Gustavo Gutiérrez facing Two-thirds World oppression. Could Christian faith have something special to contribute in the face of the unprecedented challenge of twenty-first century slums? At the least, given the numbers of those in need, Christians are required to find responses to slums that are both relevant to the needs and faithful to the historic and living Christian faith.

2.4 The precarious situation Christian minorities face in slum and squatter neighbourhoods

Many of the largest urban slum and squatter neighbourhoods have emerged from former colonial cities, such as Calcutta, Nairobi and Dhaka. Most former European colonisers considered themselves Christians. With colonialism's fall, the barriers keeping the rural poor out of cities also fell. There is simply not enough adequate housing to cope with the rising tide of poor people coming to cities to look for the urban jobs created by globalisation. Often those who are Christians in these slums are in the minority. As we shall see, almost two in three slum residents live in the geographical area known as the '10–40 Window' where Christians are least present. Not only do these Christian minorities live in difficult slum conditions, but because of Christianity's link with colonial oppression in the Two-thirds World, they often face misunderstanding, discrimination or even persecution.

What does it mean, then, to be a Christian minority in a post-Christian and post-colonial slum and squatter neighbourhood? If Christian faith is to have a positive contribution, what Good News can be incarnationally shared and accepted in such a context? How can the broader Christian community—including local and overseas churches, denominations, mission agencies and Non-Government Organisations (NGOs)—support Christian minorities without making life more difficult for them in their already vulnerable circumstances?

This book will draw from Christian theology and praxis, yet offer this faith to the broader world in a specific way, to meet a specific global need. This book seeks to find the connection between one of the key crises facing the world and what the historic and living Christian faith can offer. It is hoped that such an emphasis will encourage more engaged, strategic and Kingdom-orientated responses to slum and squatter neighbourhoods, so that more Christians will find fresh ways to respond as Christ's body to one of the most significant humanitarian crises of our times.

3.0 Assumptions and Foundations

3.1. That Christian faith has universal truth claims

There are basic truths claimed by Christians that are confessional by nature. The discipline of missiology is concerned with how this committed faith is shared in ways that are both relevant to new and changing contexts and faithful to the biblical revelation. This book will test the truths of Christianity in some ways—namely in what sense Christian faith holds truth for slums and squatter settlements—but it is assumed that God's love for the world, as evidenced in the life, death and resurrection of Jesus and the invitation to join this life and receive the Holy Spirit's empowerment to help extend God's reign in the world, has universality. This universality includes implications for today's slum and squatter neighbourhoods. It may require discipline to explicitly find and name this truth's connection, but the truths are there to find by grace.

3.2 That God is at work in the entire world

God's presence is real everywhere and all Christians are called to join God in his redeeming work. This includes the belief that God is at work in slum and squatter neighbourhoods, that there is much to learn from non-Christians and that slum and squatter neighbourhoods are not a surprise to God. The universality of Christian truth therefore needs to be tempered with the claim that all truth is God's even if found among those who do not confess Christian faith. The need for mutual respect, sensitive dialogue and freedom to choose faith is an assumption especially important when considering the role of Christian minorities in challenging circumstances. Christian minorities have a role to play in working with God, but it is not to dominate others, even if their numbers grow.

3.3 That God has a special concern for the poor and oppressed

Like the Hebrews enslaved in Egypt, God hears the cries of urban slum dwellers and is on their side (Exodus 3:7). God is just (Genesis 18:9) and therefore opposes all injustice and oppression (Amos 4:1). The Bible has over two thousand verses that implore God's people to take the side of the poor and oppressed.[31] This assumption has been especially taken up by liberation theologians of the Majority World,[32] but is being increasingly accepted across the Christian mainstream.[33]

3.4 That there is an inter-relationship between insight and action

The reflection and action cycle, often called 'praxis', assumes that insight and action inform each other. All theology has practical implications and all practice involves theology. What is crucial here is that this book assumes that theological insight has value in informing responses to slums and those responses to slums have value in informing Christian theological insight.

4.0 Research Methodology

The research for this book is an exploration in the missiological and practical theology of Christian mission relating to slum and squatter neighbourhoods. Each of these phrases helps inform the methodology engaged.

First, **missiology** is the discipline of mission studies, and uses methodologies from biblical studies, historical and systematic theology as well as anthropological and sociological insights and theories. This is because missiology involves strategic as well as theological questions about 'going out' (Latin *missio*) to those beyond the Christian church. The method of study here then is primarily missiological. The philosophical and theological issues this study raises are directly related to Christian mission in slum and squatter neighbourhoods. It uses a range of sociological, biblical and theological methodologies, but only insofar as they relate to more effective and authentic Christian mission in slum and squatter neighbourhoods.

Second, the method of study is more broadly **theological** in scope. This book explores theological challenges and answers raised by the existence of slum and squatter neighbourhoods in God's world. It seeks understandings and responses consistent with Christian faith. It uses broadly theological disciplines such as biblical studies, historical theology and systematic theology to help answer what are essentially theological and philosophical questions.

Third, **practical theology** has come to mean a particular methodology concerned with the praxis of human responses to real situations and contexts: (practical) in co-operation and connection with what God is doing (theology). The cycle of action>reflection>action that such an approach takes seriously has been crystallised for practical theological research by Richard Osmer. Osmer outlines four key tasks for practical theology, namely:

i.) *What is going on?* The descriptive-empirical task. This includes 'gathering information that helps us discern patterns and dynamics in particular episodes, situations and contexts'.

ii.) *Why is this going on?* The interpretive task. This includes 'drawing on theories of the arts and sciences to better understand and explain why these patterns and dynamics are occurring'.

iii.) *What ought to be going on?* The normative task. This includes 'using theological concepts to interpret particular episodes, situations, or contexts, constructing ethical norms to guide our responses, and learning from "good practice"'.

iv.) *How might we respond?* The pragmatic task. This includes 'determining strategies of action that will influence situations in ways that are desirable and entering into a reflective conversation with the "talk back" emerging when they are enacted'.[34]

It is true that practical theology has traditionally focused on church ministries. Practical theologies of family ministry, youth ministry and preaching have emerged in recent years as this approach has developed. The methodology also has potential for specific Christian responses to such social and global crises as the rise of urban slums. This kind of practical theological research is something that Osmer himself sees emerging:

> The scope of the field includes matters of public importance beyond the church, and often is directed toward shaping public policy and social transformation... The method of practical theology, which includes descriptive-empirical, interpretive, normative, and pragmatic tasks, may be brought to bear on *any* issue worthy of consideration.[35]

These practical theology questions are the kinds of questions that need answering if Christian responses to slums are to be discerned. Therefore, Osmer's four questions provide some focus and framing to what can be an overwhelming missiological and theological task.

The criteria for knowing whether practical theological and missiological concerns have been answered can be broad and difficult to apply. As well as a methodological outline of the four practical theological tasks, we will also ask what Good News can be identified that Christian faith and mission can offer slum and squatter neighbourhoods:

i.) Is this Good News true to biblical concerns and established Christian traditions?

ii.) Can this Good News address real concerns and challenges faced by slum residents?

iii.) Can this Good News lead to transformative action?

iv.) Is this Good News intelligent and coherent enough to understand?

Personal observations of life in Klong Toey help ground and illustrate the very human struggles this research raises, but the findings are not simply based on these. Personal experiences inform the general stance of this study, however, the significant existing data on slums and the practical missiological and theological issues they raise are the primary concerns. Therefore this is not the 'final word' on slums, with further research even needed to better consider the ideas in this book. For example, data is not collected before or after the use of the motif of enfleshed hope is applied in slums. What I aim to do here is propose and illustrate a theoretical framework; it is hoped that others can experiment and test this framework more empirically and ultimately for the People of God to move toward better transformations of slums through Jesus.

5.0 Structure and Outline

This book is structured around Osmer's four tasks of practical theology; which gives it the shape. A multi-disciplinary approach, especially drawing on missiological insights, will be used to answer the four questions. Each of the four parts will open with some personal observations and reflections from Klong Toey to help set up and ground the practical theological question or task for that part. The conclusion will be concerned with how well the Good News questions listed above were answered.

Part A. What is happening with the rise of slums? Identifying the nature and scope of the crisis of urban slum and squatter neighbourhoods.

First, an understanding of the nature and phenomenon of slums in the twenty-first century will require engagement with existing United Nations material and with the writings of other scholars and practitioners, including Christians. This will include investigating the nature, challenges and expansion of urban slum and squatter neighbourhoods, and also the Christian impact thus far. We shall begin this looking through the eyes of Klong Toey.

Part B. Why are slum and squatter neighbourhoods such a challenge to Christian faith and mission?

First, Klong Toey slum helps illustrate the ways in which urban slums raise serious challenges to Christian faith and mission. Specifically, the barriers to transformation of living conditions, church growth and poverty alleviation conditions and theological frameworks will be considered.

Second, using Langmead's three-part definition of incarnational mission as a base line, a critical survey of a spectrum of different approaches to incarnational Christian mission in regard to slums will be outlined. It will be argued that though there are strengths, there are also serious limitations to many such contemporary approaches to incarnational mission which can undermine Christian responses to slums. This clears the way for an alternative approach.

Part C. What ought to happen? Enfleshing hope as an incarnational motif to help transform urban slum and squatter neighbourhoods.

The theological motif of enfleshing hope will be proposed and examined in relation to slum and squatter neighbourhoods. This work builds on the three-part definition of incarnational mission proposed by Langmead, and especially incorporates the work of Dietrich Bonhoeffer, Walter Brueggemann, N. T. Wright and Jürgen Moltmann. Significant Christian voices from the Two-thirds World are also considered in developing this incarnational motif including those from Liberation and Revivalist traditions.

Part D. How might we respond? Strategies of transformative action that can be informed by the incarnational motif of enfleshing hope.
The ways that an incarnational approach can inform and inspire three important dimensions to Christian practice will be considered, namely, approaches to pioneering teams, local and relational place-sharing and poverty alleviation strategies. How these can become more responsive, distinctly Christian and transformative within the life of slum and squatter neighbourhoods is outlined.

Conclusions will be offered, especially testing what Good News such a practical mission theology can offer. Conclusions will also be made about the viability of the basic hypothesis of this book: that rather than being a separate kind of Christian response to slums, the incarnational motif identified by Langmead can help inspire and inform the six classical Christian responses to poverty to be more holistic, transformative and distinctly Christian in a slum context.

After each main section there is a story, pictures and a set of questions for group and personal reflection. One way to use these in a group is to have participants read the chapters of the section during the week and then come together to read the story aloud and reflect on the questions together. Please use these as a way to engage this book in a deeper, more personal way.

It is hoped that this book will contribute in a small way, not only to saving lives, but also seeing God's Kingdom come more fully in urban slums, as in heaven. Christian faith and mission will not make a real contribution to a crisis that will touch most of humanity by the end of this century unless significant changes are made. If more engaged, strategic and Kingdom-orientated responses to slum and squatter neighbourhoods can start to happen, and if more Christians can find fresh ways to respond as Christ's body to one of the most significant humanitarian crises of our times, then this endeavour will have been worthwhile.

For the love and the hate of it

I have an intense love and hate relationship with slums in general and Klong Toey in particular. Sometimes, even on the same day, I can be overwhelmed by extremes of emotion. On most days for example, in the mornings, I love to see the scurry of activities. Children scurry off to school in their freshly pressed white school shirts, day labourers rush to the Ports and even my 500 metre walk to the community centre can take half an hour as neighbours shout out my name, wanting to talk. It can feel like a big urban village. Like heaven on earth. Who would not want to live in a place where everyone knows your name… in the mornings?

Yet, by the middle of most days something else happens. It's not just that the concrete grounds above the swamp lands start to heat up like an oven or that the open sewer's stench in your nostrils reminds you that as many as 100,000 people have done their business already today. That's oppressive enough, but it's the stories that emerge of those who didn't make it out during the night that haunt you. I remember at noon one day, Jodie came rushing in the community centre, sweating and distraught. 'Nu Lek, Nu Lek, she's dying!' Nu Lek was a teenager with Down Syndrome we first met years ago as a little girl locked in her home, tied to her bed, while her grand parents went out to work. Over the years we'd helped Nu Lek learn how to wash and clean herself and she was a regular at the centre with a bright, radiating face who would squeal with delight as she met you. However, when the grandmother suddenly died, there was only the grandfather who could not cope. They moved to a smaller shack and by the time Jodie found them that midday, Nu Lek was like skeleton wrapped in skin. The family wouldn't let us in to help, authorities were not interested. 'It's our fate', the grandfather explained and by 1pm that day Nu Lek had died. Essentially from malnutrition and diarrhoea, totally unnecessarily. At those moments, deep within, you scream, this is hell on earth. How can anybody live like this?

By the evenings, as I reflect on the highs and lows of the days I often simply crash out in prayer. We know the steep rise in numbers of people enmeshed in slum living like Klong Toey. It's over a billion now and could be half the world's population by the middle of this century. As a Christian I know God wants us to do something. That the Gospels centre Jesus' ministry as 'Good News among the poor.' (Luke 4:18-19) For me then, despite feeling inadequate and overwhelmed, there is a sense that places like Klong Toey are the very frontiers where Good News is most required.

Klong Toey is not an easy place to live. It's a constantly morphing and moving living phenomenon, never stopping to take a breath. A place where anything could happen, but probably won't today. We took the plunge into Klong Toey's chaotic and at times overwhelming world in 2002, but in so many ways, 'found our lives' by losing it within Klong Toey. We have no regrets about taking the plunge into Klong Toey's chaotic and at times overwhelming world. Indeed we have, in so many ways, 'found our lives' by losing it within Klong Toey's crowded, narrow and sometimes dark laneways. [1]

---

[1] For a fuller account of our first year in Klong Toey see Ashley Barker, *Finding Life: Reflections from a Bangkok slum* (Melbourne: UNOH Publishing, 2003).

SLUM LIFE RISING

PERSONAL AND GROUP QUESTIONS:

1. When you think of the word 'slum', what are the positive and negative images that come to mind?

2. What are your hopes and fears as we seek to find responses to the rise of slums in this book?

3. How can you best prepare to allow God to speak into your heart, mind and will in the course of reading this book?

Part A

What is Happening with Urban Slum and Squatter Neighbourhoods? Their Nature, Sudden Rise, Challenges and Christian Impact.

SLUM
LIFE
RISING

Chapter One

Introducing Urban Slum and Squatter Neighbourhoods Through Klong Toey

Movies like 'The City of Joy', 'City of God' and Academy Award winning 'Slum Dog Millionaire' have recently shone the public spotlight on urban slum life. Though not without its dramatic moments, life in Klong Toey is like so many other urban slum and squatter neighbourhoods around the world—far more mundane in its daily life than the action packed dramas played out on the big screen. That said, Klong Toey is a constantly morphing and moving living phenomenon, never stopping to take a breath, a place where anything could happen, but probably won't today. On April 1st, 2002, with our daughter Amy, then aged only five, Anji and I moved into our new home in 70 Rye neighbourhood, Klong Toey, Bangkok. It was the size of four double beds and only a few doors down from where we stayed on sabbatical for three months in 1999. We quickly began to learn Thai and based our work and ministry with Church of Christ in Thailand's Klong Toey Community Centre. Our son Aiden was born in Bangkok on October 17th, 2003. Our neighbour-landlords organised a hole to be cut in our ceiling and a permanent ladder set up so Amy could climb up and use one of five separately-rented rooms upstairs for her bedroom, giving us more space for us downstairs. Like all Urban Neighbours Of Hope (UNOH) workers,[1] the thrill of leaving all we had to follow a dream would be tested over the years. To this day however, we have no regrets about taking the plunge into Klong Toey's chaotic and at times overwhelming world. We have, in so many ways, 'found our lives' by losing it within Klong Toey's crowded, narrow and sometimes dark laneways.[2]

The view from the top of Klong Toey's 'Ta Rua' (The Port) church building, a former Mafia Mansion complete with lookout, gives one perspective of our 70 Rye neighbourhood. We can look straight ahead to see a mixed mass of rusted, corrugated iron and grey asbestos-clad rooftops, with hundreds of electrical wires and TV antennae jutting out, almost to the horizon. It is one of at least twenty-one neighbourhoods making up the urban slum and squatter neighbourhoods of Klong

Toey.[3] On a good day we can see through the smog to the far edge of the slum with the blue glass skyscrapers reaching up to the clouds in the distance. On a bad day even the enormous bill-boards that hover over the freeway above Klong Toey for the benefit of passing motorists are difficult to make out. On really thick and soupy smoggy days even the thirty feet of spotlighted advertisements for the latest high-rise condominiums (complete with swimming pools and sauna) are as impossible to make out as the potential of slum residents living below to buy them.

We can never see the whole of Klong Toey from this vantage point even on the best of days. 70 Rye is really just one of her neighbourhoods. Certainly we can not see what others can from the sky:

Viewed from the air Klong Toey appears as a sprawling mass of tin roofs in a swamp, its houses built on stilts over waist-deep water, with narrow, precarious plank walkways linking the shacks to the dirt roads. Klong Toey has become a symbol of the larger problem of squatter slums which are developing throughout the city.[4]

Not unlike the shape of a skinny, crouching elephant with its trunk up, as shown in map 1 below, Klong Toey is more an archipelago of 'twenty-one settlements marked by considerable variation in history, size and socio-economic status'[5] than one, single 'mega-slum'. Somewhere between 80,000 and 100,000 residents, depending on 'who (or what) gets counted and why',[6] live in an area two kilometres square, making Klong Toey by far Bangkok's largest slum.[7]

Map 1: Klong Toey from above

Source: Rod Sheard, 'Klong Toey slum and squatter neighbourhoods shaded from Google maps', 2006   See colour version in Appendix

With the housing in a constant state of temporary renovation and adaptation, any cheap and accessible materials for building use are understood as a Godsend. From our church-top vantage point, now with its special lookout holding up a metal pole with a cross on top, we can see that rough wooden packing crates are the building materials of choice for many of the unique, strictly one-of-a-kind, second storey structures. This is for good reason. If we turn 180 degrees around we can see over a concrete and barbed-wire fence to see and feel the noise of whirling men, women and machines in the heat of the day at the Port Authority of Thailand (PAT). The workers scurry around, unpacking large pallets of wooden boxes out of the huge, primary coloured, metal shipping containers. Some of these wooden pallets and boxes, now moving from person to person to vehicle, will soon make it over the fence to help provide basic shelter for Klong Toey neighbourhoods. The rough wood which is not sold for shelter is meticulously smoothed down and varnished by eager craftsmen along the goods-train line in Klong Toey and made into chairs, tables and bookshelves for sale. Materials in abundance, so close at hand to so many, are never thrown away.

If we turn from the Port's activities back to the rooftops of the slum neighbourhood in front of us, we can see our first home in Klong Toey. It's not too hard to spot, even though it is nestled in among the masses of well-used packing crate renovations and houses with corrugated iron roofs. My daughter made sure of that with a hot pink sheet in her window to block out the harsh sunlight in her 'up-laddered' room. It provides a distinct splash of colour in contrast with what is overall a heat-faded and discoloured scene. From this view on high, what lies below us could be understood as just another mass of temporary slum housing; just a small number of the billion or more now living in similar conditions globally. Yet each of these homes represents real flesh-and-blood neighbours, many of whom I have come to love and respect like family since making our home here in 2002.

There is another view of our neighbourhood. As a Christian I can't help but remember that each and every woman, man and child living in this neighbourhood is loved and made in God's image. Further, even the neighbourhood as a place itself can be understood as an important arena for God. Eugene Peterson's words come to mind:

> In the Christian imagination, where you live gets equal billing with what you believe. Geography and theology are biblical bedfellows. Everything that the creator God does, and therefore everything that we do, since we are his creatures and can hardly do anything any other way, is in place. All living is local—this land, this neighbourhood, these trees and streets and house, this work, these shops and markets.[8]

The view from my front door step is different from the elevated views from above. A real sense of joy can be felt most mornings as children like 'Boss' and 'Best' go off to school on the back of their father's motorbike, neighbours scurry off to work in the markets or the ports and the lively conversations about football with neighbours start up. You feel like you are in a big urban village. Yet by the middle of the day the humidity rises, thick smog descends and pungent smells from the open sewers can induce vomiting. The elderly without family or those with disabilities start to emerge from their shacks and those who have done the night-shift in the bars stagger home after selling their bodies. The life of the neighbourhood by midday seems to have had the life choked out of it. The daily local life we share here at ground level is demanding, even harrowing at times, but there is something sacred about it if we can only pay attention. This neighbourhood is not just one of the many overwhelming statistics related to the rise of slum and squatter neighbourhoods. This neighbourhood is our home, where our children grow up, and is no less than a place of God's work.

Klong Toey is as good as any slum and squatter neighbourhood to consider as an example of what is really happening, not only around Bangkok, but all over the developing world. It is certainly the neighbourhood that I know best. Because of its size, notoriety, famous heroes and infamous villains, as well as its close proximity to the various centres of learning and media in Bangkok, it is also one of the most well researched and chronicled neighbourhoods in Bangkok. It is hoped that my personal experiences as a Christian worker, operating in partnership between our mission community (Urban Neighbours Of Hope) and various Thai organisations in Klong Toey (such as Church of Christ in Thailand's 'Klong Toey Community Centre', 'Ta Rua church', 'Helping Hands', 'Rom Gow Community Centre', 'Second Chance Bangkok'), will add a much needed humanising dimension to a book that could otherwise move easily to more abstract academic, and elevated views. For these reasons I have chosen to begin by briefly analysing existing research which makes clear something of the nature of this cluster of neighbourhoods called Klong Toey, as well as making some of my own observations.

1.0 Urban Slum and Squatter Neighbourhoods in Bangkok

Klong Toey must be understood within the broader context of Krungthep[9] ('City of Angels'), known internationally as Bangkok ('Place of Olive Plums'). Officially established as a city in 1782, it was developed to become the new capital of Thailand after the previous capital Ayuthaya was destroyed by the Burmese army in 1767. Built eighty-six kilometres further south along the Chao Phraya River than its predecessor, in many ways Krungthep is a river-centric city to this day. Never colonised by Western powers as its neighbouring countries were, Thailand has been proud of its ability to adapt and to stay 'free' (*thai*). Krungthep, from its founding, has been a crucial economic hub for the region, providing, for example, a port for merchants and trading that has helped Thailand leverage power and negotiate agreements.

Bangkok's population underwent rapid growth during the twentieth century; this has continued into the first decade of the twenty-first century. There were around 600,000 residents in Bangkok in 1900; in 1958 after World War II the population had grown to 1.6 million, and by 1986 the population was up to 5.4 million.[10] In 2000, the last official census, the total population of Bangkok was 6,320,174 people, which constitutes 10.4 per cent of the overall Thai population.[11] However, the unofficial figures could be significantly higher as those who are not counted can include migrants, those with residence 'up-country' but working permanently in Bangkok, and many slum residents. Further, by 2010 though the official estimate of 'the city core' of Bangkok had grown to around eight million residents, around 17.5 million lived in the wider Bangkok Metropolitan Region.[12] This figure constitutes around twenty-eight per cent of Thailand's population in 2010.

Thailand's degree of urbanisation is expected to grow from around 32.3 per cent in 2005[13] to up to forty per cent by 2025, with Bangkok's population expected to reach over thirty million people.[14] This would move Thailand toward a degree of urbanisation similar to that of countries like the Philippines, Indonesia, and Malaysia (respectively 66.4%, 53.7% and 72% urbanised in 2010[15]). The UN predicts that by 2050 the total Thailand urban population will be over 43 million.[16] If urbanisation is at 60% then these vast numbers of people would be absorbed into the Bangkok Metropolitan Region. Conservative estimates predict 60% urbanisation by 2050, but it is possible that Bangkok may reach these kinds of numbers as early as 2025.[17] Given that Bangkok is Thailand's prime city (Chiang Mai is next largest currently at around 142,000 city residents), and that its economy is similar to places like the Philippines, these kinds of figures are possible and would make Bangkok one of the world's largest cities.

Though urban slum-like neighbourhoods have been a part of Bangkok's growth since its founding, they have only really begun to be taken seriously by authorities in the 1980s. The pressure of growth from rural-urban migration, but even more so from birth rates by slum residents themselves, created a scale of slums that could no longer be ignored by planners or policy makers.[18] Sopon Pornchokchai is a fascinating and important voice tracking the developments of urban slums in Bangkok. He is the key Bangkok-based scholarly consultant for UN-Habitat, writing papers for them such as the case study of Bangkok for the 2003 *Challenge of Slums*.[19] He is also an important part of Bangkok's real estate industry; for example he is on the real estate council and is President of his own appraisal firm.[20] He is credited with breakthrough research in 1985—at a time when official authorities were ignoring the rise of slums—and with repeating his research in 1995. Dr Pornchokchai writes:

> When the author found 1,020 slums in 1985, the Bangkok Metropolitan Administration found only 500 and the National Housing Authority found 700. Newspapers put this

discovery of a thousand slums as news on their front page. The author understood that some involved in solving the problem, particularly NGOs, liked the discovery because it helped attract the interest of the general public on this issue of social problems. However, some local authorities, particularly those in the central business district, might not have agreed and questioned the definition of slum because slums might be considered an eyesore by investors. Eventually, the BMA accepted that there were slums in inner-city districts.[21]

There were significant numbers of slums in Bangkok before the 1980s. The same author quotes a real estate industry report from American consultants in 1958 that found around 48% of Bangkok's 1.6 million residents (740,000 people) were living in slum-like conditions.[22] However, policy-makers in the 1980s were forced to deal with the rise in ways that they hadn't needed to before. Chart 3 below shows only fifty urban slum neighbourhoods identified in 1968, but goes up to 1,404 by 1990.

Chart 3: Proportion of slum dwellers in Bangkok city

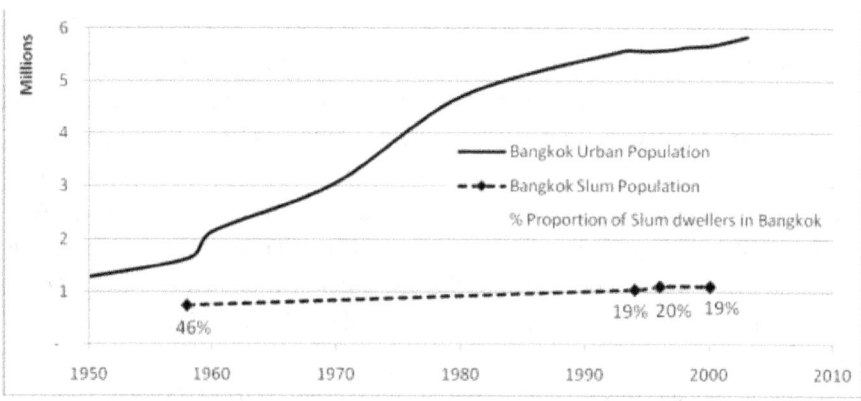

Source: Pornchokchai and Thailand census, 2000[23]

Some of the latest official figures, from the 2000 census, show that more people than ever (1.43 million) live in Bangkok urban slums; that is still 22% of the population. In 2010 one estimate has 1.5 million slum residents in 2,000 slums, but this will not be confirmed until the next census due late in 2010.[24] What can be said is that there are probably a smaller number of slum communities than 1,404, but they are housing more than 1.43 million residents. Therefore, the current density of slums, creating further overcrowding, as well as the growth in actual slum dwellers is a serious concern. Given the urban population growth expected over the next few decades in Thailand in general, and Bangkok in particular, these figures could grow to distressing levels.

Though a breakthrough advocate in researching slums, Pornchokchai denies slums are a real problem for Thailand. Citing table 1 on the following page, based on the 2000 Census, he writes: 'Thailand has a total number of slum population of 1,763,872 or some 3% of the total Thai population. This means that substandard urban housing in the form of slums does not prevail in Thailand.'[25]

Table 1: Summary of slum communities in Thailand, 2000

Urban Centres	Slums	Households	Population	Share of Total Household (%)	Share of Total Population (%)
Bangkok	796	196,354	1,099,575	8.4	17.3
Nonthaburi	60	6,994	34,970	-	4
Pathum Thani	93	17,099	85,495	-	13
Samut Prakan	207	41,456	207,280	-	21
Total Greater Bangkok	**1,156**	**261,903**	**1,427,320**	**8.5**	**14.2**
Samut Sakhon	62	8,838	44,190	-	10
Nakhon Pathom	30	3,338	15,190	-	2
Total BMR	**1,248**	**273,779**	**1,486,700**	**8.5**	**16**
Other Cities	341	62,673	277,172	-	1
Thailand Total	**1,589**	**336,452**	**1,763,872**	**2.1**	**2.9**

Source: Pornchokchai, 2003, and figures in this column are calculated using data in NSO, 2000[26]

There are a number of possible reasons the reported percentages are so small, however. Not least is that the official percentage of rural to urban population in Thailand is significantly lower than the reality as the number of 17 million residents in Bangkok (almost a third of the overall Thai population) indicates. People travel from rural areas to the city for weeks and months of work at a time, but are registered in a rural area.

It should also be acknowledged that the raw figure of 1.7 million people living in slums is a considerable number of people. Only 277,172 of these are not living in Bangkok, but this total slum population is actually bigger than the whole of Bangkok in 1958. It is true that the percentage of urban slum dwellers in Thailand is not as significant as for other Asian countries such as Bangladesh (70.8% of all urban residents were in slums),[27] but in raw numbers Bangkok has amongst the highest numbers of slum residents of any city in the world. Bangkok probably now has more slum residents than Kolkata (1,490,811) and almost twice as many as Chennai (747,936).[28] There have been various responses to these challenges, not least former Thai Prime Minister Taksin's vision to eradicate all slums in five years— discussed in Part B. The prevailing mood in Thailand, however, is still that slums like Klong Toey are a normal, accepted and economically essential part of the wider Bangkok landscape. As we shall see, Klong Toey has remained stubbornly immovable despite successive waves of public policy which have attempted to either ignore or eradicate the slum.

2.0 The Development of Klong Toey's Urban Slum and Squatter Neighbourhoods

Though the sharp rise in numbers of Bangkok slums was most noticeable in the 1980s, and though numbers have continued to increase, Klong Toey's history goes as far back as the development of the main Bangkok port. In the 1930s the Thai government rented land to construction workers to build a new port and to enable cheap labour to be available once the port was in full swing.[29] This was the founding of the Klong Toey neighbourhoods. The Port Authority of Thailand (PAT) was soon established as a state agency after construction of the port was completed. A kind of 'bait and switch' soon happened to residents as a result. The government abolished its land rental agreements with residents, giving the land to PAT. Legal renters became illegal squatters overnight.[30]

This did not stop a rising tide of new residents from moving into Klong Toey, especially from the rural poor North East of Thailand, called the Isaan region. Known for their pragmatic mix of Buddhism with animistic practices, this ethnic group still dominates every Klong Toey neighbourhood. Other residents came from other Thai regions also known for their forms of Buddhism. There are unknown numbers of refugees or migrant workers from Burma, Cambodia, Bangladesh and India who are peppered throughout Klong Toey, and because their employment is less secure they often live in some of the worst housing conditions. There are a few Thai Muslims from near the Thai-Malay border and one small mosque in the slum. Christians and Muslims are the exceptions religiously speaking, with perhaps as many as 98% of residents considering themselves both Thai and Buddhists.

Klong Toey is not only older than other slums in Bangkok, but also much larger. There are around 1.5 million slum residents currently living in Bangkok's 2,000 slums, making the average number of people per slum only 750. This average is significantly lower than the 80,000 to 100,000 residents in Klong Toey.

The kind of work Klong Toey residents do varies. The PAT hires around 3,500 workers at any one time, mostly from Klong Toey. Though what locals call 'in shipping' is the single biggest employer, the informal manufacture and sale of food, clothing and other goods is significant as a source of work. Few households have nothing to make or sell.

3.0 Ten Characteristic Challenges Slum Residents Face, Klong Toey

As the numbers of households rose in Klong Toey, so did the challenges. It is clear that each slum and squatter neighbourhood is made up of a unique constellation of people, settings and officials. Yet there are many common challenges faced by these kinds of neighbourhoods in comparison to regular, urban neighbourhoods. From my experience living in a slum and squatter neighbourhood, supported by data from reports and research, I have identified ten common challenges. These ten challenges have different levels and degrees of impact for each neighbourhood, but most slum and squatter neighbourhoods would have to confront these challenges at some stage in their development. The ten challenges overlap and have a cross-fertilising effect touching almost every part of a resident's life. All ten are experienced in most of Klong Toey's neighbourhoods. These ten challenges are explored, listed and illustrated here using examples from Klong Toey.

3.1 Challenges associated with housing security

A defining factor in slum and squatter neighbourhoods is that the homes of residents are outside the protection of law. Lack of secure housing tenure means vulnerability to forced evictions, corrupt 'landlords' and corrupt 'rental' systems in general. It also means unrecognised capital in residents' homes. Klong Toey neighbourhoods have experienced numerous forced evictions including the eviction of Lock 7-9 neighbourhoods in 2003, where over three hundred families were evicted using army personnel, police and bulldozers.[31] This vulnerability to eviction and corruption undermines people's wellbeing; the ongoing, angry and sometimes violent conflicts between those who claim ownership of homes and tenants are an immediate danger too. These conflicts occur in part because there is no legally valid place for either 'landlord' or 'tenant' to go to have disputes settled. Further, and unlike regular home owners, squatters can't use their investment in property as collateral. Economist Hernando de Soto argues that squatters in the developing world would own trillions of dollars in assets and capital if their properties were recognised. Specifically, De Soto's research calculated that if squatters gained access to a deed for their property (in the same way the first squatters did in many Western countries as they entered their country's capitalist modern era), they would be US$9.3 trillion better off.[32] De Soto voices concern about residents' long-term investment in slum homes which are 'dead' capital. In Klong Toey, the longing to find secure housing is a need we often see expressed by our church members. Housing security, then, is a central and intrinsic challenge to those living in slum and squatter neighbourhoods.

3.2 Challenges associated with poorly-built homes

The threat of eviction—even if it is not carried through—creates a sense of insecurity and vulnerability. This sense of transitoriness is reflected in the choices Klong Toey residents make about how to construct housing and infrastructure. Why would residents spend what little resources they have on buildings if they might be bulldozed tomorrow? Klong Toey homes are built with the best materials residents can afford given that there is no land security. This kind of housing is often less than ideal. For example, dangerous or hazardous construction materials may be used. Asbestos is still the roof of choice in Klong Toey because of its cheap price, despite the risks known to the broader world—that asbestos has been linked to cancer.[33] The actual land that squatter residents occupy may be vacant for good reason. For example, it may require expensive types of infrastructure and foundations before it can be deemed suitable for permanent housing. UN-Habitat estimates that 'at least three or four in every ten non-permanent houses in developing countries are located in dangerous areas that are prone to floods, landslides and other natural disasters'.[34] This is the case with many Klong Toey neighbourhoods, which often flood because they are located on low-lying marsh land.[35] The human cost of inadequate housing construction is especially high for the most vulnerable in a slum and squatter neighbourhood. UNICEF explains that there are numerous health risks associated with poor quality construction and materials. Lack of fly screens exposes children to flies and mosquitoes, and porous walls and roofing harbour rodents and insect pests. Hard to clean floors increase contact with pathogens—the agents that cause disease—especially for babies and young children.[36]

For Klong Toey, being outside of formal housing neighbourhoods means that there are usually no enforced building standards, inspectors or government officials checking the quality or safety of dwellings, and so such dangers are not averted.

3.3 Challenges associated with a lack of long-term planning for neighbourhood development

Just as with housing, there is a lack of planning for roads, paths, sewerage, water, educational and other infrastructure for slum and squatter neighbourhoods. In many ways neighbourhoods like Klong Toey are built the wrong way around. For regular neighbourhoods considerable time is spent in the planning stages before infrastructure is put in. Then housing is built. Finally, the homes are sold, the houses are furnished and people move in. It is the opposite for most slum and squatter settlements. First, people move onto vacant land with whatever belongings they have. Only then do they build and improve their shelter as they can. Finally electricity, water, paths, roads and sewerage might be put in, if it becomes clear that the neighbourhood could be there to stay. The lack of initial planning means that the space used and infrastructure installed are rarely at their most effective. Because of a lack of planning, slum and squatter neighbourhoods lack access to adequate electricity infrastructure. This, paired with the fact that homes are built with flammable building materials, makes fires a constant threat to these neighbourhoods. Further compounding the problem, the lack of planning for adequate roads makes slum and squatter neighbourhoods almost impossible to access by fire-fighters, and residents cannot quickly evacuate their homes if a fire occurs. In Klong Toey fires are a relatively common occurrence.[37] Some are big enough to make the national news, like the chemical fires of 1989 which poisoned hundreds of residents, and another in 2001 which left over 5,500 residents homeless.[38] But many do not make the news. The costs of fires in terms of lives, livelihoods and properties are significant.

3.4 Challenges associated with overcrowding

UN-Habitat uses overcrowding as one of its criteria for slums.[39] As multitudes move into cities like Bangkok from the countryside and infant mortality rates improve, there is simply not enough affordable housing for increased numbers of people. Moving as many people as possible in together is a characteristic strategy in response to this situation. In 2003, around twenty per cent of the world's urban population was living in overcrowded homes.[40] Overcrowding is not simply inconvenient; it is a health and social development hazard linked with an increase in infectious diseases, domestic abuse and hampered child development.[41] In Klong Toey this can be seen in the stress it places on our neighbours, especially children, who seem to constantly struggle with illness, violence and premature death. The most obvious effects of overcrowding include mental illness, interference with social relationships and the transmission of diseases (including the single biggest cause of infant and child death in the developing world: acute respiratory infection). Less obvious are the effects on child development, including poorer cognitive development, behavioural problems, delayed psychomotor development and child abuse.[42] Overcrowding can therefore have serious long-term negative effects on whole generations of residents in places like Klong Toey.

3.5 Challenges associated with a lack of secure employment

While slum and squatter neighbourhoods are magnets for those who dream of employment, they have in fact become catchments of labour nightmares. *The Challenge of Slums* concluded that 'instead of being a focus for growth and prosperity, the cities have become a dumping ground for a surplus population working in unskilled, unprotected and low-wage informal service industries and trade'.[43] Informal sector employment has been the subject of considerable debate, especially between promoters and resisters of globalisation and free market economies. This sector so lacks legitimacy and organisation that workers are inherently vulnerable to exploitation on a scale unimaginable to even Karl Marx and Friedrich Engels.[44] It is clear that informal jobs have higher vulnerability, higher risk, and lower levels of pay than most formal jobs. It is these jobs that are available to those living in slum and squatter neighbourhoods. The way slum and squatter residents make (or don't make) a living affects every part of their households lives. Inadequately paid work is another issue that slum and squatter residents face because of insecure work. When, for example, inflation hits food supplies, urban poor families are forced to use up to seventy or eighty per cent of their disposable income on food.[45]

3.6 Challenges associated with sanitation and related health issues

Squatter residents face greater health risks than residents in regular urban neighbourhoods because of inadequate sanitation. More than 560 million urban dwellers do not have a basic, decent toilet facility,[46] a characteristic challenge that leaves residents surrounded by urine and excrement.[47] Again, built the 'wrong-way-round', Klong Toey started with no water or sewerage system at all, and systems only began to be built over the top of existing homes once neighbourhoods had already been established. This has massive health costs to residents. For example, five diseases—pneumonia, diarrhoea, malaria, measles and HIV/AIDS—account for more than fifty per cent of all child deaths in slums globally and 'the chances of contracting any one or a combination of these diseases are compounded by poor living conditions and poor access to health'.[48] Public health expert Eileen Stagnent claims that 'every day, around the world, illnesses related to water supply, waste disposal, and garbage kill 30,000 people and constitute seventy-five per cent of the illnesses that affect humanity'.[49] A key reason for this is the lack of basic infrastructure for sewerage and clean water. In fact, 'the ratio of child deaths in slum areas to child deaths in non-slum areas is consistently high in all developing countries, even in countries that have made progress toward reducing child mortality overall'.[50] The most vulnerable in Klong Toey face these life threatening conditions, to varying degrees, daily.

3.7 Challenges associated with organised crime and corruption

Outside of the law, the slums are ripe for exploitation. While not every resident is a criminal, a common kind of exploitation comes in the form of organised crime syndicates. Because organised crime can hide in these 'shadow cities', slums can easily become a base from which prostitution and drug trafficking rings can operate without attention from authorities, or even with police cooperation.[51] In fact, few aspects of life and work in Klong Toey are untouched by organised crime syndicates. It's not simply drugs, prostitution and gambling, but also many other types of non-formal employment, such as transport and the selling of goods and services.[52] Organised crime gangs are stubbornly embedded in Klong Toey. Even former Prime Minister Taksin's three month 'war on drugs' in 2003, which saw over two thousand extrajudicial killings and had a focus on Klong Toey,[53] still did not make any significant difference in the drug trade.[54] Recently in Klong Toey organised crime syndicates have even stooped so low as to light fires in the slum to gain profits; the culprits have not been brought to justice.[55] Klong Toey residents, like those in slums around the world, have trouble protecting themselves from these dark forces. Living outside of the official law creates dangers and vulnerabilities to organised crime and corruption that are not faced by neighbourhoods which are protected by law.

3.8 Challenges associated with a lack of quality schooling and educational opportunities

While there are often more schooling options in cities in comparison to rural settings, education remains inaccessible or unaffordable to many children in slum and squatter neighbourhoods. The actual location of schools can be an issue. Schools located outside of Klong Toey, for example, can be difficult and expensive for students to get to. Yet, the few schools which are actually in Klong Toey often have trouble attracting quality teachers. Add to this slum children's increased susceptibility to illness, to missing classes and to pressures to help the family out financially by working, and the barriers to gaining a quality education soon mount up. It is not surprising, then, that a survey in a Kolkata slum revealed that 84% of school age children were not attending school. A lack of educational opportunities particularly affects girls; in countries with low overall enrolment rates, fewer than fifty per cent of primary-aged girls are enrolled.[56] Research shows that even the girls who do attend school drop out early for four common reasons: lack of finances, early marriage and pregnancy, domestic work responsibilities and poor performance.[57] While living in a slum and squatter neighbourhood has been described as an 'urban advantage'[58] in comparison to rural living, female illiteracy rates are still high in the developing world, particularly in urban poor areas.[59] Certainly those living in urban non-slum areas have much higher rates of enrolment than those in urban slum areas.[60] Again these are long-term—even generational—costs and challenges that residents in Klong Toey face.

3.9 Challenges associated with dangerous dumping grounds

Because slum and squatter neighbourhoods are outside the protection of the law, it is possible for them to becoming dumping grounds for unwanted chemicals, garbage and refuse. Industries that would not be acceptable in middle class neighbourhoods because of the dangerous toxins involved can thrive in slum and squatter neighbourhoods. These include tanning, battery recycling, casting, vehicle repair, chemical manufacture and storage. 'If natural hazards are magnified by urban poverty, new and entirely artificial hazards are created by poverty's interaction with toxic industries, anarchic traffic, and collapsing infrastructures'.[61] In Klong Toey, the succession of chemical explosions, fires and mysterious illnesses have all been linked to the environmental hazards created by such dumping.[62]

3.10 Challenges associated with despair and the 'culture of poverty'

What happens to people in Klong Toey is not simply external and material. In a ground-breaking study in the 1960s, Oscar Lewis argued that those who are in close proximity to wealth but are marginalised can be susceptible to a 'culture of poverty'. He wrote that:

> This culture [of poverty] tends to grow and flourish in societies with the following set of conditions: (1) a cash economy, wage labour, and production for profit; (2) a persistently high rate of unemployment and underemployment for unskilled labour; (3) low wages; (4) the failure to provide social, political and economic organisation, either on a voluntary basis or by government imposition, for low-income population; (5) the existence of bilateral kinship values in the dominant class that stresses the accumulation of wealth and property, the possibility of upward mobility and thrift, and explains low economic status as a result of personal inadequacy or inferiority.[63]

Clearly such an environment exists in most slum and squatter neighbourhoods, including Klong Toey. Lewis' research was with Puerto Rican immigrants in the United States. He described a number of common characteristics which constituted this culture of poverty that had developed as a result of marginalisation. These characteristics included: suspicion and apathy towards institutions; people producing little wealth; unemployment and the resulting lack of reserves of cash and food; acceptance of middle class values but individuals not living by them; hostility and mistrust of government and police; childhood that is not cherished or protected; a strong emphasis on the present and immediate gratification; and a preoccupation among men with proving their masculinity.[64]

> The marginalising experiences of most residents in slum and squatter neighbourhoods could be considered worse than those experienced by Lewis' Puerto Rican immigrants. The extremity of wealth found in most of today's cities compared with the conditions of slum and squatter settlements creates a kind of understandable despair, leading to the characteristics consistent with a culture of poverty. In regard to slum and squatter neighbourhoods specifically, Lewis researched slum dwellers in Mexico City and San Juan who did not have the added layer of oppression caused by ethnic discrimination. He found that 'on the level of the individual the major characteristics are a strong feeling of marginality, of helplessness, of dependence and of inferiority'.[65]

To the extent that neighbourhoods like Klong Toey are marginalised they have a greater susceptibility to a culture of poverty, and are therefore more vulnerable to problems such as the cycle of violence and drug use than those free of such injustice and oppression. If life seems hopeless, living for the moment is all you have and numbing the pain is understandable. Even if it is possible to take away drugs—as the Thai government attempted in 2003—this does not address the underlying social causes of drug use. Over 1,500 mostly poor people were killed in Thailand by police and gangsters during that 'war'. At least twenty were in our own neighbourhood, but no 'drug kings' were ever caught for these murders or for their involvement in the illegal drug industry.⁶⁶

Lewis argued that drugs are a result of marginality, injustice and despair, not simply the cause. As such, though slum and squatter neighbourhoods are ripe for such a culture, Lewis also argued that this was not inevitable:

> When the poor become class-conscious or active members of trade-union organisations, or when they adopt an internationalist outlook on the world, they are no longer part of the culture of poverty, although they may still be desperately poor. Any movement, be it religious, pacifist, or revolutionary, that organises and gives hope to the poor and effectively promotes solidarity and a sense of identification with larger groups, destroys the psychological and social core of the culture of poverty.⁶⁷

The topic of despair and hope and what Christians can offer in response are a core theme in this book. Its suffice to say here that although a culture of poverty is a key challenge that is understandable given the social context in which residents in Klong Toey's slum and squatter neighbourhoods find themselves, it does not need to inevitably drive responses of residents.

The dramatic rise of slum and squatter neighbourhoods like Klong Toey has created immense challenges for its residents compared with those faced by regular urban neighbourhoods or even some rural communities. Real harm and in some cases premature death can be caused by the characteristic conditions faced by residents in their neighbourhoods. These challenges are inherent to the kind of living conditions and legal status that defines slum and squatter neighbourhoods.

4.0 The Impact of Christianity in Bangkok and Klong Toey

What has been the response of Christianity to the complex and often overwhelming needs in slums like Klong Toey? Thailand has long been a predominantly Buddhist country with a minority of Muslims and an even smaller number of Christians. Christianity has had little impact on the general Thai population until recent times and even now it is hard to measure. In 1855 a diplomat noted that 'there were probably fewer than ten Protestant Christians in the country. Not until 1860 was the first ethnic Thai woman baptised'.⁶⁸ Today Thai Christians are still a very small minority. According to one of the few surveys of Christianity in Thailand there are probably only around 326,000 Protestants who are part of Thailand's over 4,000 Protestant churches. That is only 0.54% of Thailand's sixty-one million people.⁶⁹ Catholics represent a similar number, with 292,000 adherents in 436 parishes, or 0.46% of the Thai population as reported by the Vatican.⁷⁰ Together this makes for around 1% of the Thai population and fewer than 1,000 churches. This overall figure is lower than those reported in the 2000 Thai census,⁷¹ in the *Atlas of Global Christianity*⁷² and in *Operation World*⁷³, but because of the thorough nature of the Martin Visser study and the Vatican research, their figures are probably the most accurate.

What is significant for this study is that more than half of the Protestant Christians in Thailand are tribal peoples such as the Karen and others based on the Thai-Burma border. The Karen and other tribal people are not the majority indigenous Thai. As map 2 on the following page shows, there are very few Christians away from the borders.

Map 2: Per cent Christian per Amphur

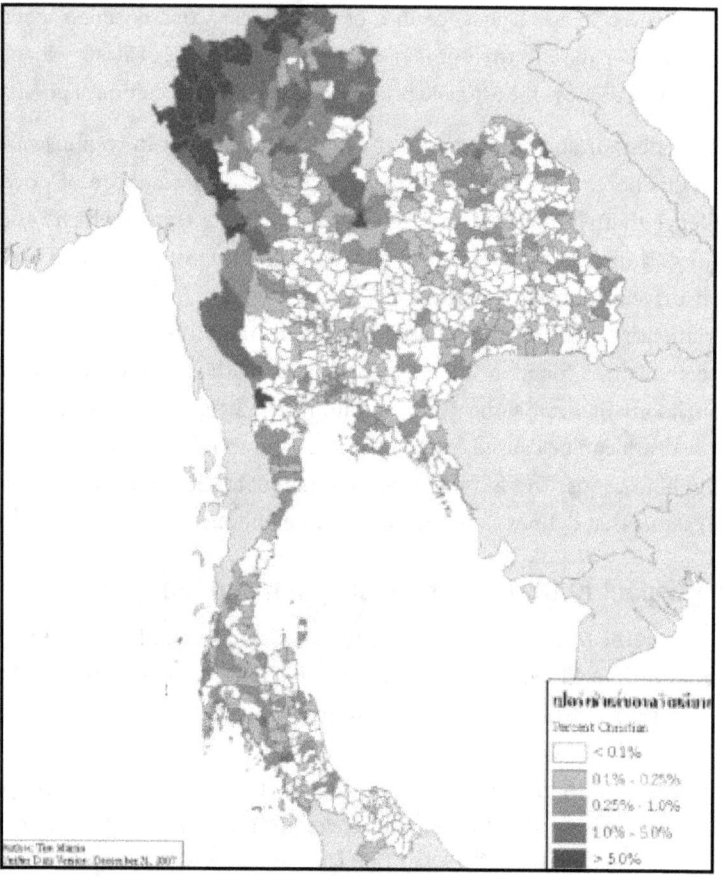

Source: Visser, 2008[74]

This trend can be clearly seen in Bangkok itself where Visser reports that there are only around 45,885 Thai Protestants in 450 churches.[75] This makes up only 0.25% of the 17 million people who live in Bangkok, which is a much lower percentage than in the provincial capitals whose populations are around 0.88% Protestant. There is no data available on Christian ethnicity; the Chinese, tribal and foreign populations may form part of the above figures, leaving few who are indigenous Thai Christians in Bangkok.

Though the data for Catholics is not as reliable or as clear, Visser argues that similar numbers are to be expected for Catholics.[76] Combining the numbers, it is clear that ethnically-Thai Christians, especially in Bangkok, are a very small minority.

Christianity in Klong Toey seems to reflect the wider Bangkok picture. Klong Toey does have some Christian churches, ministries and development agencies. These include the 'Bot Ta Rua' (Port Church) congregations based in the 70 Rye neighbourhood of Klong Toey. The Ta Rua church is a Christian movement founded by a resident of Klong Toey, Ajarn Suwat. Ajarn Suwat came from a drug and mafia background before conversion, and is a part of the Evangelical Fellowship of Thailand council.[77] Around thirty Klong Toey residents are a regular part of this Christian network. Some outreach meetings have been held in Rong Moo and Chuan Pluen (two other Klong Toey neighbourhoods).

There are also Christian meetings at a Kalana 'New Dawn' Vineyard church, which began around 2004 through a partnership with workers from St. Stephen's Society.[78] This church has a significant mixture of Klong Toey residents and people from outside the slum, with the pastor living in a nearby suburb. It has an average attendance of around forty people.

As part of the Mercy Centre and the Human Development Foundation, Father Joe Maier and sisters from the Redemptorist order have been a constant presence in Klong Toey since 1973, offering an amazing variety of development and educational programs.[79] They started running mass in the Rong Moo ('slaughter-house') section of Klong Toey slum (where Father Joe lives), to service the Vietnamese community who migrated to work slaughtering pigs, something that Buddhists would not do. Mass is held for staff and children at the Mercy centre in 70 Rye neighbourhood too.[80]

In 2008, UNOH and the Klong Toey Community Centre helped to start a small house church with parents, staff from Klong Toey Community Centre and Lock Six, 70 Rye and Rom Gow neighbours. This house church has grown, and, at the time of writing, meets in a room above the 'Second Chance Bangkok' shop on the edge of the slum, with about thirty-five people attending each Friday evening.

These churches are tiny compared with the general Klong Toey population. Certainly no more than a combined total of two hundred residents are regularly involved.

Some residents do attend churches outside the slum. The large Pentecostal church, 'Jai Sai Mon', for example, has a mini-bus pick-up service for those connected to its 'Baan Chivit My' community centre based in 70 Rye. There is also a Lutheran church that meets not far from Klong Toey slum and has a children's ministry in the Rom Gow section of Klong Toey. It is difficult to estimate the number of Christians who live in Klong Toey but attend a church outside of it; it is probably no more than a hundred residents.

This study is not just about the numbers of people who describe themselves as Christians in urban slums, however. It is about what Christians have to contribute to the transformation of urban slum and squatter neighbourhoods. Though the number of Christians who are slum residents is tiny, the actual work of various NGOs, including Christian ones, has been unusually effective in supporting Klong Toey residents. Some commentators actually credit the continued existence of these neighbourhoods—in spite of increasing land values—to these diverse groups, though there is no uniformity of access or protection.[81] Some of the NGO leaders, like Father Joe Maier (Catholic Priest who leads the Human Development Foundation), and Dawn Prateep (Buddhist educationalist, recent Senator, and leader of the Duang Prateep Foundation), have become iconic figures of national significance. As an example of Father Joe's prominence, while he was still U.S. President, George W. Bush visited Father Joe's Mercy Centre.[82] These leaders are particularly well-recognised as advocates for Klong Toey, and have certainly been extremely important. But in addition to the high-profile individuals and NGOs, below the surface there is a broad and varied collection of activist, development, educational and religious organisations at work in Klong Toey.[83]

The significance of the Christian contribution to the transformation of Klong Toey is difficult to evaluate without further, field-based research. Certainly Christianity has made a contribution in terms of children's education through the various 'annu-baans',[84] with many tens of thousands learning basic literacy and numeracy. Christians have also provided health-care and development on a scale far outweighing their small population. This is especially the case through NGOs such as the Klong Toey Community Centre (Church of Christ in Thailand), Santisuk Foundation (Pentecostal), Sunshine Centre (Lutheran), Baan Chivit Mai (Pentecostal), and Step Ahead (formally with Youth with a Mission), as well as the previously mentioned Catholic, Ta Rua and Vineyard churches.

It is clear that of the over 80,000 residents of Klong Toey, fewer than 1% would describe themselves as Christians or participate in a Christian church. Such tiny numbers are not uncommon in the slums of Asia, or in slums in cities where the majority religion is not Christianity but rather Islam, Hinduism or Buddhism. Such small numbers of Christians are common throughout slums in the broader Bangkok city, too. Bangkok's slums have never been easy areas for Christianity to take root in. In the only field study of Christianity in Bangkok slums that I could find, a 1986 Church Growth Committee surveyed 1,020 slums in Bangkok and found that only three churches and two house groups existed amongst what was then around one million residents.[85] With over one million people living in slums at that time in Bangkok there was only one church for every 333,333 slum dwellers. This may have changed only a little in Bangkok over the last twenty years as in 2010 there were only

450 registered churches to service Bangkok's estimated seventeen million residents city-wide. As I looked at the list of these 450 churches I could identify fewer than ten churches which could possibly be based in Bangkok's slums.[86] This is consistent with Viv Grigg's claims that, 'nowhere in Asia, with the exception of Korea, does the church in slums make up more than four per cent of the existing church of that city'.[87] Therefore, though *Ta Rua* church and others seem small, their existence and contributions within the slum are actually extremely significant.

4.1 What is happening in Klong Toey is not an isolated incident

The nature and the phenomenal rise of urban slum and squatter neighbourhoods is, one of the most important challenges facing humanity and, especially, Christianity. The sheer numbers and projections are difficult to comprehend—and taking any neighbourhood seriously is not an easy task as Christians. Even Eugene Peterson has trouble with this and he lives in a neighbourhood with trees!

> I find cultivating a sense of place as the exclusive and irreplaceable setting of following Jesus is even more difficult that persuading men and women of the truth of the message of Jesus. Why is it easier for me to believe in the holy (because God inspired it) truth of John 3:16 than the holy (because God made it) ground of 579 Apricot Lane where I live?[88]

Part A examined the nature of the phenomenon of slums as place and crisis both for humanity in general and Christianity in particular. What is happening in Klong Toey is unique, but not exceptional.

Chapter Two

The Nature of Urban Slum and Squatter Neighbourhoods in the Twenty-first Century

1.0 Known by Many Names: Definitions

How do slum and squatter neighbourhoods differ from regular neighbourhoods? Without a clear definition of what a slum or squatter settlement is, it is difficult to understand what is meant by this notion and to consider appropriate Christian responses. However, there is no shortage of definitions for these settlements as they have mushroomed in cities around the world, especially since World War II. Common terms and definitions are difficult not least because of the variety of languages used in so many diverse cities. UN-Habitat notes, for example, that there are fifty-four terms for slum housing from eight language groups in twenty cities around the world, and this is not an exhaustive list.[1]

Even in English there are a variety of terms and definitions. Take the most common term 'slum', for example. Some activists and scholars take exception to the term because it could be seen as derogatory. For Robert Neuwirth, the term 'squatter' or 'squatter settlement' is preferred to 'slum dweller' or 'slum community'. The term 'slum', he argues, is 'loaded', creating 'fear' and 'distance' implying that slum residents 'don't share the same principles' as other city residents.[2] Yet 'slum' is the official term used by UN-Habitat as seen, for example, in its landmark 2003 report *The Challenge of Slums* and in calling for 'Cities without slums'.[3] UN-Habitat is one of the most significant voices in defining slum and squatter settlements. This is the UN's special taskforce that works with other organisations and national statistical officers to monitor and help create policy results for slum dwellers. It aims to keep urban slums and squatter neighbourhoods on the global agenda. It succeeded, for example, in having included in the Millennium Development Goals, 'a significant improvement in the lives of at least 100 million slum dwellers by 2020'.[4]

UN-Habitat began in 1980 and has its head office in Nairobi, but also has offices in nine other cities. It sponsors conferences around the world each year, has a major meeting every ten years and commissions reports and publications. One of the most important catalysts for this research was the UN-Habitat report, *The Challenge of Slums: Global Report on Human Settlements* 2003 which provided, as then UN Secretary General Kofi Annan, wrote:

> An operational definition of slums and, on this basis, provides the first global estimates of the numbers of urban slum dwellers. It discusses the local, national and international factors underlying the formation of slums. It analyses the social, spatial and economic characteristics and dynamics of slums. And it addresses the impact of the main policies towards urban slums adopted by governments, civil society groups and international organisations.[5]

This report is especially important because it not only provides an operational definition of slums, but also estimates how many slum dwellers there are and will be in the future. Without this kind of definitional work and hard global data, the nature of slums and the trends and problems slum dwellers face would rely too heavily on anecdotal evidence.

The *Challenge of Slums* report discussed the notion of slums, surveying diverse definitions in search of an 'operational definition'. It acknowledged that 'slums, insecure tenure and poverty' are terms that 'do not have clear or universally agreed definitions'. It acknowledged that 'slum' is an especially difficult term to define:

> Efforts to propose a more 'quantitative' definition of slums have only recently been started, not only because of divergent opinions as to what constitutes the key determinants of slums, but also because of several features of the concept:
>
> * *Slums are too complex* to define according to one singular parameter.
>
> * *Slums are a relative concept* and what is considered as a slum in one city will be regarded as adequate in another city—even in the same country.
>
> * *Local variations* among slums are too wide to define universally acceptable criteria.
>
> * *Slums change too fast* to render any criterion valid for a reasonably long period of time.
>
> * *The spatial nature* of slums means that the size of particular slum areas is vulnerable to changes in jurisdiction or spatial aggregation.[6]

The report concluded in defining slums that they are 'multi-dimensional in nature' and that 'even with well-defined indicators, measurement can be very problematic, and acceptable benchmarks are not easy to establish.'[7] While the UN acknowledged there is no common term or definition, it did attempt to provide one. Whether one definition will suffice or not, most definitions cover similar issues. Residents, local governments, non-government organisations, development academics, social commentators and the UN-Habitat itself all commonly raise three factors in identifying these kinds of neighbourhoods.

1.1 Urban living conditions

Terms like 'slums'[8] and 'shanties'[9] are employed because of the tough and sometimes horrific living conditions residents endure. In Laini Saba in Kera slum, Nairobi, Kenya, for example, around one million people have little access to a few working toilets. Residents are forced to excrete into plastic bags and throw them as far as they can out of their windows.[10] The challenge of sanitation in these neighbourhoods will be taken up in more detail later, but here it is enough to say with Davis that millions are 'living in shit',[11] as both a metaphor and a reality. A term like 'slum' fits well here for it has a long history in the English language describing the harsh living conditions experienced by those facing urban poverty.

The term 'slum' probably started out as a verb meaning a 'racket' or 'criminal trade' before it became a place.[12] The novelist Charles Dickens especially helped bring the notion of slums as a place into popular use with phrases like, 'Westminster slums are haunts for thieves' at a time where 'slums' began to mean 'back-alleys or dangerous, poor urban neighbourhoods'.[13] The slums in Victorian England had similar conditions to today's low income and middle-income world slums. Friedrich Engels, for example, wrote that in Manchester in 1884, 'In one of these courts, right at the entrance of where the covered passage ends is a privy without a door. This privy is so dirty that the inhabitants can only enter or leave the court by wading through puddles of stale urine and excrement'.[14] This Victorian and Dickensian notion of slum is not lost on contemporary social commentators in describing today's urban living conditions in slums. Davis, in particular, is relentless in drawing the comparisons in his important work *The Planet of Slums*. He quotes Dickens—'I saw innumerable hosts, foredoomed to darkness, dirt, pestilence, obscenity, misery and early death'—and then notes, 'The dynamics of Third World urbanisation both recapitulate and confound the precedents of nineteenth and early twentieth-century Europe and North America'.[15] Davis further explains the development of the English term 'slum' moving from a synonym for a criminal trade around 1812 to the cholera years of the 1830s and 1840s where 'the poor were living in slums rather than practicing them', then to the idea of 'classic slum' which was understood as:

> characterised by an amalgam of dilapidated housing, overcrowding, poverty and vice. For nineteenth-century Liberals, of course, the moral dimension was decisive and the slum was first and above all envisioned as a place where a social 'residuum' rots in immoral and often riotous splendour. Slums' [i.e. 'The Challenge of Slums'

2003] authors discard Victorian calumnies, but otherwise preserve the classical definition: overcrowding, poor or informal housing, inadequate access to safe water and sanitation, and insecurity of tenure.[16]

In the 1880s the Housing Reform Movement in England began to use the term 'slum' as an operational concept for 'a house materially unfit for human habitation', and this made it possible to mark whole areas on maps as 'slum areas'.[17] The term was then imported to places like India to describe without distinction settlements such as 'bustees', 'chawls' or 'cheris' which were the Mumbai, Delhi and Chennai terms respectively.[18] It remains the most used English word to describe this notion, as the report *The Challenge of Slums* exemplifies.

'Slum' does not necessarily have the same implications for those in non-English speaking countries, unaware of the long, emotive history of the term. As we noted, these countries often have their own more colourful and precise terms for the variety of living conditions residents face. UN-Habitat notes that languages like Tagalog in the Philippines have developed six different and descriptive words for the living conditions of these residents.[19]

What all of these terms have in common is that they are describing undesirable living conditions. Like the term 'slum' these terms are not positive, but they are honest. They describe the kind of living conditions the majority of a city would not willingly choose to live in. Yet it is often the only kind of living condition that these residents can afford in locations where employment is possible. In a rapidly urbanising world where agriculturally-based industries in the countryside require fewer people, this trade-off for income is one of the few choices open to them.

The Challenge of Slums reviewed various slum definitions used by national and local governments, statistical offices and institutions involved in slum issues and public perception. From its survey it then offered the following 'attributes of slum parameters'.[20]

Lack of basic services: This includes lack of access to sanitation and safe drinking water, garbage disposal.

Sub-standard housing or illegal and inadequate building structures: This includes the use of non-permanent and/or unsuitable materials for housing given the location and climate, as well as the lack of planning approval from local government.

Overcrowding and high density: This includes low ratios of 'space per person', or 'space per dwelling'.

Unhealthy living conditions and hazardous locations: This includes lack of services resulting in visible open sewers, lack of pathways, uncontrolled dumping of garbage and pollution. It can also include the actual site being dangerous because of flood-proneness or toxic emissions.

Insecure tenure; irregular or informal settlements: This includes a lack of any formal document entitling the occupant to occupy the land.

Poverty and social exclusion: This includes low-incomes, slum conditions creating a barrier to human/social development, and stigmas such as crime associated with slums.

Minimum settlement size: This includes there being a minimum number of dwellings for a slum to be so labelled.

Most of these attributes of slums describe living conditions and environmental concerns. Outlining the multi-dimensional aspects of living conditions in slum settlements in this manner is helpful in that it provides some parameters and variety in what constitutes a slum. 'Many slum areas', notes the UN-Habitat report, 'may also show only a few of these negative attributes, while the worst may have them all'.[21] Table 2 below gives examples of six slums measured against the six parameters.

Table 2: 'Slum parameters'

Example of a Slum	Services	Structure	Density	Location	Poverty & Exclusion	Security of Tenure
Ibadan, Bogida Market	Poor	Fair	High	Hazardous	Poor	Secure
Dhaka railways	Fair	Poor	High	Hazardous	Severe	Insecure
Karachi invasion of state land	Poor	Fair	High	Not Hazardous	Severe	Secure
Karachi ad-hoc settlements	Poor	Fair	High	Hazradous	Poor	Insecure
Cairo highrises	Fair	Good	High	Not Hazardous	Poor	Secure
Durban 'informal' settlements	Poor	Poor	Medium/ Low	Not Hazardous	Severe	Secure

Source: *Adapted from UN-Habitat, 2002*[22]

In Nairobi, from October 28th to 30th 2002, the United Nations Expert Group Meeting (EGM) recommended a definition for slums for future international usage that was affirmed in *The Challenge of Slums* as an 'operational definition of slums'. It stated:

A slum is an area that combines, to various extents, the following characteristics (restricted to the physical and legal characteristics of settlements, and excluding the more difficult social dimensions):

* inadequate access to water;
* inadequate access to sanitation and other infrastructure;
* poor structural quality of housing;
* overcrowding;
* insecure residential status.[23]

This definition has indeed become the standard definition of slums. With the exception of the last dot point which has more legal concerns (and will be discussed in the next section), these characteristics are all about the kinds of difficult living conditions faced by slum dwellers. After describing these general characteristics, *The Challenge of Slums* report then sought to tie them to Millennium Development Goal indicators and definitions where possible. While acknowledged as provisional—requiring field testing and local adaptation—the definition aimed to establish a 'reliable base-line' to estimate the 'numbers of people living in slums'.[24] By using this measurement the report found that the extent of slum-residency was around one billion people in 2001 (31 per cent of the world's urban population).[25] It also predicted that if no concrete changes are made, using the same slum definition the figure will rise to two billion people by 2025.[26]

There are legitimate concerns about using the term 'slum'. It needs to be acknowledged that 'slum' can be a derogative, emotive and thus limiting label for any neighbourhood. Yet its employment by UN-Habitat and its acceptance as part of international, scholarly discourse can be potentially helpful for this study for a number of reasons. First, 'slums' can be an appropriate term used to describe the living conditions faced by the urban poor in these neighbourhoods. The kinds of characteristics identified by the UN in their definitions are not positive, but are a tragic reality for a billion slum residents. Second, the definitional work done by the UN is helpful in that it identifies specific kinds of living conditions slum residents face and how these differ from the conditions found in regular neighbourhoods. Third, the definition of 'slum' by the UN's report allowed quantification of the scope of slum dwelling.

The term 'slum', then, can aptly describe the living conditions of the urban poor when it is used in a relatively precise, descriptive way. By itself, however, 'slum' can be derogatory and therefore needs to be used in conjunction with other terms to be a more precise and rigorous term. Also there are more dimensions to these neighbourhoods and their residents than simply difficult living conditions.

1.2 Legality and security of housing tenure

Terms like 'squatter',[27] 'illegal housing'[28] and 'informal sector housing'[29] are employed because they describe the concerns of security of housing tenure these residents face. These residents live in housing that is mostly not legal in that it does not have a deed, and therefore lacks the legal protection this would provide.

The term 'squatter' is often preferred to slum because it is a more precise legal term and because it has a much longer history than the term 'slum'. For example, Argis of Sparta and Tiberius, the Roman Tribune, both argued for land reform for those who were fleeing the countryside to squat in urban areas. Both were killed by ruling urban families to stop these property reforms.[30]

Between *circa* 130 to 30 BCE, Ancient Rome doubled in size to house 800,000 people. Many could not afford the high priced housing and simply built their own. Historian C.R Whittaker noted that there was nothing 'romantic' about destitution under Tacitus' reign in Rome:

> If they were lucky they could build *tuguria*, lean-to sheds which made a sort of 'Bidonville' or shanty town, perhaps on the edge of the city, but sometimes above workshops or up against public buildings. The authorities regarded them as a fire risk and might tear them down, but they were allowed to remain if not obstructive and were even charged rent.[31]

In fact a Roman law called *usucapio* was developed to recognise squatters' rights to land they had used for long periods of time. It is a law that is still used in a number of countries today including Brazil where it is called *usucapiao*.[32]

Most medieval cities also had to deal with squatter housing. For example, in 1587 Paris had a population of around 260,000 and about 17,000 were living in shacks around the walled city. By 1787 Paris's population was over 500,000 people including 91,000 squatters.[33]

Settlement of land where colonisation took place over the last two hundred years often involved squatters too. Hernando de Soto actually calls the squatters' rights laws the 'missing lessons of US History',[34] claiming the recognition of squatters' claims for US land (e.g., the *Homestead Act* of 1862) was a crucial factor in explaining why American capitalism works there. These property laws helped protect the land claims of squatters and gave them an ability to play within the rules of the capitalist system.[35]

Some of the non-English terms which allude to legal concerns are nicknames to describe how settlements came into being. For example, the Turkish term *gecekondu* literally means 'it happened at night'.[36] This came from the taking advantage of an ancient Istanbul law that if citizens started construction of homes after dusk and had moved in before sunrise without being caught by authorities they would not be evicted without a legal fight. Around six million residents in Istanbul currently live in these *gecekondu* homes.[37]

Because squatter settlements often come under the jurisdiction and authority of city or municipal governments, there have been various attempts by the government sector to define them. *The Challenge of Slums* analysed definitions of slums in twenty-nine cities. While eight cities lacked any definition at all, the two issues most referred to were the use of poor construction materials (60 per cent) and the legality (or otherwise) of land occupancy (55 per cent).[38] Legal concerns, then, are present in the majority of definitions used by the local governments surveyed.

Local governments can have a love-hate relationship with squatter neighbourhoods because they have to employ legally binding definitions and conventions. On one hand many squatters can vote and can therefore be courted by political powers. On the other hand slum conditions can be considered a failure of government and therefore strategies of masking or hiding these settlements can take place.

For example, in the late 1980s Bangkok had an official poverty rate of only five per cent, yet surveys found that nearly a quarter of the population (1.16 million) was living in slums and squatter settlements.[39] The goal of eradicating squatters, while appealing in rhetoric, would require the definitions to be narrowed to a very tight, legal definition to have any real chance of being achieved. In reality many of Bangkok's slums do have some security of tenure, with Sopon Pornchokchai arguing that only 15% are technically 'squatters'.[40] Even the best titles, deeds and contracts are notoriously weak for even the most established housing in Bangkok. While compensation is often paid to those being removed from their homes, there is not, in most cases, adequate protection from eviction if a stronger power wants the land. So while 85% of slum residents may not officially be squatters, their legal protection is not strong.

It is clear in these examples that the term 'squatter' is a more precise term than 'slum' in that it highlights quite specific legal concerns these neighbourhoods face. It is possible to have a high standard of living conditions in a home that has no legal right to be on the land—it is outside the legal housing framework. We will argue that to add the legal term 'squatter' to the term 'slum' (with its concerns for living conditions), gives a more precise and rigorous focus for this study.

Robert Neuwirth is a passionate advocate for the use of the term 'squatter' instead of 'slum'. In his book, *Shadow Cities*, Neuwirth describes the rise of squatter settlements after spending time living in them in Rio, Nairobi, Mumbai and Istanbul.[41] He is not alone in advocating for the term 'squatter' in preference to the term 'slum'. For example, the January/February 2006 edition of *New Internationalist* devoted a whole edition to what it called 'Squatter Town'. Richard Swift's editorial of that edition sums up why many dislike the term 'slums' writing that, "'Slum" is a tricky word. It conjures up images out of control. The threatening. The miserable. The lawless. Rarely the heroic... the slums and those who live there are simply "other."'[42]

Why not just use the arguably more politically correct term 'squatter' as Swift and Neuwirth do and dispense with the term 'slum' altogether? Neither Swift nor Neuwirth explain how 'squatter' differs to 'slum' in terms of negative images. 'Squatter' is hardly a flattering or positive term and has much the same baggage as 'slums', perhaps even evoking more negative responses to 'criminal' or 'illegal' activity than the term 'slum'. Certainly the English terms 'slums' and 'squatter settlements' are consistent with very similar insider terms used by the residents themselves to describe what is happening in these settlements. In some settings these terms can seem derogatory, but in others they are not as emotive. As terms they are limited in that they cannot take into account the many positive characteristics some such settlements have. These neighbourhoods cannot be exhaustively defined or described only by their living conditions or extra-legal status. A sense of community, hope and a willingness to accept sub-standard housing for access to education and employment are rarely the first images that come to mind when describing whole neighbourhoods where shelter is inadequate or illegal. So it needs to be acknowledged that there are limits of language in describing these settlements as only 'slums', or in describing residents as only 'squatters'.

Hari Srinivas, from the Global Development Research Centre, has been active in education and advocacy with slums and squatter settlements and may provide a way forward. She uses both terms and describing these settlements in the following way:

Slums and squatter settlements represent a series of trade-offs

between

poor living quality *and* close proximity to jobs and markets

between

poor quality of houses *and* low affordable investment in housing

between

no housing *and* tenural insecurity

between

no access to infrastructure and informal *and* intermittent supply of urban services.[43]

By using the terms 'slum' and 'squatter' together as adjectives, Srinivas notes that they encapsulate different concerns. She goes on to define the distinctions between the terms 'slums' and 'squatter' thus: '**slums** refer to the environmental aspects of the area where a community resides, while **squatters** refer to the legality of the land ownership and other infrastructure provision'.[44]

Joining the UN's definition of 'slums' as being specifically defined by living conditions with the legal term 'squatter' helps to convey more fully a reality which is multidimensional. However, just using 'squatter' in conjunction with 'slum' is still too limiting and potentially de-humanising. Even Swift and Neuwirth fail to argue that the label 'squatter' improves on the tendency of the term 'slum' to stigmatise residents as the feared 'other'. Peoples' homes represent more than simply their legal status or living conditions. Spatial concerns need to be considered and included in any definition too.

1.3 Spatial concerns

Terms like 'squatter', 'slum' and 'informal' can be used as terms in their own right, but they can often also be coupled adjectively with terms like 'towns',[45] 'settlements'[46] or 'communities'.[47] How do we describe the space, locality and place that these households occupy together? There are many different types of localities. Fundamental to this is the question of whether the locality is at the core or the periphery of a city. If this is considered, then there are a whole range of agreements that can be made (or not made) with authorities that can make the slum and squatter locations different from each other. Davis, for example offers a 'slum typology' ranging from those in the 'metro core' to those on the 'periphery' and 'refugee camps', which can all be 'informal' or 'formal' creating at least eighteen types such places can be understood in relation to the broader city.[48] What such a typology highlights is the trade-offs that residents in these locations make in order to survive, as well as their opportunism. In Karachi, for example, thirty-four per cent of the poor live in the inner-city slums, compared with sixty-six per cent in peripheral slums.[49] The inner-city provides greater access to employment opportunities, but higher costs and less housing security. Some, like pavement dwellers, have no roof at all, while other areas are 'hand-me-downs', having a previous use like Cairo's former Jewish Cemeteries. A reporter noted, 'I found a young couple with four children cosily installed in a particular splendid neopharaonic vault. The tomb dwellers had unsealed the columbarium inside, finding it made convenient built-in shelving for clothes, cooking pots and a colour TV set.'[50] Some housing is made by those who dwell in it, and some is built by others who pass it on or 'sell' it. Refugee camps are another kind of slum, generally found on the periphery of cities or border-towns. Then there is diversity of size; some localities contain only a few families but in other places slums are cities in their own right. For example Neza/Cholo/Izta in Mexico City, Mexico has four million residents; Libertador in Caracas, Venezuela has 2.2 million.[51]

To find a common term to include such diversity and yet provide some precision and focus, it is proposed in this research that the term 'neighbourhood' best describes most of these occupancies, for several reasons. First, slum and squatter neighbourhoods are made up of clusters of households mostly smaller in number than districts, towns or cities. Even the largest areas for slum and squatter households have smaller, differentiated neighbourhoods. These entire neighbourhood areas should, in most circumstances, be considered part of a larger district, town or city rather than one in their own right.

Second, although these neighbourhoods are different from other neighbourhoods in their living conditions and legal concerns, this is not because they don't have a legitimate locality within a city or town. Families and individuals are living side-by-side as neighbours. These households have more similarities to other regular neighbourhoods in terms of locality than differences from them.

Third, as an urban locality of households, they are neither 'villages' where a locality of households stands alone, nor a 'community' where everyone knows each other. While a sense of 'village' or 'community' may well develop in some neighbourhoods, it is too optimistic to expect every slum and squatter neighbourhood to experience this, let alone be defined by such a sense.

Fourth, these neighbourhoods are not just settlements. They are more complex than first settlement or colonisation of land because they are often part of a larger, already settled, town or city space. These neighbourhoods may pioneer a space not used or under-used for housing in the same way some new urban housing estates settle new land. Few would describe new housing estates as 'settlements' however because they are part of cities and towns and not new ones. Mostly they are described as neighbourhoods, especially as people move in and develop their own sense of worth and identity.

Fifth, neighbourhoods can change their nature even if the same people live there. It is possible that either slum or squatter concerns in locality can be addressed in such a way that those living there can be living in just another neighbourhood in a town or city. In many ways this is the ideal: a slum and squatter neighbourhood becomes a healthy, legally protected neighbourhood. Therefore the description of space occupied needs to be such that it can allow such a possibility to exist. The term 'neighbourhood' provides for this possibility in a way that 'town', 'city' or 'settlement' does not.

Sixth, neighbourhood is a potentially humanising, yet precise, description of place. Further marginalising or stigmatising those already living in tough conditions is a very real concern here with terms that make residents 'other' than an integral part of a city. Yet, there can also be a danger of underplaying those same tough, dehumanising conditions with terms like 'community'. 'Neighbourhood' is a more neutral term, suggesting an area residents can walk around easily, and is in common with other parts of a city, which do not have the same living conditions or legal threats.

Seventh, by using the term 'neighbourhood', those who live there can be described as 'residents' or 'neighbours'. This is more humanising and less stigmatising than 'slum dwellers' or 'squatters'.

2.0 A Working Definition: 'Slum and squatter neighbourhoods'

Having discussed various terms and concerns, a working definition needs to be chosen to help address the concerns we are raising. To address the question of what Christianity can offer the process of transformation in these areas, a working definition is required. The term 'slum and squatter neighbourhood', with quite a specific meaning, is therefore chosen as a term of reference for the remainder of this book.

2.1 The adjective 'slum' is used to describe the living conditions

To highlight the tough living conditions, the term 'slum' as defined by the UN-Habitat will be employed as an adjective. The UN-Habitat definition of a 'slum' can then be included.[52]

2.2 The adjective 'squatter' is used to describe legal concerns

To highlight concerns by scholars like De Soto and journalists like Neuwirth, the term 'squatter' will be specifically used as an adjective in relation to legal/extra-legal, formal/non-formal and authorised/unauthorised housing security. What these household areas have in common is that they are outside the protection of law.

2.3 The noun 'neighbourhood' is used to describe place and spatial concerns

It was noted above that Srinivas uses the two terms 'slum and squatter' together adjectivally, and this use will be adopted throughout the research. Where this study departs from Srinivas is in the use of the noun 'neighbourhood' rather than 'settlement'. This choice is made primarily to highlight the commonality of space shared between households in relationship to the broader city. The term 'settlement', while more often used in discourse by scholars and activists to describe the space and place these households occupy, is not as helpful to this particular study as 'neighbourhood'. It does not point clearly enough to what those living in slum and squatter neighbourhoods have in common with those in regular urban neighbourhoods. Terms other than 'neighbourhood' could potentially create further marginalisation.

There are two further reasons for choosing these terms and definitions as a reference point that does help limit and focus our concerns. First, this book doesn't require its own statistical estimation of the numbers of residents living in slum and squatter neighbourhoods. This work has already been done by UN-Habitat. Using 'slum' as an adjective and not a noun keeps us in step with the UN-Habitat's 'five elements' in slum-households, but opens up the definition for the particular purposes of this study. Second, 'slum and squatter neighbourhoods' is a term that can aid the discussion of theological and practical contributions to transformation by Christians. This is our main focus of this study. A more statistically loaded definition is not required.

3.0 Explosive Growth Since World War II and its Factors

Despite the lack of affordable housing options and knowing something of the challenges of living in slum and squatter neighbourhoods, around 1.3 million people around the world will move into urban areas this week.[53] That is around seventy million people annually.⁵⁴ Since World War II the urban population has grown by 2.5 billion, a more than six-fold increase, making it one of the largest migrations in human history.⁵⁵ With few exceptions, most Two-thirds World cities have had a common trajectory over the last hundred years or so, which has created some characteristic challenges for residents. There were low growth rates for the first half of the twentieth century. Then suddenly in the 1950s, urban populations started to explode, especially in slum and squatter neighbourhoods. For example, Dhaka, Bangladesh, had a population of 110,000 in 1800, and by 1900 the figure had actually decreased to 90,000. In 1950 it was up again to 417,000. By the year 2000, however, Dhaka had a population of over ten million people.⁵⁶ African cities such as Nairobi (Kenya), Khartoum (Sudan), Abidjan (Ivory Coast), Dar es Salaam (Tanzania) and Lagos (Nigeria) increased their urban populations on average sixteen-fold between 1950 and 1980.⁵⁷ As table 3 below shows, this is a common phenomenon around the world.

Table 3: The fastest growing large cities 1950 to 2000, according to average increment per year in population

Urban Centre	Country	Population (Thousand)				Compound Growth Rate, 1950-2000	Average Incremental Per Year, 1950-2000 (Thousand)
		c.1800	c.1900	1950	2000		
Tokyo	Japan	492	1,497	11,275	34,450	2.3	464
Mexico City	Mexico	137	415	2,883	18,006	3.7	304
Sao Paulo	Brazil	f	240	2,334	17,099	4.1	295
Mumbai (Bombay)	India	174	928	2,857	16,086	3.4	265
Delhi	India	125	209	1,369	12,441	4.5	221
Dhaka	Bangladesh	110	90	417	10,159	6.6	195
Jakarta	Indonesia	92	115	1,452	11,065	4.2	192
Karachi	Pakistan	14	136	1,047	10,020	4.6	179
Seoul	Repuublic of Korea	190	201	1,021	9,917	4.7	178
Kolkata (Calcutta)	India	200	1,085	4,513	13,058	2.2	171
Manila	Philippines	85	204	1,544	9,950	3.8	168
Lagos	Nigeria	5	42	288	8,422	7.0	163
Al-Qahirah (Cairo)	Egypt	260	595	2,494	10,391	2.9	158
Rio De Janeiro	Brazil	43	967	2,950	10,803	2.6	157
Istanbul/ Constantinople	Turkey	570	900	967	8,744	4.5	156

*Source: Satterthwaite, 2007*⁵⁸

If the nature of these slum and squatter neighbourhoods is to be understood we need to consider why such unprecedented urban growth has happened in the second half of the twentieth century. What has changed? What are the push and pull factors—reasons for leaving the countryside and factors attracting people to the city—for what is predicted to be two billion people living in these neighbourhoods by 2025? We can briefly identify five of the most important factors creating the rapid growth of slum and squatter neighbourhoods, before considering their impact on residents.

3.1 Major ideologies fell and brought down with them walls impeding access to cities

Three ideologies employed in the running of nation states were responsible for the intentional creation of walls around cities to keep rural people at bay. These barriers mostly fell or loosened up by the second half of the twentieth century. The ideologies of colonialism, communism and military dictatorships in different ways restricted the internal movement of people, including movement to cities. The case of Nairobi illustrates this well. Nairobi was originally a tiny Masai tribal village prior to 1899,[59] before it was built up by the British to serve as a base for construction and servicing of a railroad. It was conceived as a European city to serve only the white settlers. In fact, the only Africans allowed to walk the streets there were those who had labour skills needed by the colonial class. Nairobi was systematically racially zoned in the plans of 1905, 1927 and 1948.[60] It was also an odd location for a city to be developed, as Neuwirth explains. Its 'terrible drainage and water shortages plague it to this day' he wrote, 'and the early administrators actually considered knocking it down and moving the entire city to a more favourable location, but the idea was simply too costly. Warts and all, Nairobi would remain Kenya's number one city'.[61] The local African population was still required for labour, and by the 1930s they had rough homes just outside of the downtown area and down by the Mathare River. These areas had none of the infrastructure of the settler neighbourhoods. Even so, at times even these settlements were considered a threat, as demonstrated by the 1953 demolition of 7,000 homes in the Mathare River area by British police in search of Mau Mau rebels.[62]

With the fall of British colonial rule in 1964 racial access restrictions to Nairobi were lifted. While colonial-style bureaucracy remained (just taken over by locals), a principal barrier to moving to Nairobi was gone. Its dire location and planning, however, already a problem in the time of colonial rule, would cripple its ability to cope with more than six million people who, now free to move, flooded into Nairobi in search for work, including nearly two million into slum and squatter neighbourhoods.[63] UN-Habitat reports that in 1971 there were fifty such neighbourhoods with 167,000 residents, but by 1995 there were 134 with some 1.8 million residents and that 'the share of informal-settlement village inhabitants rose from one third to an estimated 60 per cent' of Nairobi as a city.[64] Some of these slum and squatter settlements are the world's largest, including Kibera, which has over 800,000 residents and was made famous around the world after being the setting for the Hollywood film, *The Constant Gardener*.[65] Not only did the fall or partial fall of the ideologies of colonialism, communism and militarism lead to the easing of restrictions concerning where people could live, it opened up access to cities for the growing numbers of rural poor. Chart 4 below shows the dramatic increase in size of Africa's cities since the 1950s and 1960s when many African countries won independence.

Chart 4: Population growth for African's largest cities in 2000 over two centuries

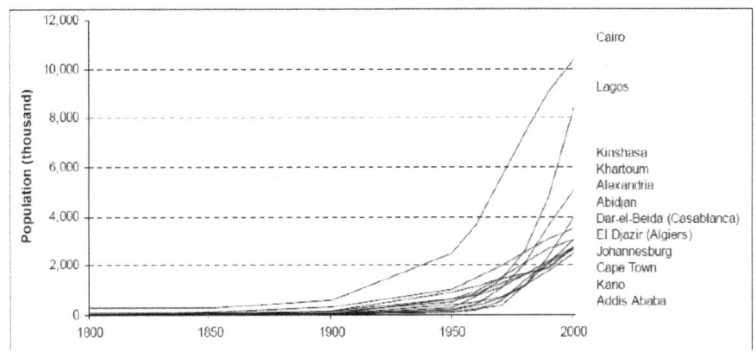

Chart 3: Population growth for African's largest cities in 2000 over two centuries

Source: Satterthwaite, 2007[66]

3.2 Urbanisation's link with globalisation's rise

Ideas of democracy, globalisation and free-market economies filled the ideological gap left by colonialism, communism and militarism for much of the developing world. Helped by the UN and World Bank economists, much of the Two-thirds World has moved to some form of free-market economy over the last fifty years. Even those considered Communist, such as China or Vietnam, have liberalised their economies. Yet during the same period of time improved technologies and agricultural practices have meant that the world does not need as many rural people producing food as in the past. For example, in the US, the number of people engaged in farming dropped from seventeen per cent of the total workforce in 1940 to six per cent by 1960.[67] The lowering of barriers and freedom of movement to chase employment, coupled with the smaller percentage of the population required to produce food has a logical conclusion for millions of rural people: go to cities in the hope of better jobs, education for children and housing. The influential economist Jeffrey Sachs explains the link between economic growth and urbanisation in two ways.

The first is that agricultural practices improve so that 'As food production per farmer rises, an economy needs fewer and fewer farmers to feed the overall population'.[68] This cheapens food and raises the income of farmers—then fewer farmers are required.

The second is the advantages urban areas have for finding non-agricultural-based jobs. 'Once the labor force is no longer engaged mainly in food production, it is natural that the bulk of the population will relocate to cities, drawn by higher wages that in turn reflect the higher productivity of work in densely settled urban areas.'[69] For Sachs the pull and the push of the city is a natural and expected consequence of a growing free-market, global economy. The question of why this same free-market cannot provide adequate neighbourhoods and affordable housing for these people to live in is an important, but often overlooked discussion. It is at the heart of Davis' thesis that the failure of global capitalism and the intentional withdrawal of the State is the primary cause of the lack of affordable urban housing that produces urban slum growth.[70] To be fair to Sachs he sees the connection and has personally been involved in the Millennium Development Goals taskforce monitoring the progress toward slum changes. In the foreword to a recent report Sachs writes that it identified 'strategies needed to meet one of the most important challenges of our time. Cities in developing countries need to improve the lives of slum dwellers and manage a projected near doubling of the urban population over the next three decades'.[71]

Here it suffices to say that rapid urbanisation is a natural consequence of the ideology of globalisation and free-market economies, in a way that was not true in the age of colonialism, communism and militarism before the second half of the twentieth century. This can especially be seen in fast-growing Asian cities, shown in chart 5 below, where cities like Tokyo literally grow off the chart to reach over 34 million residents.

Chart 5: Population growth over two centuries for Asia's largest cities in 2000

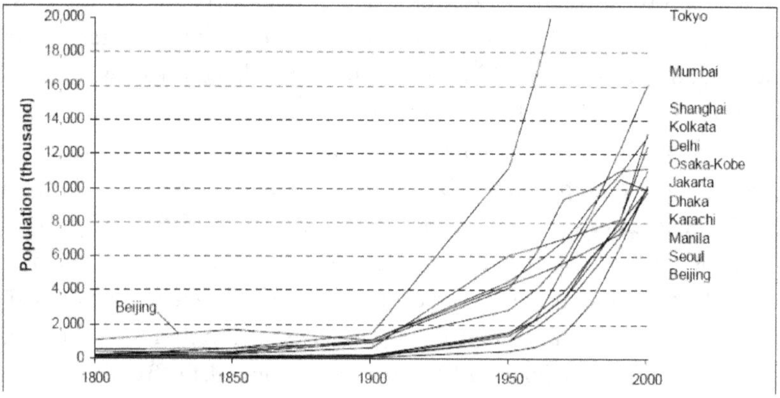

Source: Satterthwaite, 2007[72]

3.3 Numbers of people able to flee, or return from, persecution since World War II have risen

Many residents of slums are in fact refugees or internally displaced people, fleeing persecution elsewhere or returning to a city after persecution. This internationalisation of slum and squatter neighbourhoods is markedly different to what happened in cities before World War II. For example, some of the world's largest slum and squatter neighbourhoods are in fact little more than refugee camps. In the 1990's, Goma slum in Zaire had over 700,000 Rwandans before many died of cholera mostly due to the slum's poor sanitation conditions.[73] The Gaza Strip, with more than 750,000 residents, is a more complicated case because of competing national claims and the neighbourhoods being isolated politically. Residents there have a well-founded fear of persecution and are considered refugees; two thirds are living on less than US$2 a day.[74] The movement of refugees is not a recent phenomenon, but in 2011 there are 15.1 million refugees worldwide, with over half living in urban areas.[75] Access to a greater range of cheaper transportation options than prior to World War II, as well as better UN protection of refugees, helps to explain the rise.

3.4 Overall rise in population growth since World War II

It took until 1820 for the world population to first reach one billion people. By 1930 it was two billion and then by 1960 it was three billion. Between 1960 and 2000 the human population doubled to six billion people.[76] This rapid world population growth rate, especially since World War II, has a natural flow-on effect on the growth of slum and squatter neighbourhood populations. There are a number of factors of population growth which affect the growth of slum and squatter neighbourhoods. These include the higher birth rates of existing slum dwellers, lower child mortality rates and higher average life expectancies. Not only are more people being born, including being born into slums, but more people are living longer, including living longer in slum and squatter neighbourhoods. This can be seen in table 4 below, which outlines the exponential growth in numbers of urban dwellers.

Table 4: The declining time needed for one billion additional urban dwellers

World's Total Urban Population	Time Taken
0 to 1 billion urban dwellers	10,000 years (c. 8,000 BC-1960)
1 to 2 billion urban dwellers	25 years (1960-1985)
2 to 3 billion urban dwellers	18 years (1985-2003)
3 to 4 billion urban dwellers	15 years (2003-2018)

Source: Satterthwaite, 2007[77]

3.5 Rise of environmental problems since World War II

There are two major dynamics here that affect the growth of urbanisation and slums. First, environmental disasters such as earthquakes, famines, floods, droughts and volcanic eruptions are problems that are increasing in places of human activity. Residents can only flee to the city to start again or to try to rebuild. Many choose to relocate to slums rather than try to rebuild.

Second, growing urban populations and industries require more water, fossil fuels, electricity, land and places to dump their waste. None of these resources can be found in urban areas and so rural people are stripped of these resources or at least restricted in their access to them. Rapid urbanisation is such an issue in India, for example, that more than 50,000 hectares of valuable croplands are lost to urbanisation each year.[78] This urban encroachment on environmental reserves affects both urban people as their regional food and water supplies become polluted, but also those who have farmed rural regions for generations. Rural people are often left with little choice but to become part of cities, and are only able to afford slum housing. Chart 6 shows the rapid population growth of key Indian cities, whose growth is putting a strain on environmental forces.

Chart 6: Population growth over two centuries for India's largest cities in 2000

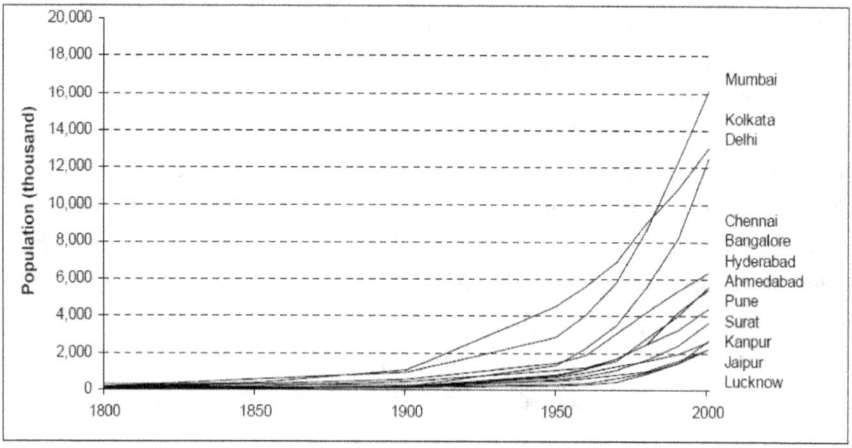

Source: Satterthwaite, 2007[79]

Lack of environmental sustainability is one of the key factors in the rise of slums, but also could increase the density of slum living. Cities like Bangkok, for example, are on low-lying clay-based land that is sinking. Even small rises in sea levels could claim large areas of slum residents' homes, creating further overcrowding. Some predict that this could happen in Bangkok within ten to fifteen years[80]—and Bangkok is just one city with slums that are affected. The Associated Press reported that, 'Of the 33 cities predicted to have at least 8 million people by 2015, at least 21 are highly vulnerable' and these 'include Dhaka, Bangladesh; Buenos Aires, Argentina; Rio de Janeiro, Brazil; Shanghai and Tianjin in China; Alexandria and Cairo in Egypt; Mumbai and Kolkata in India; Jakarta, Indonesia; Tokyo and Osaka-Kobe in Japan;

Lagos, Nigeria; Karachi, Pakistan; Bangkok, Thailand, and New York and Los Angeles in the United States'.[81] Issues of environmental sustainability are connected to the future of all humans. A recent *National Geographic* article on human population growth said succinctly,

> The central challenge for the future of people and the planet is how to raise more of us out of poverty—the slum dwellers in Delhi, the subsistence farmers in Rwanda— while reducing the impact each of us has on the planet.[82]

There is no indication that the five factors considered to have helped fuel the rapid creation of urban slum and squatter neighbourhoods over the last fifty years will come to an end any time soon. Unless something dramatic forces changes to these factors—like billions of deaths through nuclear war, pandemics of infectious diseases or the collapse of global capitalistic ideologies and their replacement by ideologies global restraint—then the numbers of slum residents will continue to increase.

Each urban slum and squatter neighbourhood is made up of a unique constellation of personalities and settings. Yet, as we saw in Chapter One, there are many challenges common to these neighbourhoods. From my experiences living in a slum and squatter neighbourhood (and supported by appropriate data) we identified ten characteristic challenges faced by residents of these neighbourhoods. These challenges have different degrees of impact on residents, but because of their nature, most slum and squatter neighbourhoods have to confront these challenges at some stage in their development. Compared with regular urban neighbourhoods, characteristic challenges faced by slum residents include those associated with: housing security and threat of eviction; poorly built homes; long-term planning; overcrowding; sanitation and related health issues; lack of secure employment; organised crime and corruption; lack of quality local schooling and educational opportunities; dangerous and toxic 'dumping grounds'; despair and the 'culture of poverty'. Real harm and in some cases premature deaths can be caused by these characteristic conditions. Anna Tibaijuka, the director of UN-Habitat says:

> Global intra-city statistics clearly show that slums are amongst the world's most dangerous places to live. Their people are victims of crime and violence, and suffer a greater incidence of disease. Child mortality is much higher than elsewhere, life expectancy is much lower, and slums are fast becoming breeding grounds for AIDS. In Nairobi—where over 60 per cent of the urban population live on 5 per cent of the land—150 out of every 1,000 children die under the age of five, compared to 83.9 deaths per 1,000 children in the formal areas of the city and 113 in rural areas.[83]

These are not just vague numbers, but real lives (and deaths). Watching a person die unnecessarily is amongst the most harrowing of human experiences, and a deep, despairing futility can easily emerge. Urban slum and squatter neighbourhood residents regularly face these challenges because they are inherent to the kind of living conditions and legal status that defines their neighbourhoods as part of rapidly growing urban populations.

This chapter outlined the basic definitions, nature and challenges of the rise of slum and squatter neighbourhoods. With this in mind, the impact of Christianity can now be examined.

Chapter Three

What Are Christians Doing? The Current State of Christian Response to the Rise of Urban Slum and Squatter Neighbourhoods

Christian faith and mission faces a new urban world. What is Christianity doing to respond to this sudden rise and phenomenon of urban slum and squatter neighbourhoods? It is difficult to get an accurate overall picture, not least because the kind of global census of slums carried out by UN-Habitat has not been embraced by Christians as part of their mission. For example Todd Johnson, editor of *Atlas of Global Christianity*, explains that slums are difficult places about which to find accurate information in general, but information about Christianity in slums is even more difficult to obtain:

> Estimating the number of Christians in the slums of the world is difficult because data are not collected specifically on religious affiliation in slums. Church statistics are also problematic because of the fluid nature of slum populations and the lack of ecclesiastical infrastructure. Strategies to reach slum-dwellers are best worked out on the ground where changing circumstances and shifting populations can be addressed directly.[1]

Though there is a lack of co-ordinated hard data about the numbers of churches and Christians in urban slums, we can get a rough picture from a specific city's research and anecdotal evidence. From these sources some broader trends can be detected and we can seek confirmation of these from urban Christian experts and some anecdotal evidence.

1.0 Christianity in Urban Areas Generally

Although Christianity began in the rural villages of Galilee, it grew to be an influential movement throughout Roman cities and urban centres. From its early beginnings in Jerusalem, to its growth in Roman colonial cities like Ephesus and its eventual status as the official religion of the Roman Empire, Christianity has a history of adapting to urban conditions and finding resonance among urban populations. Christian faith even sees its eschatological end in the city of 'New Jerusalem' (Revelation 3:12). However, this urban influence has been mixed. At its best, for example, during the plagues in Roman cities when Pagan priests and most who were able to flee did so, the courage of early Christians to stay with the afflicted is credited as an important dimension in the rise of Christianity.[2] The credibility of a Christian faith underpinning such acts rose too.[3] However, Christianity can also be seen at its worst when entwined with the dark spectre of European colonisation. Certainly this became the case when Christianity became the official religion of the Roman Empire, but also later the British, Dutch, Spanish and Portuguese Empires—which intertwined the tasks of 'civilising' and 'Christianising'—were an especially oppressive force upon indigenous populations around the world and cities became important places for this to be based from.

Almost certainly Christianity's urban influence began to wane prior to 1900. According to Barrett and Johnson's 'Status of Global Mission', cities seem to have been tough places for Christianity to find resonance in since then. For example, they note that in 1900 urban Christians made up over 68% of the global urban population, but by 2004 the figure was 39.67%, with projections at just 36.90% for 2025.[4] The decline can be seen in chart 7 below.

Chart 7: Proportion of Christians in global urban populations

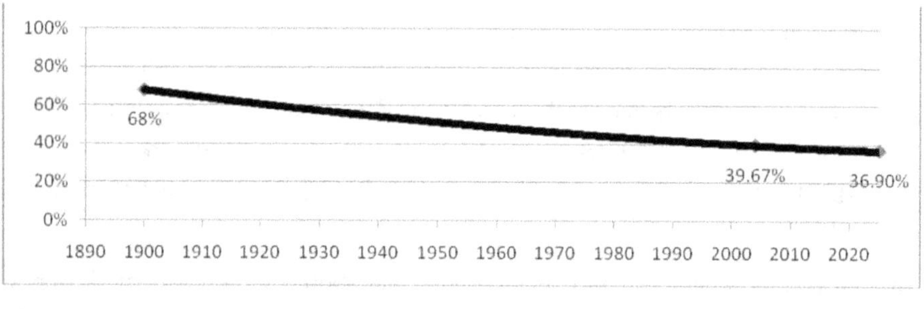

Source: Status of Global Mission, 2004[5]

In 1910, the world had only twenty mega cities (cities with a population of over one million). *Atlas of Global Christianity* notes that the largest ten were each over 95% Christian, as shown in table 5 on the following page.

Table 5: The largest cities in 1910 and their percentage Christian

Size Rank	City	Country	Population	Christians	Percentage Christian
1.	London	Britain	6,958,000	6,680,000	96.0
2.	New York	USA	5,405,000	5,135,000	95.0
3.	Paris	France	3,854,000	3,777,000	98.0
4.	Berlin	Germany	2,966,000	2,906,000	98.0
5.	Chicago	USA	2,300,000	2,208,000	96.0
6.	Vienna	Austria	1,739,000	1,670,000	96.0
7.	Philadelphia	USA	1,654,000	1,588,000	96.0
8.	Buenos Aires	Argentina	1,464,000	1,435,000	98.0
9.	Ruhr	Germany	1,406,000	1,378,000	98.0
10.	Manchester	Britain	1,425,000	1,368,000	96.0

Source: Atlas of Global Christianity, 2009[6]

Only five of the twenty mega cities were minority Christian in 1910. By mid 2010, however, there were 498 mega cites with 266 considered 'non-Christian'. By 2025 projections have numbers of non-Christian mega cities at 300 out of a total of 650 mega cities.[7]

Further, numbers of new non-Christian people in urban areas are rapidly growing. According to David Barrett and Todd Johnson, in 1800 the number of new non-Christian urbanites per day was 500 people. By 1900 it was 5,200 per day. By 2004 it was 138,000 and by 2025 this figure is projected to rise to 200,000 per day.[8] This growth can be seen graphically in chart 8 below. By most measures, then, urban Christianity has shrunk as an influence in comparison to the rapid population rise of cities over the last two hundred years.

Chart 8: Number of new non-Christian urban dwellers per day

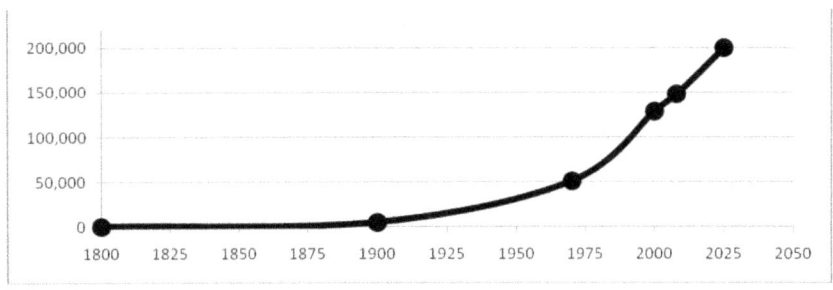

Source: Status of Global Mission, 2010[9]

80 SLUM LIFE RISING

We also know that there are certain kinds of cities where Christianity is stronger, and others where Christianity struggles to make a numerical impact. This can be clearly seen in data from the *Atlas of Global Christianity*. For example, there are cities like Mexico City where 95% of the population describe themselves as Christian. On the other hand, cities like Mogadishu are 96% Muslim. Maps 3 and 4 below show the cities where Christianity is strongest and where other religions are stronger.

Map 3: Largest cities by religious adherence, 2010

Source: Atlas of Global Christianity, 2009[10] *See colour version in Appendix*

Map 4: One hundred cities with the most Christians, 2010

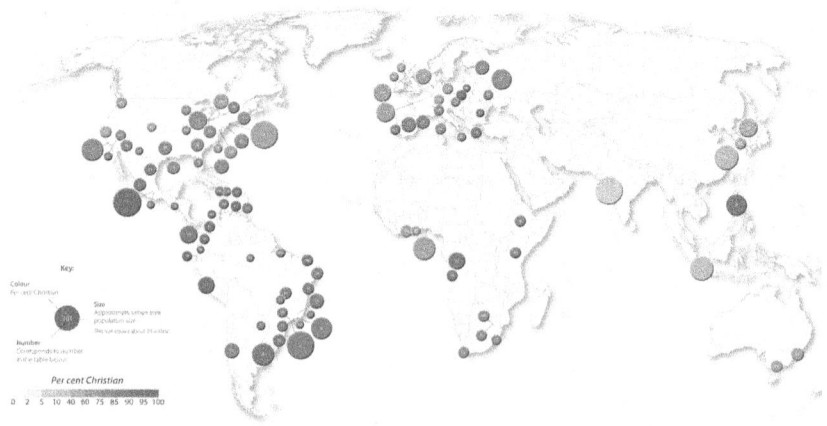

Source: Atlas of Global Christianity, 2009[11] *See colour version in Appendix*

There are a number of common factors here. First, Christianity is struggling in the cities of nations which are still undergoing rapid urbanisation but which are not under communism. Christianity is strongest in cities where urbanisation rates have stabled or are even in decline. At a regional level this can be clearly seen in table 5 below. Consider the urban rates of change, the percentage of the population that is urban, and the percentage of the population that is Christian. With the exception of Sub-Saharan Africa, in regions where the urban rate of change is higher than 2%, the population is less than 8.6% Christian. This trend can especially be seen in many Asian cities, like those found in India, Pakistan, Afghanistan, Thailand and Cambodia. North Africa is another place where urbanisation has not yet peaked and where Christianity is numerically weak. In many cities where rates of urbanisation have stabilised, however, Christianity is doing numerically better. This can especially be seen in Western cities like Los Angeles, US (80% Christian), Rhine Ruhr, Germany (73%) and Melbourne, Australia (69.1%).[12] Christianity is even doing better numerically in cities whose countries have recently stabilised their urbanisation rates, such as cities in Latin America (for example, Bogota 93% Christian, Mexico City 95.3% Christian), South Korea (Seoul 45.7% Christian), and the Philippines (Manila 93.8% Christian).[13] The exception to this rule is Sub-Saharan Africa, which still has high growth rates of urbanisation, but also has a high percentage of Christians. The history of colonisation in Sub-Saharan Africa is a part of the reason for this being the case.

Table 6: Urbanisation and Christianity

Region	Urban Rate of Change			Percentage of Urban Population			Percentage Christian 2010
	1950-55	1970-75	2005-10	1950	1970	2010	
World	3.12	2.56	1.92	28.83	36.08	50.46	33.2
Europe	2.06	1.35	0.40	51.27	62.84	72.78	80.2
North America	2.67	0.95	1.31	63.90	73.80	82.13	81.2
Oceania	2.85	1.82	1.28	62.00	70.80	70.22	78.5
Latin America	4.52	3.67	1.60	41.38	57.06	79.63	92.5
Asia	3.93	3.38	2.28	16.33	22.73	42.17	8.5
North Africa	4.40	3.67	2.45	24.78	36.22	51.15	8.5
Sub-Saharan Africa	4.88	4.83	3.71	11.10	19.50	37.30	82.0

Sources: Urbanisation rates and percentages from United Nations, 2007[14], Christianity percentages from Atlas of Global Christianity, 2009[15]

Second, urban Christianity struggles where colonisation did not leave a majority of citizens Christian. Thus, Christianity is relatively strong in the urban areas of North America, Australia, Manila, Latin American and Sub-Saharan Africa. However, urban Christianity is far weaker numerically in most cities of Asia, Northern Africa and the Middle-East. It should be acknowledged, however, that the kinds of Christianity that State religion and colonisation can produce can be characterised by high levels of Christian nominalism. This is not just the case in the Two-thirds World, but also where there are still official State churches in Europe. So while large sections of a population may identify themselves as Christian, what that identity means is more difficult to measure.

Third, Christianity is currently not strong numerically in cities where there is already a major religion other than Christianity, and that religion is the majority. Cities in this category include Cairo (82% Islam), Bangkok (78% Buddhist) and Delhi (78% Hindu). However, where Christianity is the majority, or even where there is a variety of religious expressions, Christianity fares better. For example, in Oceania, Europe and North America, there are strong numbers of urban Christian adherents. Further, where there is more pluralism (like many cities in China, South Korea or Indonesia), Christianity is able to survive, even thrive.

Fourth, Christianity in general struggles in the region known as the 10/40 Window—including in the cities of this region. Map 5 below shows this geographical area, which extends from West Africa across the Middle-East to Asia, between 10 degrees north and 40 degrees north of the equator.

Map 5: The 10/40 Window

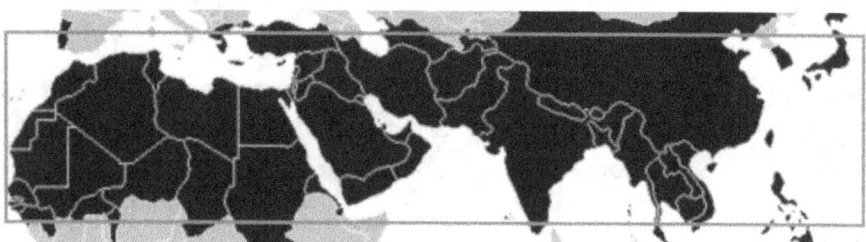

Source: The Joshua Project[16]

Evangelical strategist Luis Bush and the Joshua Project, following the AD2000 movement, have been especially focused on this region and its cities, identifying it as the least evangelised part of the world. They contend that: 'The top 50 least evangelised megacities [i.e., cities over one million] are all in the 10/40 Window'.[17] Bush estimates that: '97 per cent of the 3 billion people who live in the 55 most unevangelised countries live in the 10/40 Window.' This not only 'constitutes the core of the challenge of reaching the unreached',[18] but is also geographically significant in terms of poverty, with over 2.4 billion people there earning less than $500 a year and where 'only 8 per cent of all missionaries work among these people'.[19] The 10/40 Window is also the focus of attention for geo-political reasons. For example, the US-based Foreign Policy Research Institute wrote an article entitled, "The 'Mega-Eights': Urban Leviathans and International Instability" which looked at the mega cities of this region where 'socioeconomic challenges are the most daunting', and where 'turmoil and violence are unavoidable. Without doubt, unchecked growth in the "10/40 Window" will change the face of the global map in the twenty-first century.'[20]

The 10/40 Window only has 8.5% of all Christians (352 million people).[21] Given that over 140 million of these Christians live in Eastern Asia (which includes South Korea and China),[22] the numbers become far starker for the other parts of Asia, and for Middle-Eastern and North African cities.

In summary, then, cities with an existing dominant major religion other than Christianity, cities which have experienced colonisation and cities with high rates of urbanisation and are in geographically located in 10/40 Window are less likely to have a strong urban Christian population. As we shall see these are the kinds of cities where the majority of slum residents live.

2.0 Christianity in Urban Slum and Squatter Neighbourhoods

If Christianity struggles in urban areas under certain conditions, it seems also to have had little impact numerically in the majority of urban slum and squatter neighbourhoods. This can be seen by comparing the following three maps, which show human population density, Christian population density and slum population as a percentage of human population. We saw earlier that the rural population has already peaked as a percentage of the human population, and that the Two-third World's urban areas, including slums, will absorb almost all future population growth.[23] Maps 3 and 4 below compare current human population density and Christian population density. Map 6 shows where slum-dwelling is more and less common within a population. Compare all three maps and Christianity can be seen as weakest in the areas where population density and slum percentages are highest.

Map 6: Concentration of human population, 2010

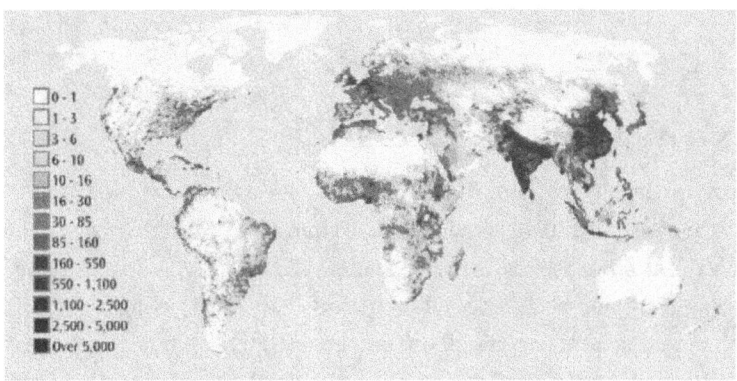

Source: Center for International Earth Science Information Network, Columbia University, 'Gridded Population of the World'[24] See colour version in Appendix

Map 7: Concentration of Christian population, 2010

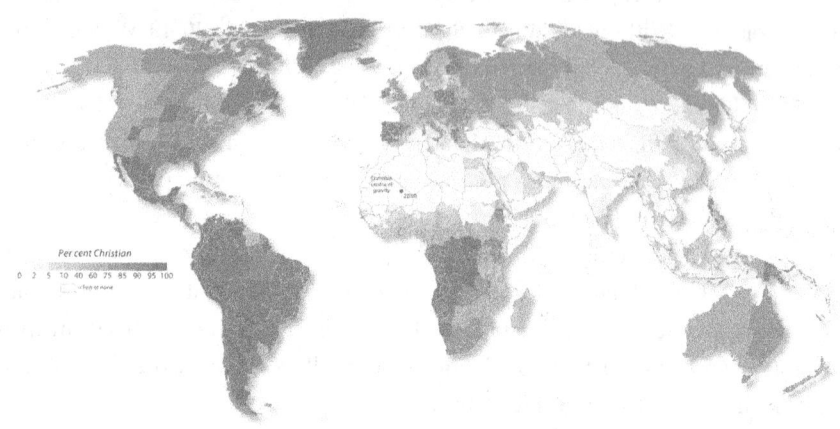

Source: Atlas of Global Christianity, 2009[25]   *See colour version in Appendix*

Map 8: Share of slum population as percentage of human population, 2003

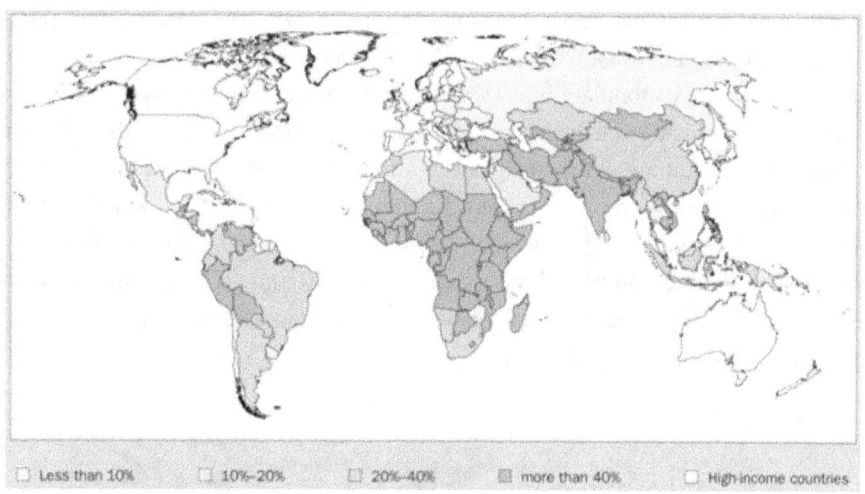

Source: UN-Habitat 2003   *See colour version in Appendix*

Few Christians live in many of the cities where slums are most prevalent. This is especially the case in the 10/40 Window, where almost two out of three slum residents live. What is unknown is how many of the few Christians who live in these cities live in urban slum and squatter neighbourhoods. For example, for the ten Indian cities with populations of over a million, we have estimates of how many Christians there are (*Atlas of Global Christianity*), and how many slums residents there are (*2001 Indian Census figures*)—but we can't tell how *many* Christians live in slums in these cities. As Chart 9 below shows, with only two exceptions (Bangalore and Chennai), even in the unlikely event that all the Christians in these cities *only* lived in slums, with none living outside of slums, Christians still represent only a small fraction of residents living in slums there. Christianity may well be doing better in slums than outside of slums, but this premise can be neither supported nor denied by the currently available data.

Chart 9: Proportion of slum dwellers and Christians of total Indian populations in Indian cities over one million people

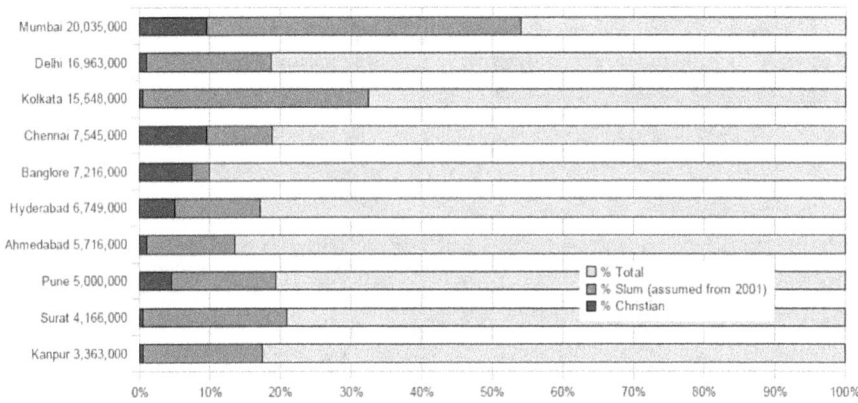

Source: based on Indian Census 2001[26] and Atlas of Global Christianity 2010[27]

Factors that contribute to the overall and continuing trend of few Christians in areas of high human and slum populations include the following. First, in countries where rapid urbanisation continues, slums are to be expected. Rapid urbanisation is also one of the contexts in which Christianity is weakest. One example is Dhaka, Bangladesh, which between 2005 and 2010 had a national urbanisation rate of 3.45%, and a slum population of 3.4 million,[28] combined with a Muslim population of 90%.[29] Similar numbers can be seen in many Asian and North African cities where annual urbanisation rates are often double the world average.

Second, slums are prevalent in post-colonial cities which were left with a minority Christian population. Consider cities in Pakistan, for example, where between 35 and 50 per cent of the urban population lives in slums known as Katchi Abadis. Pakistan's *Daily Times* noted that 'The growth of these informal settlements in the two mega cities, Karachi and Lahore, has particularly been massive. In the former, these settlements increased from 212 in 1958 to more than 500. In Lahore, there are more than 300 Katchi Abadis, while in Faisalabad, at least 40 per cent of the population lives in these Abadis'.[30] The percentage of Christians in Karachi, Lahore and Faisalabad is tiny, with over 93% of these cities Muslim.[31] Similar trends are found in post-colonial cities where Christians were a minority across Asia, the Middle East

86 SLUM LIFE RISING

and North Africa. All cities like these have low percentages of Christians as well as high numbers of slums. Chart 10 below shows the fifty largest cities in Asia and their religious composition. Only three of these cities have significant percentages of Christian residents. South Korea's Seoul and Pusan have very few slums, leaving Manila as the only Asian city in the top fifty to have both large numbers of slum residents and a large Christian population.

Chart 10: Fifty largest urban areas in Asia by total population, 2010

▼ Key for religion bars below

Agnostic	Christian	Jain	Sikh
Atheist	Confucianist	Jew	Spiritist
Baha'i	Daoist	Muslim	Zoroastrian
Buddhist	Ethnoreligionist	New Religionist	
Chinese folk	Hindu	Shintoist	

	Urban area	Country	Population	Largest	%	Religions Adherents by percentage
1	TOKYO	Japan	35,467,000	Buddhists	56.0	
2	Mumbai	India	20,036,000	Hindus	69.0	
3	Delhi	India	16,983,000	Hindus	78.0	
4	Shanghai	China	15,790,000	Chinese folk	30.0	
5	Kolkata	India	15,548,000	Hindus	69.0	
6	JAKARTA	Indonesia	15,206,000	Muslims	65.0	
7	DHAKA	Bangladesh	14,625,000	Muslims	90.0	
8	Karachi	Pakistan	13,252,000	Muslims	93.0	
9	MANILA	Philippines	11,799,000	Christians	93.8	
10	BEIJING	China	11,741,000	Agnostics	36.0	
11	Osaka-Kobe	Japan	11,305,000	Buddhists	55.0	
12	Istanbul	Turkey	10,546,000	Muslims	95.0	
13	SEOUL	South Korea	9,554,000	Christians	45.7	
14	Guangzhou	China	9,447,000	Agnostics	36.0	
15	Shenzhen	China	8,114,000	Agnostics	35.0	
16	TEHRAN	Iran	7,807,000	Muslims	95.0	
17	Chennai	India	7,545,000	Hindus	83.0	
18	Wuhan	China	7,542,000	Agnostics	36.0	
19	Tianjin	China	7,468,000	Agnostics	38.0	
20	Hong Kong	China	7,416,000	Agnostics	37.0	
21	Bangaluru	India	7,216,000	Hindus	76.0	
22	Lahore	Pakistan	7,201,000	Muslims	97.0	
23	BANGKOK	Thailand	6,963,000	Buddhists	78.0	
24	Hyderabad	India	6,749,000	Hindus	83.0	
25	Chongqing	China	6,690,000	Agnostics	38.0	
26	BAGHDAD	Iraq	6,593,000	Muslims	93.0	
27	Ahmadabad	India	5,716,000	Hindus	86.0	
28	Ho Chi Minh City	Viet Nam	5,698,000	Buddhists	43.0	
29	Pune	India	5,000,000	Hindus	75.0	
30	Shenyang	China	4,952,000	Agnostics	40.0	

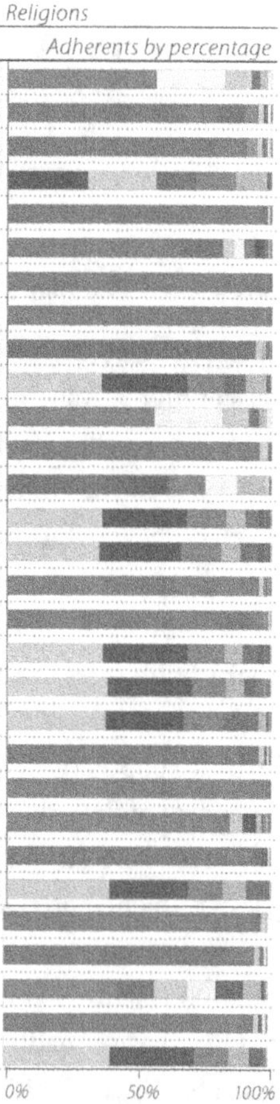

*Rate = average annual growth rate, per cent per year, between dates   0%   50%   100%

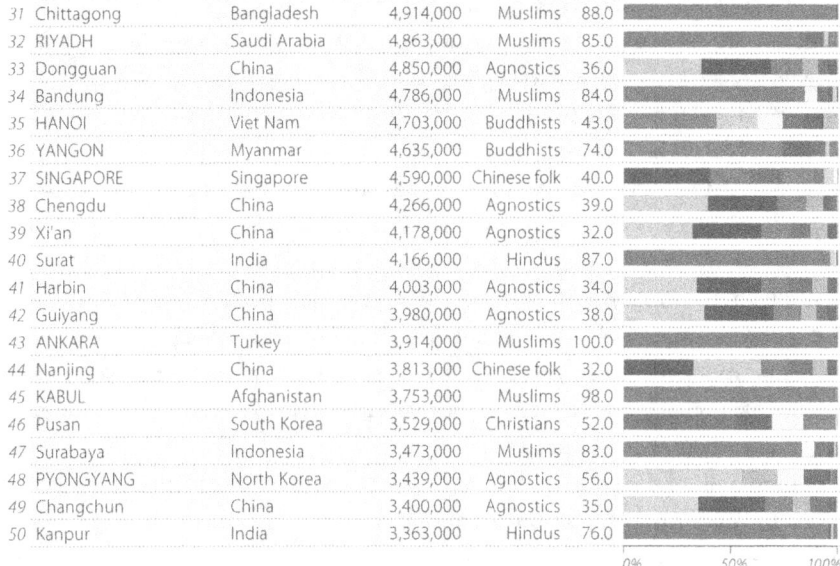

31 Chittagong	Bangladesh	4,914,000	Muslims	88.0	
32 RIYADH	Saudi Arabia	4,863,000	Muslims	85.0	
33 Dongguan	China	4,850,000	Agnostics	36.0	
34 Bandung	Indonesia	4,786,000	Muslims	84.0	
35 HANOI	Viet Nam	4,703,000	Buddhists	43.0	
36 YANGON	Myanmar	4,635,000	Buddhists	74.0	
37 SINGAPORE	Singapore	4,590,000	Chinese folk	40.0	
38 Chengdu	China	4,266,000	Agnostics	39.0	
39 Xi'an	China	4,178,000	Agnostics	32.0	
40 Surat	India	4,166,000	Hindus	87.0	
41 Harbin	China	4,003,000	Agnostics	34.0	
42 Guiyang	China	3,980,000	Agnostics	38.0	
43 ANKARA	Turkey	3,914,000	Muslims	100.0	
44 Nanjing	China	3,813,000	Chinese folk	32.0	
45 KABUL	Afghanistan	3,753,000	Muslims	98.0	
46 Pusan	South Korea	3,529,000	Christians	52.0	
47 Surabaya	Indonesia	3,473,000	Muslims	83.0	
48 PYONGYANG	North Korea	3,439,000	Agnostics	56.0	
49 Changchun	China	3,400,000	Agnostics	35.0	
50 Kanpur	India	3,363,000	Hindus	76.0	

Source: Atlas of Global Christianity, 2009[32] See colour version in Appendix

There are many post-colonial cities that do have high numbers of slum residents and high rates of Christian identification, however. This is especially the case in Latin America, Sub-Saharan Africa and Manila. However, as noted above, colonially-instigated Christianity is difficult to measure. If Christian community participation is one indicator of genuine Christianity, then we see mixed results in slums. In Manila, for example, which has a Christian identification rate of 93.8%,[33] and where there are 3.3 million slum residents, Viv Grigg found that there were 677 churches in 1998 and over 1000 by 2004, but only 3% of these were in slums.[34] Grigg did find higher rates of churches in slums, however, in other post-colonial cities like Lima, Peru. Lima has 2.7 million slum residents and 594 churches, and 90% of these churches are located in the slums.[35] In summary, in the slums of post-colonial cities with high rates of Christian identification there are reports of both high and low levels of church participation—so it is difficult to make a generalised statement about the state of Christianity in the slums of these cities. What we can say is that, to our knowledge, there are no reports of high rates of church participation in the slums of post-colonial cities where there are few Christians overall.

Third, slums are also prevalent in large numbers in cities where one of three 'other' major religions (Buddhism, Islam and Hinduism) are a majority. We can see, for example, in Appendix A that Bangkok slums have over 1.5 million residents, are mostly Buddhist, and have fewer than ten churches. Large Muslim cities like Dakar (Sengal) have over one million slum residents[36] but few Christians, as 89% are Muslim.[37] Hindu cities like Delhi have 1.5 million slum residents[38] but few Christians (78% Hindu).[39] Majority Hindu, Muslim and Buddhist cities all have very few Christians, but many have large numbers of slum residents.

Where poverty is most concentrated—and that includes where the most slum-residents live—Christianity is struggling most. As we have seen the so-called '10/40 Window' has been highlighted as a geographical area where poverty is extreme and Christianity is weak. This region also accounts for over 630 million slum residents, where almost two out of every three people, are slum residents.[40] Yet Christians comprise only 8.5% of the population in that region, a total of 352 million.[41] Indian cities like Mumbai, for example, have 3.2 million slum residents, Delhi 1.8 million and Kolkata 1.5 million,[43] and those cities have tiny percentages of Christians. Similar stories can be told throughout Asia and Northern Africa, where all three urban conditions identified earlier—rapid urbanisation, post-colonialism and the existence of another world religion in the majority—help to ensure a large number of slums, but with few Christians living in them.

The kind of hard data required to make more accurate assessments of the state of Christianity in slums is simply not yet available. Having examined the bigger trends, however, we can also turn to some expert opinions that lend support to the trends we have considered.

3.0 Anecdotes and Opinions From Urban Christian Experts

The struggle for Christianity to take root in a context of rapid urbanisation has been identified by many Christian scholars. Urban Christian scholar-activists like Harvie Conn,[44] Ray Bakke,[45] Robert Linthicum[46] and Colin Marchant[47] built on the more polarising work of Jacques Ellul, who viewed the city as inherently cursed by God.[48] By comparison Harvey Cox's view of the 'secular city' was optimistic (almost utopian) in the 1960s and 1970s.[49] There was a real concern about the lack of resonance that contemporary forms of Christianity were finding in urban areas, but it was possible for urban Christians to find 'a theology as big as the city', to use Bakke's phrase.[50] A common theme in these scholars' writings was the assumption that Christianity struggles to adapt to urban areas generally and the urban poor particularly, and that there is a need to take an urban Christian theology seriously. For example, Roger Greenwood contends that: 'The urban poor constitute the largest unclaimed frontier Christian missions has ever encountered. The urban masses have not yet heard of the Gospel of Jesus Christ or seen it demonstrated in ways that affect their lives... Their living conditions are largely unseen except in printed statistics and photographs. The causes of their poverty are barely understood by the vast majority of mission minded Christians.'[51]

Viv Grigg, a New Zealand urban Christian activist, writer and speaker who has pioneered a number of organisations that have focused on reaching the urban poor, has long argued that Christianity has neglected urban slums and does so at its peril. His books *Companion to the Poor* and *Cry of the Urban Poor* helped to at least put slums on the missiological radar. He argued that: 'More nightmarish than the poverty and its staggering growth is the fact that most political, religious and social actors have not yet turned their attention to address this global crisis... Since squatters and slum dwellers constitute an immense people group, we must make the urban poor the primary thrust of missions.'[52] Grigg has attempted to catalogue Christianity in urban slums as few others have done. For example, Grigg estimated that, 'nowhere in Asia, with the exception of Korea, does the church in slums make up more than four per cent of the existing church of that city'.[53] If current trends continue, the rise of urban areas with few Christians living in them—including slums—will be the norm. The Geneva Sector Intelligence's report, *Urban Slums Worldwide*, is an especially significant report commissioned by Grigg. It provides various statistics, opinions and anecdotal evidence to suggest that Christianity in the slums is not only a tiny minority, but that it is having serious trouble in engaging urban slum and squatter neighbourhoods. For example, the report cites The Cities Resource Network of the AD2000 and Beyond Movement (disbanded in 2000), which counted 1,736 'least evangelised cities' (with populations in excess of 100,000), all of which had large numbers of slum residents. 'While almost each of these cities had a handful of churches, none had sufficient numbers of believers to effectively evangelise their cities, let alone their slums.'[54] Grigg not only argued for a focus on slums, but questioned the current focus of churches and Christian NGOs. The report claimed that many Christian agencies are simply 'unequipped to deal with the challenge of urbanisation. No wonder most humanitarian agencies and Christian missions still concentrate most of their ministry and development efforts in rural and small town areas'.[55] The report also claimed that 'church growth in urban slums of many cities remains slow' with cities like Kolkata but one example where: 'Local church leaders agree that only an estimated 10 to 15 congregations in Kolkata can be considered slum churches. With a slum population of 6.5 million, this equates to 520,000 residents per slum church.[56]

Voices for urban Christianity such as Viv Grigg, Ray Bakke and Roger Greenwood, as well as Two-thirds World voices with first hand experiences in urban slum and squatter neighbourhoods, all call for deeper and more engagement with slums.[57] All testify to the importance, but near impotence, of the church in urban poor areas.

Grigg also offered table 7 below as a summary of his research on the church in the slums of various cities. Grigg acknowledges that his statistics are now out of date, but nevertheless his findings do lend support to the existence of the trends discussed above.

Table 7: The church in the slums

	Slum/Squatter Population	Slum/Squatter Percentage of Population	Number of Slums in City	Number of Churches in City	Number of Churches in Slums	Percentage of Churches in Slums
ASIA						
Kolkata, India	6+ million in one family per room 3.15 million in bustees, 48,000 on streets	57% 33% in bustees	1,000+	145	3 plus 10 house churches, several middle class churches where poor people attend	4%
Manila, Philippines (1st city in Asia where the poor movement of churches is happening)	3.3 million	38%	1,000+	15,000	677 in 1998, 1,000+ in 2004	6%
Bangkok, Thailand	1.2 million in slums now being re-housed in housing projects 600,000 prostitutes 500,000 drug addicts	17% in 1885, 6% in 2004, with 11% housed in concrete high rises, one family per room	1,024	156	3 + 6 house churches 2 ministries among prostitutes 3 ministries to drug addicts	2%
Chennai, India (Madras) (1st city in India turning to Christ)			2,000	4,000	1,500	37%
LATIN AMERICA						
Sao Paulo, Brazil	3 million in corticos, 1.5 million favelados, 700,000 street children	17% in slums and corticos, 24% poor	1,086	15,000	10,000	60%
Lima, Peru	2.7 million	55%	598	610	594	90%
Mexico City, Mexico	2.7 million	15-25%	500	2,500	1,500-2,100	60-80%

Source: *Viv Grigg, 'Where Are the Churches of the Poor?'* [58]

It's not just churches, though. When we look at overall trends of where Christian workers are located, we observe a similar trend. The areas where the most slum residents live have the lowest numbers of both international and national Christian workers. This can be clearly seen in maps 9 and 10 on the following page, which highlight the density of Christian workers per head of population. Where the majority of slum residents live is where the minority of both national and international Christian workers serve.

Map 9: National Christian workers (per million population) by country, 2010

Source: *Atlas of Global Christianity, 2009*[59]

Map 10: International Christian workers received (per million population) by country, 2010

Source: *Atlas of Global Christianity, 2009*[60]

92 SLUM LIFE RISING

This same observation can be made by looking at where Christian workers are coming from and going, shown graphically in chart 11 below.

Chart 11: Foreign missionaries sent and received by UN region, 2010

Quadrant meanings (numbers correspond to the following chart):

+	These quadrant lines represent the total global missionaries sent (per million affiliated Christians) against the total global missionaries received (per million population).
i	These regions send more missionaries per million affiliated Christians, and receive fewer missionaries per million population, than the global average.
ii	These regions send more missionaries per million affiliated Christians, and receive more missionaries per million population, than the global average.
iii	These regions send fewer missionaries per million affiliated Christians, and receive fewer missionaries per million population, than the global average.
iv	These regions send fewer missionaries per million affiliated Christians, and receive more missionaries per million population, than the global average.

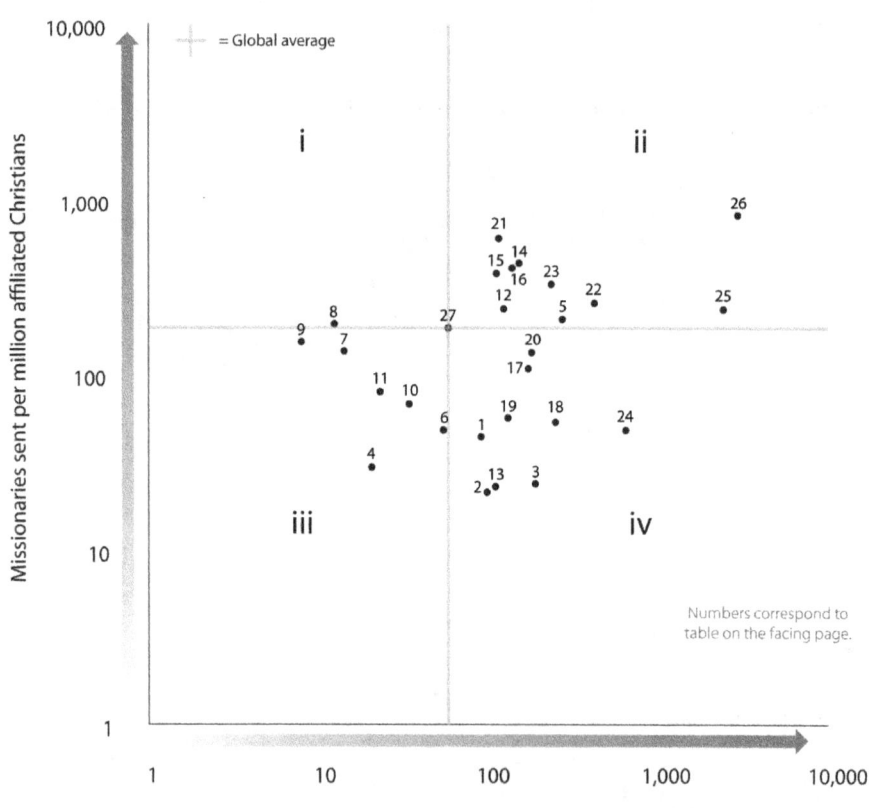

Numbers correspond to table on the facing page.

Missionaries sent and received					
1.	Africa	11.	Western Asia	21.	Northen America
2.	Eastern Africa	12.	Europe	22.	Oceania
3.	Middle Africa	13.	Eastern Europe	23.	Australia/New Zealand
4.	Northern Africa	14.	Northern Europe	24.	Melanesia
5.	Southern Africa	15.	Southern Europe	25.	Micronesia
6.	Western Africa	16.	Western Europe	26.	Polynesia
7.	Asia	17.	Latin America	27.	Global total
8.	Eastern Asia	18.	Caribbean		
9.	South-central Asia	19.	Central America		
10.	South-eastern Asia	20.	South America		

Source: Atlas of Global Christianity, 2009[61] *See colour version in Appendix*

Regions in quadrant iii receive and give fewer missionaries; these are North Africa, Western Africa, Asia, Eastern Asia, South-central Asia, South-eastern Asia and Western Asia. Given two out of every three slum residents live in these regions it is fair to say Christian worker involvement in these regions is under-represented for the needs.

These maps, opinions and figures cannot tell the full story, however; they can tell us only about the bigger picture geographically and not socially. Most probably fewer Christian workers would be working in slums than located in these regions overall.

To confirm these general opinions and trends, we can look closer at individual anecdotes and case studies of where Christian mission and development agencies are sending workers. For example, the Churches of Christ/Christian Churches is a growing strand of the Stone-Campbell movement with a long history of inspiring mission responses around the world. In the US alone there are over 1,144,000 members in 5,552 congregations.[62] Its annual National Missionary Convention has often had over ten thousand participants in recent years. Doug Priest, Executive Director of Christian Missionary Fellowship found, however, that the focus of their mission agencies on slums has been minimal, with a few exceptions. He told of a survey he took among the four largest mission sending agencies in the United States among the Restoration Movement (independent Christian Churches/Churches of Christ), to determine the number of missionaries whose major ministry focus is those living in urban slums outside of the USA. Table 8 on the following page outlines the survey's findings.

Table 8: Number of US missionaries with a major ministry focus in urban slums outside of the US

Number of Missionaries Serving Outside of the US in the Four Agencies	Number of Missionaries Among These Agencies Whose Major Ministry Focus is These Living in Urban Slums Outside of the US	Number of Those Who Have Been Engaged in This Ministry For Two Years or Longer
636	26	21

Source: Doug Priest, 2010[63]

Only four per cent of these US missionaries had a focus on slums, and this did not necessarily mean living in them. Fortunately at least, eighty per cent of these had been serving for longer than two years. The figures from this survey lend support to our earlier assessment: that very few Christian workers—overseas or national—are focusing on slums in comparison to other needs.

Similar trends are also in evidence for Christian development agencies. International Non-Government Organisations (INGOs), including Christian ones, have had real trouble investing in community projects in urban slums. For example, as shown in Chart 12 below, in 2004 World Vision International had an overall expenditure of just over US$1.54 billion in cash and goods with $1.27 billion of that amount spent on international programs. A WV report—So, *Where Are Those Urban Programmes?*—found that US$112 million (7.27%) of the overall budget was focused specifically on their 669 identified urban projects. Many of these urban projects, however, were in places like Eastern Europe with few urban slums, and some were infrastructure projects that helped whole regions. The projects specifically named as focussing on urban slums cost around US$21 million or 1.3% of the overall WV budget.[64]

Chart 12: World Vision expenditure, 2004

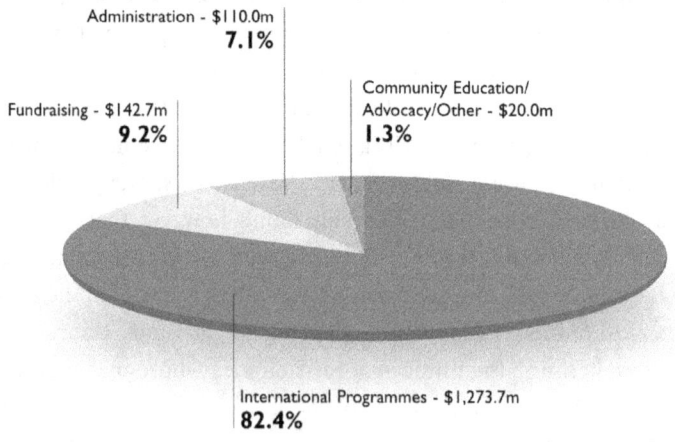

Source: World Vision 2004 annual report[65]

That WV, the world's largest Christian development agency, would spend such a small percentage of its funds on urban projects generally and in urban slums specifically is significant, not least because WV has a history of engaging with urban development issues. People like Rob Linthicum and Ken Luscombe, when with WV's Urban Advance, published some important work in the 1980s and 1990s; this was influential for contemporary understandings of urban development.[66] Yet, WV has had trouble translating this into practice on the field. One WV task force report concluded that: 'Perhaps 15-18% of WV's programming is located in urban settings, but for the past ten years the WV Partnership has had no urban strategy. The last approved WVI Board urban policy and strategy was twenty years ago.'[67]

Though Part B contains a fuller discussion of the reasons urban community development is so difficult, let it be noted here that the methodologies which have been successful in rural settings, like child sponsorship, have been less effective in urban slums. The same WV task force, for example, found the following: 'Initial research shows us that child sponsorship is not incompatible with the range of urban project settings, but further research is required to more accurately establish the risks, opportunities and costs.'[68] Building up child-centred and community-based institutions and keeping track of children accessing these services are extremely difficult tasks in the fragile squatter lands that slum neighbourhoods occupy.[69] This is especially the case in comparison to rural village settings, where WV strategies have often been implemented with minimal expenditure and maximum effectiveness.[70]

What is true of WV is also true of other International nongovernmental organisations (INGOs). A survey of fourteen other major INGOs by WV's David Kupp found that only one had a majority focus on slums. He summarised his findings thus:

INGOs have a clear history of rural activity and, many would argue, a bias against working in urban settings... on the whole, INGOs are primarily rural organisations playing catch-up in the face of rapid urbanisation.[71]

It is difficult to empirically back the claim of a governmental or NGO bias against working in urban settings, because there is a serious problem in identifying and tracking the balance of development work in slums. This is despite the inclusion of slums in the much publicised Millennium Development Goals. For example, the only clear public record of what part of AusAID's budget could have focused on slums is in the area of 'urban development and management'. In the 2008-09 figures this item was worth A$999,000 (0.02%) in a total budget of A$3.8 billion. There could well be other areas that include slum projects, but this is not clear. In fact, even the 'urban development and management budget' may not have been focused specifically on urban slums.[72] A similar lack of clarity is found in Tear Australia's records: they could identify 15% of their funded programs as 'urban work' in the Two-thirds

World, but not all of these programs were necessarily focused on slums.[73] This lack of tracking makes it difficult to say with any authority what is happening, but it does seem clear that slums are not understood as a specialised area of development with unique needs. The indications are, however, that slum projects are not funded well in comparison to rural projects by government and NGO development agencies. As far as Christian NGOs are concerned, this is part of an overall trend reflecting Christian priorities in resourcing, especially for those who live in the 10/40 Window. With few Christians to draw on in the majority of slums, Christian mission and development agencies have trouble finding traction.

David Barrett has also called attention to distortions in Christian resourcing. What he calls 'World A' (unevangelised) and 'World B' (only partly evangelised)[74] are the regions in which the majority of slums are found. Barrett found that in 2010 World A received only 0.5% of US dollars given to Christian missions;[75] 'World B' received only 5%.[76] Even this small percentage of funds is not necessarily directed toward ministry in urban slums; we can ascertain only that it goes to those areas in general. Contrast those figures with the US$1.6 billion spent on short-term mission trips by Americans in 2006.[77] Further, in 2010 'World C' (the Western Christian world) received 94.5% of money given to Christian mission.[78] Though we can't access specific details, it is clear that overall only a small fraction of Christian mission, development and ministry resources are being focused upon seeking transformation in urban slum and squatter neighbourhoods.

4.0 What Kind of Christianity is Growing in Slums and Where?

Though the overall picture of the state of Christianity in slums does not seem positive, it is important to highlight some signs of growth and health where Christians are serving in slums.

First, we can see that Pentecostalism and Evangelicalism is growing in the slums of Latin America, Sub-Saharan Africa and the Philippines. This is consistent with the conditions and factors we considered earlier, but positive conditions still need to be intentionally responded to and maximised. Pentecostalism has been especially effective in urban centres around the world in the latter half of the twentieth century and into this century. Even left-wing political activist Mike Davis acknowledges the growth of such movements.

> With the Left still largely missing from the slum, the eschatology of Pentecostalism admirably refuses the inhuman destiny of the Third World city that Slums warns about. It also sanctifies those who, in every structural and existential sense, truly live in exile.[79]

Though conditions conducive to the growth of urban Christianity are not usually found in the 10/40 Window, Grigg does offer some examples in India that are worthy of further investigation. In Chennai, a city with 747,936 slum residents,[80] 'the ACE church of 15,000 continues to multiply cells in slums. There is now spontaneous combustion of church growth across the city and particularly among the poor.'[81] There is also anecdotal evidence which suggests that these kinds of church planting movements are flourishing: 'In Mumbai [it has grown] from 40 slum workers in 1986 to 400 churches in 2004[;] there are at least 800 [churches] in the slums'. The 'effect of a million people pouring out of the slums to hear Benny Hinn a couple of years ago is undocumented, but we estimate another 800 slum cells have occurred from this. These are largely indigenous, Pentecostal, but some have been able to access resources on their terms from elsewhere to sustain indigenous growth.'[82]

Second, Christian communities and liberation theology seem to be significant in the slums of Latin America, as well as in other cities where colonisers were majority Catholic, such as in East Timor, Manila or francophone Africa.[83] However, it is far weaker in places where Catholicism has not been part of a colonising power. Again it must be stressed that simply because conditions are positive for Christian engagement, it does not mean that Christianity thrives. In this case, it is clear that Catholicism, via liberation theology and basic Christian communities, has been able to adapt and make positive contributions in these conditions. Certainly one of the themes of liberation theology is the challenge to the partnership between Christianity and colonising powers. In fact, the focus on the oppression and inherited power originating with colonisation is a central theme.

Third, some Catholic orders are moving from institutionally-based responses to more incarnational approaches that can adapt to the slums. Large institutions like schools, orphanages and hospitals have been an important strategy of many Protestant and Catholic missions over the past two centuries. In the beginning these institutional responses were difficult to establish in congested slums due to a lack of space and stability. There have been many adaptations to engage slums since the 1950s, however. Perhaps Mother Teresa of Kolkata and her Missionaries of Charity are the most prominent. *Time Magazine*, for example, named Mother Teresa as one of the most powerful twenty-five women of the last century, noting that 'her start-up missionary community of 13 members in Kolkata (formerly Calcutta)' has grown 'into a global network of more than 4,000 sisters running orphanages and AIDS hospices'.[84] Many of these 4,000 sisters and many tens of thousands of volunteers are serving in urban slums like their founder.

The Missionaries of Charity, however, are just one of many hundreds if not thousands of Catholic communities finding more flexible approaches to respond to slums. The combination of local parishes—often based in slums—with specialised workers recognised as having as a vocation in a specific religious community has often proven to be impressive. In Nairobi, Kenya, for example, an area with some of the largest slums in the world, the Exodus Kutota network of Catholic parishes working in slums has been able to make a significant impact. The story of their impact is told by Christine Bodewes.[85] Map 11 below shows where eighteen parishes are located (higher density of slum residency is shown by darker colours).

Map 11: Exodus Kutoka and slum density, Nairobi, Kenya

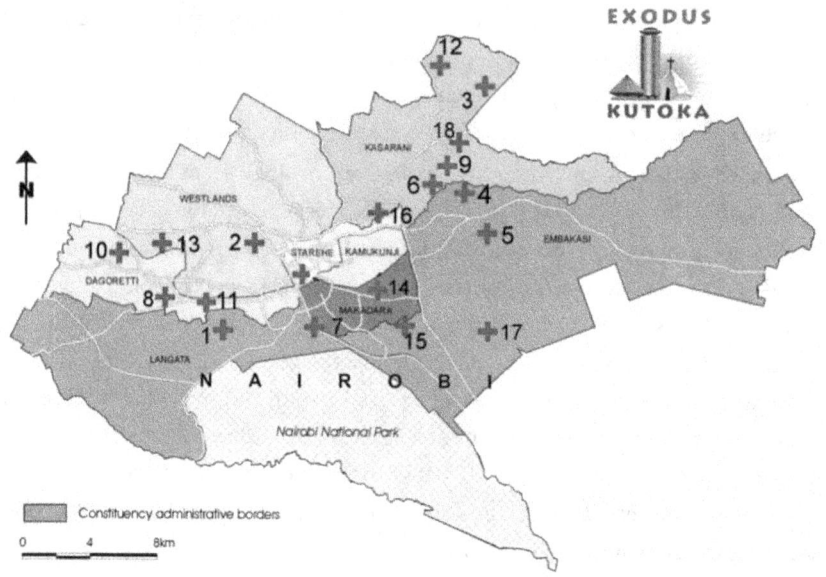

Source: Exodus Kutoka[86]

Father Joe Maier in Klong Toey[87] and Father Benigno Beltran in Smokey Mountain, Manila,[88] are other examples of neighbourhood-based responses in slums. What all these examples have in common is a kind of entrepreneurial sensitivity combined with a deeply spiritual stance in their slums over long periods of time. While these kinds of ministries may seem to be personality-based and to revolve around heroic characters, they often have quite sophisticated organisational and formation processes for workers and projects.

Fourth, the 'New Friars' movement is of note. 'New Friars' is an umbrella term for a new wave of post-colonial mission organisations—mostly ecumenical communities—that focus on the urban poor, living in urban slum and squatter neighbourhoods. Given where slums residents are located, there is a great need for cross-cultural, credible, urban ministers able to relocate to engage slums with Christianity; these groups aim to do just that, and their experimentation is significant. Paul Pierson describes the need for these kinds of groups:

Viv Grigg and others are advocating the formation of communities of believers who live in an incarnational ministry among the poor. It is a growing movement that requires great sacrifice similar to some of the best of the Roman Catholic orders... We must consider those kinds of choices if we are going to take seriously the mission of the cities.[89]

Scott Bessenecker has written extensively on this movement, which includes groups that Viv Grigg helped to inspire or start—such as Servants to Asia's Urban Poor, Servant Partners, and Encarnação Alliance. There are others, too, including Inner-Change, Word Made Flesh and Urban Neighbours of Hope. Bessenecker identified five 'signs' common to these groups. They are marked by being devotional, missional, communal, committed to the marginal and incarnational. These are communities that are emerging, most with less than two decades of experience. They are also not a very large group of workers in slums. Bessenecker estimates that in 2010 there were 'no more than a couple of hundred' workers living in slums with 'perhaps as few as 100' who had served longer than three years.[90]

While small in number these workers and organisations are, however, located in strategic places. Bessenecker writes that to his awareness they are in at least eleven 10/40 Window cities. These include 'Khartoum, Phnom Penh, Bangkok, Dhaka, Addis Ababa, multiple locations in India, Jakarta, Myanmar, Amman, and Manila. There are likely others I am not aware of.'[91] I have written elsewhere that what holds these groups together is a common concern for incarnational approaches to life and mission among the urban poor.[92] What informs the kinds of devotion, mission, ministry on the margins and community strategies chosen is an *incarnational* approach. These groups will be cited often when examining what an incarnational approach can mean in Part B of this book.

Grigg also networks with a group of non-Western mission workers who relocate to developing world slums; they call themselves The Encarnação Alliance of Urban Poor Movement Leaders.[93] Grigg estimates that in 2010, within networks he was involved with, there were perhaps as many as 20,000 Christian workers from non-Western backgrounds serving in slums. Once they move into slums, he contends, few actually leave. Grigg writes the following about his recent involvement in training non-Western Christians, with the aim of raising-up 50,000 Christian workers in slums:

One hundred and ninety-eight trained in Uganda, 250 round Hyderabad, 300 commissioned last year from ACE in Chennai, 56 graduating each year in the slums of Kibera in Nairobi, 110 church plants I have been able to count as a direct result of grassroots training two years ago. Now multiply that by 40 cities where we know training is happening and at least that is 8,000, but that is only what we know.[94]

Compared to the number and continuing increase in slum residents, even all these figures combined do not represent large numbers of Christian workers. Their places of location are significant for this study, however, because if these kinds of ministries are not embraced, few urban slum residents will have Christians among them.

Summary

The impact of Christianity on large sections of a rising number of slum and squatter neighbourhoods cannot be known with a great deal of certainty. The evidence we have considered above, however, suggests that the impact on the majority of slums and their residents has not been significant. It also seems that there is a lack of priority given to finding new and appropriate ways to respond. Christian faith's inability to make a positive contribution is significant because of the rapid growth of slums and the universal truth claims of Christian faith. Why Christianity struggles in many slum contexts and the diverse ways in which incarnational mission can be approached can now be examined.

SLUM LIFE RISING

What stops us?

Shane Claiborne once surveyed a group that described themselves as 'strong followers of Jesus'. He asked, 'Did Jesus spend time with the poor?' Around eighty percent of the group replied 'yes'. Just think for a moment about who Jesus spent his life, miracles, death and resurrection with, and it is shocking that 20% missed what should be obvious. Shane then asked this same group, 'Do you spend time with the poor?' This time only 2% replied 'yes'. My question is not so much if these numbers are a true reflection of the broader church, though I think they might be. It's the question, 'why this reality for this group of strong followers of Jesus?' Why is there such a gap between the stated priorities of Jesus (Luke 4:18-19) and his contemporary disciples? We certainly saw that gap reflected in those maps where slum residents live compared to where the majority of those who consider themselves Christians live. In most cities actually you could draw similar maps where the majority of those who describe themselves as Christians live and are often not where the majority of the poor live.

So why so many Christians avoid the urban poor? We could talk about lack of time, bible reading, compassion or even identifying poverty as more than lack of cash, but perhaps a key reason comes from seeing others in misery and not knowing what to do about it. That moment of cluelessness can strike such fear in the human heart that even Christians can try to organise their lives around avoiding it. I am not immune to this sense of awkwardness, even fear around poverty. Even though I have been serving the urban poor for over twenty years that fear can still strike me when I least expect it. Like anyone else living in a world of so much poverty, I can easily be overwhelmed by what I see and freeze.

I was once on the back of a motorbike when I went past a neighbourhood in Klong Toey I hadn't really seen before. I mean, I'd been past it, but I really only saw it for the first time. A long diesel goods train chugged past, so we waited for it to pass by with a crowd of motorbikes. That's when an elderly lady caught my attention. She was sitting cross legged, grey hair held back, eating some rice in the doorway of her home. The "house" was really just a shack made out of plywood shipping boxes. As I looked up, I realised this ladys whole neighbourhood was really just plywood boxes: no water, no electricity, harsh smells, rubbish and dog and human feces scattered outside the rough rows of shacks hugging the train-line. Then the smell hit me hard and I tried to hide my gagging reflex. In an instant I was reminded of two quotes. Mike Davis' *Planet of Slums* which said 'today in slums one billion people (one in six) are living in shit'. This is true, both physically and symbolically, around the world and specifically in this lady's experience. A second quote from 1 John 3:17-18 came to me: 'If any one of you has material possessions and sees a brother or sister in need but has no pity on them, how can the love of God be in you? Dear children let us not love with words of tongue but with actions and truth.' Overwhelmed by both what I saw and was processing, I tried not to stare at the old lady. We exchanged glances and smiles, but I looked away with relief as we sped off. This just doesn't seem an adequate enough response to the misery this lady was experiencing and I was haunted by the look in the lady's eyes as I left.

That night I read Henri Nouwen's challenge about the kind of 'love' that can 'cast out all fear' (1 John 4:18) that these moments bring:

> Let us not underestimate how hard it is to be compassionate. Compassion is hard because it requires the inner disposition to go with others to the place where they are weak, vulnerable, lonely, and broken. But this is not our spontaneous response to suffering. What we desire most is to do away with suffering by fleeing from it or finding a quick cure for it. As busy, active, relevant ministers, we want to earn our bread by making a real contribution. This means first and foremost doing something to show that our presence makes a difference. And so we ignore our greatest gift which is our ability to enter into solidarity with those who suffer. Those who can sit in silence with their fellow man, not knowing what to say but knowing that they should be there, can bring new life in a dying heart. Those who are not afraid to hold a hand in gratitude, to shed tears in grief and to let a sigh of distress arise straight from the heart, can break through paralysing boundaries and witness the birth of a new fellowship, the fellowship of the broken.[1]

When we'd rather be competent, than fools for Christ, we miss sharing our 'greatest gift' of vulnerable, personal solidarity with Jesus among the poor where the transforming Spirit is released. To minister to the "fellowship of the broken" we need the help of other Jesus-fools so we can keep finding, learning and growing in Christ-like responses. Institutional responses will not be enough; we need to take poverty personally in community.

It was a few weeks later some of our volunteers taught English down by the railway track again and tried what they could to serve in Jesus' name. Eventually the MacCartney family relocated their home just near there. Kellie and Adam Crosse have moved there too. Even now though, with UNOH workers living in this neighbourhood, a kind of futility enters my soul when I think of this lady. I'm just not sure what difference we make sometimes in such a stinking ocean of poverty.

Despite the risk of fear, despair and cluelessness, through Christ I must keep getting in urban poverty's face. It is where the anointing of the Spirit and true purpose is found. I know too that such poverty is far more painful and awkward for the lady by the railway track than I could ever imagine or experience. If I can just look beyond myself to Jesus, I can hear him whisper 'as you do it to the least of these, you do it to me' and know that somehow I meet Jesus in the embarrassment of poverty. (Matt 25:31ff)

We simply can't ignore the plight of the urban poor around us. Whether we live in a slum in Bangkok or the suburbs in the Western world, the poor cannot be made into an 'abstraction' to care about in general terms. Real compassion is found for those neighbours who are poorer than us when we see actual people, made in God's image, when we truly receive the anointing of the Spirit and risk ourselves in faith to know and love them in Christ Jesus.

---

[1] Henri Nouwen, *The Way of the Heart: Desert Spirituality and Contempary Ministry* (New York: Seabury Press, 1981) 34.

SLUM LIFE RISING

PERSONAL AND GROUP QUESTIONS:

1. What most strikes you about the challenges that those living in urban slum and squatter neighbourhoods face?

2. Where have you seen urban poverty as a lack of freedom to live life as God intends? How is this different from a mere lack of cash?

3. What fears do you have about sharing life with those living in urban poverty?

4. What are the main barriers for you in going deeper in sharing life with those facing urban poverty? How can you respond to them better in and through Christ?

5. Have you stepped out beyond fear to better engage others not like you before? If not, why not? If so, how has that benefitted you and those you engaged?

6. Why is this saying true or false? 'Pity weeps and walks away, but compassion comes to help and stay'? (Art Beals)

7. What is one thing you can do to overcome barriers to better engage Jesus among the urban poor?

Part B

Why Are Urban Slum and Squatter Neighbourhoods Such a Challenge to Christian Faith and Mission?

Chapter Four

Klong Toey and Barriers to Transformation in Urban Slum and Squatter Neighbourhoods

Christianity seems to have made little impact in the majority of urban slum and squatter neighbourhoods. Only a small percentage of Christian resources seem to be focused on reaching these neighbourhoods despite their size, growth, challenges and often lack of access to local Christian neighbours or churches. To ask why this is happening is an important interpretive task in the methodology of practical theology[1] and one that needs attention here.

Environmentally slums can be dangerous places in which to live and to live out Christian faith and mission. There are also very real strategic, cultural, socio-political and theological challenges and barriers that need to be overcome if transformation is to occur. The temporary nature of slums can also undermine the modern reliance on institution building as a means of change. As a result, the needs of slum and squatter neighbourhoods can often be seen as simply too hard to address quickly, and resources can more easily be focused to other urgent areas. These barriers can be highlighted by briefly discussing four areas that can undermine the transformation process for Christians. Klong Toey slum is used here to help illustrate the critical practical questions. This helps to earth issues that can also apply more generally to similar neighbourhoods.

1.0 Slums and Living Conditions

Residing in a slum can be a health hazard. The living conditions, as described by the ten characteristic challenges faced by slum residents in a case study with Klong Toey are confronting. I know something of this at a personal level. Even though I have a level of access to choices and power that many of my neighbours do not, this doesn't stop me from having some firsthand experiences of Klong Toey as a testing place in which to live and work for broader change. For most residents, it's not just the regular floods, oppressive heat, ghastly smells, cramped living conditions and habitual illnesses, but also the boredom between actions. Add these altogether, sometimes on the same day, and life can quickly become overwhelming, even at times paralysing. Our first six months of living in Klong Toey were particularly harrowing for me. Dysentery, dengue fever (four times) and all kinds of mystery tropical illnesses took their toll as my body and immune systems were bombarded until they finally adjusted.[2] Even as I write today one of our UNOH Klong Toey workers is in bed with the dengue virus as a fresh outbreak is unleashed on Klong Toey. In eight months there have been 70,902 cases nationwide with 87 reported deaths.[3] These kinds of living conditions are not easy for anyone to cope with and adjust to. That few Christian workers choose to relocate to live in slums should not be a surprise.

Slums can be physically, mentally and spiritually exhausting. Faith does not immunise Christians from vulnerable and at times dangerous living conditions, high crime-rates and even premature death. In my case, however, the fact that illnesses like dengue fever didn't stop my income, and the fact that I had access to quality hospitals, meant that the cycles of debt and poverty my neighbours would have experienced were halted before they began. Mine was a difficult introduction to life in Klong Toey, but still I did not have to experience the long-term debilitation that illness can mean for my neighbours and their families.

What is especially difficult for all residents in slums is that the fragile nature of slum neighbourhoods makes for a kind of shadowy, unpredictable life. A person or even a whole neighbourhood can be thriving one day, but evicted the next. Living in survival mode, it can take a significant amount of time before residents are ready and able to share real life and Christian faith with their neighbours, most of whom are Buddhists. Time to build momentum and trust is a precious commodity, and is critical in order for real change to occur. Yet time and stability are the very resources that are in short supply in urban slum and squatter neighbourhoods.

Where life is different for Christians is that Christians believe spiritual resources can help them stay and see change come to their neighbourhood. These spiritual resources, however, are often only found when we come to the end of our own resources; they are not easily found within many of today's contemporary and popular Christian theologies. It's one thing to say from an American TV studio, 'God will give you all the riches of heaven if you just believe'. It is quite another to live in survival mode in a slum and find a faith that can sustain individuals and be used by God to see communal change happen for those around us. A more robust and deeper theology and spirituality are required if the personal barriers of slum living conditions are to be overcome in a long-term way. Few seem willing to pay the cost required to find them.

2.0 Slums and Church Growth Conditions

There is some consensus about the conditions which can help churches to grow. One of the reasons Christian faith often struggles to grow in slums like Klong Toey is that these conditions are not often there. Donald McGavran is one author who identified some of these conditions for church growth. Drawing inspiration from missionaries concerned with indigenisation, such as John Nevius[4] and Roland Allen,[5] McGavran went further to explore sociological factors that affect the growth of Christianity and churches. [6] The church growth movement in more recent years has moved away from focusing on anthropological and sociological reasons for growth, becoming more concerned with management and marketing theories.[7] Nevertheless, *Understanding Church Growth* is still considered a foundational text for church growth and missions to this day. McGavran's ideas have been given a fresh lease of life, helping to inspire and inform the emerging-church movement as it grapples with what Christian mission means in Western, post-modern contexts.[8] Sociological analysis in more mainline settings has become common practice.[9]

What makes McGavran helpful to considering the impact of Christianity on slum conditions is his theoretical framework which helps us to understand why some environments are more open to Christian church growth and mission than others. For those willing to use basic sociological tools, these classic church growth theories can help identify some of the strategic challenges that face Christian faith in slums. Conditions that are especially relevant to church growth in slums like Klong Toey include the following.

Conquest affects responsiveness:[10] Though Thailand was spared Western colonisation, most slums, especially those in the 10/40 Window, were not. Even in Bangkok there is still a strong stance against what is often viewed as Western imperialism and this is an added barrier to Christianity's resonance in places like Klong Toey.

Nationalism affects responsiveness:[11] Thai nationalism is often associated with Buddhism. 'To be Thai is to be Buddhist' is a common expression. Few residents of Klong Toey want to reject or be treacherous to their nation.

Freedom from control affects responsiveness:[12] Though free from village life, slum residents quickly form allegiances that can often be even more controlling. Organised crime syndicates, debt, prostitution and sweat shops are common experiences for residents in Klong Toey.

Halting due to redemption and lift:[13] For those who do find a level of personal security and Christian faith, their new-found ability to protect themselves and their children from negative influences can cut them off from the broader neighbourhood. Churches can quickly become small enclaves where few members have non-Christian friends; sometimes members also move away to safer parts of town.

McGavran also offered a scheme that describes how likely a church is to grow, using five lines of distribution or axes.[14] The further to the right of the axis, or the higher the number, the more likely it is that the church will grow. The five axes are as follows.

a. *Dependence versus Independence*

1.	2.	3.	4.	5.	6.
Heavily dependent, spiritually and materially, on its founding mission					No external funding, able to effectively minister locally and further without help

b. *Individual versus Group Conversion*

1.	2.	3.	4.	5.	6.
Church has arisen by pure individual decision					Church has arisen by pure group decision

c. *Proportion of Total Population*

1.	2.	3.	4.	5.	6.
Church forms 1% or less of class or tribe concerned					Church forms 90% or more of class or tribe concerned

d. *Speed of Growth*

1.	2.	3.	4.	5.	6.
Church has grown at less than 10% per decade					Church has grown at more than 90% per decade

e. *Indigeneity*

1.	2.	3.	4.	5.	6.
Church has been formed in mould of foreign founder					Church has been formed in indigenous mould

It is difficult to make general comments about the likely receptivity and resistance of slum and squatter neighbourhoods to such a scheme. Of the five factors, two ('a' and 'e') are internal to the way a church is set up and could have a variety of answers according to the individual church in question. The three external factors ('b', 'c' and 'd') could be significant as we would be expect their scores to be low for Christian churches in slums. Let us consider the *Ta Rua* church in Klong Toey as an example.

Ta Rua has some level of indigenisation in the sense that the founder/leader is Thai, and some group conversions have happened in the sense that much of the church's membership is related to either Suwat or U Ping, though support has come from churches in South Korea, Norway and Australia. This level of indigenisation aside, all other factors would be considered very low, especially the small proportion of Christians in the population ('c'). The latter is the case across Asia and much of the 10/40 Window where the majority of slum residents live. Though low scores in external factors ('b', 'c' and 'd') are likely the norm for most slum and squatter neighbourhoods, there may be an exception: urban slums in majority Catholic countries and slums in South America and the Philippines. McGavran would not be surprised if it is in these environments that some church growth has been reported. As colonisation becomes less of a factor in succeeding generations of slum residents' minds and economies—such as in places like India and China—receptivity could well become more possible.

Church growth theory predicts that any growth will be slow and difficult in most slum and squatter neighbourhoods until a kind of critical mass can be reached. Places like Klong Toey have some natural environmental conditions that can be real strategic barriers for the growth of Christianity. Significant time and people-resources will be needed to help bring about the necessary environmental changes for slums to become more receptive. There is both a serious challenge and a real opportunity to consider afresh the kinds of methodologies Christian faith uses in urban slum and squatter neighbourhoods. McGavran was not unaware of this and was an early advocate for Christians to rise to the challenges of a new urban world. He wrote, for example, that:

> Discipling urban populations is perhaps the most urgent task confronting the church. Bright hope gleams that now is precisely the time to learn how it may be done and to surge forward in actually doing it.[15]

Nearly forty years after McGavran first wrote these words, the time to apply them may never have been more urgent.

Slums can be difficult places for individual Christians to live, but they can be challenging contexts for Christian churches too. The strategic challenges above, on their own, can make it difficult for churches to even know where to start in seeking broader transformation. This can actually be enough for churches to avoid slums altogether. Though Ta Rua church may seem small with its three congregations and four house groups, it is actually an unusually significant occurrence.

There are approaches to ministry that have connected with slum dwellers around the world. The rise of Pentecostalism, particularly in Latin America, is an important example, and Ta Rua church is actually part of this tradition. To what extent these traditions transform slum communities is, of course, debated. The large numbers of adherents to the Pentecostal tradition do not necessarily correspond to the transformation of slums which have large numbers of fundamentalist Hindi or Muslim residents.

In summary, Christianity's impact in slums could be limited because conditions are not generally conducive to strategic church growth. McGavran's above-mentioned conditions for church growth are not present for most of the church in Thailand in general, or in Klong Toey slum specifically. These social conditions can change, but to see new kinds of receptivity to Christianity in slums will take significant people resources and time.

3.0 Slums and Poverty Alleviation Conditions

Christians, the church and slums themselves are part of much bigger social systems. The study of international development—like the church growth movement—is a relatively new discipline, but one that can help us to identify more strategic challenges for Christians in regard to the social conditions they find in slum and squatter neighbourhoods. While definitions, approaches and focuses are hotly debated, the most basic aim of international development is to apply strategies that can end, or at least alleviate, poverty.[16] Beginning after World War II, numbers of both government and non-government agencies taking up the cause have rapidly grown, especially over the last two decades. In the United States alone the numbers of registered NGO international aid groups grew from 6,000 to 26,000 in the 1990s.[17] The international aid and development industry is now worth about US$70 billion a year, and the West has spent more than US$2.3 trillion over the last five decades.[18] With such significant investments being made by so many, it is understandable that serious research, theories and evaluations of effectiveness have emerged around the field of development. Stake-holders such as donors, governments, organisations and practitioners need to know if their efforts are working or wasted.

There is no shortage of voices to consider here. These include those writing from a Christian development perspective such as WV's Robert Linthicum,[19] Bryant Myers[20] and Jayakumar Christian.[21] We will focus, however, on the work of one particular researcher to highlight some specific theories on strategic development challenges as they apply to slums like Klong Toey: Thomas W Dichter. Dichter is not the only voice to seriously critique international development strategies,[22] but as someone with more than thirty-five years experience in planning, managing and evaluating projects in various Two-thirds World settings for numerous NGOs as well as for the US Peace Corps, USAID, UNDP and the World Bank, he provides insights that should not be ignored. With a PhD in anthropology, Dichter's varied insights come together in his book, *Despite Good Intentions: Why development assistance to the third world has failed*. The book is comprised of case-studies paired with analysis.[23] Dichter's theoretical and practical insights are particularly helpful when applied to developing world slums like Klong Toey, as they help us to understand why strategy in development terms are such a serious challenge for Christians who want to respond positively to the rise of slums.

Real optimism about alleviating poverty has emerged in recent times. The rise of various NGOs, governments, the UN, church leaders, economists such as Jeffery Sachs and celebrities has created almost utopian expectations.[24] The overall picture of the international development industry's effectiveness in alleviating poverty has not been encouraging, however. For example, the West spent US$2.3 trillion on foreign aid over the last five decades, but has not managed to enable basic help such as getting 12 cent medicines to children to prevent half of the million malaria deaths a year, or enabling poor families to purchase $4 bed nets to prevent most malaria deaths.[25] Despite the many plans, technologies and more than two trillion dollars, there are more people living on less than $1 per day this year than last year.[26] Ditcher writes bluntly,

> No other large scale publicly funded effort for such duration could have got away with such poor performance, certainly not the private sector or even ranks of government. Yet, all the players in development assistance are still in business.[27]

Of particular importance to this study is that although such enormous sums of money have been spent since the 1950s in strategies to alleviate poverty, the rapid rise of urban slum and squatter neighbourhoods has actually accelerated. In 1900 there were only twenty million slum residents, by 1970 there were 260 million, and now there are over one billion with 88,000 new slum residents still arriving each day.[28] In the face of such rapid slum growth it is fair to say that development strategies have overall been impotent.

That someone like Dichter claims that most development strategies are failing the Two-thirds World—and slums in particular—is important for Christians to consider. He highlights the very real strategic challenges that those in development have discovered over the last fifty years. These conditions are briefly noted below in regard to Klong Toey.

3.1 The need for significant process—time affects poverty alleviation

Dichter argues that most processes, time-frames and objectives of development plans are flawed because of the complexities of poverty and the time required for any real change to occur. The introduction to his book begins with a quote from Leonard Frank explaining what his multinational team of six needed to do in North-West Africa: 'We've got four weeks to come up with a project for, say, thirty million dollars. Routine'.[29] In contrast to this picture, the achievement of real change in a community requires a significant time investment to search out possible solutions, plan, localise the process, set-up and evaluate. Cultural change that goes deep within a community can take generations. Sufficient length of process time is important, not just for when a project starts and an agency is involved, but also to ensure longevity of results decades and even generations after the first intervention. For example, key objectives like a micro-enterprise start-up and repayment of a small loan may be met in the two to five year period for an average project that donors support. Yet, the real questions about alleviating poverty centre on what is happening five to ten years later, or even in the next generation. It is possible, for example, that if a micro-enterprise failed within a few years then the individual in question could soon be in a worse state of debt than before. But as long as the loan was paid back initially, the story about the same individual could be written up as a success in a report by the sponsoring agency after their two years of involvement is completed. Dichter argues that only significant time will tell how effective such an interventionist strategy is, and the patience to wait for this kind of evaluation is something that few governments, donors or agencies have.

Klong Toey's slum neighbourhoods can be demolished at any moment and so any long-term planning and institution building can be undermined. This lack of security in housing tenure makes sufficient time for proper process almost impossible. For example, when Klong Toey's 'Lock's 9-12' neighbourhoods were bulldozed in 2003 to make room to store more Port Authority shipping containers, residents knew the demolition was coming. Most didn't believe it would happen. Whatever development for poverty alleviation may have been planned fell with the 3,000 shacks in those neighbourhoods as residents scurried to find new housing. If significant time for process is needed to build trust and assess assets in a community as well as to search for, find and evaluate appropriate responses to help alleviate urban poverty, then real change for these residents was undermined by the nature of their neighbourhood. Lack of time for long-term planning for poverty alleviation is a problem central to the nature of slum conditions.

3.2 The forces of dependency affect poverty alleviation

Issues of power and dependency are constantly woven throughout Dichter's book.[30] The desire to move from charity 'band-aids' to more 'sustainable', 'accountable' and 'participatory' development was a significant philosophical shift since World War II. Dichter notes that the motivations of even the most 'tough-minded' development agencies such as the World Bank stemmed mostly from a genuine instinct to help. Anger and resentment toward them when help stopped, however, nearly always emerged:

> The quantum of 'feel-good' we get from giving them help is so large that they are getting the short-end of the stick in the exchange. To make it right, they need to ask for more, and at some level they do not want to.[31]

The psychological dimension of 'resentment' (rancour expressed against benefactors), coupled with the economic dimension of reciprocity (something needs to be returned for the gift) can create an extremely toxic dynamic of dependency for both residents and agencies. Combined with a third factor of close proximity between development workers and slum residents, these three powerful forces can undermine the freedom sought by all involved. Dependencies, real anger and a sense of exploitation can be felt on all sides.

In urban slums like Klong Toey these forces can be exacerbated even more than in the most extreme rural development projects. This is because development initiatives in urban slums are easily assessable by donors and potential donors in a way that rural villages are not. Close to international airports and hotels, it is not uncommon for a constant stream of donors to visit urban-slum development projects. It's only natural then that those doing the work on the ground each day would want funds from donor-visitors in return for sharing their experiences of poverty. In fact, one development worker in the large Kiberia slum Nairobi said, 'our extreme poverty is our greatest natural asset'.[32]

Another urban factor helping to create dependencies is the swirling economic currents found in cities. These include the roles of the formal sector such as local, national, multinational and global business competition as in most cities, but in slums they can also include large informal sector and organised crime interests. These deep and swirling currents often compete together in slums in ways that are mostly unheard of in isolated villages. For example, even starting up a small food or transport business is potentially a complex, expensive (compared to a Western city) and even dangerous proposition because of the diverse legal and illegal competition and interests that must be understood and negotiated.

Urban residents also live in an economy where they rely fully on financial income to survive. Unlike their rural counterparts, it is difficult to supplement any income with home-grown food for themselves or for bartering. In rural areas the ability to produce one's own food is a kind of safety net that naturally limits dependence. An income generation project in an isolated rural village may work or not, but if the family already has access to its own rice and eggs it is not as big a risk to be involved in the project as it would be for urbanites. Development success can be a bonus for the rural poor, whereas the urban poor are dependent on project success for their survival.

A key economic factor for urbanites is time. As we have seen, significant time is needed to build trust, confidence and skills as well as to find and evaluate solutions, if long-term change is to happen in a community. Where the urban poor are disadvantaged in development projects, therefore, is that time literally equals much needed money. The kinds of seasonal rhythms and traditional family set-ups that allow rural people time to volunteer in churches, committees and associations are often impossible for the urban poor. If employment is the difference between eating or not, and you are surplus urban labour, then you must take work whenever you can get it. This economic reality can bankrupt the kind of 'social capital' that communities need to be communities. Development work in such contexts can't rely simply on local volunteers, but requires salaries and income if residents are to leave paid work to join in. The need to pay for the time of participants obviously makes it easy to create dependencies. The project works while there is an income stream for local staff and stops when that dries up.

Dependencies can undermine transformation and create conflict. If alleviating poverty is about the freedom to choose real life, then this is significant. This struggle between residents and agencies can be seen visually in Klong Toey where on one end of the central arterial there is an section known locally as 'NGO alley' because of the cluster of large aid and development agency buildings based there. Tour buses of donors, ready with cameras, are a common sight. There is even a bicycle tour that takes tourists through the slum to show them its poverty. At times residents complain that their neighbourhood 'feels like a zoo'.

A WV case study from Urban Advance also pointed to ongoing funding as an issue in an urban project that was showing promise.[33] In Sao Gabriel District, Belo Horizonte, Brazil, WV was seeing real changes happening with housing, health and schooling. Using a sophisticated community organising strategy aimed at empowering locals and moving on, WV's Urban Advance saw: 200 homes built with Habitat for Humanity; a primary school built; electricity and street lighting put on by the government in one slum; health care and two health stations; three water reserves built; public bus services so that residents could take jobs in the city; public telephones installed; streets paved by the government; and a coalition which provided job training, employment opportunities, schooling, health care, and counselling to street children.[34] However, these results were not enough to save the project from funding cut backs. As well as high staffing turnovers, difficulties in matching needs with local interests and broader networking,[35] the report noted 'low salaries of staff', 'threats of closing', 'limiting funding' and 'there was not enough innovation used in developing funding streams appropriate to urban settings to generate support.[36] The program closed and momentum was lost.

Forces of dependency are especially complex in slums like Klong Toey. For the basic needs of residents to be met educational and health institutions are needed, but these are expensive in cities and permanent space is difficult to find in slums. Few are able to achieve self sufficiency using short term 'seeding grants'. Once donor funds dry up, for example with a small school, it is not normally possible for slum children to pay enough fees to cover the costs of the whole school's annual budget. Given that governments often see these neighbourhoods and residents as 'illegal', where can the extra funds come from except for current or new donors?

There can also be a kind of double standard here between donors and their expectations of recipients regarding dependencies. For example, most Western countries do not expect 100% of the funding for their schools to come only from student fees, or for 100% of hospital costs to be covered by patients. Few in the West would argue that they are 'dependent' because they do not cover 100% of their own education or health-care costs, but similar institutions in the Two-thirds World are viewed with suspicion if they are not able to quickly become self-sufficient.

The development industry in slums also struggles with another double standard. Projects are often expected to become self-supporting within a few years, while the same agencies are dependent upon this same supporter-base. For example, a development agency may support a project by advertising and raising funds for it from their supporter-base as well as by helping to plan and evaluate the effectiveness of the project. For this service the INGO takes a percentage. Yet when the funding period finishes, the project that has raised funds receives no more funds, but the development agency still depends on the same supporter-base for a percentage of the next project. This double standard is rarely lost on the local project workers or residents over time.

Some International NGOs and Mission agencies have tried to avoid this dynamic by partnering with or setting up very large community based non-government-organisation (CBNGO). This can help deal with increasingly complicated legal and donor obligations and can help the INGO support many different projects through the one organisation. The development workers and CBNGO are still dependent on funds, however, and need to find new projects in order to survive. The agenda for funding new projects is often still on the partnering International NGOs terms, however, so CBNGO workers need to keep finding ways to fit the funding criteria. This may not have anything to do with the actual needs and assets of slum residents toward transformation.

Culture is a further complicating factor in terms of dependence. For example, the Thai cultural value of the hierarchical relationship of *Pi-Nong* (benefactor-recipient) is intentionally a dependent relationship. This cultural value certainly exacerbates dependencies in Klong Toey, where *Pi-Nong* relationships can often be a kind of survival strategy. Who your benefactor is (the one who can look after you) often determines your income security and status. In Klong Toey the role of *Pi* to Nong applies as much to heads of extended families as to the heads of organised crime syndicates; heads of churches as much as heads of local NGOs. So concerns about competing for a *Pi's* role as well as making others further dependent on existing *Pi's* are real challenges for any Klong Toey poverty alleviation strategy that aims to be sustainable over a long period of time. Because wealth is difficult to generate in slums, many Klong Toey residents can be dependent on non-government aid and government organisations, as well as organised crime syndicates.

3.3 The need for stability affects poverty alleviation

The morphing and moving nature of slum and squatter neighbourhoods like Klong Toey provides another strategic challenge to Christian mission, especially in the establishment and growth of churches, institutions and effective poverty alleviation strategies. Dichter states that:

> Nothing is worse for development than instability, especially the kind development practitioners were becoming accustomed to—that prompted by famine, flood, economic disaster and capital flight, or religious and ethnic wars.[37]

A recent Red Cross report claimed that slum residents experienced the five worst natural disasters between 2000 and 2010, and warned of the increased risks urban slum residents face compared to other populations.[38] But there are also other reasons why instability is a key ongoing challenge to slum and squatter neighbourhoods' development processes. First, the opportunity for people to solve their own problems together can only happen when people can stay together long enough to trust each other and move forward together. Second, any kind of real searching, evaluation and critical thinking about responses needs people to be together through the various cycles of a common project. Third, as we have discussed, the critical ingredient of significant process time depends on the stability and consistency of participants.

Stability in slums can be undermined by many factors in inherent to slums. These can include: infectious diseases that cause ill-health; turnover of residents seeking more secure housing; demolition or threat of demolition; regular fires and floods. Such unstable conditions notes Dichter, undermine some of the most successful marketing of international development projects. With 'child sponsorships', for example, the need to identify, gather and maintain children to keep up with the demand for child sponsorships can create a cycle of dependency for NGOs in this methodology.[39] However, a key issue for children in urban slums is that many do not live in a neighbourhood long enough to be sponsored for any significant length of time. The funding strategy only works because of the stable connection between the sponsor and 'one child living in poverty'. If a sponsor's 'child' moves away without any information as to why then the sponsor's trust and confidence in the project, and therefore their willingness to fund it, is undermined. WV's David Kupp writes:

> Child drops represent the most significant risk of cancellation in any support office (i.e., up to 40% for UK). Therefore, ... there is a potential for WV to be more vulnerable to increased cancellations as it moves to increase its number of urban ADPs (Area Development Programs).[40]

This has certainly been the case in Klong Toey. Numerous children were sponsored at the Klong Toey Community Centre's (KTCC) pre-school by Compassion International at one time, but because of high turnover rates the sponsorships stopped. The withdrawal of sponsorships almost led to KTCC's closure in 2002.[41]

Slums like Klong Toey are amongst the most unstable of neighbourhoods. Even local institutions like schools, medical clinics and businesses are often established outside of official channels and face a vulnerability that those in regular neighbourhoods do not. They could be closed at any time and therefore investing in these institutions is fraught with difficulty.

3.4 Broader socio-political and cultural factors affect poverty alleviation

The broader social context of where poverty alleviation takes place is of great significance to how any given development strategy can be applied (or not). Socio-political, cultural and even geographic factors are involved which can help development in one place, but may undermine it in another. Ditcher explains that there is a well recognised continuum from hard to soft factors that affect whether a country will be rich or poor. From the hard end there are factors like 'geography, topography, size, climate, soil, natural resources (water, minerals, fauna and flora such as forests, and so on), population growth and density'.[42] The 'softer' factors combine with the harder ones and with each other. These include: history, trade, internal movement, human/cultural factors and health. Then further along the softer end of the spectrum are the institutions of a society that include: law, justice, finance, government and formal religion. How effective or even how corrupt these institutions are will have a direct affect on how healthy a nation can be economically. Finally, Dichter points to the very soft end which includes culture and worldview and such ideas as individuality/community, the status of women, family networks, 'national character' and how 'social capital' is formed and maintained. 'And, as all cultures adapt and change, how is that change taking place? Back the loop goes to history and the 'hard' physical factors'.[43] To not take all these factors into account, as can often be the case in slums, is analogous to the 'blind-man-touching-the-elephant problem', where each agency touches a part but describes a different beast.[44]

A similar theme is taken up by Paul Collier, who identifies five 'traps' or factors that ensure the poorest billion people continue to live in the worst conditions. These are: conflict, lack of natural resources, being land-locked with bad neighbours and bad governance.[45] Dichter, however, goes further in discussing not just the 'hard' traps as Collier does—such as roads and laws—but also the 'softer' ones such as how the poor are viewed:

> It is hard enough to face how little the conditions of poverty can change unless the positions of poor people in those societies change. But because the large forces (and

stakes) behind feudal landownership system or behind a caste system are so intertwined, it is close to impossible for outside agencies to do much to change them. While the poor who are kept in their 'positions' by those forces can be helped temporarily, they remain where they were.[46]

Broader social and cultural factors in a local context, then, create a real challenge to any strategy, model or response to slums. In fact, Ditcher argues that 'development has always involved interacting forces too complex to be planned or engineered'.[47] He goes on to note that interactions have included the transactions and interactions between local forces of culture, human psychology, climatic changes, differences in climatic zones, new technologies, external influences through trade and wars, kinds and patterns of crops, markets, roads, epidemics that affect crops and people, changes in prices and more.[48] Any new initiative by residents of slums is not made in a vacuum, but in an extremely complex cultural, social, economic and political environment.

Klong Toey is a local context affected by many broader socio-political-cultural forces. These include government policy, the Port Authority of Thailand, diverse businesses and NGOs, as well as the worldview of residents. For example, one NGO leader in Klong Toey identified the following 'personality characteristics of slum people which are obstacles to development work'. These included: A persistent belief in *wenkam* (personal fate or karma) to explain misfortune; an acceptance of government authority and respect for officials; an acceptance of phuyai and phunoi (hierarchy) and *lukphi/luknong* (patron-client) relations; the fact that people don't listen to those of equal or lower status than themselves; love of independence (*rak issaraseri*) and fun (*sanuk*) and therefore a lack of discipline; a desire for freedom but a dislike of working in groups or teamwork; a tendency to forgive and forget easily; extravagant tastes and competition in displaying possessions; and a desire to build personal influence and honour.[49] To ignore these forces in searching for strategic responses to poverty is to ignore a fundamental factor that helps determine the potential effectiveness of development.

3.5 Investment by those who will most benefit can affect poverty alleviation

Dichter often notes how transient and temporary the development industry and development workers can be, but that conscious efforts have been made to see more participatory development. The ideal is that the poor themselves not only have a stake, but are the experts in what change is possible for them.[50] Ownership and participation from the 'bottom up'—from primary stakeholders—is now understood as essential if development is to work.[51] Partnership with secondary stake-holders is crucial too, but if development workers do not have a personal stake in the success of development they are at a disadvantage as workers compared with local residents.

This is often the case in the interaction of slum and squatter neighbourhoods like Klong Toey with outside organisations. Barriers for external workers can include: barriers of access and not really knowing who the key players are and what is really happening; barriers of affluence and not being trusted because the project is only a sideline, as well as issues of jealousy and resentment; barriers of credibility and not being respected by residents because they don't really know what is going on or what it takes to see change happen; barriers of health and sustainable lifestyle and not being able to spend the required time needed in slum neighbourhoods because their immune system is not able to cope.

The barriers to poverty alleviation discussed above are experienced regularly by most residents in places like Klong Toey, especially if they try to bring about change. The unfavourable conditions for poverty alleviation are also a significant obstacle to outsiders who attempt to see transformation. Similar discussions around indigenisation and dependencies can be seen in classic church growth theory as well. Take the barrier of health, for example. Because of the poor living conditions of slum residents, local church participants and workers can fall seriously ill with all kinds of diseases. This is not only an issue from the perspective of each person's wellbeing; it can also seriously affect income generation, causing families to spiral into debt. Ill health can also be a serious barrier to stability and momentum for churches and development projects. In the case of Klong Toey, the *Ta Rua* church has many people in its congregation who are extremely sick; in fact several members die because of preventable diseases each year. Health concerns are just one of many very real barriers to the role that an 'outsider' can play in bringing about long-term change, especially if they have no stake in its outcome.

The issues for outsiders listed above, such as jealousies, resentments, lack of knowledge and power, are also normal experiences of residents, especially those seeking change. What is perhaps unusual is that someone would choose to be in such a situation and to stay if they didn't have to. That said, even the choice to go or stay is perhaps no longer as unusual in urban slum areas because moving away to start again or to return to a village home is now not uncommon.

Perhaps even the status of 'outsider' in an urban slum can change over time in ways not possible in stable, rural villages. This is especially the case if a development worker's home is in the neighbourhood and if they can find ways for their family to have a stake in the success of projects. As we have seen, the mobility of urban residents can mean they come from all kinds of places and they may not stay long in one urban place. A person who lives in an urban slum neighbourhood for more than five years can often be considered a long-term resident. Length of residency compared with neighbours does not necessarily guarantee that 'outsider' barriers will be overcome for people born in another country, but urban slum and squatter neighbourhoods are not closed, dormant communities, and they therefore offer the opportunity for outsiders to become at least more like insiders over time.

Askew's work explored the complexity of Klong Toey residents participating together and the role of various NGOs and the ethos *kansuanruam* (togetherness/cooperation). These are complex relationships, marked by the collision of competing interests and values. For example, the self-interest of individuals took such priority that no help was given when a nearby neighbourhood faced demolition.[52]

The alleviation of poverty, like the growth of churches, requires the presence of certain conditions that are often outside the control of those seeking transformation. Even with government and non-government cooperation, the attempt to see Bangkok become a 'city without slums' has so far failed. For example, soon after the Taksin government came to power in 2002, the new Prime Minister made a short visit to Russia. Impressed by the affordable public housing he saw there, Taksin announced a bold new public approach to slums. By World Habitat Day—October 5th, 2005—a buoyant Prime Minister Taksin vowed 'to wipe out city slums by 2008'.[53] Just before Taksin was deposed in a military-led coup on September 4, 2006, the Housing Authority of Thailand admitted that the task was 'tough'[54] and it was never fulfilled. By 2010 Codi reported that over the five year period it had 'benefited 88,000 families in 1,457 communities in 76 provinces in Thailand', that few of these were actually new homes, and that few of the developments were in Bangkok itself.[55] With the figure of Bangkok slum residents currently around 1.5 million, Taksin's dream fell a long way short in terms of any significant impact.

To be fair to successive Thai and Bangkok governments, finding the right policies for slum transformation is difficult. At least real attempts have been made to address slums, even if the ambitious goals instigated by Taksin were not achieved. A UN taskforce on slums states that overall:

> Official attention to the slum dwellers of the world has been largely a matter of inaction, inappropriate action, or insufficient action. The most common government policies over the past 40 years have been to ignore slums or, when they are on valuable land, to bulldoze them.[56]

Slums can, at the same time, be fragile, combustible and contagious ecosystems. It is a complex and sensitive task, therefore, to find appropriate urban development strategies and policies for slums that do not cause harm. Even seemingly good strategies and projects that are well funded can too easily become more about donor, business or electorate satisfaction than long-term transformation in slums themselves. This theme is taken up by Steve Corbet and Brian Fikkurt in *When Helping Hurts*. A parable told by their African Christian friend Miriam Adeney underlines the point. An elephant went to a party with his friend a mouse. The elephant had the time of his life, drinking and dancing until at last he turned to his mouse friend who, to his horror, was squashed to death. 'Sometimes, that is what it is like to do mission with you Americans,' the African storyteller commented. 'It is like dancing with an Elephant'.⁵⁷ The elephant did not intend to harm, but he did not understand the effects he had on the mouse. To alleviate poverty and share Christian faith in fragile urban slums can become a great dance for large and powerful governments, NGOs, Christian agencies and churches. Residents, too, can get 'squashed' in the 'dance'. While there may well be good intentions, the long-term wellbeing of slum neighbourhoods can easily be undermined.

4.0 Slums and Theological Challenges

Like an iceberg, the most obvious above-the-water-level challenges raised by slums may well be at the personal, strategic and social level. Perhaps, however, even more substantive challenges lie below the surface in the form of deeper, more fundamental questions about Christian faith and mission. The conditions may be difficult, but why do so few Christians seek faithfulness and relevance to God's concerns about the rise of the urban poor? That slum living conditions exist and few Christians respond raises serious philosophical and theological challenges to the very heart of the Christian faith. These include the challenge to adopt what can be described as an incarnational approach to transformative mission.

Some of the most exciting and innovative Christian workers today describe their approach to mission as *incarnational*. Given the inability to rely on institutionally-based responses and post-modern sensitivities to 'progress', it should not be a surprise that new, more informal and relational ways forward are sought. The term 'incarnational' is used frequently in the emerging-church conversation,⁵⁸ amongst new friars⁵⁹ and in liberation theology,⁶⁰ as well as by more mainstream missiologists over the last thirty years.⁶¹ Langmead explores various incarnational missiologies found in such diverse Christian traditions as Anabaptist, radical evangelical, liberation theology, Moltmann's theology, Catholic and Anglo-Catholic sacramental theology, as well as Ecumenical and Eastern Orthodox theologies.⁶²

The term 'incarnational' is used in many competing, diverse and contradictory ways. In fact contemporary uses have become so slippery that it can be easily dismissed before its important call to sustained faithfulness and relevance for Christians in slums is even considered. It is in danger of becoming clichéd, losing any real meaning at all. Our life in Klong Toey is an example. Some think because we moved our family into our new home in a poorer part of Klong Toey slum we are therefore incarnational, that is the 'same as' the poor. However, just look into the harrowing eyes of little Nat*, a thirteen year old girl, who has already had two aborted pregnancies to her dad. Deeply scarred inside and out, her formative foundations are so undermined even before they've begun. I mean even Jesus couldn't be the 'same as' young Nat and He was the Incarnation! If we or Jesus can't really be the 'same as' Nat, what then can an incarnational approach mean for us however? Jesus was *incarnatus* (made flesh) as in John 1:14. When applied to us in the way used to describe the God who became human, the metaphor of 'enfleshment' has real limitations.

Further, slums in particular have been a lightning rod for debate around the limits of incarnational approaches, especially in relation to Western Christians. First, the increasing Western expenditure on mission as compared with the extreme poverty often found in urban slums is an emotive and complex issue.[64] With increased global banking, travel and internet use, it is now far easier than ever before for the poor to access the financial support of other Christians in richer parts of the world. An increasingly wealthy Western church wants to do something, to get their 'hands dirty', and can now move quickly to provide urgent, much needed aid and development responses almost anywhere in the world. 'What is the answer to poverty? It is money', says the senior pastor of one of Australia's largest Christian churches.[65] As we have seen however, the power dynamics, expectations and resentments that the use of wealth can create often undermine long-term transformational efforts, especially in places like urban slums. As Jonathan Bonk argues, this kind of extreme wealth compared to the poverty of the urban poor has become a serious barrier to Christian witness. He argues for an incarnational model where Jesus 'became poor' because 'abandoning the incarnation as a model for its own life and mission, the affluent church has assured its fundamental spiritual impotence'.[66] Taking up this incarnational model is not as simple as it seems, however. It is one thing if one of your neighbour's child needs food and some medical help that would only cost you a few dollars to fix. It is quite another when there are 80,000 neighbours with children and relatives who are malnourished and need urgent medical attention. Who gets help and who doesn't get help and may well die is not just a theoretical dilemma. It is a reality that is faced almost immediately by any Christian worker who wants to respond to poverty in slums. These real issues are picked up by people like Michael Duncan, who describes this as being forced to 'play God' in acts of mercy.[67] How helpful is the model of the Incarnation when Christians are not God and don't want to be put in such a predicament?

Second, the rise of Western Christian expectations of living standards compared with the extreme living conditions in slums is a source of discontent. Ronald Sider,[68] Jonathan Bonk[69] and Michael Duncan[70] have been particularly provocative in this struggle, asking how rich Christians should live in a world of hunger. The so called 'expat lifestyle', where Westerners can often access more luxury than they could 'back home' is particularly tempting in developing world cities, even for Christian workers. There can be real embarrassment, guilt and even bewilderment at the gap between Western lifestyle expectations and how the urban poor next door live. 'How would

Jesus live when there are so many living in slums in my city?' is rarely asked, but it is classical incarnational question. The real challenge is that the implementation of answers to this question is almost impossible. Ken Baker, for example, has pushed back, asking what is realistic and sustainable for incarnational identification with the poor.[71] Can trying to be the 'same as the poor' be dishonest and strategically counterproductive?

Third, the welfare of the children of Christian workers living in slums is an especially emotive issue. Children simply don't have the choices their parents do. Duncan, for example, tells from personal experience that slums can even be a fatal environment for Christian workers' children, as with death of his son Joseph.[72] Even Bessenecker, apologist for the incarnational approach to slum transformation, has reservations about applying this approach in slums for parents with children, saying that 'likely it will require healthy, educated men and women without children willing to take up residence in urban hovels'.[73] Grigg, too, is cautious about Christian workers bringing their children into slums.[74] Jesus did not have any children of his own and was not faced with such dilemmas. If an incarnational approach is not possible for Christian families, however, how helpful can the approach really be? It is true that every child is subjected to their parent's values and lifestyles growing up—intentionally or otherwise, but is a worker's choice to live in a slum a risk worth subjecting their children too?

The above three charged emotional realities, coupled with some ambiguous understandings of what an incarnational approach to mission can mean, have created real confusion and frustration, especially for Christian workers serving in slums. It is therefore important to consider that there may well be serious inadequacies in some of these understandings. There can be a real lack of confidence for Christians to step out and take sacrifices on the basis of an incarnational approach when other, easier options are available to them. Defaulting to less risky and more accepted 'spiritual' approaches can result.

Some versions of incarnational approaches also don't make sense to Christians who want to take a long-term approach to facing overwhelming challenges in slums. These versions of incarnation do not inspire, inform or invite real responses at all; some can even create real barriers for sustainability, credibility and transformation. For example, Baker—ministering in severe poverty in Africa—wrote an article entitled 'The Incarnational Model: perception of deception?' that was published in the Evangelical Missions Quarterly and reproduced in a *Global Urban Reader* to help prepare Christian workers for the slums. In the article Baker tells of fellow missionaries in West Africa who were approached by village elders after only a few months of living in their village were requested to leave their hut and build a 'city house'. They were the 'object of ridicule', causing 'shame' to the village.

> This creates a dilemma for those seeking to follow the incarnational model. Do the missionaries assume they know better and ignore the request because they believe that someday the people will come to understand and appreciate their identification and belief in Christ?[75]

If such an important philosophical underpinning is not clear or helpful in cases like this, then confidence and sustainability can be undermined, to the degree that even attempting an incarnational approach can be dismissed before it has started. Distant, professionalised and non-enfleshed approaches that see 'spiritual needs' as the only legitimate ones, can quickly become the most important—even only possible—responses that Christians can offer. Cases like that of Baker above are based on one tightly-defined way of taking an incarnational approach: relocating and seeking to be the 'same as' villagers. This is just one use of the incarnational metaphor in mission, however. As we shall explore, there are other definitions such as Langmead's which are not only possible, but also far more helpful in seeing needs addressed and opening up the possibility of transformation.

5.0 Different Understandings and Possibilities of Incarnational Mission

Despite its limitations and controversies, the incarnational approach should not be discarded in relation to slums. Rather, it can be used as a theological motif to help invite, inform, and inspire a new generation of Christian workers to reach the lost and poor. Ross Langmead, in his published dissertation *The Word Made Flesh*, surveyed the different ways the term is used in diverse Christian traditions. He developed a three-part definition that is slowly becoming the standard of an incarnational approach to mission. He contends that incarnational mission includes: a) following Jesus as the pattern for mission; b) participating in Christ's risen presence as the power for mission; and c) joining God's cosmic mission of 'enfleshment' in which God's self-embodying dynamic is evident from the beginning of creation.[76]

To build from this base definition and to help outline the ways in which an incarnational approach to slum transformation can be understood, possible uses of the incarnational metaphor in mission can be identified and examined. A metaphor is a 'figure of speech whereby we speak about one thing in terms which are seen to be suggestive of another'.[77] What is especially common in religious language is that there is a movement from a broad metaphor to a more specific, tighter meaning, as new ideas are proposed and examined. As Suzanne Langer explains,

> Every new experience, or idea about things, evokes first of all some metaphorical expression. As the idea becomes familiar, this expression 'fades' to a new literal use of the once metaphorical predicate, a more general use than it had before.[78]

Langmead says that 'we need to acknowledge that we cannot divide language neatly into the literal and the metaphorical, because it lies on a continuum between more literal statements and more strongly metaphorical statements'.[79] Therefore, while the metaphor of incarnation is best known in Christianity to describe 'The Word becoming flesh' where God becomes human in Christ, the various ways in which the metaphor of incarnation can be used in mission by God's people need further investigation.

Table 9 below shows a spectrum of understanding from more literal, concrete uses of incarnational mission through to more philosophical, 'lighter' uses. At one end of the spectrum there is the possibility that the metaphor of enfleshment has no relevance for Christian mission in slums. This can be considered the 'lightest' and least concrete end of the spectrum. At the other end is the idea that enfleshment is a very specific, literal methodology or model. There are more figurative understandings can which fit between the two poles such as the incarnational as one value or quality among many. A more intentional 'middle way' is proposed, however, building on Langmead's three-part definition. Both ends of the spectrum will be discussed first to pave the way for the more nuanced versions, with a middle way 'enfleshing hope' outlined in Part C of this research.

Table 9: A spectrum of four possible understandings of an incarnational approach to slum transformation

	Method or Model for	Motif Informs and Inspires	Value as Part of	No Relevance
Key ideas and uses of incarnational metaphor in mission	'Relocation', 'Identification', 'Movement starting', 'Church', 'Devotional imitation', 'Friendship evangelism', 'Simple lifestyle', 'Contextualisation', "Political liberation'	'Enfleshing hope', 'Following Jesus as a pattern for mission', "Participating in Christ's risen presence as the power of mission', 'Joining God's cosmic mission of enfleshment in creation'	'One stream to help spiritualise', 'One aspect of humanising', 'One sign for postmodern missional paradigm', 'One value in missional organisation'	'Rejecting the flesh', 'Only God can enflesh'
Metaphor used...	More literally	Middle way	More figurative	Not used in Mission
Some aspects of this view can be seen in the writings of...	V. Grigg, A. Hirsh, M. Frost, J. Perkins, J. Hayes, D. Harris, D. Andrews, M. Duncan, R. Warren, J. Stott, C. Sheldon, Francis of Assisi, Mother Teresa, J. Rayburn, Romero, C. Boff, R. Sider, J. Bonk, J. Sobrino	D. Bonhoffer, N.T. Wright, J. Moltmann, R. Langmead, A. Root	W. Wink, M. Borg, D. Bosch, R. Foster, Emerging-Church, New Friars	D. Hesselgrave, W. Simson, K. Kostenburger, K. Baker, T. Chester, R. Fung

Some considerations should first be noted about the limitations of this scheme before the possibilities are examined. First, these five theoretical possibilities assign descriptive titles in specific ways. Because activists and scholars alike often use terms like 'method', 'motif' and 'model' almost interchangeably in regard to incarnational metaphors in mission, their meaning can be confusing. For example, a writer may use the term 'model', but actually mean 'method' as described in the scheme offered on the previous page.

Second, activists and scholars may hold to more than one possibility. John Hayes, for example, explicitly argues that the incarnational approach has four meanings: 'a method', 'a message', 'a model' and 'a spiritual discipline'.[80] He often uses these categories differently from my scheme, but this is a clear example of a writer who understands the use of the incarnational metaphor in mission in more than one way.

Third, there can be overlap between possibilities. It is sometimes difficult to identify, for example, when an understanding of the metaphor of enfleshing becomes more a model than a specific methodology. Here we can only admit that on a continuum there is often overlap.

Fourth, the key reason this scheme is offered is to help identify how incarnation can best be used to inspire and inform transformative and distinctly Christian responses to slum and squatter neighbourhoods. By comparing and contrasting possibilities it is hoped that the way can be cleared for a more precise and helpful use of the idea of incarnational mission in slums. With this in mind the strengths and limitations of each possibility will be considered in relation to the context of slums and alongside Langmead's three-part definition.

Chapter Five

Unenfleshed: Rejections of incarnational approaches to mission

Incarnational approaches are as enthusiastically denounced as they are embraced. Some critical voices are more credible than others, but they span the theological spectrum. There are Fundamentalist evangelical positions which reject anything not focusing on the 'spiritual destiny' of individuals, but there are also more nuanced rejections of an incarnational approach from people such as Raymond Fung[1], Andreas Köstenberger,[2] David Hesselgrave,[3] Ken Baker,[4] and even the UK social activist Tim Chester.[5] All raise legitimate and important points that argue against the use of an incarnational approach in Christian mission. Here two general reasons why the incarnational metaphor is rejected for mission will be addressed before dealing with specific objections to more literal incarnational approaches in the next chapter. This then opens the way to propose the use of a 'motif of enfleshing hope' to inform missional responses in slums.

1.0 Rejecting the Flesh of Incarnational Mission

Christian mission can be seen by some as primarily seeking a kind of spiritual transaction between God and individuals. What Jesus' ministry on earth did, especially on the cross, enabled people to be invited to have a personal relationship with God and go to heaven when they die. That Jesus is God-Made-Flesh is only important insofar as that it enabled Jesus to really suffer and die on the cross to take away the sins of the world. Any incarnational metaphor, it is argued, is therefore irrelevant for today's Christians because no-one else can suffer and die on the cross for the sins of the world. That particular ministry has been uniquely completed by Jesus of Nazareth. Followers of Jesus today are to simply 'represent' Jesus as ambassadors and to issue invitations to take up the offer of eternal life for when they die. According to this perspective, to try to enflesh Jesus' priorities or to take up the broader social concerns of Jesus' earthly ministry are a waste of time. Why shuffle society's deck chairs on the Titanic that will soon be no more? Why feed bodies whose souls will soon go to hell? Christian mission in this view is solely about rescuing people from a Christ-less eternity.

There can also be an eschatological dimension to rejecting incarnational approaches. For example, in *The Starfish Manifesto*, house church advocate Wolfgang Simson asks a series of questions to argue that Christian faith is about 'discipleship, not development':

> Does Jesus expect that the world will be transformed before or after his return? After. Does he indicate that the character of this world, its soul, its nature, its ethos, can ever be transformed? No. Did he authorise his disciples to transform the world? No. Did he advise his disciples what methods they should use to transform the world? No.[6]

Any kind of real social and physical transformation, then, can only be expected after Jesus has returned, not in the present time. To emphasise that physical transformation is a waste of time, Simson states, 'Let's face it: developed pagans are, yes, better pagans—but they are still pagans'.[7]

Yet, the transformation Jesus saw in his direct ministry years included the physical, which makes it possible to answer in the affirmative these questions about seeking change before Jesus' return—we *can* seek physical (not simply spiritual) transformation. Further, and as will be discussed later, Jesus' physical resurrection as part of inaugurating the Kingdom undermines negative, 'unenfleshing' answers to these kinds of questions.

Some reject an incarnational approach because they see it as being part of a 'social gospel' conspiracy, or as distracting Christians from the 'real work' of 'preaching the gospel and saving souls'. Even well known missiologist Hesselgrave writes that incarnational mission cannot be the continuation of the mission and ministry of Jesus Christ.

> What then was his mission? What is ours? To answer these questions, incarnational missiologists tend to drift toward less scripture-centred ways of thinking.... Undoubtedly many of those who were enamoured with this kind of Christianity didn't realise that they were 'profiting' at the expense of the truth— the real gospel'.[8]

For Hesselgrave, this 'incarnationalism' can be understood as part of a liberation theology agenda which, he argues, leads to violent revolution. He writes with concern about a colleague who heard 'a self-acclaimed "evangelical liberationist" assert that, when following Jesus in Latin America today, "bullets are as important as Bibles."'[9] Hesselgrave traces the rise of incarnational approaches in mission to John Stott.[10] He sees a specific conspiracy whereby Stott infiltrated the Lausanne movement in the 1970s with the aim of 'mediating' between 'social gospel' and 'proclamation' evangelism, 'a project that he and his followers were still working at over quarter a century later'.[11] Typical of Hesselgrave's concerns is how Stott uses John 20:21 to justify an incarnational approach to mission because it becomes not about 'representing Christ' and 'preaching the gospel', but says 'since the church is to be salt and light, it has failed if a community deteriorates socially or physically'.[12] Hesselgrave argues that it is better to look to Paul as the model to follow today, rather than Christ. 'There would be no gospel, no church, and no mission apart from Christ, but it was Paul, acting as Christ's *ambassador* (from *presbeuo*, 'to act as a representative'), who explained the gospel, extended the church and exemplified mission'.[13] Only by preaching forgiveness of sins and repentance can true representatives of Christ be salt and light in the world today.

While concerns similar to Hesselgrave's are taken up in a wide variety of ways in contemporary Christianity, some versions are cruder than others. Some versions which hold that representing Christ to invite spiritual transaction is the only legitimate form of mission can play out especially tragically in urban slums. For example, some Christians view seeking to address physical and social needs in places like slums as legitimate only if these efforts are used as a kind of 'evangelistic bait' to do the 'real mission' of inviting conversion. It's not uncommon in Klong Toey, for example, to see Christians visit to offer free rice or medical services with the understanding that recipients are required to sit down with an evangelist and listen to a 'gospel presentation'.[14] The Thai idea of *kreng jai* (obligation) means that few recipients are able to resist signing up to become Christians. Of course, once out the door, few recipients want to participate in the life of such a church. The real cost of receiving the social program is understood as the vulnerable recipient's soul.

There are, however, more nuanced and sophisticated views which are not so easily dismissed. One example is Andreas Köstenberger whose *The Missions of Jesus and the Disciples According to the Forth Gospel* is, in part, a reaction to the views of people like Stott, who argue that 'the only kind of authentic mission is incarnational mission', and who point to John 17:18 and 20:21 as the most important, but 'most neglected' of the 'great commission' mandates.[15] In his response to these claims, Köstenberger seeks to explore what these two commissions really meant for the first disciples and what they mean for Christian mission today. He concludes that the disciples should 'bear witness to Jesus in an evil, hostile world' and 'pronounce forgiveness or retain people's sins' but that the emphasis on 'service to humanity and on human need' is—'contrary to Stott's assertions' and those of 'contemporary mission practice'—'not presented in the fourth Gospel as the primary purpose of either Jesus' or the disciples' mission'.[16] Hesselgrave acknowledges Köstenberger's insights in his argument that Paul, not Jesus, is to be followed because Paul represented Jesus in ways that we Christians also can today.[17] Table 10 contrasts incarnational and representational views of mission.

Table 10: Hesselgrave comparison of incarnational and representational views of mission

Jesus: Son of God and Saviour	
Incarnationalism	**Representationalism**
Jesus as missionary model	Paul as missionary model
Continuity	Discontinuity
1. Liberator of society and/or	1. Ambassador and
2. Transformer of culture and/or	2. Evangelist
3. Saviour of people	3. Church planter

Source: Hesselgrave, 2005[18]

Putting aside temporarily how Hesselgrave and Köstenberger define incarnational mission, an important and widespread assumption of anti-incarnational views can be seen. Many have an extremely negative view of this world and physicality in general. The world is understood as being 'hostile' and 'evil'. The natural consequence of this view for mission is that efforts are concentrated on offering forgiveness, verbal witness and otherworldly salvation, to be fuelled by private, personal and spiritual piety. None of these actions require any real physical contact with others or their physical needs; this view does not consider the broader world and its systems causing people physical suffering.

The Christian faith traditionally stands against such negative views of physicality. Jesus was the Incarnation, fully God and fully human, not, as Docetists thought, merely 'seeming' to be a flesh-and-blood human or even, as Gnostics thought, avoiding the evil of assuming material existence. That God valued flesh-and-blood people in a real society so much that 'the Word became flesh' is crucial to the kind of mission Christians engage in because it values the physical world. This theme was especially taken up in the early Christian tradition by people such as Irenaeus in the second century. Irenaeus famously wrote against the Gnostics' devaluation and rejection of good creation that 'the glory of God is the human person fully alive'.[19] Jürgen Moltmann is a modern example of a scholar who sees the importance of God using the 'means of creation', especially becoming flesh and blood in Christ. Moltmann writes:

> By becoming flesh, the reconciling God assumes the sinful, sick and mortal flesh of human beings and heals it in community with [Godself]... In his taking flesh, exploited, sick and shattered human bodies experience their healing and their indestructible dignity.[20]

God-Incarnate did far more than simply die on the cross for spiritual or ecclesial reasons. There are a number of arguments which support the assertion that Jesus has a continuing ministry in the world and values flesh and blood today.

First, Jesus lived and ministered in ways that caused his crucifixion. If Jesus' mission was simply to ensure a spiritual transaction via the cross, then Jesus would not have had to live very long at all. A baby's death would have sufficed. Yet, Jesus lived and ministered in a particular way, seeking to do and show the will of God in the world. It was this very physical life and ministry that put Jesus at risk. Without living such a real and provocative life, why would authorities conspire to kill Jesus? What Jesus was showing, setting up and instigating was the priorities of the Kingdom of God in his life and ministry 'on earth as in heaven'. Without this premise the moral teachings of Jesus in the Sermon on the Mount, as well as the meaning and power of healings and deliverance stories, make no sense. Jesus had a very practical agenda that threatened the established powers of that day and this. It's hard to read Jesus' inaugural address in Luke 4:18-19 without seeing the potential conflict with those in power.

In John's Gospel, which is the focus of Köstenberger's concerns, Jesus' public and very physical ministry is in constant conflict with the powers. It is John, for example, who has Jesus clearing the temple of money changers early in the narrative (John 2:13), as distinct from later as in the Synoptic accounts (Mark 11:15-19, Luke 19:45-48). John records this in an especially provocative manner: 'Making a whip of cords, he drove all of them out of the temple, both the sheep and the cattle. He also poured out the coins of the money changers and overturned their tables' (John 2:15). Jesus quickly found himself in conflict with the Judeans (John 2:18) and identified himself with the temple, pointing to his own 'destruction' but also to being subsequently 'raised up' (John 2:19-22). Jesus seemed to know early in this account that the consequence of living such a life was death, but also that this was the life that God affirmed. Jesus was not only killed by the powers because of the life he led; he was also raised again by God because of it. God's raising of Jesus from the dead was a divine 'yes' to the life Jesus lived.[21]

To use John's most famous verse, because 'God so loved the *world*' (*kosmos*), Jesus was given (John 3:16). Those who 'believe' in Jesus therefore cannot retreat from seeking to follow the compassion of God through Jesus into the needs of the cosmos. Jesus is specific about this, explicitly 'sending' (Greek *apostello*) the 'believers' into the world just as Jesus was sent (John 17:18, 20:21, see also Matthew 28:16-20). This sending out is despite the potential consequences of living out the priorities of Jesus' life in the way of discipleship (John 15:20). Believers are promised what Jesus experienced in resurrection: this way of living can even overcome persecution and death (John 16:33). That is the kind of 'eternal life' Jesus talks about in John, not a spiritual place inhabited by body-less souls after death.

Second, Jesus does invite (as well as send) his disciples to follow him and participate in his ministry. Disciples are not simply representatives. In John's Gospel, Jesus explicitly says, 'Whoever serves me must follow me, and where I am, there will be my servant be also. Whoever serves me, the Father will honour' (John 12:26). Peter begins to 'follow' Jesus (John 1:35) and comes to understand that such following will cause him real physical pain, even death like Jesus (John 21:19-20). None of the calls to follow Jesus make any sense if Jesus was just performing a spiritual transaction to which Peter had only to give verbal and spiritual assent. Jesus' followers were (and are) also called to be threats to dominant, oppressing powers; they may well experience physical threats because of the life and priorities they have, which are also the priorities of Jesus (John 16:33). In Mark's Gospel, to follow Jesus means to: 'Deny yourself, take up your cross daily and follow me' (Mark 8:34).

This theme of incarnational mission as following Jesus is taken up by many Christian traditions, not least by the Anabaptists.[22] They note that 'follow me' is one of the most common and archetypal invitations by Jesus, occurring six times in John and fifteen times in the Synoptics. Similar mandates can also be seen in other New Testament writings too, with Jesus an 'example' to 'follow in the footsteps of' (1 Peter 2:21). If Jesus didn't want people to follow him, why would this invitation be repeated so often? Given the frequency of these invitations to continue following Jesus, compared with the one time that Jesus in John's Gospel invited disciples to offer forgiveness of sins (John 20:23), it is difficult to substantiate Köstenberger's claim that representing Christ by verbal witness and offering forgiveness is the sole meaning of Christian mission. If Jesus simply commissioned the disciples to offer private, spiritual piety, he would not have had lived as he did or called his disciples to live out his Kingdom priorities too.

Further, the resurrected Jesus explicitly commissioned the disciples to 'make disciples' who 'obey' what Jesus commanded in the cosmos (Matthew 28:18-19). Discipleship that does not include following Jesus is inconsistent with the incarnated word. Jesus did not call people to make disciples of Paul, but of himself. Paul even explicitly forbade people placing him before Jesus as a leader to follow in the factional Corinthian church (1 Corinthians 1:10-17).

In John's Gospel the last words of the resurrected Jesus were to Peter with the repeated commission to 'follow me' (John 21:21). Far from there being no evidence of Jesus inviting his disciples to join him in service for the Kingdom's sake, these ideas are consistent with the commission of John 20:21: 'As the Father sent me, so I send you'. An authentic, real and physical following of Jesus should not be ignored by any Christian approach to mission. This is especially the case with those suffering real misery in urban slums.

A third reason for seeing Jesus' ministry as continuing to be embodied today is that Jesus is not dead and God continues his enfleshing ministry through Jesus in the power of the Spirit. That followers join, follow and participate with this risen

Jesus does not undermine the uniqueness of Jesus or his divinity. In fact, joining, following and participating with the risen Christ helps make sense of why Jesus didn't complete his ministry in the grave. Why would Jesus rise again if his mission was already completed with his sacrificial death? Orthodox Christianity sees Jesus' resurrection as physical, but in a new kind of physicality, inaugurating a new world. Jesus continues his ministry and does not stop at the cross. Further, N. T. Wright argues that eternal life is not on another planet with disembodied spirits, but that Jesus' resurrection was the first of the fruits of the new creation (1 Corinthians 15: 21-28). Just as Jesus' body was transformed, so too will be the believers and the whole cosmos. It is not just renovating the building before its demolition for a spiritual world. Christians are to seek God's Kingdom 'on earth as it is in heaven' (Matthew 6:10). The Kingdom is inaugurated by Jesus' life, death and resurrection, and will be completed when all is put to rights.[23]

This view of inaugurated eschatology and the importance of the physical resurrection of Jesus as taken up by Wright will be discussed in more detail later in this research. For now we simply note that what we do physically in this life matters because good works—like giving alms to relieve suffering—last for eternity (Luke 12:31-34). Nothing that is done in Jesus' name that is good and true will be wasted. Somehow these efforts in Christ are transformed and live on for eternity. These efforts have some role in the basic assessment of our lives (Matthew 25:31). Those things that are bad and false will not last. The fact that Jesus promised that this will happen and required his followers to keep investing their best time, energy and creativity in such physical service, is at odds with an unenfleshed view of Christian mission.

The view that anything physical is not as important as disembodied souls is not uncommon for many slum churches and versions of slum Christianity. The importation of Western forms of dualistic fundamentalism to the developing world has found resonance in many slum neighbourhoods. As we have seen, urban slums have tough living conditions, where the most vulnerable often get sick and die prematurely and unnecessarily. Most experienced urban missioners in the West or developing world have experienced the premature or preventable deaths of people they know first-hand. The otherworldly emphasis of many Christians in the developing world can be understood as a desire to transcend their experiences of physical sickness and death—experiences that many in the West cannot even imagine. Putting such suffering alongside the complexities of seeking transformation in slums can easily lead residents to feeling overwhelmed and powerless. To overcome that feeling it is not unreasonable to try to escape this world for another spiritual one which can be controlled. It is hard for slum residents to resist an emphasis on life after death given the accessibility of imported materials from wealthy Christian media ministries, the simplicity of the spiritual message, and the sense that what comes from the West is best. Confidence and power are attractive when so many have this in short supply. An unseen, untouched, spiritual world seems better than no world at all.

The widespread denial of the value of real flesh and blood, however, has some serious negative consequences in relation to slum residents. It may well be one of the key reasons why Christianity struggles to make a transformative impact in slums in many parts of the world. Brian McLaren, for example, visited Rwanda and Burundi and wrote about a workshop he did with church leaders there. It was not long after the genocide where more than 800,000 people had died and more than two million became refugees.[24] What was especially tragic for McLaren and these church leaders was that it was Christians who had slaughtered other Christians after years of revival. Rather than being a force for good, this Christianity was co-opted to become an integral part of the problem. These church leaders, wrote McLaren, identified the otherworldly emphasis of the gospel, along with domination and colonialisation, as a key factor explaining why Christians failed to prevent the genocide.[25] A strong emphasis on this life as opposed to the one after death is an important counter to the potentially destructive and almost Platonic or Gnostic thinking that can form the basis of arguments against incarnational mission. To focus on this life only, however, can lead to avoidance of facing the reality of death or the issue of life after death which need to be themes for urban practitioners and will be considered when we look at the enfleshing hope motif.

Without an emphasis on enfleshment, what Christians have to offer the transformation process in slums can too easily be minimised. As Bonhoeffer proclaimed during the Nazi regime, without an active call to follow Jesus a kind of 'cheap grace' can occur which 'amounts to a denial of the living Word of God, in fact, a denial of the Incarnation of the Word of God'.[26] Offering 'cheap grace' in praying a prayer to go to a disembodied heaven after death does not change the complex challenges people faced in Nazi Germany, or the challenges people face in a developing-world urban slum. Jesus lived physically in a way that led to his crucifixion, not only to die, but to rise again, to invite people to follow him. A denial of the physicality of the Incarnation and its implications for Christian living cannot be considered an adequate basis for a Christian response to the rise of slums.

2.0 Only God Can 'Enflesh'

The second argument objects to the metaphor of enfleshing in mission because enfleshing metaphors should only be used of Jesus Christ. To use 'enfleshing' in relation to Christian mission is seen as unhelpful because humans are not the 'divine Word made flesh' as Jesus is. It is not so much that the flesh is evil, but that it is blasphemous for humans to equate themselves with God or Jesus. Only Jesus is Lord, so to use the incarnational metaphor is profoundly unhelpful and can undermine what Christians can do in mission today.

Messiah complexes are often legitimate concerns, especially among those bold enough to go to live and seek transformation in slums. A kind of overconfidence and lack of humility can be a common characteristic of those who feel they can personally go and do something about slums. As Jayakumar Christian argues, God-complexes are a serious part of the problems which cause poverty and the oppressive relationships that do not work for justice.[27] Encouragement of zealous young people to become messiahs for the urban poor can undermine transformative efforts in slums.

These kinds of objections are raised by Köstenberger and Hesselgrave, but can also be found in the advocates of the New Reformed movement which is expressing a neo-Calvinism for today.[28] Some of these are conservative voices, but they also include Tim Chester and Raymond Fung, who do not fit a conservative-fundamentalist mould. Despite supporting social justice and mission among the poor these last two are against the use of the term 'incarnational' in mission. Chester, for example, argues that 'Incarnation is a precise theological term that... refers to a divine being taking on humanity. I can't do that!'.[29] Proponents of this view argue that the Incarnation is a central and defining Christian doctrine and is the basis of the metaphor of enfleshing. That is, the Divine Word was 'made flesh' in Jesus in ways others cannot be (John 1:14).

There are however, some ways to address this legitimate concern. By the capitalisation of 'I' in 'the Incarnation', for example, a convention can be maintained that points to the unique, once-and-for-all, salvific event of God becoming human in Jesus Christ. The missional use of the metaphor by Christians can then be (small 'i') 'incarnational'. Raymond Fung, in correspondence with Langmead, however, is also dissatisfied with this: "There are no others with a small "i". Speaking theologically and precisely, incarnation is not a methodology. It is not an adjective (such as incarnational)'.[30]

What happened in the Incarnation is unique, impossible for others to do, but there are still ways to use broader, enfleshing metaphors for Christians in mission. Indeed, even in contemporary broader society the term 'to incarnate' or 'to be the incarnation of' something is used widely and has nothing to do with the Divine becoming flesh in Jesus. A brave footballer can be described as 'courage incarnate' or a particularly vile sex offender 'evil incarnate'. The term suggests that unseen or abstract qualities or characteristics have become real, authentic, embodied or personified. As we have seen, this is actually the original linguistic sense of the Latin term *incarnatus*. To enflesh, then, can mean to make real, not necessarily to make divine.

God 'makes real' his character and will on earth in more ways than only in the Christ Event. As Langmead maintains, there has always been an 'ongoing incarnational dynamic of God in creation'.[31] This can be seen in creation itself, but also specifically in humanity, and in the presence of God among the people of Israel. The metaphor is used beyond Jesus in the New Testament too. For example, God's people can be understood as the 'body of Christ' (1 Corinthians 12:12). Paul is clearly using an enfleshing metaphor here that can be applied to Christians today. He is not saying humans are gods, nor even that the institutional church is now Christ incarnate, but explains that the possibility exists for Christians to work together to continue the ministry of Jesus in the world, thus embodying God's outgoing, vulnerable love.

This theme has helped many engage with poverty today. For example *Christianity Today* magazine reported Rick Warren's experience of poverty in Africa, where he found 'those 2,000 verses on the poor' and following the apostle Paul's metaphor, prayed 'God, would you use me to re-attach the hands and the feet to the body of Christ, so that the whole church cares about the whole gospel in a whole new way—through the local church?'[32] These wider uses of enfleshing metaphors are different to 'the Incarnation', but are nevertheless legitimate. This usage picks up Langmead's second use of the term 'incarnational mission', that of participating with Jesus as part of the body of Christ. To some degree it also picks up Langmead's third use—joining with what God is doing.[33] Therefore, this wider use of the adjectival enfleshing metaphor is legitimate, with a small 'i' for 'incarnational'. This can be a helpful differentiation for those who can hear the metaphor used in two different ways.

Chester and Fung argue that Christians today cannot be 'God in the flesh' for others in the way Jesus of Nazareth was, and any attempt to claim this is grandiose. It is mistaken, however, to place limits on the use of this metaphor when there are strong arguments that God is enfleshed—or takes shape—in broader ways than in the Incarnation. Certainly the term 'incarnational mission' can be misused, but to reject the possibility that God can enflesh hope through people, for example, misses an important motif for Christians engaging in slums, that of allowing God's love to become visible through the body of Christ.

The term 'incarnational mission' is used frequently today in diverse and sometimes unhelpful ways. As we have noted, the emerging-church, the 'new monastics' and the 'new friars', as well as more mainstream missiologists, have gravitated to the term, but to such a degree that it is now used in such diverse and contradictory ways that it is in danger of becoming clichéd. In fact so slippery has the term become that it can be easily dismissed before its important call to sustained faithfulness and relevance in mission is even considered.

Misuse of incarnational metaphors should not be considered such a barrier as to exclude Christians from employing them appropriately. To deny that God can enflesh, make real or embody hope in all kinds of ways in slums can restrict our understanding of God. Finding more appropriate and precise uses of the term incarnational mission, however, is not an easy task.

Chapter Six

More Literally Incarnational: A specific missional methodology or model to emulate

If one end of the incarnational spectrum sees no value at all for Christians in an incarnational approach to slum transformation, then the other end has a far more concrete and literal understanding of how crucially the Incarnation relates to Christians in mission. This can be seen in at least two kinds of ways.

First, Christ's Incarnation can be understood as a particular methodology that has specific steps which Christians can follow and apply in mission. This methodology is often raised in reaction to less credible, unenfleshed methodologies, such as attracting people out of poor neighbourhoods to middle class churches, or visiting poor communities to make 'evangelistic raids' only to return to their nice, safe neighbourhoods. John Perkins sums up the common reaction to these kinds of methodologies in the following statement:

> Jesus relocated. He didn't commute to earth one day a week and shoot back up to heaven. He left his throne and became one of us so that we might see the life God revealed in him.[1]

Incarnational mission here is often about pragmatic concerns about using the best methodologies possible and the methodology of the Incarnation is quickly cited as a justification. John Hayes, founder-director of Inner-Change, for example, cites 1 Corinthians 9:20-23 as giving practical reasons for an incarnational methodology: 'Living with and like the poor hastens language and culture learning, helps demonstrate that we are for real, and places us near the heartbeat of poor communities'.[2] As another example, Dave Andrews provides five specific steps, developed with reference to Philippians 2:4-8. They are:

Step one—move into the locality
Step two—remember our humanity
Step three—empty ourselves
Step four—serve others
Step five—embrace suffering.[3]

Those who hold the incarnational position can differ in their opinions as to what specific steps and aims are involved in an incarnational methodology. What they have in common, however, is that they not only take seriously the idea of 'following Jesus as a pattern for mission', to use Langmead's definition, but they also go further and make incarnational mission a specific methodology. They use the enfleshing metaphor based solely on the Incarnation of Christ and in a more literal way than other understandings we will consider. The provision of a variety of specific steps required for the methodology to be followed is another feature of this understanding, so it is possible to clearly assess whether a method is incarnational or not according to their definition.

Second, incarnational mission can be understood as a specific model to emulate or copy in mission strategy, more than simply a methodology to apply. A 'model' in this sense is about using a demonstration to make logical future predictions. The Incarnational event then can be viewed as the true prototype for specific models of Christian mission today. Modelling after this event is not only about 'true discipleship' of Christ, but also expects to result in lives being transformed just as Christ transformed lives, because it is the 'true mission' of the church, too. These approaches can often fit within one of the three parts of Langmead's definition as 'following Jesus as a pattern for mission', though there can be great diversity of opinion about what following this model means.[4] This can include models of devotion, contextualisation, simple lifestyle, friendship evangelism or social liberation. In fact, such a variety of understandings of what the specific model of Christ in mission is and how it should be copied today in slums makes it difficult to group these approaches together. As John Stott writes, however, what they have in common is the following assertion:

> Jesus did more than draw a vague parallel between his mission and ours. Deliberately and precisely he made his mission the model of ours, saying 'as the Father sent me, so I send you'. Therefore our understanding of the church's mission must be deduced from our understanding of the Son's. Why and how did the Father send the Son?[5]

The theological focus here is almost exclusively on the model of the Incarnation of Christ. Such an incarnational model is often weaker in identifying how the two other parts of Langmead's definitions relate to incarnational mission (if at all). Joining with the Creator's ongoing incarnational dynamic in creation and participating with the Sprit for empowerment in mission is not often an integral part of any specific part of an incarnational model of mission.[6]

These more literalist views of an incarnational approach as a special method or model to emulate can be seen at least in part in most Christian traditions, but are often a particular focus in Anabaptist,[7] radical evangelical[8] and liberationist[9] missiologies.[10] In the spectrum of incarnational mission we outlined these are clearly on the more literal end of the spectrum. Perhaps the grouping of incarnation as a model is less prescriptive than identifying a particular methodology as *the* incarnational approach, but both try to tie any methodology in with the specifics of Christ's model for mission. In this sense 'method' can be further left of our spectrum than 'model', though for sake of space the two will be considered together.

In what sense, then, can the Incarnation be understood as the specific method or model for Christians in mission today in urban slum and squatter neighbourhoods? What is the method or model the Incarnation provides for the transformation slums? The following incarnational methodologies and models are just some examples of how this position can be seen in relationship to urban slum and squatter neighbourhoods.

1.0 Incarnation as Relocation

Incarnational mission can be seen as a methodology of moving home to live and serve, 'as Jesus did', in another neighbourhood. John's Prologue is important as a basis for this methodology. Eugene Peterson paraphrases John 1:14 as 'moving into the neighbourhood'[11] because *skenoo* comes from a family of words which means to 'pitch a tent', 'encamp', 'live', 'dwell', 'tabernacle'.[12] Following Jesus into mission, therefore, is viewed as requiring a methodology of literally moving to live and make one's home in another place. Philippians 2:5-7 is another key relocation passage. Jesus 'gave up' the location of heaven to be 'born a human' in a particular location on earth. Similarly, and as discussed above, Andrews and Perkins see the first step in an incarnational methodology as 'moving into the neighbourhood', not simply 'commuting' or 'visiting'.[13] The Incarnational event can also mandate risking ourselves to physically go to the 'other side of the road', like the Good Samaritan (Luke 10:25-37) or as in John's 'great commission' (John 20:21) relocate 'as' Jesus did.

An incarnational methodology such as relocation has been especially advocated by Christians working and living among the poor in recent times. Relocation is often contrasted in frustration with methodologies used by Christian workers who commute from middle class suburbs into poor neighbourhoods. The methodology Christians choose, it is argued, can undermine the message Christians preach. Dorothy Matheson (formerly Dorothy Harris) describes the early experiences of her colleagues in Servants to Asia's Urban Poor where neighbours said that 'Jesus can't live in the slums, but only in the nice big middle class churches'. This raised-up a 'commitment to prove otherwise' and that 'Jesus can live in the slums'. Matheson noted that, 'After ten years of church planting, community development, health care, non-formal education, income generation, etc., we are more convinced that the slums are not abandoned by the Father'.[14] Perkins also sees Philippians 2:5-8 (as well as John 1:14) as a call to relocation in inner-city America: 'He came and lived among us. He was called Emmanuel—God with us—the incarnation is the ultimate relocation.[15]

That incarnational mission requires the method of relocation can be a controversial view, especially amongst Christians who do not relocate. Michael Duncan, while living in a Manila slum with his family, raised this idea at the Lausanne Congress on World Evangelism in Manila in 1989, and faced strong opposition. 'Should all missionaries who are working with the poor live in slums?' he was asked. 'In the end I simply encouraged all missionaries to reread their Bibles and seek the Lord on the matter,' but admitted that,

> I was upset over the fact that hundreds of missionaries were residing in some of the best residential areas of Manila while the majority of Manila's inhabitants were reduced to living in inhumane slums... They would have preferred it if I had simply said each to their call. But the intensity of feeling created over my answer suggested that I needed to explore this matter further.[16]

Duncan would go on to study and reflect further on the matter at Oxford's Centre for Mission Studies. After considering key texts and motivations for incarnational mission as relocation, he concluded that where Jesus focused his life and ministry implies Jesus' priorities and gives 'textual help in terms of how to relocate and what is needed in relocation', though he did conclude that, 'even though on the one hand scripture doesn't command us to relocate, scripture on the other hand is very much supportive and helpful in choosing this option. Relocation, therefore, is not solely a matter of personal choice and human effort.'[17] Relocation and incarnational mission are still intrinsically tied together here.

Incarnational mission as a method takes up the idea of 'following Jesus', but often in a narrower and more literal sense than other views we will consider. As we shall see there are limits to identifying with Jesus metaphorically in this way. Is where the Christ lived before his human birth in Bethlehem really analogous to a middle class neighbourhood? It can also neglect the other two parts of Langmead's definition of joining and participating with Christ, which don't necessarily fit with the one specific methodology of simply moving house.

2.0 Incarnation as Crossing Cultures

Incarnation can also be viewed in relationship to culture. As a method it can be understood as how a Christian worker joins a particular people group, seeking to become 'one of them' or an 'insider'. This method may or may not include relocation of home, but also draws heavily on Philippians 2:5-7. Just as Jesus truly became a particular kind of human—a Galilean—to reach humanity, so too should Christians 'have the same attitude as Christ' and identify with the community they want to reach. Former Bangkok slum worker Rob O'Callaghan writes that the philosophy of ministry of his organisation, Word Made Flesh, commits them to an 'incarnational methodology' but asks, 'How are we to imitate God becoming human'? One of his answers is by 'identifying with the poor': 'To serve the poor in the way of the Incarnation means being willing to embrace poverty. It might mean eating things that we would normally throw out as unfit. It might mean coming into contact with filth. It might mean jeopardising our social standing'.[18] This use of incarnational mission as a methodology of identification can often be found in broader missiological literature. For example, the *Dictionary of Mission Theology* notes:

> We should, like Jesus, identify ourselves with the people of a receiving culture without losing our own integrity or compromising our Christian convictions, values and standards. 'To the Jew I became like a Jew… to the weak I became weak' was Paul's way of identifying with those he wanted to win (1 Corinthians 9:20-23).[19]

This is also evident in the writings of many emerging-church authors, such as Michael Frost and Alan Hirsch, who view incarnational mission as a specific methodology including 'identification'. In their influential book, *The Shaping of Things to Come*, contrasts are made between 'attractional' and 'incarnational' methodologies. The attractional method is where the 'church bids people to come and hear the gospel in the holy confines of the church and its community'.[20] In contrast, the Incarnation provides a method going in the opposite direction, where Christians go out and identify with a people group: 'The Incarnation provides us with the missional means by which the gospel can become a genuine part of a people group without damaging the innate cultural frameworks that provide that people group with a sense of meaning and history… Incarnational mission will mean that in reaching a people group we will need to identify with them in all ways possible without compromising the truth of the gospel itself'.[21]

Whereas incarnational mission as a methodology of relocation mostly focuses on Christians 'moving downward' to poorer neighbourhoods, it is worth noting that incarnational mission can be viewed more broadly than just moving toward the the poor. Hirsch and Frost contend that 'The practice of incarnational identification with a group of people… should apply to all forms of genuine mission whatever the context. Not only because it "works" but because it somehow reflects that primal act of identification that was an intrinsic part of Christ's Incarnation'.[22] The view of incarnational mission as a methodology can lead us to employ strategies of identification and service with a particular target group to further the Kingdom of God among those people.

Whether such identification with those of another culture is possible needs further consideration. Most cross-cultural missionaries are aware that while they can do much to show that they love and stand beside those of another culture, they ultimately remain outsiders, or semi-insiders. They are never 'natives' but are always in some ways strangers bringing gifts.[23] This is certainly true of those who move from a rich country to a poor slum and squatter neighbourhood. Incarnational mission as methodology can lend itself to 'participating' with what God is doing within a culture, but to claim to be the 'same as' people born into other cultures or sub-cultures is to claim more than Jesus did. He was born into one human culture of first century Palestine. Modern Christians who identify with a sub-culture not their own are not the 'same as' Jesus at that point. There is potential for practical helpfulness in this kind of methodology, but there are also inadequacies that will be considered shortly.

A slightly less literal understanding of the Incarnation in relationship to culture focuses on Jesus as a model for contextualisation. That God sent Jesus Christ to become a Jewish person can be seen as the model for all cross-cultural missionaries. David Livingstone famously said, 'God only had one son and he made that son a missionary'.[24] Jesus spent over thirty years a part of the Jewish culture, playing a particular role in family and work, before his public ministry began. Cross-cultural Christian workers, it is argued, should not take the host culture they go to live amongst any less seriously than Jesus' model.

This understanding has been particularly important in helping Christians move away from colonial models of 'civilising' local cultures with European Christianity. Nevertheless, cultural arrogance, even racism, can still emerge today, especially in cross-cultural settings. Jesus' model of humility in crossing cultures is an antidote to this. Rob O'Callaghan makes the point: Jesus' Incarnation 'reminds us that we cannot divorce our witness from the specific cultural context within which it takes place'.[25]

Judith and Sherwood Lingenfelter are prominent advocates of Jesus as the model for cross-cultural ministry. Taking a Christian anthropologist's approach to incarnational mission, they develop a specific 'incarnational' model of relating contextually. From Philippians 2:6-7 they argue that:

> This text suggests that Jesus was 100 per cent God and 100 per cent human. If we can imagine it, Jesus was a 200-percent person... those who minister cross-culturally should seek to become 150 per cent persons—75 per cent birth culture and 75 per cent incarnate in the culture of ministry.[26]

Ideas of humility, a learning posture and 'growing up' in a new setting can be a helpful description of what is required in adapting to new cultures. Often cross-cultural workers need to shed identities and limit differences which can be barriers to their new host culture. Also, psychologically, cross-cultural workers can often feel as if they do not belong 100 per cent in any culture and so aiming to be 75 per cent at home in each is a realistic expectation. There are issues we will come to shortly when

Christ's deity and pre-existence is identified with a new culture, however.

Incarnation as the model for contextualisation can also be seen in many Catholic post-Vatican II models of mission, where the idea of incarnation, inculturation and indigenisation are similar. As part of the decentralising, localising and vernacularising of the Catholic church the Incarnation was used as a justification. For example, at the SEDOS research seminar in 1981 the following view was shared: 'If proclamation sees mission in the perspective of the Word proclaimed, inculturation sees mission in the perspective of the flesh, or concrete embodiment, which the Word assumes in a particular individual, community, institution or culture'.[27] The barriers God broke to engage humanity in the Incarnation can inspire Christians today, but real problems remain in using the Incarnation as the model for cross-cultural mission. One such problem is the Lingenfelters' description of Jesus as being a 200 per cent person, which is mathematically impossible. Further, to have a 200 per cent Jesus that is 100 per cent God plus 100 per cent human actually makes Jesus only half human and half God. This comes close to the ancient Nestorian heresy of Jesus being 'two sons'. Todd Billings is an example of one who has some serious objections to this formulation of Christ. He not only agrees with Hesselgrave that Jesus' ministry was unique and cannot be replicated by Christians today, but he also raises one objection not yet considered: 'The divine nature is not a "culture" and we cannot (and should not) see ourselves as analogous to the pre-incarnate Word that then takes on humanity'.[28] Since Deity is not the same as culture there are dangers in Christians identifying Christ as our model for crossing cultures. The Incarnation as a model for cross-cultural ministry has real limitations when applied like this, but as Billings argues, 'We should identify with the culture so that our lives offer an intelligible witness to the one Redeemer of peoples from all cultures, Jesus Christ. It is not enough to bear witness to Jesus as the model for crossing cultures. Jesus is much more than a model'.[29]

At best, the model of the Incarnation for cross-cultural ministry can pick up one of three themes identified by Langmead in incarnational approaches. That is, 'co-operating with God's incarnational activity since creation'[30] because God is at work in a particular culture and that Christians can join in with God in the ongoing transformation process is different from confusing divinity with culture. The limitations of this model lie in its potential to blur the uniqueness of Christ, to fail to see the differences between culture and divinity, or to set up Christian workers to try to do work which only the Divine can do. To identify cross-cultural mission as analogous with the Incarnational event is problematic and ultimately unhelpful in seeking the transformation of slums.

3.0 Incarnation as Influencing Others

The Incarnational event can be viewed as a classic methodology or model to see change in people and even see whole social movements emerge from among the host people group of a Christian worker.

First, particularly found in youth ministry circles, an incarnational approach to mission can be synonymous with following Jesus' model of personal influence via friendships. Jesus left heaven and primarily focused his ministry on inviting twelve apostles to share life with him. That journey together influenced their lives, identity and destiny. Once these men became disciples of Jesus, they were then able to influence others to become Christ's disciples through the means of their personal relationships.

Andrew Root studied this approach to youth ministry.[31] He credits Young Life founder Jim Rayburn with creating a breakthrough in youth mission in America in the 1940s and 50s that has set the model for many contemporary youth ministry approaches.[32] Rather than expecting young people to come to church (or even the evangelistic crusades that many churches and youth organisations ran at the time), Young Life concentrated on developing influential relationships within high schools and would then invite students to events like Bible clubs. Rayburn soon discovered that if he could 'accrue a currency of cool by incarnating himself within distinct youth culture' he could receive 'cool capital from the most popular students' that would influence others.[33] Root observes that initially Rayburn did much of this kind of ministry intuitively. As Young Life perfected this approach and soon became a national and then international phenomenon, however, Rayburn began to reference the Incarnation as the model of relational influence for the gospel's sake:

> Using the incarnation as a pattern, an example of how ministry could be done, Rayburn positioned the incarnation as ministerial justification (rather than theological explication) of ministry. Because of this perspective, relational ministry to this day is infused with this understanding of the incarnational as solely a pattern for ministry.[34]

Real and relevant ways to connect with young people were found, but in a survey of youth ministers Root also discovered a darker side. A kind of cool, Christian ghetto quickly emerged from following such a model. One where young people sometimes felt their friendships with leaders were a commodity. Root is particularly critical of those who don't see any intrinsic value in Christians 'sharing place' unless it leads to church participation.[35] Seeking out relationships with vulnerable adolescents only as a means to get them to come to events and make Christian decisions is ethically problematic. Is the cost of this intentional friendship a young person's soul? Not only is this practice ethically dubious, young people and urban slum residents can often smell a hidden agenda and withdraw.

Relational model imitation as incarnational mission has potential inadequacies around grace, creativity and the ongoing incarnational work of God. There are, however, deeper questions. Not least is the question of whether incarnational mission is primarily a model to justify personal persuasive powers in 'friendship evangelism'? Jesus of Nazareth did share life with his disciples and others in a way that can inform how Christians can relate to others, but what kind of model is Jesus in these relationships? This model of incarnational youth ministry outlined above claims to be based on how Jesus approached relationships, but when the Gospels are considered, few if any people with 'cool currency' are found in Jesus' friendship circles. In fact, Jesus' closest friendships were with Galileans, fishermen and Jewish tax collectors who were all amongst some of the most despised people of Palestine (Matthew 9:10-11, Mark 2:15-16, Luke 5:30). Further, rather than Jesus seeking to be paid back for his friendship by having 'friends' join his group, Jesus commands his disciples to love others 'expecting nothing in return' (Luke 14:7-14). When modern friendship evangelism aims to influence young people to join their in-groups via the currency of friendship, it faces a serious problem in justifying this on the basis of the Jesus' model of sharing relationships. Jesus' life and teachings may well be useful as a pattern to help inspire new ways and models of just and compassionate relationships, but they are not coercive or exploitative. Root especially points to Langmead and Bonhoeffer to help develop a broader, more appropriate incarnational approach to youth ministry.[36] Sharing life 'through the risen Christ', rather than striving to copy Christ's relationships as the right model, has particular relevance to Christians with slum neighbours; this will be taken up in Parts C and D of this book.

At the end of this chapter, further group considerations and evaluations will be made about the Incarnation viewed as one specific model of mission, but here we can simply say that incarnational mission needs to be more than a model of friendship evangelism.

Second, the Incarnation is the model of the ultimate movement initiator and instigator in slums. Jesus discipled the apostles and sent them out into the world to continue the movement (John 20:21). Following Jesus' way in the Incarnational event may include identification and relocation, but it can also be understood as a method of initiating Christian faith indigenised through a 'people movement'. This view, often cited by emerging-church, house church and church growth activists,[37] can especially be seen in the writings and ministry of Viv Grigg in regard to slums. For example, drawing on John 17, Grigg outlines Jesus' incarnational strategy of discipleship as 'a new sociological paradigm—a new small-group structure and a new pattern for birthing a movement. Based on these building blocks we can develop patterns for forming churches'.[38] Referring to social change movements such as the rise of the Black Panthers and Pentecostalism, Grigg calls for Christian slum movements: 'Movements grow from the communication of a positive and convinced faith. They tend to be absolutist in their beliefs, to have a strong esprit de corps, and tend to reject other groups because of it.'[39] Yet such movements bring the possibility of transformation:

> The aim is not missions,
> Nor is it the planting of churches,
> The aim is not the multiplication of churches.
> The aim is to multiply fellowships
> In such harmony with the soul of a people
> That movements are established of disciples
> Who know this movement is Christ's answer
> To the cries of this people's heart.[40]

Grigg sees incarnational involvement as an indispensable part of a methodology of raising-up such Christian movements in slums: 'Is incarnation essential? For church planting, the leadership of the church in the slums must be incarnate in the community. The missionary, in order to train others in such pastoral work, must set the pattern of identification and model the incarnational lifestyle'.[41] This methodology can call up images from all three dimensions of Langmead's definition. Church planting movements can require Christians to follow, join and participate with the risen Christ. Whether the claim that the Incarnation justifies this approach—or should be limited to this particular strategy or model—is defensible, however, needs to be considered, along with other weaknesses that will be discussed regarding incarnational mission as a methodology in general.

4.0 Incarnation as Simple Lifestyle

In a context where the increased wealth of Western missionaries is paired with the rise of urbanisation where rich and poor can live side by side, affluence has been described as a barrier to real engagement with those facing urban poverty. Roger Greenway contends that when Christians keep accumulating possessions in front of poor people, 'They are communicating a message about their values, priorities, and the deep affections of their hearts. And that message contradicts the gospel'.[42] In the face of such challenges, the Incarnational event is drawn upon as a specific model for consumer lifestyle choices in mission among the poor. Paul's call to have the 'same attitude as Christ' (Philippians 2:1-11) is a mandate for an incarnational lifestyle because God became a poor person in Galilee for humanity's sake. Homeless, with 'nowhere to lay his head' (Matthew 8:20), Jesus prioritised the needs of others above his own. His example calls Christians to be intentionally sacrificial and downwardly mobile rather than consumerist and upwardly mobile. As a model for living Paul is often cited as 'becoming all things to all people' (1 Corinthians 9:22) in the way Jesus also modelled. Thus Christians are to reduce any socio-economic barriers that thwart their ability to relate to those facing poverty because that is what Jesus modelled.

The view of incarnational mission as a simple lifestyle model has been taken up by many contemporary Christian writers and activists,[43] but perhaps its best known and most controversial advocate is Jonathan Bonk. His book *Missions and Money: Affluence as a missionary problem* generated significant debate between Western and non-Western missionaries and church leaders. Central to Bonk's thesis is that affluence is a barrier that must intentionally be addressed by the inherently powerful Christian worker. Hebrews 4:15 is a key verse in an incarnational model for Bonk because Jesus is able 'to sympathise with our weaknesses tested, as we are, yet without sin'. This view can be a call to follow Christ's lifestyle as a pattern to focuses on sustainability, generosity and relationship, rather than hoarding resources. How, asks Bonk, can missionaries, who seem to be a group of people who do not have any needs, connect and identify with the 'needy' poor and vice versa? Bonk argues that Christian workers can often model an inversion to the Incarnation depicted in Hebrews 4:15. If the missionary's lifestyle is dramatically different from the lifestyle of their neighbours then the medium of their lifestyle can undermine the message of the Christ who was poor but generous.[44]

Further, Bonk argues that the test for Christian fidelity in lifestyle and message is not the sincerity of intentions of the Christian worker, but what the receiving community actually understands the missionary's lifestyle to be saying. Bonk asserts: 'By abandoning the Incarnation as a model for its own life and mission, the affluent church has assured its fundamental spiritual impotence'.[45] Credibility and authority are undermined if a sacrificial lifestyle similar to that of Jesus is missing.[46] Bonk concludes that the communicators' lifestyle, not simply the words they say, is the key to sharing what the Incarnational event means. Words, even great words, can be easily dismissed, but a life 'lived up close and personal' modelled on Jesus is hard, if not impossible to ignore. Paul's 'all things to all people' then is a call to downward mobility.[47]

The New Friars often argue for a special kind of spiritual dynamic in returning to Christ's simple lifestyle. John Hayes from Inner Change cites Jesus' example in John 1:14, his call to the disciples in John 17:18, and the directives of Paul in Philippians 2:5-7 and 2 Corinthians 8:9, to argue that a return to following Christ in simple lifestyle and like Francis 'follow naked the naked Christ' is crucial to church reform. 'In fact', writes Hayes, 'my research indicates that nearly every reform or period of revitalisation in Church history is marked at least in part by a profound conviction to simple lifestyle.[48]

Hayes also describes why imitating Jesus' model of simple lifestyle works, by considering the call to the rich young ruler (Matthew 19:21) and the commissioning of the seventy (Luke 10:3): 'In both of these examples, living simply among the poor acts as a spiritual discipline. It helps wean us away from self-reliance to God reliance'.[49] At a time when words can be cheap, without the message and medium congruent, the gospel itself can be cheapened: 'The world doesn't need more words, not even more "right words". The world needs more words made flesh. The world needs more people to live the good news incarnationally in a way that can be seen, heard and handled'.[50]

The lifestyle challenges raised by mission in slums are not issues only for Western missionaries in the developing world. The Thai Christian community in Bangkok, for example, is predominantly wealthy and so the gap between those living in Klong Toey slum and most Christians in Bangkok can be acute. It's one thing, for example, for a Thai Christian to drive a Mercedes into Klong Toey to share a Christmas message and then drive back home to a mansion. It is quite another to consider how the life and teachings of the Jesus who was born in Nazareth relate to the lifestyle of those both sharing and receiving the Christmas story. This incongruence between medium and message may be a major barrier to the transformation of slums in Bangkok.

Bonk and Hayes are right to raise the growing gap between the messenger, the medium and the message in slums. Whether the Incarnation needs to be used to justify responses or to reduce incarnational mission to a specific lifestyle model, however, needs further thought. Several problems exist, not least that many specifics of Jesus' core lifestyle model are impossible for a contemporary Christian to emulate in a slum or elsewhere. The way a first century, single Jewish male, with a vocation as an itinerant Rabbi, prophet and Messiah lived cannot be repeated. Even if culture, dress, vocation and gender roles are put to one side, how helpful would it really be for the transformation of an urban slum neighbourhood if each Christian family took up Jesus' itinerant lifestyle and constantly moved around? Interestingly, even Jesus asked people not to follow his itinerant lifestyle model as exemplified by the healed demoniac (Mark 5:18-19). Jesus' unique mission required a specific lifestyle that was vastly different even from his contemporaries. Could it therefore be unhelpful for contemporary Christians, including contemporary Christian families, to live in slums using Jesus as their model for lifestyle? If incarnational mission is to be transformative in slums it needs a broader definitional base than just what is or isn't part of Jesus' lifestyle model.

5.0 The Church as Christ's Continuing Incarnation

Another view of incarnational mission understands the Incarnation to continue through the method of the institutional church. It rests on a literal reading of the metaphor of the body of Christ (Romans 12:4-5, 1 Corinthians 12:12, 27). This view has become an important justification for the crucial role that local and denominational churches play in mission and was a particularly strong theme in Catholic theology before Vatican II, where Jesus was often seen as exclusively continuing his Incarnation through the church. It is still a strong theme in many slum versions of Catholicism. For example, Johann Adam Mohler wrote:

> The visible church... is the Son of God himself, everlastingly manifesting himself among men (and women) in a human form, perpetually renovated, and eternally young—the permanent incarnation of the same, as in Holy Writ, even the faithful as called the body of Christ.[51]

Despite the real changes in Catholic ecclesial theology since Vatican II, some would still hold to a variant of this position. Even the Catholic catechism still states that, 'Believers who respond to God's word and become members of Christ's Body, become intimately united with him' and this happens through 'Baptism' and 'Eucharist'.[52] In general, Protestants and Post-Vatican II Catholics have been keen to differentiate between any institutional church, the broader 'people of God' and the even broader Kingdom of God. Narrowing and blurring these demarcations in an effort to justify the paramount importance of the institutional local church as the primary manifestation of the continuing Incarnation is not uncommon. For example, in China, church leaders have had to justify the importance of the local church in the face of severe persecution at times. Witness Lee, for example, who was a co-worker of Watchman Nee before helping to establish a church movement of over 20,000 people in Taiwan, argued that 'The universal church is simply the sum total of the local churches, and the local churches are simply the local manifestations of the universal church'.[53] What Lee affirms here is what many local church ministers feel all over the world in different ways: one aspect of their lives, the belonging to and leading of the local institution of their church, is actually being Christ incarnate. They may not be persecuted, but in Western countries churches may still feel under siege and under-resourced as Lee does. Given that a growing number of Westerners identify themselves as Christians but are not involved in any local church community, coupled with the fact that more aggressive Christian NGOs, media ministries and conferences now compete for Christian participation using more sophisticated means, the rhetoric of the local church as Christ incarnate is understandable. Warren, for example, writes that:

> The Bible calls the church 'the bride of Christ' and the 'body of Christ'. I can't imagine saying to Jesus, 'I accept you, but reject your body'. But we do this whenever we dismiss or demean or complain about the church.[54]

To identify the institutional local church as the sole, even ultimate, expression of the 'body of Christ' is a common, but potentially problematic, use of the enfleshing metaphor in relationship to the Incarnation. Not least is the potential problem of institutional abuse of power and organisational self-centredness. Because few Christians feel comfortable saying 'no' to Jesus, if Jesus is identified with an institution then its survival can come above all else, whether it is right or wrong. This can especially be the case in slums where local churches amongst vulnerable people can often be run on authoritarian lines.

Any institution that claims to be Jesus Incarnate can also be in danger of idolatry, making itself Lord. At best, a high value on the local church institution can draw on Langmead's incarnational use of 'following Jesus as a pattern in mission' in that Jesus of Nazareth lived and served in a committed community. Local pastors and missions are rightly concerned that in an increasingly individualised and consumer-driven society the call for more committed fellowship with other Christians is important. Langmead's notion of 'participating with the risen Christ's continuing incarnation in the world' can be especially helpful in reinforcing this point, but note that this idea of Langmead's is a more modest calling than that of the church as the continuing Incarnation. It is dangerous for any institution to claim to be the literal Body of Christ simply because institutions are run by people who are at least partly flawed. The abuse of power that could be unleashed by adopting such a dangerous position could undermine the fidelity, credibility and work of Jesus through a local group of believers. This is especially so in the vulnerable context of urban slum and squatter neighbourhoods.

6.0 Assessing Incarnational Mission as a Specific Methodology

Incarnational mission can be understood as a particular methodology or model and we can begin to further assess such approach's strengths and weaknesses in relation to slums.

6.1 Some common ground

The Incarnational event is used as a specific methodology, strategy or model to emulate and so some common assumptions emerge. Potentially helpful and consistent with Langmead's definition, some aspects can also be at odds with a sustainable and helpful understanding of incarnational mission in slums.

First, for this group an incarnational model or method cannot be an optional strategy in authentic Christian mission. Although some advocates of incarnational mission are exceptions in that they remain open to the possibility of other authentic strategies (e.g., Duncan), these other methodologies are not considered to be consistent with God's methods. To remain 'outside' and not to live among the people as 'insiders', for example, is clearly non-incarnational. To use non-incarnational methods is not to do God's mission. Since these methodologies are claimed to have been employed by Jesus they become mandatory for authentic mission because this is what God did in Jesus and what Christ passes onto Christians to do today. Frost and Hirsch summarise their reasoning for the incarnation as the method of mission for Christians when they write 'it was the missional mode in which God himself engaged in the world; it should be no less ours!'.[55]

Second, the Christian activist is the one who implements a specific methodology or model. Those committed to 'incarnational mission as method or model' are seen primarily as those who are relocated, Christian activists who identify with a particular people group. Therefore, only those who have crossed cultures or moved geographically or are committed to implementing this specific strategy or model can be considered Christians doing incarnational mission and those people who have not are not incarnational. It is clear therefore who is and is not doing God's mission by the methods or model they choose.

Third, the incarnational methodology or models have universal application. Methodologies of identification and relocation for example, can be used in any people group, rich or poor alike.

6.2 Potential strengths

A number of potential strengths can be seen in this way of drawing attention to the new challenges of urban mission.

First, a specific incarnational methodology can highlight the importance of locality in the new, globalised, urban world. Attention is drawn to the need for personal investment in a specific location for community transformation. We know from sociological researchers that urbanisation has increased mobility and diluted the glue that holds communities together. The loss of proximity, belonging and availability caused by increased mobility and commuting in particular has lessened the 'social capital' a neighbourhood draws on for its health and growth. Robert Putnam, for example, notes that for every ten minutes spent commuting, a person loses 10% of their social capital for others.[56] It is timely for the incarnational method of relocation to remind us that Christ was 'Jesus of Nazareth'—a person who belonged to a particular place—and that Christian workers need to be the same in urban neighbourhoods today. Commuting in and out of neighbourhoods just to run programs fails to build the kind of social capital and connections that are required if transformation is to occur in slums.

Second, a specific methodology of incarnation highlights the importance of praxis in the urban world. Committing in challenging, tangible ways to serve people facing urban poverty has forced Christian workers to reflect on the orthopraxis required in community transformation, not just orthodoxy. In a time when adults want to keep all options open, specifically committing to identify with real people facing poverty in concrete ways reminds us of Jesus' call to love our neighbour as we love ourselves.

Third, incarnation as a specific methodology has highlighted the importance of lifestyle priorities. The message and the lifestyle of the messenger are intertwined.

This is a crucial issue in cities today where Christian workers can choose their neighbourhoods and often choose some of the most comfortable.

Fourth, attention is drawn to following Christ's life and ministry priorities. Many models and methods of ministry today can be based more on marketing, public relations and even popularity than on the priorities of Jesus. The attempt to centre an approach on who Jesus is and what he did can unleash all kinds of creative and prophetic responses. This includes ministries in slums. However, such an emphasis does not need to be described as patterned or modelled after the Incarnation. A model can be better described as seeking to be 'centred on Jesus' who is still alive and working in a slum, rather than importing and copying exactly what Jesus did in first century Palestine.

Fifth, as a specific model or method for ministry attention is drawn to Christ's sacrificial service. A willingness to sacrifice something for the sake of others is especially required by Christians serving in slums. If God in Jesus had not sacrificed for others, then it would be difficult to argue that Christians should as well. Again, whether this needs to be justified as copying the Incarnational model is debatable. Christians can, for example, be willing to sacrifice comforts because the same Jesus who died on the cross calls them to come and follow the risen Christ into the slums today.

Sixth, this specific ministry model draws attention to the very real sociocultural barriers that often need to be overcome. God in Jesus Christ overcame barriers to ensure the salvation of the world. In that broad sense, to reach those living in slums does require the qualities of humility, compassion and initiative that Jesus had. If God did not first love us, would Christians love others enough to move away from what is comfortable? Christians do need to step out in faith and cross barriers to reach slum residents. Again, whether this requires pointing to the Incarnation as a specific model for its justification is arguable.

6.3 Limitations and weaknesses

The view that incarnational mission is a specific methodology or model for mission has limitations which can be grouped into a number of objections. This does not mean that the methodologies proposed here have no value. They may actually be the best methods available to Christian workers. However, the claim that a specific methodology or model is the incarnational approach to mission has serious problems.

First, is it legitimate to take a theological metaphor about Christ and use it literally to uphold one specific methodology or model as the way for Christians in mission? There are real problems with taking most theological metaphors too literally and this is the case when the Incarnational event is 'seen as' the 'Word becoming flesh'. The metaphorical intention seems to be that God has become visible in human form, embodied amongst us. This is not analogous to what Christians can do today in slums. Specific strategies and actions can be helpful or even Christ-inspired, but they do not require legitimating as analogous to the Incarnation to be acknowledged as such.

Second, methodologies and models in slums need to differ from the Incarnational event. Jesus was not actually an 'outsider' adult in the same way that adult cross-cultural workers are when they relocate. As a human Jesus was born a Jewish boy and grew up in that particular time, culture and place. Jesus had very few cross-cultural ministry opportunities and was never 'immersed in' or 'identified with' an 'outside' Gentile culture. Christians in slums often need to do things that Jesus of Nazareth did not need to do.

Third, can non-poor Christians really be the 'same as' poor people? God in Jesus did become an 'insider' to humanity in general and a poor community in particular, but matter how hard non-poor Christians try to identity with those born into poverty, their advantages, connections and privileges as people growing up outside of poverty remain. Unable to recognise real differences from their neighbours (and Jesus), Christian workers can undermine their own credibility and effectiveness. This is because at the very least workers can be naïve as to the needs and starting points of their poor neighbours. At worst Christian workers can be judgemental, uncaring and bitter toward neighbours who don't make the same choices they think they would in the same circumstances. Whatever the feelings of workers or perceptions of them by the poor, the claim to be the 'same as' without acknowledging differences in starting points can create barriers between Christian workers and their neighbours.

Fourth, can Christian workers' 'home culture' be equated with heaven? Jesus' pre-existence is not the same as a Christian workers' original location. This is an important limitation to acknowledge in applying incarnation as methodology because if Christian workers want to see the 'Kingdom come on earth as in heaven' they need to avoid encouraging conformity to their original lifestyle. Rather than liberating the poor to become the unique people God intended them to be in a given location or culture, Christian workers may unwittingly seek to colonise them. For example, I really like Melbourne, the city where I was born, but it is not heaven, nor the model for Klong Toey to be conformed to.

Fifth, can the emphasis on Jesus' birth (and life) as the basis for the incarnational method and model down play Jesus' ministry priorities and the work on the cross as an integral part of the Incarnation? Other than associations with the cost of the methodology, there is very little discussion as to how the ministry, death and resurrection of Jesus relates to the incarnational methodology. This can limit the scope and priorities of Christian mission as well as the uniqueness of Christ's sacrifice and resurrection. If a method of identification, for example, can be equally applied to the urban poor as well as to the urban rich, then Jesus' ministry priorities for the poor and for justice can be ignored. Jesus did minister to those who were rich and powerful, but did so from a place of solidarity with the poor. It was this solidarity with the poor that threatened the elite and helped cause Jesus to be killed. So, if defined as a multi-use methodology of identification for all classes and types of people, this could ignore the incarnational pinnacle of the cross and resurrection which resulted from Jesus' ministry priority for the poor.

Sixth, if only certain individual Christians can relocate or identify with a specific people group, isn't there a danger some incarnational workers will believe themselves to be a messianic elite? Use of these methodologies and models can create a kind of arrogance and unrealistic pressure to perform as Messiahs. Inevitably, crushing disillusionment follows. For those not using this methodology or model, a sense of resentfulness toward those who follow it and the Messianic claims they make can be created.

Seventh, isn't it possible to use methods and models but miss God's incarnating dynamic? For example, I may have relocated my home into Klong Toey, but I know sometimes I am not awake to what Jesus is doing and requiring of me. Incarnational mission therefore needs to be more than just using the 'right' methodology or model.

Eighth, can these methods and models be considered the only authentic method of Christian mission? This is not only elitist, but also limits what strategies can be employed in some locations and contexts. This is especially the case in many 'closed' slum and squatter neighbourhoods where methods like relocation and identification are not possible for 'outside' people. Sometimes the only mission strategies open to Christians to connect with people in these neighbourhoods are more 'attractional' or 'commuting' strategies. Engaging these contexts can be far more dangerous than relocating into safer slum neighbourhoods. Incarnational mission then cannot be limited to one strategy to be authentically Christian.

Ninth, can the model of the Incarnation really be imitated by all Christians? Jesus is limited and restrictive as a role model whether for a cross-cultural worker, lifestyle, friend or devotee. The unique place Jesus has as fully human and fully God, not to mention the specifics of Jesus of Nazareth's life and ministry context, means that no Christian today can actually use Jesus as a specific model for themselves. This limitation is certainly relevant for life and ministry in a slum, which often requires aspects of life that Jesus of Nazareth did not experience. These can include spousal partnerships, families, a non-itinerant and stable home life and the need to learn another language as an adult from a position of power, none of which Jesus actually had or did. Therefore if incarnational mission is the emulation of the model of the Incarnation, no one can actually do it.

Tenth, should individual Christians really seek to emulate the model and role of Messiah? 'What Does it Mean to Be Incarnational When We Are Not the Messiah?' is the title of a chapter written by Jude Tiersma-Watson.57 Tiersma-Watson examines the case of heroic Christian workers in her central Los Angeles neighbourhood and notes the unhealthy internal drivers as well as the expectations of others that can undermine transformation. Jesus' life had many qualities that can inform our contemporary ministry models and vocations, not least that he knew who he uniquely was in first century Palestine and what God required of him in that context. If individuals identify themselves as closely following Jesus-Messiah they can actually move in the opposite direction and set expectations for themselves and others that cannot possibly be met.

Eleventh, where is Christ now? The lack of emphasis on the Incarnation's resurrection is a significant loss. It is one thing to seek to follow the model of Jesus 2,000 years ago, but quite another to join, participate and follow what the living Jesus is doing today. Why the risen Jesus is so important to Christian mission will be discussed later, but we can say that without the resurrection Jesus' contemporary call to discipleship is severely restricted—it becomes only discipleship of a character in an old book. With the resurrection of Jesus, however, all kinds of new and creative initiatives are possible in slums today. To limit following Jesus to modelling themselves on what Jesus did in first century Palestine limits what new things God can do in slums today.

Twelfth, is following Jesus sustainable or even possible without the invitation, authority and grace of the risen Christ? This objection also picks up the importance of the resurrection, for only the risen Christ can give to disciples 'all authority in heaven and earth to go into all the world' (Matthew 28:18-19). This authority from Christ includes God's authority for life and ministry in slums. Without this authority, the slavish copying of Jesus can only be done in a Christian's own strength. Duty without Christ's grace ensures any enthusiasm and passion for life quickly grows cold. The empowerment of the Spirit and the joining with God's eschatological finale of creation are also often missing dimensions. The Incarnation as a specific ministry model to emulate, without focusing on what the risen Jesus is currently doing, is therefore simply not sustainable for even the most devoted Christian.

Chapter Seven

Too Figuratively Incarnational: One value among many in Christian mission

There are more figurative uses of enfleshing metaphors in mission than we have considered so far. A grouping can be made where the incarnational is one mark, principle, stream or quality among many in Christian responses to the world. The incarnational here is employed in a similar way to business management's use of 'core values' for organisations. Like one component in a moral compass, an incarnational value can be used with other values to help direct Christians in how to respond to needs.

It must be acknowledged that this diverse grouping is more difficult to draw together than others considered. How scholars and activists use incarnational metaphors in a less literal way among many others values can differ significantly. What this grouping shares, however, is that they view the enfleshing metaphor as one of many important impulses to consider in mission. How they define this impulse can be different (and even contradictory) but they are still far less literal in their use of the term than those who understand incarnational mission to be a specific method or model. Unlike the first position considered on the spectrum, this position does view incarnational metaphors as useful in Christian mission, but does not see them as central (a position to be discussed in the next section of the book.

This more figurative use of incarnation in mission needs to be noted and can be seen in at least four ways.

1.0 Incarnational Mission as One Stream to Help Spiritualise the Physical and the Ordinary

Enfleshing metaphors can be used to help ensure that the spiritual or sacramental is honoured in the physical realm. God used matter in this world, most obviously in Jesus, but also in the arts, sacramental rites and rituals that God's people have participated in through the centuries. Richard Foster's *Streams of Living Water* has been influential in offering this view. Exploring six Christian traditions which act like tributaries flowing into the river of discipleship, Foster argues that one of these is the 'incarnational' tradition which 'concerns itself with the relationship between spirit and matter. In short, God is manifest to us through material means. One of the main functions of matter is to 'mediate the presence of an infinite God to finite minds' and examples are 'the Ark of the Covenant', 'the Tabernacle' and 'Messiah as a babe in a manger'.[1]

This incarnational tradition can have an expressly religious physical dimension (baptism, communion and liturgies) but can also be expressed in spiritualising or sacramentalising in 'the arena of everyday life'.[2] Foster draws from great spiritual writers such as Evelyn Underhill, Brother Lawrence and Martin Luther, as well as some Catholic and Eastern Orthodox liturgical traditions.[3] Foster also uses examples of Susanna Wesley's life, as well as former UN Secretary General Dag Hammarskjöld's 'ordinary' vocation. These 'ordinary' lives 'make present and visible the realm of the invisible spirit'.[4]

This approach has the potential to inform transformative slum life and ministry. It uses the incarnational metaphor to describe a way of sacramental living where 'we experience God as truly manifest and notoriously active in daily life'.[5] That the work, worship and even the physical place of a slum can all be considered holy to God is something of prophetic stance against Christians who devalue matter, but also the secular materialist who denies the spiritual dimension. The parable of the 'sheep and the goats' (Matthew 25:31-46), which describes a spiritual encounter with Jesus 'among the least of these', is actually common language which points to the sacramental nature of sharing with neighbours in radical hospitality. Mother Teresa applied this idea in the slums of Kolkata. She wrote of her community taking literally the words that Jesus is found among the hungry, naked, homeless. 'In this way we are in contact with him twenty-four hours a day. This contemplation, this touching of Christ in the poor, is beautiful, very real, and full of love'.[6] Mother Teresa and Dominique Lapierre's novel *City of Joy*, about a physician discovering beauty in Calcutta (Kolkata),[7] are some of the best known modern examples of this sacramentalising of the poor in slums.

There are limitations associated with this view, however. Idols can quickly be made to replace God. As Foster himself acknowledges, this is why the people of Israel and even Quakers today are very careful in their use of images, because 'people can fail to distinguish between a sacred object and the spiritual reality it signifies'.[8] Sacramentalism can also lead to limiting God for our own control and management. Foster encourages, 'If you want God, really want God, you must come through [the] church and its ritual system to find him'.[9]

There is a fine line here between the kind of panentheism argued for by Langmead in the third part of his incarnational definition, where God is found in creation,[10] and a kind of pantheism where God is creation. It is the line between 'everything in God' and 'God as everything'. Sacramentalism needs criteria for discerning where God is most and least present.

That the incarnational tradition is considered but one of many Christian impulses also needs consideration. If incarnational theology cannot at least inspire and inform, for example, the other traditions Foster outlines, such as the contemplative, holiness, charismatic, social justice and Evangelical traditions, is it truly Christian incarnational theology? Incarnational mission, then, can quickly become but one tradition or value among many to take or leave from a Christian theological buffet. This can both broaden and weaken the focus of an incarnational approach to mission. At the very least it can fail to retain the Incarnation event as central to Christian faith and witness.

2.0 Incarnation as One Mark in a Post-Modern Missional Paradigm

The Incarnation can be used as one of many marks, values, signs or principles that make up a new paradigm of missional engagement. As Darrell Guder argues, the potential of incarnational language is especially attractive for Christians in a post-modern world for two reasons. First, it can be used in the critique of the modern missionary movement.[11] Second, incarnational language can be attractive today because Christians now understand the Jesus of history better.[12] Guder is right to draw attention to two of the drivers for more integrative mission in a post-colonialist age, but opinions about exactly how incarnational language is used as one marker in this, and what other markers should be clustered together with it, vary. Some examples of this can be seen below in the theology of David Bosch and the organisational cultures of New Friars.

2.1 Transforming mission

David Bosch, one of the most influential voices in contemporary missiology, argues in his book *Transforming Mission* that mission must be rooted in biblical faithfulness, but requires broad, diverse and complex responses to today's needs. Not everything Christians do today is Christian mission, however. Bosch points to the Incarnation of Christ as one of many images for an adequate paradigm of mission. To help Christian mission 'to be multidimensional in order to be credible and faithful to its origins and character' he suggests six major 'salvific events'. Along with 'the Incarnation of Christ' there is also 'his death on the cross, his resurrection on the third day, his ascension, the outpouring of the Holy Spirit at Pentecost, and the parousia'.[13] Although he notes the diversity in how Eastern, Roman Catholic and Anglican scholars have pictured the Incarnation, Bosch points to an incarnational approach within the liberation theologians' call to solidarity which emphasises

> the Incarnate Christ, the human Jesus of Nazareth who wearily trod the dusty roads of Palestine where he took compassion on those who were marginalised. He is also the one who today sides with those who suffer in the favelas of Brazil and with the discarded people in South Africa's resettlement areas. In this model, one is not interested in a Christ who offers only eternal salvation, but in a Christ who agonises and sweats and bleeds with the victims of oppression.[14]

Although such an incarnational picture urges the new, post-colonial world towards a radical solidarity with the poor, the Incarnation of Christ is but one of the six pictures in Bosch's paradigm. The incarnational 'practice of Jesus' is separated and put alongside five other events: the cross, resurrection, ascension, Pentecost and Parousia.[15] This raises the question of how the Incarnating of God can be separated out from these five other events.

This view is not without problems. For example, to separate the Incarnation of Jesus' life from the cross, resurrection and continuing ministry limits incarnational theology and its implications for today. It is hard to see, for example, how a dead Jesus without resurrection could side with residents of today's favelas except in a vaguely spiritual way. Unless all of these dimensions are considered part of what the Incarnating God does, believers do not have the authority of the Spirit to join, participate and follow Jesus into such situations and neighbourhoods. To separate the Incarnation from the cross is especially problematic, and risks leading to the Docetic heresy where Jesus only seems to be truly human for redemption's sake.

Moreover, this scheme can feel a little like a spiritual buffet where you get to pick and choose the image that most suits you. Though Bosch insists that all these events must be taken together,[16] his schema divides the Incarnation. The Incarnation includes Jesus' life, death and resurrection if it is to really be the Incarnation. Taken to mean only Jesus' birth and life, it misses the power, uniqueness and integrative nature of the Incarnation and reduces what it is that Christians join, participate in and follow.

We must also insist that the Triune God incarnates. Bosch's schema does not take seriously the way the Creator, Redeemer and the Advocate continue to be incarnate in the world today. It limits the use of the incarnational metaphor in mission in unnecessary ways.

2.2 The Emerging Church, the New Friars and the New Monastics movements

Many contemporary mission authors identify incarnation as a common mark of new missional movements in a post-modern world. Scott Bessenecker's book, *The New Friars*, is an important example because he groups together specific Christian communities attempting to engage with urban slums. In confronting the serious gap between modern missionary organisations and the plight of the urban poor, Bessenecker identifies 'signs' in previous historical eras of a wave of new communities which were 'incarnational, missional, marginal, devotional and communal'.[17] Groups like Inner-Change, Servants to Asia's Urban Poor, Servant Partners, Word-made-flesh and Urban Neighbours Of Hope are identified as attempting among the urban poor what the first Franciscans did in their time. Bessenecker picks up the raw and honest frustrations of wrestling with the incarnational approach. Fresh from graduation, for example, he quotes David Von Strong's reflections on his time in a Bangkok slum where 'incarnation is a choice he must make every day'.[18] Bessenecker sees the freedom to serve inside the slum informed by this value.[19]

Even amongst New Friars, however, what this incarnational sign means in comparison to other signs is not uniform. John Hayes, for example, draws on Isaiah 58:6-7, to argue for a 'mark' that 'enhances the Christian's personal growth by cultivating godly dependence and dethroning consumerism, which distracts from intimacy with God'.[20] God is not only encountered among the 'least of these', but also in the downward journey itself, which is one mark of a new spiritual dynamic operating in the world. Tom Pratt, Servant Partners' founder, views 'incarnation' as part of a three-fold approach to ministry that also includes 'Evangelism and Church Planting' and 'Community Organising and Transformation'. Incarnation for Pratt means that 'Squatter slum workers live among the people as close to the conditions of the squatters as possible. This builds trust and helps workers contextualise the gospel to the specific squatter slum community'.[21] This is a specific method, but it is also a kind of signpost that gives direction for action.

These kinds of statements of intent can pick up on Langmead's theme of following Jesus as a pattern, and some also hint at the empowerment found in participating with God. They are real attempts to use incarnational language and can fit in with other groups discussed in this grouping because they see an incarnational approach as one sign or value among many. This incarnational approach, however, is not necessarily a central sign in relation to others. It could be argued, for example, as I do in *Living Mission*, that what is often discussed as incarnational is actually the practice of 'relocation' (moving to live in a slum or urban neighbourhood).[22] The practice of relocation may well be one of the marks of New Friars, but there is a sense in which all of the signs of New Friars can and should be informed and inspired by the God's incarnating presence. Few Christians would consider devotion, community, mission, relocation and solidarity as marks distinguishing them from other generations of mission workers. It is how the incarnational informs these marks in this new movement that provides a hope to be enfleshed in these marks.

How the motif of enfleshing hope can inform and inspire various strategies like relocation will be taken up in Part D, but here we simply note that the incarnational can have a more central and foundational place among mission markers. Rather than simply being another sign of action, an incarnational approach can inform and inspire all kinds of actions.

3.0 Incarnation as an Example of Humanisation

So far we have considered views that take as read that Jesus Christ was God in the flesh. However, the divinity of Christ has been challenged from many angles in modern scholarship and contemporary discourse. Perhaps the best known of these is the book edited by John Hick in 1977, *The Myth of God Incarnate*.[23] It is, therefore, not surprising that very different approaches to incarnational mission can be derived from these Christological discussions. Contemporary scholars like Walter Wink and Marcus Borg, for example, often use the term 'incarnational' in a much lighter, even more figurative way. Because they view the divinity of Christ in non-orthodox ways they also view incarnational approaches differently from Bosch, for example. No longer seen literally as God-incarnate, Jesus can be understood as a human like others who 'incarnated' (or made visible or threw light upon) God. Christians today, it is argued, should similarly 'incarnate' (or reflect) God. Wink, for example, writes: 'Contrary to a dogma tenaciously held, Jesus does not exhaust the possibilities of incarnating God... Jesus is neither the sole incarnation of God nor the perfect incarnation'.[24] He notes the limits of Jesus' gender, culture, marital status, illnesses and writes:

> Jesus is not the incarnate God, but a human being who incarnated God and who taught us how to do the same, through the workings of the divine Spirit within us. That is what it means to incarnate God.[25]

While Jesus is not God-incarnate, argued Wink, he did incarnate God, just as all people can today in their unique ways. To use alternative terminology, the incarnational event in Jesus could happen to anyone. Jesus was the Human One who showed people how to become divine through humanising actions, and we can follow his lead.

Marcus Borg has a variation on this theme by not only taking up what he calls a historical 'pre-Easter' position on Jesus, like Wink, but also drawing on the idea that God is present in the world in a panentheistic way. Panentheism (from Greek *pân* 'all'; *en* 'in'; and *theós* 'God': 'all-in-God') differs from pantheism, which equates creation and God. Panentheism is especially contrasted by Borg with many contemporary versions of supernaturalist, theistic and transcendent understandings of God. Borg argues that:

> I see Jesus as the embodiment and incarnation of the God who is everywhere present. But he is not a visitor from elsewhere, sent to the world by a god 'out there'. He is not

different in kind from us but as completely human as we are. In the fully human life of this utterly remarkable Spirit person, we see the incarnation of God.[26]

For Borg, Jesus of Nazareth is not a unique or climactic enfleshment of God offering salvation. It can be argued that following this 'Spirit man' is easier, but it is not possible to be a co-participant with a purely historical 'Spirit man' from the past.

While there is a growing impetus for this kind of approach in secular and scientific circles, it can hardly be described as a traditional Christian approach. The once-and-for-all uniqueness of Christ can easily be undermined. In the Christian tradition the Incarnational event is unique and cannot be repeated. Guder is right to contend that incarnation as only a moral value or ethic can 'dilute the uniqueness and centrality of the life of Christ'.[27]

Unhinged from the specific Incarnational event, this approach to incarnational mission can quickly become less than Christian. Whereas other views in this grouping have various perspectives of where and how the Incarnation event can fit into a broader cluster of values, this view understands Jesus' life in a quite different, far less literally incarnational way. This view could also be placed in the grouping that sees Jesus as a 'model' for humanity because Jesus can be understood as quite literally showing what a human being can really do. I have however, chosen to put this view on the less literal side of the spectrum because it represents a more figurative understanding of the Incarnational event. A too figurative view of the pre-existent Word made flesh can water down what incarnational Christology can bring to transformation. It can also lead to unrealistic expectations about what humans have the power to do in their own strength today.

4.0 Assessing the Incarnational Emphasis as One Value Among Many

There are real possibilities for slum transformation found in the many diverse views in this grouping. Some who address post-modern concerns, such as the New Friars and Bosch, draw attention to following Jesus as a pattern for mission. Foster calls for sacramental joining with creation and empowerment for mission in this too. Others, such as Wink and Borg, identify strongly with joining God's ongoing incarnational creative dynamic, which focuses on exploring God's current activity in the world.

There can be real inadequacies, however, where an incarnational approach is simply one value amongst many in mission. The following are some issues this grouping raises.

First, how easily can one of the many other values in mission be unhinged from the incarnating God and remain Christian? An incarnational value quickly becomes a vague adjective that can exclude the power and authority Christians can find in the atoning death and resurrection of Jesus if it does not inform all of our actions.

Second, can potentially competing values cancel out the centrality of the

Incarnation? For example, could a value of tolerance be in serious tension with some of Jesus' strong claims for exclusivity? There can be serious concerns about modernist reductionist tendencies in this regard. Jesus can just be a good person and teacher, but not Lord of Life. To reduce the Incarnation to only one moral aspect or value of the Incarnational event is a reduction too far. There is a need for empowerment and solidarity that can only come from the incarnating God.

Third, is being a mere value too weak in using 'incarnational' in Christian mission? While it is true that moral values can direct community actions and policy, they can also be expressed as business platitudes, such as 'We value our customer'. The incarnating God is more than an organisational flavor. This God can be an effective guide and inspiration for missional action in slums.

Summary

There are diverse and even competing views on how the Incarnational event and the metaphor of enfleshing can be used in Christian mission toward slums. Each has some potential strengths and deficiencies, as we have seen. I have also argued that to define and justify one methodology or model on the Incarnation has real limitations both theologically and practically. A more integrated and theologically robust understanding needs to be sought if Christians are to respond more faithfully and credibly in slums.

Can incarnational mission be defined and enacted along more helpful lines? We can now propose and explore what a motif of embodied hope can mean in relation to slum transformation, against the backdrop of Langmead's three-part definition of incarnational mission.

Not the Same?

There are differences between my family and our slum neighbours, but God also provides common desires for change.

Some think because we moved our family into our new home in a poorer part of Klong Toey slum we are therefore incarnational, that is the 'same as' the poor. However, just look into the wide eyes of little Lek*, a four year old girl, smiling a toothless grin through the dirt on her face and matted hair, her tiny hand wrapped around our son Aiden's plastic 'Ben 10' on our floor. Surely the blood stained spots on her ripped dress and dark purple bruises on her arms and back tell me I cannot even imagine identifying with her? With her formative stages of life so dislocated, Lek's foundations have already been undermined before they've really begun. I mean even Jesus couldn't be the 'same as' little Lek and He was the Incarnation!

If we can't really be the 'same as' Lek (and of course Lek can't be the 'same as' me or Jesus in so many ways too) is incarnational mission a costly, but misguided approach? Jesus was the incartio ('made flesh') as in 'The Word became flesh and blood and moved into the neighbourhood' (John. 1:14 The Message), but this metaphor of enfleshment has real limits when applied to us. What then can an incarnational approach mean for us that is possible?

We can live inspired and informed by an incarnational approach if we see that the incarnating God invites us to follow, join and participate in seeing God's kingdom come on

Fortunately for Manow (pictured above), her life circumstances are more positive compared with the story of Lek*. Photo: Jackie Rado

earth as in heaven. As we take up this invitation we don't become mini-gods, special people or even the same as those suffering, but rather we begin to find the special presence of Christ and en-flesh, make real, the promises of God. Such en-fleshed hope can change the trajectory of people's lives and in fact the whole of creation's destiny. This is the good news we have to offer the Lek's of the world. For Lek's life doesn't have to follow a predictable path after all. If we follow, join and participate with Christ on the side of what is right and just now, we will see all wrongs put to right, instigated by the resurrection of Jesus, on that promised day. This promise can come alive and can be seen now 'in the flesh' through us.

This is not an easy approach to take. It is easier to hide behind a grand institution or program. The idea that an institution and program do the work for us in Lek's is simply not an option here. So, as UNOH workers we covenant together to, 'share our lives and resources in solidarity with those living in urban poverty'. We can't do this from a safe distance or behind a desk. Martin Luther-King Jr once said 'unearned suffering is redemptive'. Any of the hard things of living up close and personal with those in need is nothing compared to the sense of purpose and meaning our lives are injected with by seeing hope rise in lives of the little Lek's of our neighbourhoods. Moving to a slum home then is a small price to pay to be able to have the best opportunity possible to en-flesh such hope both now and forever.

We are different to everyone, especially those whose misery we cannot share, but there is also a common desire. It's a desire for a God given freedom that lives in each human heart. The apostle Paul wrote, 'Where the Spirit of the Lord is there is freedom.' (2 Corinthians 3:17) This is the work of the Spirit and can emerge in the most unlikely places and circumstances if we are ready for it. In November 2011, for example, floods in Thailand left over 800 people dead with millions of homes and lives affected. Es is originally from Klong Toey slum where we live and is part of the Ta Rua church, but now lives in northern Bangkok where the floods hit hardest. His motorbike, car, tools for work and all he owned were submerged in his home.

With some of our neighbours from Klong Toey we went out with Es to his neighbourhood to help give medicines, food and water, wading in with small boats to those hard to get at places. It was a special time, not least because the men in our neighbourhood, who are so often looked down upon, were the ones giving help this time. We had to get them all special printed blue t-shirts so flood victims didn't think they were a gang of looters!

'Hey thanks! Where are you guys from?' came a shout from a second story home after receiving much needed food.

'Klong Toey!' Gung replied.

'Klong Toey? Really?'

'Sure. Keep fighting on! Don't give up!'

Very few of these men can swim, two crocodiles had just been caught there from a local croc farm (with over 200 still loose!) and the smelly brown, often neck deep water was putrid. Courage does not do justice to describe how these men responded so freely.

If poverty is not just about lack of cash, but a lack of freedom to live life as God intends, then there is a feeling that our men began to break the cycle of poverty in their own lives by stepping out (and under!) to help others. Many of us got serious illnesses from the flood water and we don't wish floods on anyone, but in crisis there can be an opportunity to find life and confidence as we respond as Christ would in the power of the Spirit. It is the Spirit who gives this freedom to respond.

Please keep praying for Thailand. The floods have subsided and we are grateful our Klong Toey neighbourhood was spared, but we still are a long way from healthy, with literally tens of thousands of Leks still suffering here. We need more Spirit empowered courage for freedom.

Incarnational mission then is not based on institutions, but it is not a special method or model. Rather it's about living in ways that detect and en-flesh the special presence of the risen Jesus. No matter where we're called to live I pray we can all find ways to join and make real the hope only found in the Incarnation, the crucified and living Lord Jesus Christ, who invites us all to 'come, follow me'. To follow, join and participate with this Christ is to find our true lives.

SLUM LIFE RISING

PERSONAL AND GROUP QUESTIONS:

1. In your encounters with the misery and suffering of others, how different and how similar were you? Why can your own experiences help or hinder transformation?

2. How is this incarnational approach similar and different to institutional or program based approaches to sharing life with those who are suffering?

3. What are the costs associated with an incarnational approach? What are the benefits to make it worth the costs?

4. No-one starts life at the same starting line. What have been important benefits and challenges that have helped shape what you have to contribute in life?

5. One of the characteristics of a 'culture of poverty' (Oscar Lewis) for those who live in poverty are that men can feel socially castrated and act out, seeking to 'prove their masculinity'. Where have you seen men in bondage, acting out? Where have you experienced God intended freedoms in mature men? What can help or hinder God's intended freedom in masculinity?

6. Where have you detected the incarnating God in the life situations of others?

7. Where have you seen a common desire for freedom? What is one thing you can do to help others join with others in Jesus' name?

Part C

What Ought To Happen? Toward a Trinitarian Incarnational Theology of Urban Slum and Squatter Neighbourhood Transformation

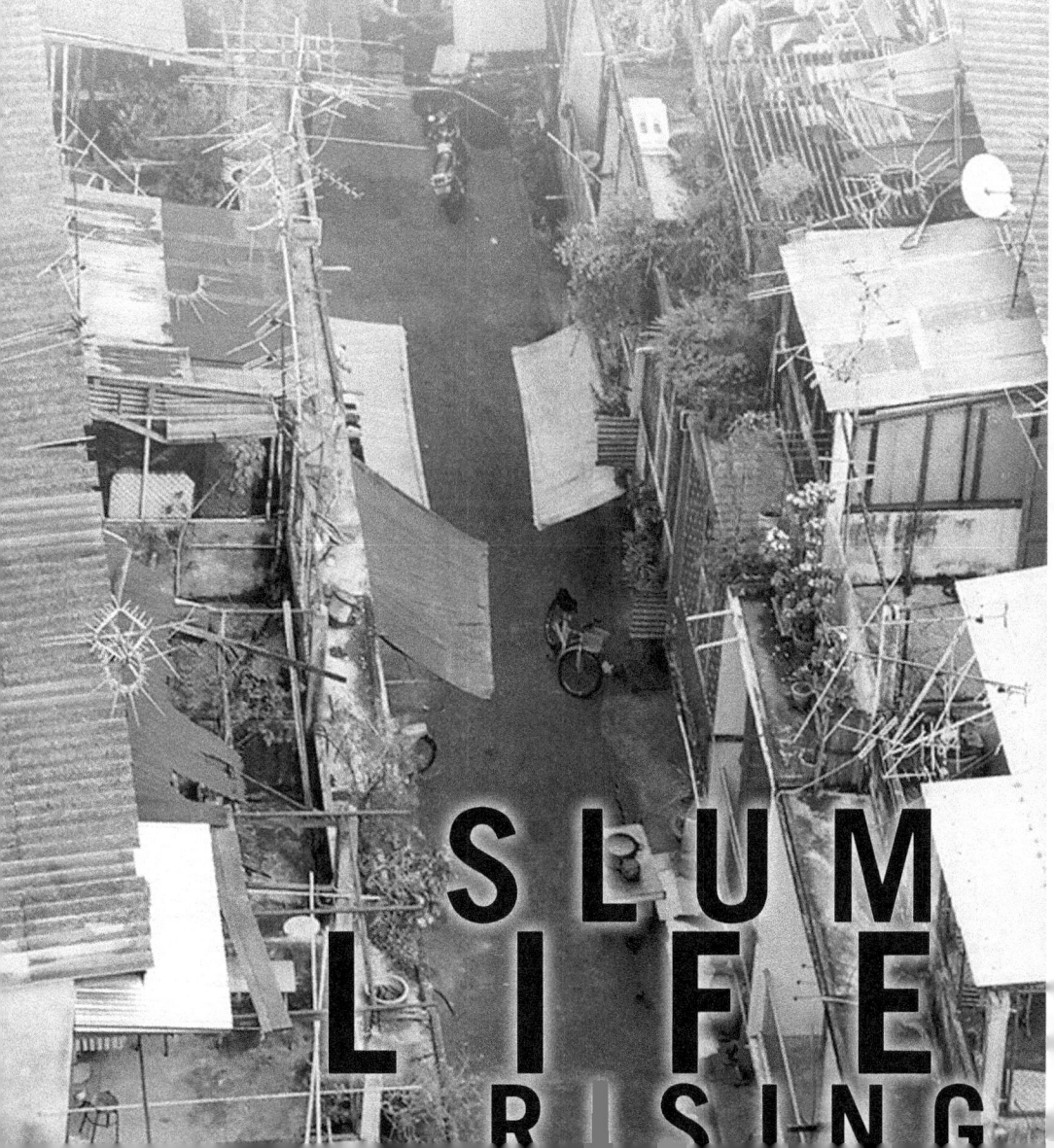

Chapter Eight

The Creator Incarnates: Joining God's invitation to make real creation's promise

The Creator has not abandoned creation. As Langmead contends, God has always had an 'incarnating dynamic' and so an incarnational approach to mission requires 'joining' this dynamic. This is because an incarnational theology, not simply an incarnational Christology, 'integrates our understanding of God as Creator and Redeemer, and because it articulates well the human experience of God's relationship to creation'.[1] Therefore, while the metaphor of incarnation is best known in Christianity to describe 'the Word becoming flesh', the broader meaning of the metaphor for a trinitarian incarnational theology of mission in slums raises important questions for this study. In particular, has God used an incarnational dynamic before and after the Incarnational event? If God 'self-enfleshes', in the broadest sense, then this has implications for how God's will can be done in slum and squatter neighbourhoods today as in heaven. We can see three important ways the Creator incarnates that has implications for slums.

1.0 The Creator Enfleshes Hope 'In' Good Creation

There is debate about how to balance God's immanence and transcendence in regard to creation. The consequences of any sharp separation between God and creation are of particular concern to Moltmann. He points to the secularising forces of the last few centuries and notes that 'the ruthless conquest and exploitation of nature which fascinated Europe during this period found its appropriate religious legitimation in that ancient distinction between God and the world'.[2] N. T. Wright also worries not just about the pole of pantheism (where God is everything) but also that a kind of dualism can occur that can undermine real change, including in places like slums. He writes: 'The proper response to idolatry is therefore not dualism, the rejection of space, time, or matter as themselves evil or dangerous, but the renewed worship of the Creator God, which sets the context for the proper enjoyment and use of the created order without the danger of worshipping it'.[3]

As well as in Wright and Moltmann's work, an integrated view of God in creation is also highlighted by Bonhoeffer and Langmead. All four reject both poles of God 'as creation' or a dualism where God is not present in creation. Instead they seek a middle way that takes both the immanence and the transcendence of God seriously. For Bonhoeffer, God, while not the same as creation, is constantly present and personally 'upholding the created order'.[4] Moltmann, at times, holds this line too: 'As God's work, creation is not essentially similar to the Creator; it is the expression of his will'.[5] But Moltmann goes further in arguing for a kind of panentheism, where God 'in' creation means that 'Creation is also the differentiated presence of God the Spirit, the presence of the One in the many'.[6] N. T. Wright's view is closer to that of Bonhoeffer; Wright worries that Borg and Moltmann's panentheism (God 'in' creation) is too close to pantheism, acknowledging that God will be 'all in all' eventually, but not yet:

> God intends in the end to fill all creation with his own presence and love. This is part of an answer to Jürgen Moltmann's proposal to revive the rabbinic doctrine of zimzum, in which God as it were retreats, creates space within himself, so that there is ontological space for there to be something else other than him. If I am right, it works the other way around. God's creative love, precisely by being love, creates new space for there to be things that are genuinely other than God.[7]

What is widely agreed upon is that God is constantly present in the world, reaching out in love and hope to creation in various, ongoing and relational ways. These manifestations of God's love are kinds of sacraments and symbols that reveal both the transcendence and immanence of God's presence, which is not completed yet. This is where Langmead lands, arguing that an understanding of God requires an incarnating dynamic in creation which can 'highlight the link between God's creative self-pouring in creating the material universe and God's self-pouring in the redemptive act of becoming flesh in Jesus Christ'.[8] Further, 'God is creative, reconciling love. Creation and incarnation are therefore intrinsically related through God's mission of enfleshment and incarnation'.[9] Christian theology best understands God as being, by nature, involved in creation from the beginning and constantly working for its completion. That is, the incarnating dynamic of God is not only expressed in Christ's Incarnation, but has a wider meaning, describing God's very nature and ongoing hope alive in creation. This God is a constantly enfleshing presence and is active in all creation, including slums.

What is problematic with the Creator who is present in creation is the existence of evil in place like slums. If God is everywhere, must God also include evil? This is especially true in slums where at times it can feel as if one moment God is tangibly present in the close knit buzz of community life, but then violence quickly erupts and shatters this sense in the very next moment. One way to answer this problem is to see that what God did and continues to do in creation is to provide a space and promise of love returned. That space can be rejected now, but one day will be fully filled in a renewed, completed creation. These ideas can be especially seen in Wright's understanding of God's good but incomplete creation where evil is still possible.[10] There are a number of points to make briefly here in relation to slums.

First, if there is 'space' between the identity of God and God's creation then God can be alive in creation, but not the same as creation or evil responses. God can still 'cover the sky with clouds, provide the earth with rain, and cause grass to grow on the hillsides' (Psalm 147:8-9). This is not God growing himself, but rather sustaining creation, and this space is a crucial for the choice either to return love or to rebel. Slum residents and neighbourhoods, then, can have access to God who is not themselves nor is evil, but is both immanent and transcendent.

Second, if God is love and created the heavens and the good earth in love, then offering humanity to return love freely back to God is possible. Slum residents to not need love to be a new kind of slavery, so freedom to return love requires an opportunity and possibility to reject love. This possibility of the freedom to reject the Creator God creates the space for the potential infiltration of evil in places like slums. It is not that a loving God is not present in Klong Toey; rather, the freedom to choose evil and cause suffering shows that a loving God is present.

Third, if humans are designed by God to have a unique role in creation as God's image bearers and stewards, then this co-vocation with God can continue today. This also comes with a promise of provision and sustainability (Genesis 1:28-30). These promises come directly from a God deeply involved in creation. The mandate to be God's image bearers, stewards and guardians, helping to reproduce, nurture and grow creation, is a central purpose and role for humanity in God's good creation. This mandate was accompanied by the promise of sustenance to enable humans to be good stewards. God would provide people what they needed to live and to fulfil their role in creation. God's promise and mandate for humans is something he continues to seek to fulfil throughout the biblical witness and can apply to each of today's urban slum residents. Slum residents are more than economic production units; they are created in God's image to be stewards of God's good destiny for creation.

Fourth, if the option of evil exists, it is an option that exists in slums. The creation narrative in Genesis 2 and 3 tells of two symbolic trees in the centre of the garden, but God forbade humans to eat from the tree of the knowledge of good and evil (Genesis 2:16-17). Humans rejected God's only restriction, and therefore his love. This rejection unleashed what was previously only the potential power of rejected love and allowed evil and death to infiltrate creation. This evil especially makes toxic the relationships between humans and God, between humans and each other and between humans and the environment. This disharmony warps humanity's role to care for and maintain creation in relationship with God (Genesis 2:15). The complex suffering seen in places like slums, then, is a result of rejected love, but not of a rejecting God.

In Genesis the humans are banished from the garden and cut off from the second tree, the tree of life, which is confined to Eden. But this is not the end of the story. What God promised and mandated in the beginning God had always intended to fulfil through humans. God has not taken away the original purposes, promise and possibility of love in creation, nor humanity's cultural mandate. On the contrary, God's hope is like a cord that pulls humanity's good future forward where this can all be fulfilled without the parasitic powers of evil that lead ultimately to decay and death. This idea of hope can be seen with the use of *hwqt tiqvah* which is one of fifteen Hebrew words that can be translated 'hope' and which sometimes clearly means a 'cord' or 'rope' (as in Joshua 2:18).[11] Thus, biblical hope can have the metaphorical sense of a cord that can connect, pull and bring forward the good future God intends. This metaphor of hope as a cord is taken up in the New Testament, too, when the writer of Hebrews encourages readers to 'hold fast to the hope set before us' (Hebrews 6:18). This hope is in the Christ event as the future of creation is drawn to the present.

Therefore Creation was 'good' in the beginning, but will only be completed when evil is defeated and creation is fully alive with the glory and knowledge of God 'as the waters cover the sea' (Isaiah 11:9). Just as the sea is already water, God's presence will one day be 'all in all' (1 Corinthians 15:28). Hope for the renewal of creation is fundamental to Christian ideas of both love and hope. According to N. T. Wright,

> One day, when all the forces of rebellion have been defeated and the creation responds freely and gladly to the love of its creator, God will fill it with himself so that it will both remain an independent being, other than God, and also be flooded with God's own life. This is part of the paradox of love, in which love freely given creates a context for love to be freely returned, and so on in a cycle where complete freedom and complete union do not cancel each other out but rather celebrate each other and make one another whole.[12]

God by nature infused people and other creation with his presence, but one day the space made for love will be returned. Time and space which is now inhabited by rebellion will one day be filled with the Lord's knowledge and glory. God is present in creation (including in people) before this hope is fulfilled, but the incomplete presence and intensity of God's glory is crucial to recognise in places like slums. It is the presence of God who seeks to fulfil the full hope for and through creation, but has not done so yet.

What is important to note here is that the Creator will overcome the barriers of rejection that allowed death and the power of evil the space to make toxic the core relationships of creation. What the first Adam could not do, God, first within his covenant with Israel and then ultimately in Christ, will complete (Romans 5:14; 1 Corinthians 15:22, 45).

There are many implications of understanding a God who enfleshes hope in a good but unfulfilled creation, from the beginning and in a continuing way today. These include the following.

First, God's love and freedom toward creation are the fundamental reason for the responses of God in slums. God takes personally the rebellious chaos in creation and is affected by its suffering too. The infiltration of evil in a good creation not only causes the suffering and death of slum residents, but also tortures and crucifies God again. The Christian God is understood as the Creator who lives in the slums and is absorbing the pain experienced there.

Second, God is not absent from slum and squatter neighbourhoods, no matter how dire circumstances may seem. God may well be unseen, but he is nevertheless a present, sustaining life and witness to all that is happening. If neighbourhoods are primarily responsible for their own health, safety, environment, economy, food, children and care, then as John McKnight and Peter Brock argue, they will be able to effectively steward these things with the sustaining presence of God.[13] For McKnight and Brock, even the poorest neighbourhoods can fulfil these responsibilities by accessing the abundance found through neighbours giving their gifts, associations coming together and the compassion of hospitality.[14] Without a sustaining God, giving gifts and drawing people together as neighbours and strangers to fulfil responsibilities would not be possible. All kinds of outside aid, development and missional interventions become obsolete if neighbourhoods are intrinsically places of God's sustaining abundance rather than places lacking his presence, intrinsically places of scarcity. More than mere glimpses of hope, it would be possible to see love and a sense of community through God in the lives of residents. How neighbourhoods can access this together will be discussed in Part D, but here we can say that these kinds of neighbourhood responsibilities and localised sharing are not only possible, but ought to be pursued because God is present.

Third, the God who has an incarnating presence in slums has not yet completed the project of creation and creation's redemption. The Creator God is looking to incarnate his promises for a world without the miserable side of life in slums, but this is as yet unfulfilled. Just as God heard the cries of his people and sent Moses, so too does God look for a people of shalom to join him in creation's fulfilment. This joining will be completed as we shall discuss, but seeking to join and be on God's side as creation's destiny unfolds is no small thing. Just because slum neighbourhoods, or any other, cannot be fully perfected in this life it does not mean that joining God in this ongoing, incarnating dynamic is wasteful. Indeed, it is perhaps the greatest privilege a human can have to be part of the perfecting process of creation, including humanity's habitat in places like slums.

Fourth, God is already present in slum and squatter neighbourhoods before any Christians get there. Christians do not bring God with them and then let God loose once they have arrived. This belief has many implications for the approach Christians take and do not take in such neighbourhoods. At the very least it requires respect of the 'holy ground' Christians walk on when they join a new slum community, and a careful listening to what has gone before them. Joining, rather than inventing or importing, the God who is already present in these neighbourhoods is to join in what the incarnating God is already doing. An arrogance that tries to try to be the Creator who redeems, rather than join the Creator in redeeming, must be resisted.

2.0 The Creator Enfleshes Hope Through Covenants

The rise of the Hebrew nation is well chronicled in the Hebrew Bible, with its promise and possibility majestically prophesied in Isaiah (Isaiah 61, 42, 44). While the nation's rise and fall can be understood as a journey of unfulfilled promise toward God, it can also be read as God's continued determination to fulfil his side of the covenant promise. After various covenants collapse[15] God then turns to Abraham and offers to make his promises for creation real through him. As Walter Brueggemann writes, this covenant becomes the Hebrew Bible's 'central and defining theological affirmation'.[16] More than just a kind of contract,

> The covenant is at the same time a theological idea, a liturgical practice and a durable public institution in Israel. In its largest sweep, the covenant affirms that the God of all creation has made an abiding commitment of fidelity to this chosen people, Israel.[17]

In many ways the early creation and covenant stories told in the Hebrew Bible intended to give some context to the reasons for the birth of the Hebrew nation. From the beginning, the Hebrews were founded, formed and shaped by God's promise to change the toxicity of evil in the world through a flesh and blood people and their land. Rather than destroy creation, God works to see the whole of creation's redemption. This can be seen in the bilateral commitment of God in covenants in Sinai (Exodus 19-24), as well as in unilateral covenants with Abraham (Genesis 15:7-21) and David (2 Samuel 7:1-16). The fulfilment of these promised covenants is especially embodied in the raising up of a nation from an unlikely family into an unlikely land. God's promise is enfleshed in Abraham and his descendants who come from God's explicit invitation and initiative. This can be seen in Genesis 12:1 where God calls Abram out of his own country to a new land with a new family so that 'all the families of the earth will be blessed'. With slavery under the Egyptians at one end and the captivity and exile of the Hebrew people at the other, only a small window of Hebrew freedom punctuates God's rule in Canaan. Yet from this tortured reality still comes the hope for a creation where evil is exiled for good. Christopher Wright notes that a triangle of integral relationships between God, people and land can be identified as a renewing remnant of the larger creation project between God, people and creation.[18] The Hebrew nation was to be a smaller, healthy relational triangle between God, Israel and their land. From this small triangle, the whole world would be blessed. But these relationships were never only for the sake of the Hebrew people and their land. This small triangle would usher in a new, all encompassing triangle of the Lord, a new humanity and a new earth.

Yahweh's presence or glory is incarnated among the Hebrew people with the promise of more glory and presence. This can especially be seen in God's leading (fire and clouds, 'anointed' kings and prophets), in the Torah (Psalm 119) and in the Temple (Shekinah glory of God manifested in the ark and temple). It is within this framework of the promised 'new' that the hope in the panentheistic and covenant-making God can best be understood when examining the Incarnation in the New Testament. The Incarnation, which is the climax of God's enfleshment of hope, can also be seen as a new fulfilment of promise. Not only does Christ fulfil the promise given in creation and covenant but also in the expectation of a coming Messiah. The Christ event is consistent with the God revealed among the Hebrew people. As N. T. Wright notes regarding Jesus' final week, it focuses on the 'two great incarnational symbols' of Judaism, the temple and the Torah, and Jesus 'upstages' the first and 'outflanks' the second:

> Approach the incarnation from this angle, and it's no category mistake but the appropriate climax of creation. Wisdom, God's blueprint for humans, at last makes herself become human.[19]

After the Incarnation, then, nothing can be the same. God personified promises in the form of a human being. The significance of the Incarnation is that it is the fulfilment of God's promises in creation through the covenant made with the people of Israel in quite unexpected ways. The meaning and implications of such a central event to Christian faith will be explored further in the next chapter. Here we can simply note that the ongoing incarnating dynamic of the Creator God is not only found in creation, but also in Yahweh's covenanted relationship with Israel. What can these enfleshed promises given for Israel mean for the transformation of slums?

First, there is a *precedent* in finding hope in the God of promise. The suffering of the Hebrews was not only heard by God, but God acted to join with and liberate them. God took the initiative, chose the small nation of Israel, and empowered them to be his agents of change. In this relational and covenantal way, God promised and physically fulfilled the kind of change that can inspire and encourage those who are oppressed or alienated in slums today. The Creator God's very character is an active hope and love and thus can be trusted by those who are suffering in slums. What God has done in seeking out Israel and freeing them from Egyptian oppression, for example, God can do again for slum residents in their fight for freedom and in moving towards the way God intends their neighbourhood to be.

Second, there is a *warning* to those who are oppressing and benefiting from oppression in slums. Given the inter-connectedness of urban slums within the global community this is a serious caution to all humanity. God is neither neutral to injustice nor distant from evils. Rather, God feels, sees and joins with the oppressed, ready to see real transformation occur as part of his concern for all creation. The theme of God siding with the oppressed as a precedent and as a warning is a characteristic theme of liberation theology. What God did with Israel, God can also do with residents from slums, freeing them from all kinds of our slavery.

Third, those in slums are part of a *continuance* of concrete promises that empower. Slum residents can join the story of what God is doing to renew and fulfil creation. Slum residents can be involved in seeing a new heaven and new earth come together in the ways that God has always intended. As we shall see, this was inaugurated in Jesus, but the promise of a New Jerusalem which has no misery is the promise that those in slums can hold on to as well, just like the Hebrew nation. This promise of urban utopia is especially important in the face of today's rapid and unstoppable force of urbanisation. The future location of humanity is not on a cloud in the sky, but in a neighbourhood of a city. Participating in the direction God desires for creation, rather than trying to vacate or flee from it, can be a source of authority and power for change.

3.0 The Creator Enfleshes Hope Through Raising Jesus from the Dead, Inaugurating New Creation

It is God who raised Jesus from the dead (Romans 10:9) and so inaugurated the promise of new creation (1 Corinthians 15). A distinctive feature of eschatological Christian hope is that it is intrinsically linked with the resurrection of Christ. N. T. Wright, in his scholarly treatment of Christian origins, as well as in *Surprised by Hope*, makes explicit these links with Christian mission today. In the latter he writes that 'The mission of the church must therefore reflect, and be shaped by, the future hope as the New Testament presents it.' For Wright this means that areas such as 'justice, beauty and evangelism' should be understood in terms of

> anticipation of God's eventual setting to rights of the whole world, we will find that they dovetail together and in fact that they are part of the same larger whole, which is the message of hope and new life that comes with the good news of Jesus' resurrection.[20]

The need for hope the Two-thirds World has is especially taken up by liberation theologians, such as Jon Sobrino, a Jesuit priest from El Salvador. A recent collection of his writings edited by Stephen J. Pope is entitled *Hope and Solidarity: Jon Sobrino's challenge to Christian theology*.[21] As Vera Ivanise Bombonatto says, Sobrino's

Christology is 'inspired by the light of the resurrection of Jesus, which is an expression of the power of God, not only over death, but also over the injustices that produce so many victims. God raised-up the Crucified One; consequently there is hope for all the crucified of history'.[22] As a prominent theme in *Theology of Hope*, however, Moltmann see these roles as actions informing hope in God in the face of suffering:

> Christian hope is resurrection hope, and it proves its truth in the contradiction of the future prospects thereby offered and guaranteed for the righteous as opposed to sin, life as opposed to death, glory as opposed to suffering, peace as opposed to dissension.[23]

The theme of resurrection and eschatology is especially developed in Moltmann's writings. This can be traced to a formative event that occurred while he was at Duke University in America in April 1968. During an 'International Theology of Hope Conference', with over five hundred theologians, the news that Martin Luther King had been assassinated rang out.[24] Moltmann would reflect that eschatological hope is different from mere optimism.

> For if God has raised the persecuted, forsaken, assailed Jesus, who was executed by the power-holders of this world, then he brings future to the persecuted, forsaken, and damned of this earth. Christ's resurrection is the promise of a new future for the godless and God-forsaken people and not least for the dead.[25]

God's past promises are central to understanding eschatological hope that can be trusted in the face of suffering. The resurrection of Jesus, not a modernist notion of progress, is the sign that can be trusted to find a new way forward. Slum residents then need to know not only that the Creator is present, but that the Jesus who suffered and has risen, who provides the promised life and destiny of all creation, is on their side, ready to act through them as agents of change.

We must insist that this framework of hope in the Creator God's promise and coming to 'make new' the world and 'put it to right' includes the 'making new' and 'putting to right' of urban slums. If the eschaton is inaugurated with God raising Christ from the dead (Acts 4:10), then the eschaton can be considered an essential part of an incarnational approach to Christian mission in general and urban slums in particular.

To counter death there needs to be a focus on the God of Life. This is also a constant and sometimes surprising theme taken up in N. T. Wright's theology. Is what happens when we die and when all earth is filled with God's glory worth reflecting on and informing what we do now in places like slums? Wright argues that when a person dies they go to sleep before they are resurrected with all creation when Christ returns in glory. The kind of body Jesus had post-resurrection was the inauguration of what new creation will be like. New creation then is not simply a far away spiritual place, but is heaven coming to earth. The new kind of flesh seen through the risen Christ looks to the day when all heaven and earth will be joined together. The hope found in Christ's prayer—'Thy will be done on earth as in heaven'—is about the world being put to right both now and forever. The dark spectre of death can be pierced through the risen Christ now, but will eventually be fully banished when 'all the earth is full of his glory' (Isaiah 6:3).

What happens after death becomes extremely important for putting this life in perspective. Wright argues that when humans die there is first a kind of sleepful bliss until the final day when Christ will come and all will be raised from the dead and a new heaven and earth will be fully formed.[26] Understanding this resurrected 'life after life-after-death' is of crucial importance to the present for Wright. For what happens physically in this life is not simply thrown away in the next. All those activities done 'in Christ' can live on in an enhanced way when the great day of renewal comes and that is for Wright 'the logic of the mission of God'.

> God's recreation of his wonderful world, which began with the resurrection of Jesus and continues mysteriously as God's people live in the risen Christ and in the power of his Spirit, means that what we do in Christ and by the Spirit in the present is not wasted. It will last all the way into God's new world. In fact, it will be enhanced there.[27]

Such an understanding of life after death gives hope and purpose to life now, not least for those living and serving Christ in slums. Death is not the final word because this eschatology sees even death transformed (1 Corinthians 15:54-55). Nothing invested in the 'least of these' is done in vain or wasted (Matthew 25:31-46; 1 Corinthians 15:58). On the contrary, it becomes meaningful in an ultimate sense because the faith, hope and love poured out by Christians remains forever (1 Corinthians 13:13).

Premature death is a real barrier to transformation in slums. Loss and grief are some of the most painful realities of being humans in a fallen world. Yet, when the young die, especially when their deaths are easily preventable as is often the case in slums, the tragedy is dramatically intensified. Something could and should have been done about the premature loss of any person made in God's image. The God of Life invites people to join him in completing the promise all people have.

Any adequate Christian response to urban slum and squatter neighbourhoods therefore needs to address issues of life, death and the inauguration of new creation. As we have seen in this chapter the promissory and anticipatory hope can be found in joining the Creator of Life. This is not least because 'The Lord is good to all, and his compassion is over all that he has made' (Psalm 45:9). The goodness and compassion of the Creator God is an important source of hope that Christians can experience and then bring to the transformation process in slums. Without it, God's transformation remains far off, but with it God's renewal of all things is on its way and we can all join in on seeing all creation's promised fulfilled.

Chapter Nine

The Redeemer Incarnates: Following the risen Jesus into the hidden life of urban slums

Jesus Christ, the Incarnate One, makes real God's promises in the world. Langmead's three-part definition of incarnational mission focuses on following Jesus as a pattern for mission[1] and can also help frame a Christian response to slums. As Langmead outlines, a Christo-praxis centre can help Christians focus on what it can mean to embody Good News to the poor, share vulnerable love and follow the way of the cross.[2] As we shall see, these incarnational dimensions are distinct to Christianity and have the potential to provide real courage and creativity in slum neighbourhoods.

If God has always had an ongoing, 'incarnating dynamic of hope' in the creation and through a covenant with the Hebrew people, what, then, is the special meaning and importance of the Incarnation of the Redeemer? Perhaps the most explicit and developed use of the metaphor of enfleshment to describe the Incarnational event can be found in John's Gospel and the Johannine Epistles.[3] Particularly important, and from where the very term 'incarnation' is derived, is John 1:14:

> And the Word (*logos*) became flesh (*sarx*) and dwelt (*skenoo*) among us, and we have seen his glory (*doxa*), the glory (*doxa*) as of a father's only son, full of grace and truth.

Four Greek words here—'flesh' (*sarx*), 'dwelling' (*skenoo*) and 'glorification' (*doxa*) of the 'Word' (*logos*)—can help inform in what sense the Incarnation can provide a motif of enfleshing hope in slums as especially seen in Johannine writings.

A Johannine use of *sarx* ('flesh') here and elsewhere can be contrasted with the typical Pauline use. For Paul, *sarx* is a metaphor used fifty-four times, mostly describing base human nature, driving people to be in constant rebellion with God.[4] 'The flesh', then, is something Paul calls readers to resist by the grace of God (Galatians 6:8). For John, however, *sarx* is but one metaphor employed to describe the mystery of God's salvific purposes in Jesus Christ. Jesus says in John's Gospel, for example, I am 'the light' (John 1:4-9), 'a good Shepherd' (John 10:11-14), 'the door'

(John 10:7) and 'the way, truth and life' (John14:6). In his Prologue John introduces the metaphor that the 'Son of God' is 'the Word' (*logos*) who 'was God' and was 'with God' and who helped create the world (John 1:1-2). It is this logos that is then personified (made *sarx*) as Jesus. The eternal Word is not only made flesh, but **dwelt with us**—John uses the verb *skenoo*, which is also metaphoric language denoting the pitching of a tent like the tabernacle, in a particular time and place as a human being. This is significant in that the literal dwelling place of the eternal Word is quickly identified by John as the town of Nazareth, a marginalised place from where 'nothing good' can come (John 1:46). Jesus was 'in the world, and the world was made through him, yet the world knew him not', and even though he was rejected 'by his own people' in that place where he lived, he still invited 'all who received him, who believed in his name' to have 'power to become children of God' (John 1:10-12). With this opening, John uses poetic metaphors to prepare the reader for the good news that God becomes human in Jesus Christ to redeem the world (John 3:16). This is the central event of the New Testament, of the Christian faith, and the event that is developed explicitly in John with incarnational metaphors.

It is worth noting here that a strictly literal, non-metaphorical *logos* becoming *sarx* is almost impossible to imagine. Just as with other Johannine metaphors where Jesus cannot literally be light, bread, true vine or door, neither can Jesus literally be a spoken word made of sinewy skin and human meat without bones. Taking Christological metaphors literally can create real confusion, not clarity, about Jesus.[5] Metaphor helps us 'to see as' something else and is used throughout Scripture and theology to point to realities.[6] This does not mean that the Incarnation event is imaginary and not historical. We simply note that by using a mixture of inspiring metaphors, including 'the Word became flesh', John describes a mysterious, unique salvific event which is difficult to express literally. As is often found in Johannine scripture, this metaphor reveals eternal realities.

Jesus' glorification is a rarely considered dimension of incarnational theology. 'Glory' can sound so spiritual and otherworldly, almost the opposite of the messy and dirty 'flesh and blood'. Yet it is a key concept that informs John 1:14, perhaps the most obvious incarnational text. That Jesus enfleshes God's glory is introduced here in the Prologue, but it's a theme that weaves its way throughout John's Gospel with 'glory' (*doxa*) used fifteen times. At its root *doxa* means 'favourable opinion', as in what a person thinks or decides about someone or something.[7] It can also be used in a final eschatological sense that draws on the Hebrew idea of *kabod,* often translated 'honour' (Daniel 12:3, Isaiah 40:5). That is, God's glory can be God's final word or opinion that comes with God's honour and power. In John's Gospel *doxa* is often used to contrast the glory and positive opinions sought from other humans (John 5:44) or for oneself (John 8:50), where the only real *doxa* that lasts comes from God

(John 12:43). Jesus' 'first sign' turned water into wine, which first 'revealed his *doxa*' (John 2:1). These signs build in the course of the narrative so that by chapter eleven John has given us six signs that in Jesus, God's glory is revealed.[8] Jesus' crucifixion and resurrection is the final and fulfilling seventh sign. This is 'the hour' that came for the Son of Man to be glorified (*doxazo*) by the Father (John 17:1). Jesus' way of living, healing and sacrificing himself for others illustrates the path for others to follow and to be therefore *doxazo* and approved with honour by God too (John 17:22, 24).

For John, Jesus, the Word-who-created-the-world, now 'tabernacles among us' (*skenoo*). The promised Messiah is present and replaces what the Temple—and all it represented for Israel—could do for God. In Israel what God, the land and the people had was only on a small, limited scale. Jesus fully reconciles God, all people and creation together. This is all creation full of God's **glory**.

N. T. Wright draws attention to the way John uses Genesis creation language not only in the Prologue, but also in the stories of Jesus' death and resurrection. The Creator's schedule of working for six days and then resting is reflected in Jesus' final words on the cross: 'It is finished' (John 19:30). In the tomb, Jesus, like the Creator, has his Sabbath rest so that on the seventh day Jesus arises 'rested from his completed labour. The Word became flesh, and slept among us; we beheld his glory, glory as of the loving God who has finished the work of redemption'.[9] It is in this new and redeemed creation that Jesus invites his disciples to follow him (John 20:19, 21). It is no accident that the risen Jesus is first mistaken by Mary for a 'gardener' (John 20:15), or that just as God breathed Adam into life and gave him his mandate (Genesis 2:7), so too does Jesus breathe the Holy Spirit into the disciples and give them their mission. The mandate, 'As the Father sent me, so I send you' (John 20:21) invites the disciples to follow Jesus' pattern for honouring God. In John's Gospel Jesus' final words to Peter are simply 'follow me' (John 21:22).

Christians need a clear reference point for action in slums. Our own *doxa* (opinion) of ourselves or from others or even about a God who used to dwell among humans is too vague and limiting if slums are to be transformed. Rather, by the invitation to follow Jesus in loving obedience to the Father we can share in Jesus' glory, a glory ultimately expressed in Jesus' life, cross and the resurrection. As Paul wrote to the Colossians, it is 'Christ in you' that is 'the hope of glory' (Colossians 1:27). This guiding light leads us into appropriate action if we sacrificially serve and follow Christ. As Jean Vanier writes of John's ending:

> This passage reminds us to be humble shepherds,
> Not seeking power, wealth or our own glory
> But to be servant-leaders,
> Ready to give our lives and to share our lives with the poor,

> To live simply with the poor,
> To serve Jesus,
> Who remains present in the daily ordinariness of our lives
> And who calls us to become 'beloved'.[10]

The psalmist hoped that God's glory would fill the heavens and earth (Psalm 108:5). In Christ it has finally been inaugurated. Hope enfleshed both in Jesus and in our invitation to follow Jesus is possible because Jesus is the 'first fruit' of a new era (1 Corinthians 15). In Jesus, transformation of the worst suffering, even death, via his obedience as the authoritative new Adam is possible. Jesus is putting all creation to right. Hope enfleshed in Christ—seen through the concepts of *sarx*, *skenoo* and *doxa* of the logos—provides a theological motif and framework to help inform and focus Christian responses in urban slum and squatter neighbourhoods.

John's Gospel is a high point in an incarnational theology of mission, but over the centuries there have been various ways to understand the meaning of the Incarnation as a salvific event. Some of the fiercest debates among Christians in the first few centuries were around how best to define the person of Jesus in relation to God. Perhaps the most accepted and lasting definition is the declaration of the Council of Chalcedon in 451. This Council reaffirmed the Nicene Creed and rejected two popular formulations. These were Nestorianism (Jesus seen as two distinct people) and Eutychianism (Christ's humanity absorbed into his divinity).[11] It also clarified that Christ was fully God and fully human, God incarnate.[12] There have been recent scholarly challenges to this understanding of the meaning of the Incarnation, especially over the last hundred years and mainly focused around the term 'substance'. Langmead, for example, draws attention to the diverse ways in which Jesus can be understood as God-made-flesh in traditional and contemporary Chalcedonian terms where Jesus is understood as 'the same essence as the Father'. Building on Sarah Coakley's work, Langmead outlines seven senses of incarnational Christology, each option claiming less than the first, Chalcedonian, view.[13] These include more speculative contemporary expressions that hold some promise for being able to describe the complex relationship between the person Jesus and divinity.

While there are different ways to express how and in what sense the Incarnation works in the world, a Christian understanding affirms both Christ's humanity and divinity. Jesus is unique in this sense and therefore this can help inform a distinctive Christian response to slums.

The Christian doctrine of the Incarnation is unique. It can be contrasted with other major religious traditions such as Buddhism and Hinduism, for example, which have notions of incarnation, where gods become human for short periods of time. These are more re-incarnational events, however, than the Incarnational event portrayed in the Gospels and developed in orthodox Christian theology. In the Incarnation the supreme God became fully human in a once-and-for-all salvific event. Islam does not recognise the divine Sonship of Jesus or his unique role in salvation. In Christian tradition Jesus is more than a prophet and none other than God Incarnate.

Further, what Jesus' Incarnation includes is distinctive in its own right. Throughout history there have been people who have claimed divinity but who did not live and die as Jesus did. Jesus' distinctiveness is not least because of his crucifixion, death and resurrection as God Incarnate. This is unlike any other religious or political figure. As Hans Küng, for example, explained:

> It is not indeed as risen, exalted, living, divine, but as crucified, that this Jesus Christ is distinguished unmistakably from the many risen, exalted, living gods and deified founders of religion, from the Caesars, geniuses, and heroes of world history.[14]

What God Incarnate as a theological concept unique to Christianity can mean for slums, and whether other people can accept it, is to be discussed later, but here we can establish that in the Incarnation, Christianity has something distinct to offer the world. The Incarnation was developed from gospel times, is at the heart of Christian orthodoxy and is therefore crucial to Christian self-identity and thus distinctive Christian responses.

1.0 What Does the Incarnation Include?

What scope does the term 'the Incarnation' encompass? We will insist here that the Incarnation is the Christ event in full (including its continued work today), though this is not the only view of the Incarnation. Langmead, for example, outlines three main schools of thought among scholars that define the boundaries of this unique 'Incarnational event'.[15] The first sees the 'Word became flesh' as referring only to the actual birth of Christ (which may also simply include the conception).[16] The second view sees the Incarnation as referring only to Jesus' birth, life and teachings—the other aspects of Jesus' life belong to other categories.[17] The third view sees the Incarnation as the Christ-event, including Jesus' birth, life, ministry, death and resurrection; this is the view to which Langmead adheres.[18]

Why insist that the Incarnation include the cross and resurrection as essential for Christian hope in slums? Paul saw the bodily death and resurrection of Christ as so crucial to the Christ-event that he could write, 'If Christ has not been raised, then our preaching is futile and your faith is empty' (1 Corinthians 15:14). Why would Paul hold this view? Why not include other elements of the Incarnation like the birth of Jesus or the ministry of Jesus? What is argued below is not only that the cross and resurrection is a climax to the enfleshing dynamic of God, but that if these events did not occur 'in flesh and blood' to Jesus then Christian faith loses its hope for real transformation in the world. If such transformation is not possible in the world then hope for change in neighbourhoods like urban slums is indeed 'futile' and 'empty'.

First, that God experienced real suffering and death is impossible without Jesus' real humanity. To devalue the suffering work of Jesus on the cross is to lose the power and authority of the incarnate and crucified God. The ideas of Gnosticism and Docetism, where Jesus only seemed human, were rejected by the early church. These ideas have no value in the concrete situation the world finds itself in today. Moltmann states:

> As the people of the crucified Christ, the church originated in the particular earthly events of the oppression and liberation of Jesus, and exists in the midst of a divided and mutually hostile world of inhuman people on one side and dehumanised people on the other. Its concrete language must therefore take this difference into account, and its action must be that of commitment.[19]

The real suffering of God in Christ is passionately taken up by liberation theologians. Jon Sobrino talks of taking the crucified Christ in oppressed people off the cross.[20]

Crucially, if the torture and execution of Jesus is excluded from the Incarnation event, then not only is solidarity with humanity diminished, but it cannot be said that God suffers with us. God could suffer emotionally 'in creation', as when God saw the Hebrew people in slavery, but only a body can physically cry, bleed and die in suffering. God was not distant and 'other' in Christ, but suffered and hurt more than most human beings in history. Paul, in his majestic poem in Philippians, picks up this theme (Philippians 2:5-8). A breakthrough in the relationship between the fallen creation and its Creator required, as it were, a punch through the barriers of evil from the human side of the relationship. That breakthrough would not be possible if Christ was not really human, following God's will to the end. Evil would not have been broken and defeated if it were not for the real, sacrificial martyrdom of God-in-the flesh, who resisted evil and finally stared it down from the cross.

Second, that God raised Jesus in flesh and blood from the dead gives the ultimate affirmation of the life and ministry of Jesus. Jesus died because of the life he lived and was raised as a sign that this is the God-filled life. The second part of such an affirmation would not be possible if Christ's body was only spiritually raised. The biblical writers clearly use the term 'resurrection' in similar ways to the Pharisees, referring to what pagan writers thought was impossible. Neither did the New Testament use of 'resurrection' simply mean Jesus was resuscitated and then would die again as Lazarus did. The risen Jesus was also not a ghost, as shown in Matthew 28:9 where the disciples grab hold of Jesus' feet, and also in John's Gospel where Thomas touches the torture scars of Jesus (John 20:27). In Luke's account the idea that Jesus is a ghost is explicitly denied by Jesus himself (Luke 24:36-43). A ghost could not do the physical actions that the resurrected Jesus did, as described in the Gospels.

Jesus rose from the dead in the flesh, yet it was not flesh as we know it. The risen Jesus had the ability to walk through walls and to appear and disappear at will (e.g., Matthew 28:9-10, 16-17; Luke 24:34; John 20:11-17, 21:1-2; Acts 2:32, 3:15, 4:20, 10:40-41, 13:30-31; 1 Corinthians 15:5-7). Jesus seems to have been able to disguise his appearance so that close friends could not recognise him after having spent hours together, and then reveal himself and disappear altogether (Luke 24:13-32). What kind of flesh was this? Regular flesh and blood cannot do this. Clearly, Jesus had a new and improved body free of death and decay as the 'first fruits' (1 Corinthians 15) of the new creation humanity can eventually have too.

The theme of Jesus' resurrection as 'first fruits' was considered briefly in the last chapter where God raised Jesus from the dead to help inaugurate the new creation. This is a theme taken up by Wright when he argues that in Jesus' resurrection we see not simply an afterlife of a distant, spiritual heaven, but rather, as in Mark's Gospel, 'Jesus is raised, therefore there really is life after death'. The point is, 'Jesus is raised, therefore you'd better go to Galilee and see him there'.21 The truth and climax of the whole creation project is found in the Incarnation of Jesus; this was underlined and affirmed for the disciples by the resurrection. Jesus therefore is affirmed as Israel's Messiah because he was raised from the dead. Without such verification Jesus was just like the many other would-be Messiahs of that day, whose execution sealed their movements' failures. As the disciples walked away from Jerusalem they probably thought that was the case, that Jesus was a sham, or mistaken. With Jesus risen however, the fulfilment of the promises God gave to Adam (as a human in God's image) and Abraham (the whole world blessed) is possible. When the disciples met the risen Lord one of the things they did was 'examine the scriptures' to see how Jesus fulfils Yahweh's hope for world (Luke 24:44-48). Jesus' resurrection, then, is an integral part of God's fulfilment of the many promises made through Israel for the whole world, including slums.

Third, that God defeated death and evil is impossible without Jesus' real humanity in the cross and resurrection. The freedom of humanity to love, and the problem of evil and death, required a radical act of God to put things right. Jesus needed to be fully human to follow the will of God, even to a sacrificial death. To go on to actually defeat death, absorb it for others and then come out the other side required an unprecedented physical resurrection. The veil of death that kept humans and fallen creation in darkness could only be broken by someone who came back from the dead. As Peter proclaimed at Pentecost: 'God raised him up, having released him from the pains of death, because it was not possible for him to be held in its power' (Acts 2:24).

Fourth, it would be impossible for Christ to have all authority over heaven and earth without Jesus' real humanity in the cross and resurrection. Paul proclaims this clearly in his letter to the Philippians (Philippians 2:8-11). Jesus would not be Lord and Saviour of all without these physical acts in 'heaven and earth'. Jesus' authority was not just in a spiritual place somewhere else. His authority was here on earth, breaking the barriers between heaven and earth. This Lordship of Christ on earth is what led the early church into trouble and persecution. Fidelity to Jesus over Caesar and all other gods was not based on mere ideology or a desire for a safety net in heaven. Real fidelity to Jesus flowed from the authority found in the only person who defeated death and who invites humans to join his new reign. This living Lord is not separated out from earth, but offers his presence as disciples go about expressing his reign, because 'all authority' has been given to Jesus and Jesus can give his authority and presence to the disciples in the whole world (Matthew 28:18). God's reign in Christ is not simply for another time and place, such that all we can do is resist the current evil age. God's reign has begun afresh in the world now because Jesus was raised from the dead.

Fifth, God's inauguration of the new heaven and new earth is not possible without Jesus' real humanity in the cross and resurrection. Jesus is the 'first fruits' of the new creation. With the bodily resurrection Jesus fulfils the themes of God's enfleshment from the beginning of creation. This is especially taken up in John's Gospel as a climax; it is the reason why the Word that created the world became flesh. The risen Jesus is the new Adam, risen on the first day of the (new creation) week to pick up the cultural mandate that Adam dropped. It's not surprising, then, that he is actually mistaken as 'the gardener' by the first woman at the tomb. The role Adam was to have in Eden is now taken up by Jesus for the renewal of all creation. This is why the body of Jesus is of a new and different kind, one that humans can eventually gain too.

2.0 The Incarnated Redeemer and Slum Transformation

What Jesus did in Nazareth and inaugurated eschatologically in the cosmos ensures that there is a continuing presence of the risen Jesus able to be followed for God's redemption in slums. Jesus has a deep solidarity with and understanding of what slum residents are facing (Hebrews 2:18, 4:15); he can also now offer his Spirit for new empowerment (Acts 1:7) and liberation (2 Corinthians 3:17). This is the reconciling power of Christ for all creation (1 Corinthians 5:17-21). Jesus' comprehensive redemption and reconciliation must include slum residents and their worlds. The ministry of reconciliation, then, is a key response to what Christians can offer in slums, following the Christ who redeems.

It is no small thing to nurture a stance of reconciliation. Yet, this intentional nurturing of a committed relationship with the Incarnated Redeemer is often a theme in Thomas Merton's writings. He defines contemplation as, 'That life itself, fully awake, fully active, fully aware that it is alive'.[22] It is this kind of awakening that Christians must find in the often hidden life of slums. Merton goes on to say, 'He answers himself in us and this answer is divine life, divine creativity, making all things new'.[23] To follow Jesus in slums as Merton proposes, a person echoes Christ's ministry of reconciliation as Word in the world as they encounter Christ. To love only the idea of Jesus or devotion without the existential reality of Jesus as a person is to miss the presence of the Redeemer.

Without both the cosmic and local dimension of Jesus to follow, Jesus can quickly become a local deity to be domesticated or a distant deity to be ignored. The spectre of indifference, racism or provincialism can be held at bay, however, if Jesus belongs and is Saviour and Lord of the whole world. We are to have no competing interests in God's redemption, but rather are all God's children with whom God wants reconciliation. Motivation for costly hospitality and compassion for the stranger, alien and the outcast can quickly be found when we see our sibling loyalties within the cosmos. The God who is reconciling the whole world to himself through Jesus invites us to follow him by being agents of reconciliation too.

The rise of urban slums challenges Christian fidelity. With the risen Jesus found in local, cosmic and redeeming actions, it is possible to follow Jesus into transformative, faith-full actions in slums, but it is also possible to reject or ignore this invitation. These kinds of themes around fidelity and infidelity to Christ are seen throughout the New Testament, especially in contrast to the Roman Empire; they inform decisions to stay and face those violent powers or not. At the time the Book of Revelation was written, for example, the myth of *fides* (trust, loyalty, Greek *pistis*) was foundational to life in the Roman Empire; it was a kind of 'reciprocal loyalty' between Caesar and his subjects. Caesar would provide for their welfare in exchange for their *fides*.

> Conquered peoples would offer their fides to Rome, where it involved a total surrender to the discretion of the emperor. Faith could not be divided. It was either given to Caesar or not. Not to give to Caesar was an act of gross insolence. It might even amount to a declaration of war.[24]

If Jesus embodies *fides*, there is a radical alternative to faith in Caesar and his equivalents today. The English word 'faith' has often been domesticated to mean a mere private belief in God by an individual. But the writer of Revelation goes to great lengths to further explode the myth of faith in Caesar as illusory and transient compared with faith in Jesus, a faith that calls for both relevance and faithfulness to Christ. We see this in the words directed to the Pergamum church who live where 'Satan's throne is' and yet 'hold fast' as the martyr Antipas did (Revelation 2:13).

Alongside the practical difficulties for Christian living and development strategies that slums pose, these 'below the surface' challenges go to the nature of Christian faith in a world facing complex globalised oppression. These injustices are more than simply an issue of who has the most power, but a reflection of 'relationships that don't work, that are not just, that are not for life, that are not harmonious or enjoyable'.[25]

To follow Christ as a pattern for mission in a place like Klong Toey is to believe that these kinds of relationships can be mended, but not without personal costs. Issues of solidarity, justice, oppression and how power relates to different individuals, groups and systems are complex and costly to address. I experienced this first hand on May 19th 2010, when rioting and looting broke out across Bangkok.[26] The global and local relationships clearly did not work for those living in slums, and the looting and burning down of Bangkok buildings were evidence of this. Would we stay or go in the chaos? We prayed and felt staying with Jesus in the chaos with our neighbours was a practical and symbolic response of fidelity. Inherited and developed power needs to be locally sacrificed if the goal of globalised justice is to be realised.

To follow the Redeemer who incarnates into the life of slums and to stay long enough to see change is costly and risky. This is especially the case where Christians are a minority and where institutions are difficult to build. As we have seen, this is the situation where two-thirds of slum residents live. The power of being a majority and the security of institutional order cannot be a foundation for a Christian response to these slums. A radical, lived trust in a sense of call by Christ may be all that a Christian can rely on.

Christian faith, however, has a rich tradition of adherents who have risked their lives in faithfulness to God in the face of oppressive and chaotic contexts. It is significant that the Greek word for 'witness' can also be translated 'martyr'. Archbishop Romero of El Salvador is one such martyr. Challenging Christians to faithfulness to Jesus just moments before he was assassinated, he said:

> If they kill me I will rise again in the Salvadorian people. I tell you this without boasting, with the greatest humility… As a pastor I am obliged to give my life for those I love, who are all Salvadorians, even those who are going to murder me. If they fulfill their threats, as of now I offer God my blood for the redemption and resurrection of El Salvador… Martyrdom is a grace I do not think I deserve. But if God accepts the sacrifice of my life, let my blood be a seed of freedom and the sign that hope will soon become a reality.[27]

Christianity owes a great deal to liberation theologians like Romero who saw justice as integral to following Jesus with their lives. The stakes to see God's Kingdom come seem to have been raised further, however, as the numbers of those living in slums globally grow by nearly 100,000 a day.[28] The personal cost can rise too and that can be a real litmus test for authentic Christian discipleship today in relation to slums.

That Jesus has inaugurated the coming of God in the Incarnation is therefore crucial for slums in a number of ways.

First, without this promise fulfilled there would be no hope in a Christian sense.

Hope in the possible defeat of the death, demonic forces and despair that are so embedded in slum life would be unfounded. Without the promise enfleshed as 'first fruits' of creation's renewal (1 Corinthians 15:23), resistance would be futile (1 Corinthians 15:17). Yet, because of Jesus, residents in slums can not only know about God but can follow the risen Jesus personally. God is not a vague force, but is known through Jesus.

Second, while the life Jesus lived in Nazareth was unique, in seeking to find and follow this risen Jesus today new possibilities open up. We can affirm with Langmead that Jesus is a pattern for mission, but he is not a static one. Rather, the risen Christ continually moves ahead of Christians, inviting responses already begun by God. This is especially the case in slum and squatter neighbourhoods where sudden and abrupt changes are not a surprise, but are anticipated by Christ. The need for spiritually sensitive detection of what the risen Christ is doing in such situations is of special importance.

Third, without the Incarnated Redeemer, this trinitarian expression of incarnational theology is incomplete. God's promises can be fulfilled in the lives of residents in slums because of the redeeming and reconciling work of Jesus. This helps provide a much needed theological framework that can be accessed and activated by following Jesus, in the power of the Spirit, for the glory of God the Creator. Christians might be washed away by the surging floods of suffering that neighbours face in slums if there were not such deep, concrete and robust theological foundations.

A motif of enfleshed hope calls Christians to 'join' the Creator and 'follow' the Redeemer and can provide a direction, framework and orientation for action in slums. Yet, a power and authority for action is needed for transformation that can only come from participating with the Spirit who incarnates. In the next chapter we will give attention to this theme, often neglected in incarnational missiology, and apply it to slums.

Chapter Ten

The Advocate Incarnates: Participating with the Spirit's transformative presence in slums

The Holy Spirit's role can be considered a third element of an enfleshed hope motif for slum transformation. Just as the Creator and the Redeemer incarnate themselves into the world, so too does the third person of the Trinity. What the Advocate does incarnationally not only helps to fill out a trinitarian framework for a Christian response in slums, but also centres actions on participation that empowers for transformation. The Spirit's role, though often overlooked in incarnational missiological discourses, should be considered a key part of an incarnational theological framework for slum transformation. It is proposed that all of the Trinity is intertwining its activities in people and in the world. What is crucial for this book's argument is that participation with the Spirit makes possible God's promise for wholeness and eternal life in urban slums.

The incarnated Spirit is a significant aspect in Langmead's three-part definition of an incarnational approach to mission. The work of the Spirit is a neglected incarnational theme, but for Langmead 'the role of the Spirit is central in any attempt to express the actions of God in Jesus Christ'.[1] This is an essential part of a trinitarian approach which 'speaks of the Holy Spirit as the means through which God continues the mission of Jesus in the world today, therefore linking the Spirit-centred incarnation with a Spirit-centred Christian mission'.[2] In Langmead's incarnational approach the Spirit especially highlights the grace of God that enables Christians to do God's will as revealed in Christ.[3]

Christianity, building on Judaism, understands itself as a monotheistic faith (Exodus 20:1-17; Deuteronomy 5:1-21; Romans 3:30; Galatians 3:15-25). How the Holy Spirit works within a unique relationship with the other two persons of the Trinity is a complex and at times controversial issue. The level of controversy is evident in the Orthodox and Catholic split in 1054 over whether the Spirit proceeded from the Father or just the Son.[4] While a lot of the early church's attention was given to formulations of Christ's divinity, it was not until 381 that the Spirit's divinity was actually named in an explicit way by an ecumenical Council.[5] The Nicene Creed of 325, for example, simply stated a belief 'in the Holy Spirit' and that was felt to be all that was needed.

Langmead draws attention to the theology of Moltmann as an especially important bridging role in linking traditions of 'following Christ' with 'joining the Creator' in mission contexts.[6] 'Moltmann's significance', Langmead insists, is 'in articulating a view of incarnational mission in terms of conformity to Christ as both a criterion and power for mission which justifies his inclusion as an individual theologian in the middle of a survey which otherwise examines Christian traditions'.[7] Langmead considers 'following Christ' as a key theme in Anabaptist, radical evangelical and liberationist incarnational theologies of mission, just as 'joining the Creator' is considered a key theme in Catholic, Orthodox and ecumenical missiologies. Only Moltmann, however, is named by Langmead as the bridge between the two that focuses primarily on the incarnating work of the Spirit.

To focus on the incarnational work of the Spirit with only Moltmann's insights might, however, be too limiting. Can Revivalist traditions like those of contemporary Pentecostal and Charismatic movements, for example, be explored for their insight into the role of the Spirit in incarnational mission today? These are broader traditions than Moltmann's theology alone, although at times their perspectives can overlap.[8] Given that many classified by Langmead as 'radical evangelicals' (such as Charles Ringma, Viv Grigg and Michael Duncan) also have explicit Charismatic backgrounds and understandings of mission,[9] perhaps Pentecostal and Charismatic scholars and activists can make a real contribution to an incarnational theology of the Spirit in mission. Could this tradition, as seen in early urban Pentecostalism, and more recently in developing-world Pentecostal voices and contemporary Pentecostal scholarly discourse—to which Moltmann is a regular contributor—help inform our engagement with the Spirit in slums?[10]

A Revivalist tradition, however, is notoriously difficult to define. Often there is more of a focus on common experiences than on the diverse doctrinal statements or ecclesiological organisation that the tradition has produced.[11] The eighteenth and nineteenth century revival movements in Europe and America have impacted how the Holy Spirit can be active in the church and society,[12] but we can limit our study to contemporary revival movements within the Pentecostal and Charismatic tradition. 'Pentecostal churches are intent' writes Douglas Peterson, 'on demonstrating how their fundamental doctrines work their way out practically in the life of the people'.[13] What holds this tradition together then is an emphasis on the role of the Spirit to directly fill, animate and empower flesh and blood Christians to do Jesus' mission, including the use of spiritual and supernatural gifts.[14] This is especially the case for Pentecostals—both historically and contemporarily—among the urban poor.[15]

It must be admitted that some aspects of Pentecostal and other Revivalist traditions seem anything but related to incarnational mission. Pentecostals are stereotypically seen as otherworldly and spiritually minded, not enfleshing or socially engaged. A Revivalist tradition of the Spirit incarnated, however, should not be ignored for a number of reasons.

First, the global rise of Charismatic and Pentecostal Christianity is especially prevalent in Two-thirds World cities that have large numbers of slum residents. Those influenced by Pentecostal denominations and those who are Charismatic amongst the Catholic and other mainline churches have grown from less than one million in 1900 to over 612 million adherents world-wide in 2011.[16] In Latin America alone there are as many as 156 million adherents, with 162 million in Africa and over 179 million in Asia.[17] Maps 12 and 13 from the *Atlas of Global Christianity* show the concentration of these so-called 'renewalists' in the Two-thirds World, as both a percentage of the population and a percentage of Christians.

Map 12: Renewalists by province, 2010

Source: *Atlas of Global Christianity, 2009*[18] *See colour version in Appendix*

Map 13: Renewalists by country, 2010. Percentage of Christian population

Source: Atlas of Global Christianity, 2009[19] *See colour version in Appendix*

The emphasis of the Spirit in the rise of one of the few Christian movements to find resonance among urban slum residents is especially significant and relevant to us. Second, the roots of Pentecostalism have much in common with what many residents in urban slums face today. This is not only true of the famous Azusa Street revival in inner city Los Angeles led by an African American and son of slaves, minister William Seymour (1906 to 1908), but also in Pentecostal revivals in India and Korea that started around the same time.[20] In the case of Korea, the rise of Pentecostal Christianity in the revivals was primarily an expression 'from below' of ordinary people emboldened by the Spirit. This soon filtered up through a predominantly Buddhist society, transforming it in significant ways. South Korea today, for example, stands as one of the few places in Asia where the numbers of slum residents have rapidly declined at the same time as percentages of Christians have risen sharply. Consider that in 1910 South Korea had only 50,600 Christians in total (0.5% of the population), but by 2010 had 41.4%,[21] with the main cities of Seoul, Pusan, Incheon and Taegu all around 50% Christian with few, if any, slums.[22] The Pentecostal roots in a case like this should not be ignored as a factor in these transformations.

Third, Pentecostal and Charismatic scholars have a growing sophistication in their pneumatology. More mature and creative expressions are found as the cycle of the movement moves from the first combustible fires to more considered responses. As Moltmann observes, with the rise of globalisation and greater access to important and broader theological networks, Pentecostals have become a more confident part of more formal academic institutions and discourses over the last twenty years.[23] The quality of scholarship has dramatically improved and especially includes a growing number of Two-thirds World Charismatic and Pentecostal scholars.[24] These voices place a distinctive emphasis on Charismatic experiences and understandings of the Spirit's work, and are now more focused on how these relate to social issues. Such developments need a closer examination in a study like this.

Fourth, some of the most important incarnational insights in slums are coming from Charismatic writers. We have already cited Christian writers and activists like Jackie Pullinger, Dorothy Matheson, Charles Ringma, Viv Grigg and Michael Duncan in regard to Christian mission in slums. While Langmead is right to name these as prominent voices focused on the incarnational call to radical discipleship,[25] their insights about the Spirit's work in slums, however, are probably as distinctive as their calls to radical discipleship.

Fifth, Moltmann himself recognises the importance of Pentecostal experience and theology in mission today. He writes of Pentecostalism, that a 'new formation in Christianity is being heralded' and 'has come of age', one that 'expands our gaze to the activity of the Holy Spirit in nature, and in different cultures and religions'.[26] Moltmann credits the German healing Revivalist Christoph Blumhardt (as well as Bonhoeffer) with informing his theology of the hope of the empowering Spirit.[27] He goes on to criticise Karl Barth for 'replacing' Blumhardt's influence with that of Kierkegaard in the second, 1922 edition of his commentary on Romans.[28] Moltmann is also personally involved with the contemporary Pentecostal movement. This includes participation in small Pentecostal churches in Nicaragua, and in Yonggi Cho's one-million-plus Yoido Full Gospel (Pentecostal) church in Seoul, South Korea.[29] Moltmann speaks regularly at various Pentecostal forums[30] and contributes to Pentecostal publications.[31] He writes, 'Whereas social-critical analyses explain why people sink into poverty, misery, and sickness, the experience of the Spirit enables people to emerge from social misery and to ascend the social ladder'.[32] Moltmann may well be a helpful bridge in Christian mission between the incarnational work of the Spirit and that of the Creator and the Son, but he is not alone.

1.0 The Significance of the Incarnated Advocate in Slums

What then can be the theological significance of a Holy Spirit who incarnates into the life of slums and invites Christians to participate for empowerment? What can Revivalists, especially though not exclusively, contribute to an incarnational framework for slum transformation?

1.1 The Spirit incarnates by empowering Christians to continue Jesus' Kingdom ministry

The work of Christ and the Holy Spirit are often intertwined in the New Testament. Pentecostals especially draw attention to the idea that the same Spirit who anointed Jesus for ministry continues to do this through God's people today until Christ returns again.[33] Luke's Gospel and Acts focus on Jesus who was anointed and empowered by the Spirit for Kingdom ministry (Luke 3:22, 4:1, 14, 8-19, 10:21). The risen Jesus then ensured the disciples received this same Spirit which was promised to be poured out on 'all flesh' (Luke 3:6; Acts 2:17) to enable the disciples to continue Jesus' Kingdom ministry 'to the ends of the earth' (Acts 2:1). In John's Gospel the Spirit was also upon Jesus (John 1:32-33). Once Jesus was glorified, that is he went to the cross, the Spirit was promised to be like 'living water' coming out of the believer's heart to give real and authentic life (John 7:37-39). When this Spirit came upon them the 'advocate of truth' would guide the disciples into right action (John 14:17, 26, 15:26, 16:13). After his death on the cross the risen Jesus breathed on disciples and they received the promised Spirit into their bodies (John 20:22). This image draws on the Hebrew word for Spirit, ruach, which literally means 'breath' or 'wind'[34] of the God who gives life. This references Genesis creation stories and the God who breathed Adam into life from the dust of the ground (Genesis 2:7). Jesus also said to his disciples as he breathed the Holy Spirit into them that it would empower them to do 'even greater works' than Jesus himself did (John 14:12), and that they were to continue the ministry he was sent by the Father to do (John 20:21). The risen Jesus wants his followers to collectively continue, in the power of the Spirit, what he began as a person: reconciliation of the world to himself. Paul describes the Holy Spirit as the 'Spirit of Christ' who can 'dwell in' people's bodies (Romans 8:9; Philippians 1:19). For the same Spirit that had the power to raise Jesus bodily from the dead can now indwell believers' bodies to empower them to take up Christ's life in the world (Romans 8:11). What the unseen Spirit does, then, is to enable and empower Christians to participate in fulfilling Jesus' ministry in the world.

Moltmann is conscious of these biblical and experiential impulses for the new work of God by the Spirit. He focuses especially on the continuing life that is possible through the Spirit:

> Where the Holy Spirit is present there is life. That is what the Acts of the Apostles and the apostolic letters tell us; for where the Spirit is, there is joy at the victory of life over death, and there the powers and energies of eternal life are experienced. So in this divine sense mission is simply and solely a movement for life and a movement of healing, which spreads consolation and the courage to live, and raises up what wants to die.[35]

Without the connection the Spirit has with Christ, and without the Spirit's incarnating into and through Christians, the capacity to follow and take up the continuation of Jesus' Kingdom ministry—to see God's will done on earth as in heaven—would not be possible. In the power of the Spirit, however, there is real opportunity to experience and share the real life Jesus instigated. This is a life that those living in slums often miss out on.

1.2 The Spirit incarnates by filling Christians and channelling spiritual gifts into ordinary life

To be 'filled with the Spirit' is an often used metaphor in Pentecostalism to describe an intense spiritual experience that Christians can have beyond their initial conversion experience. As Frank Macchia contends, from the early years of Pentecostalism, 'The dominant focus was on the divine calling for humanity to bear the divine Spirit, or the *inhabitatio Dei*, the indwelling of God through the reception of the Spirit'.[36] Though Macchia notes that Pentecostals have always had 'a strong Jesus piety', the experience of Christians 'filled with the Spirit', 'possessed by the Spirit' or 'baptised with the Spirit' is one of the defining marks of the contemporary Pentecostal and Charismatic tradition.[37] The metaphor of being 'filled with the Spirit' is an especially Lukan one; Luke used the phrase ten times (Luke 15, 1:41, 1:67, 4:14; Acts 2:4, 4:31, 7:55, 9:17, 13:9, 13:52). Paul, too, instructs Christians not to be 'drunk with wine', but 'filled with the Spirit' (Ephesians 5:18). There is potentially an eschatological dimension to the Greek word *pleroo* which draws attention to being 'filled up' and 'satisfied', but also 'to running out' and 'to end'.[38] So to be filled (*pleroo*) with the Spirit can point to the completion of God's will, that people are so Spirit-full that what God plans for the future of life will overflow into the present. 'In the last days', prophesied Joel, 'the Spirit will be poured out on all flesh' (Joel 2:21). This is a theme in John's Gospel, where Jesus speaks of the Spirit, from which 'out of the hearts of believers will flow streams of living water' (John 7:38). Ezekiel, too, prophesied that when God's promised Spirit comes, God 'will remove from your body the heart of stone and give you a heart of flesh' (Ezekiel 36:26). These are incarnational images of hope which point to the Spirit enfleshed and promises made real in the life of the believer for the world.

The Spirit's infilling, however, is not for self-fulfilment. The purpose of God's infilling of humans is to enable them to be channels for action in the world. 'Spirit baptism was an endowment of the Spirit as power for service, a power that opened the believer up to multiple extraordinary gifts of the Spirit'.[39] That this democratisation of power includes slum residents was not lost, for example, on Duncan in the slums of Manila. He writes,

> Experiencing the gifts of the Spirit can transform community life and empower the poor… It is an immense gain to break the culture of silence which is so crippling in a slum. Today, the poor are discovering their voice again. They now believe that their speech can convey something worthwhile. This revolution of speech is being facilitated in part by the gift of tongues. As the Spirit enables them to speak directly to God, so they discover that these words from their mouths count for something and are workers of God. The powerless discover a new power in prayer.[40]

The Spirit enables slum residents to be used as a channel for God to speak and to act.

This can help to quickly mobilise and involve even those with little formal theological or academic background. To find a voice and to witness out of one's own experiences of God gives an authority beyond one's own background into everyday life.

1.3 The Spirit incarnates by emboldening Christians to cross barriers in the face of opposition

From early on in the Pentecostal tradition the Spirit has been understood to embolden Christians to break down barriers, even barriers beyond human control. The Day of Pentecost itself can be seen as reversing the curse of Babel, so that all people could be one in Christ, able to understand the good news of Jesus. On that day the Spirit's coming did what Joel had prophesied: slavery, age hierarchy and gender could be overcome. Koo Dong Yun analyses the *minjung* (people) and how barriers were broken.

> The people (*minjung*) who have been oppressed and subjugated will receive the same or even more of the Spirit's blessings in these last days. With the outpouring on the day of Pentecost, the oppressed *minjung* with charismata were enabled to become the center and subjects of God's salvation history.[41]

The Spirit so filled the early disciples that they were characterised by 'boldness' out of proportion to societal expectations of them. (Acts 4:13, cf. 4:29, 4:31, 28:31) This kind of confidence was also experienced symbolically and dramatically at the start of the Azusa Street revival. In segregated America at the turn of the twentieth century, a racially mixed leadership headed by African-American William Seymour was both rare and confronting. The revival was reported at the time as scandalous, and was considered 'foolishness' because 'white women, perhaps of wealth or culture' and 'strong buck niggers' shared common experiences of the Spirit.[42] Participants in this revival also came from diverse, often polemical, theological confessions that under the intense experiences of the Spirit became less important than unity.[43] In recent years, too, the phenomenon of 'speaking in tongues' has been identified as a unifying work of the Spirit for a 'new humanity'.[44] It can point to both an immanent experience of God who is using the speaker as a channel to make sound, but there is also a consciousness that words are too limited for the God who transcends even doctrinal categories. Attempts to recover these unifying dimensions of Holy Spirit empowering have emerged to find their place again in Pentecostal spirituality and mission.

That the Spirit unifies is an especially important dynamic in urban slums where there are mostly plural and often oppositional forces at work. This can be contrasted with some rural village environments, for example, where it can be possible for one group or even one development worker to help mobilise the whole village leadership to identify and find responses together. Rarely in large complex urban slums, however, will there be just one dominant group, organisation or church, or even one philosophy of development or ministry. Fiercely competitive Christian workers or organisations are not uncommon in slums as limited resources and priorities are fought over. The kind of transformation required in slums needs a kind of supernatural cooperation between all the main actors and people of good will, including Christians. Such unity of purpose requires a work of the Spirit who incarnates to bring unity.

The Spirit also emboldened and directed participants to cross geographical barriers to see unity in Christ among the nations. The dreams and visions so often seen in Acts as a fulfilment of the Spirit's coming (Acts 2:16-18) directed the early disciples out from their home towns and villages. The connection between Holy Spirit filling and the receptiveness to follow visions that call for sacrificial journeys for the sake of the gospel are a common occurrence throughout history. Just some include: Paul's call to the Gentiles (Acts 9:10-12, 11:5, 12:9, 16:9-10, 18:9, 26:19); Peter's call to move beyond his cultural prejudices (10:3-19); Patrick's call to return to Ireland after a vision of Victoricus holding 'countless letters' pleading for him to return to Ireland, and the Celtic movement that changed Europe after the fall of Rome;[45] Count Zinzendorf and the Moravian Pentecost of 1727 that sparked a family-based mission movement around the world;[46] and Wesley and Finney's revivals, which also had visions which led participants to American frontiers for missions.[47] In the case of the Azusa Street revival the Spirit baptisms so unified and empowered the initial group that as many as two hundred missionaries went out to at least fourteen countries in those first few years of the revival, most going with little more than a 'one way ticket'.[48] Some died and others returned early, but within only a few years similar revivals had broken out across the world. As Timothy Tennent notes, 'within the first one hundred years of Pentecostalism the movement has grown from a few scattered revival meetings to a major global force of a half a billion adherents, second in size only to Roman Catholicism'.[49]

Given that two out of three slum residents now live in cities with few Christian residents, there are real geographical and cultural barriers to cross today. Since little can be offered in the way of finances or fame for the required relocation, a focus on the Spirit's emboldening may be a crucial mobilising factor. Without a deep confidence to cross barriers Christians will simply not go to slums. If Christians only look to the aid and development industry for answers, then slums may simply seem too hard. The strategy of 'paying only local institutions' to do transformation alienates Christians in the majority of cases because there are simply too few Christians to pay, and their institutional capacity is insufficient to cope with large donations and projects. New kinds of Christian activists are needed; activists motivated by the Spirit and by a sense of call to move their lives to slums and to find ways to adapt to the conditions. This kind of participation with the Spirit offers far more than climbing up a development career ladder ever could, but the costs are not to be taken lightly. A sense of call may well begin in intense spiritual experiences, directing Christians with visions to follow

Jesus into particular slums no matter what happens, come what may. To be led like this in boldness is real evidence that the Holy Spirit is leading and filling a Christian.

1.4 The Spirit incarnates by animating Christians to instigate new actions

The Pentecostal tradition is also characterised by a confidence that the Spirit 'does a new thing' (Isaiah 43:19) and is 'making all things new' (Revelation 21:5). This nouven of all things opens up never before known possibilities. Creative new Christian responses, including new responses to slums, are at the core of the Spirit's work in the world. These are in many ways eschatological terms with new kinds of actions required in the in-between times before Christ's return in full glory. That new actions are expected brings new hope that the promises of God for the future are made real in the new now. Whereas incarnational mission limited only to 'following Jesus as a pattern' can quickly limit Christians to focusing on what happened two thousand years ago, the constantly renewed dynamic of the Spirit can open up the horizons of opportunity and hope for new kinds of change.

Douglas Peterson, who has been an important Pentecostal voice for social change, especially makes this point. He acknowledges that Revivalist traditions in Pentecostalism can sometimes stifle creativity and become too formulaic, but is nevertheless convinced that participating with the Spirit can inform a creative 'new morality and imagination'. Pentecostalism is well placed to do this both socially and theologically, argues Peterson because Pentecostalism has always had a 'democratisation of religious life, promise of physical and social healing, compassion for the socially alienated, and practice of Spirit empowerment' which can come together as a 'powerful moral imagination' able to 'address the concerns of the disinherited, frustrated, and assertive persons who in large part make up the movement'.

> For the Pentecostal community of faith, a moral imagination saturated with spiritual discernment and supernatural empowerment becomes a powerful tool for creative thinking and action to practice all that 'Jesus said or did'.[50]

Tetsunao Yamamori and Donald Miller found this imagination in the slums among Pentecostal Christians in a way found in few other strands of the Christian church. What they called 'Progressive Pentecostals' saw this kind of real change as coming from the bottom up.[51] Such passion and imagination for new kinds of responses among those in slums is crucial if transformation is to occur. The world has never had so many urban slum residents before. There are no proven and tested responses available. Therefore, the Pentecostal impulse to participate with God's Spirit in instigating new and creative responses is a crucial dynamic, much needed in any Christian response to slums.

Moltmann is well known for his concerns for God's newness in the coming of the Spirit.[52] He pushes the term 'new', however, in ways that are not often understood or are even rejected in revival circles. Moltmann for example, writes, 'The Spirit is the principle of creativity on all levels of matter and life' and 'creates new possibilities… In this sense, the Spirit is the principle of evolution'.[53] By the Spirit, God is not only in creation and in people, but especially makes *new* and is not just renewed. This is where the Creator and Spirit are intertwined, and where some Pentecostal scholars have trouble with Moltmann's panentheism.[54] Rather than rejecting the Creator who incarnates into creation, however, God the Spirit can be understood as a kind of 'first instalment' for what the Creator wills to come (2 Corinthians 1:22). For Moltmann (and others) the Trinity is *perichoresis*, like a kind of constantly moving 'circle' (*peri*) 'dance' (*chorsis*) to join in with. These metaphors can enable Pentecostalism to see beyond its own traditional boundaries that can sometimes become dualistic. As Sean William Anthony notes, 'Jürgen Moltmann's pneumatology serves as an incredible corrective and contribution from which Pentecostals can [gain] great knowledge and testimony and of God's power'.[55]

2.0 The Incarnated Advocate and Transformation in Slums

In Langmead's three-part definition of incarnational mission, 'participating' in the Spirit can often be understood as discerning and joining the risen Christ in action now. Langmead acknowledges that the attraction of Moltmann in this is that 'no other writer is as influential in putting forward a missiologically orientated theology with a strong christocentric focus'.[56] This is certainly how Andrew Root linked Langmead's idea of 'participation in the presence of Jesus' with Bonhoeffer's question 'where is Jesus?' (see table 10), and its implication for relationships between people in community.[57] Having explored how the incarnated Spirit was understood in the Revivalist traditions, however, we can now broaden the focus to participating with the distinctive person of the Holy Spirit: It is participating with the Spirit as the source of authority and empowerment for Kingdom engagement. Identifying this distinctive role of the Spirit may help us to uphold a biblical understanding of the unique work of the Spirit, and a traditional Christian trinitarian monotheistic faith. In the Christian's own flesh, Paul reminds us, we do not have the required strength or abilities to see real change take place (Galatians 6:8). For even if we join the Creator and follow the risen Christ our flesh still needs to be transformed to do God's will. This is the transforming work of the Spirit 'in' and 'through' people and creation.

The invitation to be indwelt and empowered by the Spirit to participate with the risen Christ's mission has many important implications for slums. Not least is that through the resurrected Christ's authority which defeated death, his followers can be empowered by the Spirit to overcome evils that lie unseen in an urban slum, even the causes of premature death. We can also highlight two other ways in which an in-Spirited Christian can overcome real obstacles for transformation in slums.

2.1 In-Spirited to overcome despair

Futility breeds a dark despair felt by many residents in slums. Urban poverty, when slammed right next to extreme urban wealth, can exacerbate a slum resident's feeling that fate, or karma, is against them and that they are intrinsically cursed. This can even be seen in Christian writings. Ellul, for example, argued that urban residents are cursed by God for a life of despair, demonic oppression and eventually death. This is because cities are by nature filled with humans who try to progress beyond and in compete with the Creator-God. Ellul saw no redemption or reformation for cities by God in the same way individuals can be redeemed and reformed, no matter how hard Christians and others of good will may try. Citing various Hebrew prophets[58] and the book of Revelation,[59] Ellul outlined the destiny of all cities as simply that 'the city cannot be reformed' and 'they are all cities of death, made of dead things, condemned to death, and nothing can alter this fact.. She has become the house of the demons who haunt the desert'.[60] What can the Spirit do in urban slum and squatter neighbours if they are ultimately places of God's curse? Are cities intrinsically places of deep despair, absent of any real promise and hope? This is how it can often feel living in slums.

As we have seen poverty can be defined in terms of oppression, and disempowered relationships that do not make for life. What empowerment by the Spirit can do is open up the possibilities for empowered people to take initiative and find ways to reject the city's curses. This is intrinsic to the role the Spirit can play in the believer's life. As Aubrey Johnson suggests, drawing on the Jewish idea of *ruach*, it is only as we take 'a really deep breath' and are 'filled with the Spirit' that we can fully express 'the whole range of (our) emotional, intellectual and volitional life'.[61] Being made alive and awake like this by the Spirit can counter the natural despair slum residents can face.

New actions led and guided by the Spirit of truth may well be costly, but they are not wasted. If these acts are empowered by joining, following and participating with Jesus, despair can be overcome in a number of ways. This includes Christians able to invite and offer empowerment to overcome despair with hope enfleshed. The curses of urban life in a fallen world, experienced so fully by slum residents, need no longer be a permanent state. Creation, out of kilter and causing suffering, has begun to be put right through the life, death and resurrection of Jesus. Resistance to despair in this urban life therefore is not futile because the risen Jesus broke through barriers between heaven and earth, God and humans have begun to be reconciled in creation. Suddenly there is a lot more to live for in this life than just clenching our teeth and enduring our lot. The hope of glory has opened up the windows and doors of the heavenly reign, giving humans the role of stewards on earth. That Jesus rose from death and offers his Spirit makes possible for all people to break free of the predetermined paths that evil prescribes.

Moltmann also sees the 'fruits of the Spirit' such as 'joy' (Galatians 5:22) as an important dimension. The 'rapturous joy' from the Spirit is much needed in slums as elsewhere: 'When the Spirit of the resurrection is experienced, a person breathes freely again, and gets up out of the defeats and anxieties of his or her life… It far outdoes the disappointments and hurts which reduce our love for life and weigh us down.'[62] When overwhelmed by slum life this new love for life, this new kind of joy, is a most needed quality. Given what slum residents face each day, a new kind of disposition is needed, one only found by participating with the Spirit of God who makes alive and animates new responses to dark and often troubling circumstances.

Despair is a real and understandable temptation, but it does not give life. Finding an alternative to despair, even if the action seems small, is possible through the Spirit. Such actions (whether it be standing up to a Mafia leader or pleading the case to a local government official) may not 'fix' the problem. There may be even more suffering as was true in the case of Jesus and the early church in the power of the Spirit. Yet, these actions, birthed in prayer and enfleshed in hope have had a lasting impact beyond their death. As Brueggemann observed,

> We have to acknowledge our thirst for certitude and then recognise that if you had all the certitudes in the world it would not make the quality of your life any better because what we must have is fidelity.[63]

If fidelity with Christ is more important than certainty, then the worst that can happen to a Christian in this life is death, which Jesus has overcome for us. If the fear of death is taken in Christ we can be empowered by the Spirit for creative, prayerful and hopeful responses to suffering. Participation with the incarnated Spirit then can give courage, gifts, fruit, creativity and boldness to overcome even the most despairing of circumstances.

2.2 In-Spirited to overcome the demonic

Participation with the Spirit can also empower Christians to engage and overcome demonic forces. As Ellul and others have highlighted, there are fallen spiritual powers that prey on vulnerable urban people, causing confusion, chaos and suffering in whole cities.[64] These oppressive powers, however, are not an equal army to God. This is a key problem when war analogies are made in regard to the battles as the Kingdom comes,[65] or in discussions of spiritual warfare.[66] Exploration of the nature of these kinds of spiritual dynamics in cities has grown in the last few decades, leading to the development of various understandings as to the nature and dynamic of these powers and what can be done about them. Thomas McAlpine helpfully groups these into four basic understandings: 'Anabaptist', 'Third-wave', 'Reformed' and 'Social Science'.[67] All offer some important ways of understanding the nature of invisible, dark forces in slums.

To explore one example briefly from the social sciences we can see real potential for change in slums. Echoing another Christian anthropologist, Alan Tippett, Paul Hiebert calls for three kinds of power encounters. At the lowest level there does need to be an 'empirical encounter' that addresses the nature of humans and their relationships with each other and the natural world. This is an encounter aiming to win over those holding the secular worldview that Ellul would call the idolatry of humanity's independence from God. At the highest level Christians also need to engage in 'truth encounters' about the ultimate story of God and fidelity to Jesus as Lord to win over those holding other religious mindsets. Hiebert contends that it is vital that Christians engage in 'power encounters'. These encounters, however, cannot be understood in the Indo-European worldview.[68]

How can there be 'power encounters' that are both true to a Judeo-Christian worldview and understandable to those with other worldviews? Hiebert suggests a three-step process of investigation when spiritual battles seem to going on:

Phenomenology: What do people think is going on?

Ontology: What is really going on?

Missiology: How to bring people from where they are to where they should be?[69]

In urban neighbourhoods residents often hold a tribal or animistic worldview and so spiritual phenomena present as a part of daily life. I have witnessed what seem to be some extreme forms of supernatural phenomena in Klong Toey. For example, neighbours once interpreted an older lady in a trance to be her dead mother, who screamed out obscenities about the bad conditions and how disappointed she was that they 'lived like rats'. Such channelling is unusual; a more common supernatural occurrence is for neighbours to see the ghosts of dead people, especially in dark rooms or homes. All these events are experienced as being very real, fear-inducing phenomena, interpreted by those who experience them as being initiated by the spirits of tormented dead people. Such interpretations are reinforced by a large number of traditional Thai myths as well as Thai movies. More recently Western horror movies have added to the interpretive tools that offer 'realities' that are seen as plausible. A Thai worldview often seems to have no problem mixing the animistic worldview with the Indo-European and is pragmatic enough to accept whatever interpretation works best. While most residents would describe themselves as Buddhist, the animistic stories, beliefs and ceremonies of tribal and rural peoples have never been fully rejected.

How residents interpret these phenomena is important to know, not only to respect their views but also overcome barriers in our communication. Hiebert asks Christians to start by using terms and understandings that local people use of supernatural phenomena. Of course, the Judeo-Christian worldview cannot simply leave people living in fear of spirits. There are ontological as well as phenomenological issues in considering what is really going on. If there is a debilitating fear in people's lives the Christian perspective on the demonic needs to be considered alongside the psychology of mental health. Both counselling and prayers of exorcism are potential remedies, but both require missiological insight. How to help a person move from 'seeing' a ghost is not a simple pastoral and missiological process. It requires Christ's love and truth to permeate encounters, rather than violence and further oppression.

Hiebert's model views demonic oppression as a kind of spiritual parasite—not part of the body itself, but embedded within the body, attacking and weakening the body's immune system, especially if the evil is well fed. The evil can embed itself into people, groups and systems of cities, weakening its host's will and changing its host's demeanour. The metaphor has limits but, infused with Hiebert's model, can provide some responses to the weaknesses seen in the views previously discussed.

Hiebert's model and metaphor (of the parasite) together can provide an incarnational understanding of the role of demonic oppression which can inform many possible responses to demonic oppression in urban slums. Viewing evil spirits as spiritual parasites, for example, can aid rejection of some of the fatalism about the city's demons that can be found in Ellulian thought as well as in some Anabaptist perspectives about the powers in this life. It is not the city's spirit, power or culture itself that is demonic. Rather, spiritual parasites can attach themselves to people, groups and structures and can therefore be exposed and treated by God's people in the authority of Jesus. The parasite metaphor can be seen where the Synoptic Gospel writers use the Greek word for 'to save' (*sozo*) sixteen times in regard to Jesus' healing.[70] Exorcism and healing from blindness and other disabilities have a spiritual dimension that Christ can address and heal. Salvation from evil can be concerned with healing and wholeness from evil's parasitic nature in this life; it is not just about resisting evil and waiting for it to end in heaven's afterlife.

Such a metaphor and model also provides a correction to some 'Reformed' and 'Third-wave' optimism about either saving the powers or banishing demonic powers from cities. The people, the ethos and the structures of the city are good because they reflect God's image, but their health is under attack by demonic forces. These attacks can weaken the immune system found in the city's people, ethos and structures to such a degree that they can overwhelm them. These evil parasites cannot simply be won over or banished from the city, but they can be treated by the process of 'power encounters'. Through Christ it is possible for residents to respond to the demonic by finding and addressing phenomenological, ontological and missiological issues.

The understanding of demonic oppression as parasitic also allows that Christians themselves can be affected by demonic oppression and need freedom too. This possibility is difficult to see if a kind of 'good (us)-versus-evil (them)' battle is predominant. The demonic is not just 'out there'; like all the people in a city, Christians can be weakened by the demonic 'in here' and need God's help. This view makes sense of the call to 'seek the peace/welfare of the city for in its peace/welfare we will find our own' (Jeremiah 29:7) in ways Ellulian thought finds troubling.

However we understand the nature of these dark forces, the health and wellbeing of those who live in urban slums are more vulnerable than for most. Fear, superstitions and systems and forces beyond these residents' control can help create a kind of receptive host for the most horrendous kinds of parasites. These evil forces wear down their hosts' will and strength, opening them up to further despair and disadvantage, and ultimately leading to premature death. Many residents are fighting back through Christ, trying to address the powers of darkness in their midst and in their city.

What we have seen is that if there is a spiritual conflict going on, as Christianity claims there is, then surely the front line is among the world's urban poor. Not only can cities be places where false promises are made to multitudes, creating despair, but cities also become attractive hosts to demonic forces. We must conclude, then, that any authentic Christian response to the rise of urban slum and squatter neighbourhoods must not only include effective strategy and fidelity, but also include ways to participate in the authority of Christ in overcoming the barriers to transformation such as despair and the spiritual powers of darkness. Participating with the incarnated Spirit is therefore crucial for such empowerment.

With these conclusions we complete our outline of an enfleshing motif, providing a framework of joining the Creator, following the Redeemer and participating with the Spirit incarnationally. How this motif can be practically used to inform and inspire practical responses for teams, neighbourhoods and strategies can now be considered.

SLUM LIFE RISING

Beyond Fight or Flight: Standing with the Incarnating God amidst the urban chaos

The ideology of community is a pale comparison to the tangible sense of belonging that comes from the fruit of vulnerable, loving commitment to others. This was especially evident to me on 19th May, 2010, as the UNOH Bangkok team sat around our regular communion table in the Klong Toey Community Centre late in the afternoon. All hell was breaking loose across Bangkok. Just a few minutes away an angry mob was using grenades, M-16s and machetes to fight the army and loot 7-11's, luxury-shopping malls and banks. They came closer to our slum by the minute and there was the very real threat of our slum being burnt down in the chaos. Over 50 people had already died and thousands more injured in the two month lead up to what, at that moment, seemed like an apocalyptic nightmare. Some of our team already had close calls that day. One image that stays with me is when I looked up from where I was at the Klong Toey Community Centre and saw plumes of smoke rising up into the sky from not too distant business buildings. Along with the adults and children gathered there, I was transfixed as army helicopters started to land on the very top of one of the closest, burning 'Channel 3' sky scraper, rescuing TV execs and staff, from the fires, looting and rioting going on below.

The Red Shirt protest leaders had just surrendered after the army crashed through their protest areas in downtown Bangkok with tanks. Now their supporters, some armed with M-16s and grenade launchers, were moving across the city exacting revenge. Banks who had held on to former Prime Minister Shinawatra Thaksin's assets, media outlets that had not fully supported their cause (including Channel 3), and some of the largest shopping malls were set alight and turned to rubble. Urban Neighbours Of Hope (UNOH) workers, including myself, quickly gathered together with our children at the community centre, trying to work out what was next for us and our neighbours. Even getting in and out of Klong Toey was difficult now and there was a rumour Red Shirts were coming to burn our slum down. The young men who I normally coach football with had grabbed baseball bats and machetes and even a golf club to guard the two main entrances to Klong Toey.

Since early March tensions had been rising. Bangkok's main commercial hub had been blockaded by Red Shirt protesters after exiled and former Prime Minister Shinawatra's assets had only been partially released. There had been over 50 deaths and thousands injured in Red Shirt grenade attacks and clashes with army and police during this time.

We had some close calls ourselves. Ben Rowse (a brother of UNOH Melbourne worker, Hannah Rowse) was about to step onto a train at Saladeng BTS Skytrain Station when four grenades went off. He was rushed to hospital and after a night there stayed in Klong Toey ready to continue work in Burma with just cuts and bruises. I was due to pick up the computer I am writing on now from a computer repair shop just near this station at the time the grenades went off. My computer wasn't ready in time and I was spared the trip and danger. Chris McCartney, another UNOH worker, heard shots fired and saw people fall to the ground, while he kept riding his motorbike. On the morning of the 19th May my mum was with my son Aiden at a local shopping mall when suddenly shots rang out and bombs went off nearby. They eventually found a person to help them across the road and found a tuk-tuk to take them to my office. This was all happening about five minutes motorbike ride from our home and getting closer by mid-day.

At a neighbourhood level there had been a deep divide. Even our house church had strong supporters of both Red Shirts (pro-Thaksin) and Yellow Shirts (anti-Thaksin). The Red Shirt barricades of tyres, sharpened bamboo poles and barbed wire had been in place in central Bangkok for more than two months, with battle-ready soldiers on the streets, even near our kids' schools. Skirmishes and explosions on the edge of the protest barricades had been common, but an atmosphere of quiet, anticipatory dread fell across the rest of the city until it all exploded early on the 19th May.

Perhaps these apocalyptic images of social conflict exemplify why the transformation of slums should be so important for all people today, including Christians. We know currently over 1 billion people live in slums (1 in 6 people) and this could double in the next 20 years. That the world's poor live within touching distance to the rich and famous - and are nurtured and informed by the same media marketing bombardment - yet remain without the wherewithal to access these lifestyles is a toxic cocktail of guilt and resentment. Guilt that they and their children have not been smart or able enough to have what 'everybody else has', and a deep, burning resentment of 'everybody' who can. From this perspective, the looting and destruction taken out on Bangkok's luxury shopping malls only a few kilometres from slums should not be a surprise. Christians surely have something to offer here.

How and why the rural and urban poor became radicalised as Red Shirts is also a warning. At first glance, it makes no sense for so many poor to leave what they are doing and put their lives on the line for Thaksin, one of the richest people on the planet. For this is not an 'uprising of the poor', but an acting-out on behalf of a billionaire. Even while in exile and with his official assets seized, Thaksin bought Manchester City football club and a Greek island.

Some of this can be explained by Thailand's patron-client relationships where a benefactor is sought to look after them. Thaksin offered to be a kind of mega-benefactor for the poor. Not only did he provide 500 baht a day plus food for each Red Shirt protester that signed on each day and 1500 baht a day for those on front line 'security', if they won the cause against the government there would be homes and cars for everyone who wanted them. This was part of Thaksin's appeal while in office too, though very few of his populist schemes actually worked for many people and he certainly made more money in office than as a private citizen. The sheer amounts of money on offer and the idea of such a benefactor was hard for some of my Klong Toey neighbours to reject, but it was almost impossible for many of those in rural areas like the north-east to reject. What other options are there to find the 'good life'? Messianic figures able to manipulate the masses for their own benefit should be expected as the rise of poverty and urban slums increases. There are only so many helicopters that can whisk people to safety. In world with so many urban poor, no one can be immune from the chaos.

As the UNOH team sat around our regular communion table in classrooms of the Klong Toey Community Centre late in the afternoon of 19th May, we were deeply aware of two primal impulses. Fight or flight. The impulse to flee was being echoed from the Australian government and some of the parents of our team. It's a harrowing thing to read an sms from your embassy saying they have already evacuated and basically 'good luck, you're on your own now'. As a parent with two of my children with us (Amy then aged 13 and Aiden aged 6) as well as three children of UNOH workers the MacCartney family, I was also deeply aware of the potential trauma staying could have on them.

But there was also the impulse to overstretch our role and try to be heroic in reckless ways unhelpful to the cause. Should we join our footballers for example with the baseball bats and fight the mob coming toward us? What good could we really do in this urban chaos? We were not the same as our neighbours, if we listened to the incarnating God could we be faithful?

In the end as we prayed together around that table we all had a peace to stay. While all workers were given the freedom to leave, we all committed to stay together that night at the community centre so we were in our slum together and no-one was isolated. This was what our local Thai leaders had asked of us if we did not evacuate. What we had to offer was our presence in solidarity as a team in Christ. Of course, what would it say about the Jesus we say we follow if we left our neighbours when the going got tough? Some of us did also venture out to give moral support to our friends on the front line at the entrances of our slum at different points during the night. As rioting continued during the night, over 50 more people died and hundreds more were injured.

As the sun rose early on the 20th May I did have a baseball bat in my hands at an entrance of the slums, but it was for fun, playing around with some of the footballers who had stayed awake all night. The Red Shirts had not come much further. Though there were attempts to light fires, all the fires had been put out in time and no damage was done. We lived to stand with our community another day.

As Aiden, then aged 6, rose that morning I tentatively asked, 'how you going there mate?' He looked up from a mattress on the floor in one of our class rooms and said, 'Great Dad. When can we do it all again?' With a smile I joked back, 'Next time there's a riot son'. Amy then aged 13, and I went for a motor-bike ride to survey the damage and look for something for us to do that day. 'If I get shot', Amy said matter-of-factly, 'I'd like to only get shot in the arm, because it wouldn't hurt that much, but gee I'd have a great story to tell with it!' We found a movie theatre open and with all the team went and watched the latest Shrek movie as if nothing had happened.

I am not sure what our kids will make of our faith or our world when they are adults. They have witnessed some awful, real-world things, but I doubt they'll think our faith is boring or irrelevant. I hope they can see that Christian fidelity requires we stand with people as the crucified and risen Jesus stands with us and on the side of the poor. That faith is active and alive, may well cost us more than we bargain for, but is worth it to see our lives count for something. Rarely is faith in action convenient, but anything less than giving our lives undermines the God who 'became flesh and blood and moved into the neighbourhood' (John 1:14, The Message) and calls us to 'come follow me'. Urban chaos will subside, but how we live for and with the living Christ within it lasts forever.

SLUM LIFE RISING

PERSONAL AND GROUP QUESTIONS:

1. When have you experienced a situation where fight of flight was your first impulse? What did you do? How did you respond?

2. How does the idea of a Creator God who is continually present and 'incarnates' differ from the popular idea a God who is absent and not incarnating? What difference can an incarnating Creator make in an urban riot?

3. Why does it matter that God the Redeemer became a human being that lived, died and is now risen? What difference does it make to urban riots that Jesus is alive and risen?

4. When have you been in an out of control situation, why does an inner authority matter more than external titles or other forms of power? Why would the Holy Spirit be described as an Advocate that can empower us? How can that make a difference in a situation like an urban riot?

5. Mission is discipleship - the call to be both relevant and faithful to the incarnating God in the world. Why and how can the search to join, follow and participate with this God make a difference in slums?

Part D

Toward Enfleshed Hope in Urban Slum and Squatter Neighbourhoods

How can the motif of enfleshed hope help in bringing transformation in urban slum and squatter neighbourhoods? This final section explores various practical approaches that can be inspired, informed and invited within the framework of an incarnational motif. Though this motif could inspire and inform all kind of actions, three key themes can be discerned that can make a real difference to the lives of slum residents and Christian faith in slums. These are:

Intentional teams.
Local and relational 'place-sharing'.
Poverty alleviation strategies.

These methodologies are not blueprints for transformation. Rather, they are offered more like a toolkit that can be drawn upon, adapted and used according to what Jesus' presence in a slum and squatter neighbourhood requires. A time line with suggested priorities in a team's lifecycle of seeking a neighbourhood's transformation is also offered.

This is the most speculative and yet practical section of *Slum Life Rising*. Field work is required to see how effective these methodologies can be in different urban conditions and lifecycles as compared to other responses with other frameworks. It is hoped here to provide a kind of practical grid the study can be more grounded in actual possible Christian responses to slums.

Chapter Eleven

An Incarnational Approach to Teams Based in Slum and Squatter Neighbourhoods

Jesus of Nazareth did not simply proclaim a message. He built a community in the power of the Spirit that could multiply his discipleship movement and sustain his transformative vision that God's Kingdom is at hand (Matthew 12:28; Mark 1:15; Luke 10:9; John 14:12; Acts 1:8). Jesus called people to leave family and friends to join a new set of family and friends and demonstrated that it takes an empowered, committed community to reach a community (Matthew 10:35-40; Mark 10:29-30; Luke 9:23; John 12:24-25; Acts 2 and 4). This kind of committed team dynamic is also crucial if Christians are to experience a sense of the incarnational dynamic of God and see long-term transformation take place in slums.

It can be rare, however, to find a focus on both team building and service with the poor among Christian workers who want to engage slums with an incarnational approach. Most workers seem to favour either team building or service, and this can even change over time. Jenni Craig from Servants to Asia's Urban Poor, for example, recorded their early experiences with this struggle in the slums of Metro Manila:

> Those who had been in Metro Manila for three or more years had adjusted to squatter life and as cultural and language stress eased, they needed less team support. A tension of priorities grew. Each one belonged to two communities—the slum and the SERVANTS team. Which one was to have priority? The newer arrivals depended upon the team more for their early survival. The 'oldies' needed the team less, and gave more energy to their squatter community. The two groups were concerned about different issues.[1]

Team and community are not only important for adjustment to life in slums, however. For some the very idea of community and its sense of belonging with peers in a just and right cause is especially significant and attractive. Yet it is also possible that these same people, even after adapting, can have real trouble relating to poor people and embracing the sometimes mundane and often chaotic nature of ministry amongst those living in poverty. Steve Mosher observed this in the Philippines, especially as Western missionaries struggled to relate personally to the poor:

> Privileged Western (Western European and North American) churches sent out well-educated, middle class missionaries who had trouble relating to the poor and powerless of the third world. The supposed strength of such missionaries—including myself—turned out to be weakness.[2]

Then there are those who are primarily activists, who want to forge ahead and spark real change among their friends living in urban poverty. This is often difficult at first in slums even for the most activist-minded, and relying on others is essential at first. Michael Duncan, for example, admitted that:

> The first two years in a slum are often the hardest. All manner of trials are sent to test us. Most of us have been reduced to tears out of fear, frustration or depression. The community becomes our life source. We unashamedly need each other. Most of us wouldn't have survived without this community.[3]

Yet after a period of adjustment the activists' need for others can quickly dissipate. Indeed, difficulties in being motivated to connect with and build up other relocated peers or new workers can result. Intentionally helping other new workers adjust and build their foundations can easily be neglected by activists because now 'It's all about our neighbours'. These workers can often do the task side of the ministry competently with little help from peers. However, such independence can cause workers to easily lose perspective as chaos unfolds, or can even create a kind of dependency on a ministry centred around the worker. The kinds of transformation that depend on timing and momentum are especially difficult to discern and see happen only as individuals. These activists can have trouble demonstrating the same grace that they were shown as they adapted as new workers.

Christians can be too team-oriented as well, however. An intense inward focus can drain the energy from a community of Christian workers by absorbing excessive attention. Bonhoeffer's caution is apt here:, 'Those who love the dream of community kill community. Those who love people build community'.[4] The empowering love of team and neighbour can easily be lost in the dream of what the community ought to be and do for the worker.

If the first group are primarily individualists and they dominate a mission community, the work in slums rarely finds momentum or long-term effectiveness. If the second group are primarily team-dependent and they dominate, the internal energy required by the community can suck the life out of any dynamic it might have been able to offer the broader neighbourhood. What is common is that both sets feel unfulfilled and soon become disillusioned with the way they have battered each other, determined not to do that again. Unnecessary attrition results.

Even the best Christian slum workers generally start out with a bias toward one or the other of these agendas. Yet, what an incarnational approach requires is the sustaining of both agendas—loving the mission community as well as the poor by centring on Jesus, doing God's will, in the power of the Spirit. Jesus exemplified the way of holding these two agendas together, and this can inform teams based in slums. After a night of prayer and discernment Jesus 'called to him those whom he wanted' and appointed twelve as 'apostles' (sent ones) to 'be with him' (Mark 3:14). This is the intentional community formation side. But he also sent them 'out to proclaim the message, and to have authority to cast out demons' (Mark 3:15). This is the task and action side. In many ways this first apostolic community in which Jesus called a few to be with him *and* to go out was the archetypal incarnational missional team. Jesus set important precedents for the church that should not be ignored in the face of the challenges slums present to Christians.

Jesus invited twelve people to 'be with him'. These twelve went through a three year formation process that included observing Jesus as he lived and touched lives, serving under his supervision, and being sent out on their own in pairs. In all of this, they were forged into the kind of community that could continue forward when Jesus was no longer with them in the same way. Apart from the 'nuclear family' of the Twelve, a looser and broader localised discipleship movement emerged that was not explicitly part of Jesus' itinerant community. Some, such as the healed leper or the freed demoniac, were sent home to advance the movement in more locally specific ways.

Christianity has often been at its strongest when there are groups that can nurture focused, specific commitments, which in turn cultivate more localised and inclusive Jesus-centred movements. Missiologist Ralph Winter, for example, described this dynamic as the church's 'two redemptive structures': specialised communities like the early apostolic communities (which he called 'sodalities') and the broader, localised discipleship movement (which he called 'modalities').[5] Winter argued that modern Protestants are often handicapped, in comparison to other Christian traditions, by a narrow ecclesiology that fails to understand the role sodalities played in church life. Indeed a common term for these is 'parachurch ministries' which literally means 'alongside' the church (that is, not a part of the church). In contrast missionary orders are sodalities recognised by the broader church as having a God-given charism to share with the broader church and society. This permission and recognition may involve a struggle for acceptance from authorities, but in the long-term sodalities are valued by and related to a broader church body. Winter argued that there are four ways in which mission agencies can relate to broader church structures. These are:

a) Church/denomination administered and funded;

b) Church/denomination administered and funded by direct, designated giving;

c) Church/denomination related but autonomous;

d) Unrelated to any one church/denomination.[6]

Orders are a 'type c' organisation as a voluntary society related to broader church structures. This means they have accountability and a 'voice' within a particular church structure, but a freedom and a mandate to live out their charism. In the Roman Catholic church this has traditionally been related either directly to the pope or a local bishop. Protestants, even those with autonomous congregational traditions, have often tried to centralise such organisations as 'agencies', or to create corporate or NGO-type corporate boards for them. This has not always been the case, however. Zinzendorf's 'order of the mustard seed', William Carey's 'Serampore Brotherhood' and early Methodist circuit riders are examples of 'related, yet autonomous' specialist teams. Orders have their own leadership from within and yet find ways to belong to a specific, broader church body.

There is a need to distinguish between teams in a sodality and teams in a modality because it helps identify appropriate expectations for local people as well as relocating workers and teams. An apostolic team's primary concern, for example, is not to try to help local people to join it; rather, it is to help them join, participate and follow Jesus in a local movement that is indigenous to their neighbourhood. In UNOH we have found that if we can keep clarifying the nature of our teams, then we have a better opportunity of empowering the poor too. UNOH workers are apostolic (sent out, relocated) and we do not 'own' any of the neighbourhood owned and run projects, institutions and churches from the start.

Historically, healthy sodalities found ways to respond to God's calling, challenging and equipping in ways that related to the broader church but did not replace it. They were not cults who felt they were the only ones who had the truth, nor were they manufactured by the church bodies they related to. Rather, orders were a response to God from the edges, then ratified and confirmed by the centre. God initiated a charism in the face of real needs and people responded. Those who become members of orders can have a sense of call and a challenge by God to live out the order's founding charism, and they have the grace and gifts to do this. Therefore, orders require a discernment process in deciding whom they believe God is calling, challenging and equipping to join their community. Not every person is called to live out the gospel in an order. Those who are called to be a member of one distinctive order are not necessarily called to join other orders.

Patricia Wittberg and others argue that the lack of relevance and credibility of these common commitments to a changing context can lead to the decline of orders.[7]

Their basic mission and charism may well still be relevant, but their methodologies can become mechanical and no longer serve the mission. Committed communities can be re-founded on their original vision and become enfleshed symbols again. If methods become the mission and not just the means for achieving the vision, however, then a more prophetic future becomes unlikely.

Orders often take a long-term view of their charism and do not expect instant results. This ability to embody a long-term commitment to a particular pattern of living out the gospel enables a charism to be nurtured through hardships and challenges. The durability of orders—some have lasted over a thousand years—is based and nurtured on the founding charism and the basics of the gospel. As we have discussed, transformation and development requires long-term commitment and yet many slums can be gone in a matter of days. If teams can understand their vocation and calling in broader, longer terms, then faithfulness can be evaluated in far better ways. Development's value is often only calculated on project outcomes, but orders can evaluate long-term fidelity beyond the immediate task. Such a team viewpoint is especially important in relation to slums because outcomes in development terms rarely go to plan.

New kinds of orders are needed for slum teams if they are to play a role in the transformation of slums today. The need to focus on advancing the Kingdom through apostolic service in communal, radical and sustainable ways seems especially important. These kinds of missional orders need to be apostolic in nature, not monastic or cloistered. That is, they have an emphasis on catalysing, pioneering and starting new work in slums to advance the reign of God directly in the broader society. Many of the Celtic orders, some mendicant orders (such as the early Franciscans) and some apostolic orders (such as the early Jesuits) could be considered such orders in the past. New kinds of missional orders are also required, however, to meet today's urban challenges with new and emerging charisms. The difference between missional orders and many of the other types of orders, development agencies and missionary societies lies, in part, in the common, radical and sustainable ways pioneering work is done in light of the founding charism of the missionary order. The founding stories and ethos can guide workers in ways that mission statements and objectives can't in slums. If apostolic service is 'being sent out' to the neighbourhoods where the people are, the incarnational challenge to join, follow and participate with Christ in this service can be an important dimension. Not least is that an incarnational focus can help groups to avoid defaulting to traditional organisational structures which employ individual workers for a task, rather than a community of workers.

These understandings of missional orders helped shape the founding of UNOH in relation to the Churches of Christ.[8] These apostolic teams need a strong sense of call confirmed by the broader Body of Christ because they need to be prepared to do whatever it takes to see the Kingdom come in a focused neighbourhood. Especially in pioneering work in slums there is a need for teams to be adaptable, innovative and flexible. I have written elsewhere that teams can find real traction in this kind of mission in slums if there are the following team character traits.[9] Without these, real change is difficult almost impossible for a team to see happen. They can be summarised in relation to slums and the motif of enfleshing hope.

1.0 Join with Experienced Team Leadership

An incarnational approach benefits from experienced team leadership. Those who know firsthand what it means to join, follow and participate with the risen Christ in a slum can help lead teams of those who haven't had this experience. This may sound obvious, but what so often occurs for new workers in slum ministries is a kind of 'sink or swim' experience. Duncan writes of how he 'cried' and was 'scared' after he and Ruby with their two young children were dropped off in a Manila slum home on the first day. He did not 'know the language, did not know a soul, and in this stark setting did not know how to cook, sleep, or even bathe the children', and then did not see any other team members for weeks at a time.[10] This is a common experience for new workers and in pioneering teams. Sincere and willing workers they may be, but they are often inexperienced, unsure of what is happening and have trouble adapting. This is not sustainable for most teams in slums. Some, like the Duncans, do have the resources to bond with neighbours and find ways forward by themselves. This approach should be a last resort, however. It is far better to pair new workers with experienced leaders.

It is better, for example, to partner a capable, high-potential new worker with an effective, seasoned team leader than to throw that worker into the deep end of starting a new team themselves. The extra time invested in developing team leadership helps create good leadership habits, addresses character issues and gives space to learn the practices of the Christian worker's trade. It can be unfair to apprentices and those involved if they are forced to be responsible for a team before they are ready. This is especially true in pioneering settings where inexperienced workers are sometimes asked not only to adapt to the shock of challenging cultures and living conditions, but also to lead others where they have not been. It is far healthier for teams if new workers can learn from experienced ones and then, when they are ready, start new teams themselves.

2.0 Follow Jesus in Community Formation

A community formation process is different from simply orientation or training. For apostolic teams it requires apprenticing oneself to a community to live out the gospel and experience a sense of common identity, ownership and belonging. Such formation gives the team a huge head start in working together and providing real opportunities to follow Jesus in difficult contexts. Indeed a lack of formation can drive a team apart even before the real work starts. One of our important learnings in UNOH has been that it is crucial to give newcomers to the community the space to identify if they too have been given a grace from God for this way of gospel living, or if God has called them to another vocation.

While there are many definitions of community formation, in UNOH we have found Gerald Arbuckle's definition helpful:

> The process of liberation by which, under skilled guides, the person frees himself/ herself from constraints of a personal order (sin, pride, ignorance of Christ as the centre of life, ignorance of academic/pastoral skills necessary to be part of Christ's mission today); and a social or cultural order (undue cultural pressures, prejudices).[11]

Such community formation is a process in and through community. An aim of community formation is for character, values and skill development to all come together for a person through a lived experience of a Christian community's charism that helps to identify their vocation. Such formation requires a connection and initiation into the community's founding charism that questions and affirms a person's calling. Having tasted the community's charism a person can better discern their own vocation.

The initiation rites found in many traditional cultures may well be helpful frameworks for helping teams to initiate new workers. For example, Arnold van Gennep describes rites of passage in three stages: separation, liminal and aggregation rites.[12] In the Gospels we can also see the three stages in the relationship between Jesus and the first apostolic workers as they are called, face chaos and then find the paschal mystery. Teams that relocate to slums cannot assume their workers have intuitively grasped frameworks and practices that will support their vocation. This needs to be an intentional focus if long-term transformation is to occur.

3.0 Participate with Clarified Expectations

The Spirit can move in teams as they share gifts and inspiration. This dynamic however, has its best chance to empower new workers if there is a clear common ethos and initial boundaries. This helps determine whether or not the team can work together, though the ethos of an organisation is better seen in the practice of its teams than its brochures. Unfortunately, many gifted workers end up doing their own thing, rather than harnessing the collective resources and discipline of a team.

Teams can be destroyed overnight if unfulfilled expectations are left unnamed and unmet. Finding regular times to help clarify expectations and nurture a common ethos is essential. Pioneering mission in slums is typically pursued on ground that is constantly shifting, in a fragile neighbourhood ecosystem; consequently numerous course corrections are required. Teams need to be able to check whether they are working on the right issues at the right time. Judgments are rarely made with the luxury of having gathered all the relevant information. A team must often follow intuition or a previously unrealised connection to redirect collective energies into the most strategic and prophetic tasks.

One way to help apostolic teams do this is to find common commitments and a rhythm of life together. If it takes a community to reach a community, attention must especially be given to the rhythm of community and team life. Over the years our missional order has been able to be a collective witness that has amplified the joy of the gospel in ways one person could not. Left to ourselves we have found that even the most basic commitments to pray daily can be pushed aside for more pressing and urgent concerns. Therefore we can't take chances on our individual ability to keep commitments. United in the Spirit we have found that putting the most important features of community first in our weeks enables us to be faithful to our collective vocation.

UNOH's 'common rhythm of life', for example, aims to help us as a community to live sustainable, radical and focused lives. By marking out common times together for rest, communion and prayer as well as our ministry tasks, we can make space for that which helps sustain us in the Spirit. Life amidst urban poverty can be demanding and disorientating. We can be tossed around from crisis to crisis, from demand to demand, without making any lasting impact. This is especially true for our spiritual development which can quickly be overwhelmed. Conformation to a secular rather than a Spirit-filled mindset can easily occur if we do not intentionally keep sacred space to stop and be attentive to Jesus together and individually. This renewing of mind, Paul reminds us, is central to transformation (Romans 12:2).

There is major difference here between apostolic teams seeking to follow an incarnational approach and many other kinds of mission, development and church organisations. To join this kind of sodality that seeks an incarnational approach is an all-of-life vocation that has some specific markers about what is required and when. This includes expectations around how time is spent, as well as the expectation that new teams will be started so that a large team does not create barriers to bonding with neighbours.

Team time and rhythm expectations are important, but perhaps expectations around resources are just as crucial. What can teams expect to draw from others? Even before a team starts out, to take stock of what a team has access to can help teams understand their own power and know what resources to draw on in cases of emergency or conflict. These resources can include the Spirit's gifts, talents and personality types inside the team, but they also include resource people outside the team, training options, networks, money, office supplies or buildings. To identify what resources team members have helps them to connect with each other more easily because resources that have been named and recognised in security are more easily shared.

The issue of how a team is funded to serve in a slum does need careful consideration. What has been common in other settings is to fund, through institutions, salaried roles like minister, social worker, doctor or teacher for projects. This practice faces serious challenges in slums, where institutions are essentially temporary. As mentioned previously, slums are an especially serious challenge for child sponsorship agencies. In stable, rural areas the development of institutions like schools, clinics, churches and housing can multiply the capacity for child development. The better the institutions and staffing the more children can be helped. However, slum and squatter neighbourhoods are by nature temporary urban settlements, outside the protection of the law. This means children often move around a lot without warning. The temporary nature of institutions in slums also presents a challenge to developing long-term plans. Continuity and momentum, so crucial to change, are often undermined. If children are impossible to track and partner institutions have short lives, the confidence of both donors and agencies can quickly be undermined.

These kinds of challenges face Christian institutions in slums too. This is not least because there are often few local Christians to draw on. For example, there are only ten churches based among Bangkok's 1.5 million slum dwellers and all of these have attendances of fewer than forty people. Church of Christ in Thailand, the largest denominational council (which includes Baptists, Churches of Christ, Presbyterians and Methodists) seems to have no formal churches in Bangkok's slums. With two out of three slum dwellers (globally) living in places with few Christian residents, partnering with local Christians is not simple or often even possible for institutions.

What is the alternative to funding projects or institutions? In Jesus and his first apostolic teams we have a funding model that may well work to provide the kind of flexibility and reproducibility that most teams in slums will require. How was Jesus' team funded? Luke records very clearly the answer: Supporters or benefactors, in this case women, 'contributed from their own resources to support Jesus and his disciples' (Luke 8:1-3). Jesus could have chosen a range of options to raise his support. Why did he choose other people to resource his team? Jesus' ministry required a flexibility and adaptability that even his carpentry job could not afford him; therefore instead of continuing in that occupation he turned instead to people who believed in him to resource his ministry out of their wealth. In many ways Jesus' funding needs are not unlike those required to catalyse ministries in slums. Those who are inspired by the motif of joining, participating and following Jesus and who understand the metaphor of being all-together the body of Christ do well to take note of the way Jesus was supported. People-supporting-people (rather than projects or institutions) has real potential as a funding mechanism today, keeping support connections personal as well as adaptable and sustainable in slums.

In UNOH we have found that to have supporters who stand with us in solidarity gives a freedom. If workers can raise not only a small living allowance for themselves but also 'seeding funds', they have the flexibility to help instigate ministries and respond to needs quickly. This is something that institutionally-based responses have trouble doing. UNOH workers have found that those most likely to regularly support us are those who know us, trust us and believe in what we do. When these people become regular partners with us through prayer and finances it is a sacred gift for us, our supporters and the Kingdom of God. With the growth of travel, global banking, internet and other systems bringing people closer together, the potential for worker-support-funded responses becomes an option for more Christian slum workers. This is as true for international as well as national Christian workers in slums. Child sponsorship agencies, for example, could take a more incarnational approach if they did not tie funding to child sponsorship in slums, or even primarily to projects, but rather to Christian development workers. The right Christian people living in slums can then adapt, innovate and find ways to see transformation take place through Christ. This includes church planting and projects that can come out of relationships with neighbours. From a sponsor's point of view, this would require churches or individuals to sponsor adult Christian workers rather than a child. This is less paternalistic and is a more equal partnership, a leading direction in current development practice. Few countries—Australia included—see the need for foreigners to look after their children as a positive thing. It's just that slums force this issue. Partnering adults to adults, however has great potential.

4.0 Co-ordinate Teams and Workers

The identification of different cycles in team life is important for an incarnational approach to teams in slums. What teams need at one stage is not what they need at the next. Further, small 'relocator' teams (those from outside the neighbourhood) often don't know what to aim for at different seasons in their life cycle, let alone what new relocator-workers they need. Too often a new worker is sent to an already struggling team not prepared or able to take the worker on and the whole team suffers, unable to move beyond its own struggles.

The following story from Klong Toey illustrates some of the possible team dynamics of slum transformation with an enfleshed hope motif. The story of Jet Sip Rye and the way teams went about a neighbourhood transformation[13] helps to see how enfleshed hope and the Christian's role in supporting transformation can be difficult to discern when a whole slum neighbourhood is considered. Strategically we were inspired by the team theory proposed by Jon Haley, illustrated in chart 13 on the following page.[14] Teams are not just a few workers thrown at a problem at random; rather they need to be coordinated through different times and seasons in the life cycle of transformation. Haley argued that a few workers need to start in a host community to make contacts and set up opportunities for service. Then as more workers come they share faith and the life of discipleship together in cooperation with locals, and ultimately a 'critical mass' or momentum is reached. At that point, there needs to be deployment of workers so that local leaders can take transformation to another level. The less need there is for relocated workers, the deeper and broader will be the theological and organisational capacity to see real change happen.

Chart 13: Haley and Mission Team Theory

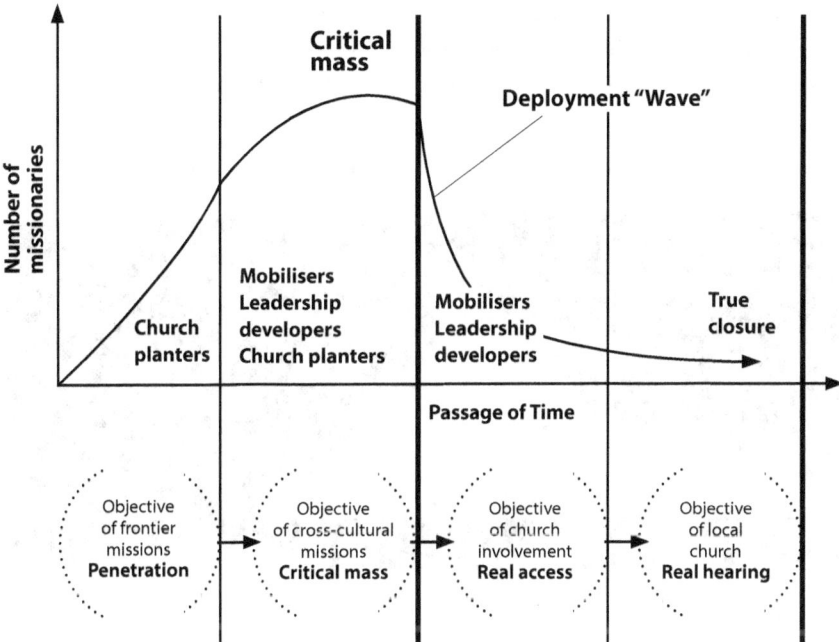

Source: Haley, 2007[15]

Anji and I relocated to live in Jet Sip Rye as the first couple in the role of frontier relocator-workers. After about eighteen months Rod Sheard joined us and then finally the MacCartney family. The real neighbourhood momentum and critical mass began almost as soon as all five of us were in the neighbourhood. This momentum was relational as well as strategic, with projects and church connections building up a strong head of steam. Rod moved out with neighbours Jim and Bu. Then, after six months, the MacCartney family moved to nearby Lock 6 and the Rom Gow, leaving only our family from UNOH in Jet Sip Rye again for another four years. These redeployments of UNOH workers meant that the local Ta Rua church and the local community projects as well as discipleship could grow as indigenously as possible. The staggered deployment of relocator workers moving in, the building of momentum with local neighbours and the redeployment of relocator workers to other neighbourhoods was crucial to seeing transformation take place. Had only one couple been there the much needed momentum, or 'critical mass' as Haley describes it, would have been difficult to establish because we alone couldn't relate to the diverse peoples and networks in the neighbourhood. The MacCartney family, for example, were able to build connections with people at one end of the street who had been shy in relating to us because we were friendly with Jim's extended family, with whom they were feuding at the time. Had all five UNOH workers been there together for the whole eight years the temptation to connect primarily with fellow Australians due to culture shock, rather than bonding with neighbours, would have been very real. Even if a critical mass for local development had started to develop, the room for local leadership to stretch its wings and grow would have been limited.

Chart 14 below has been used in various ways in UNOH's ministry strategy over the years.

Chart 14: UNOH strategic priorities: Worker deployment for 'critical mass'

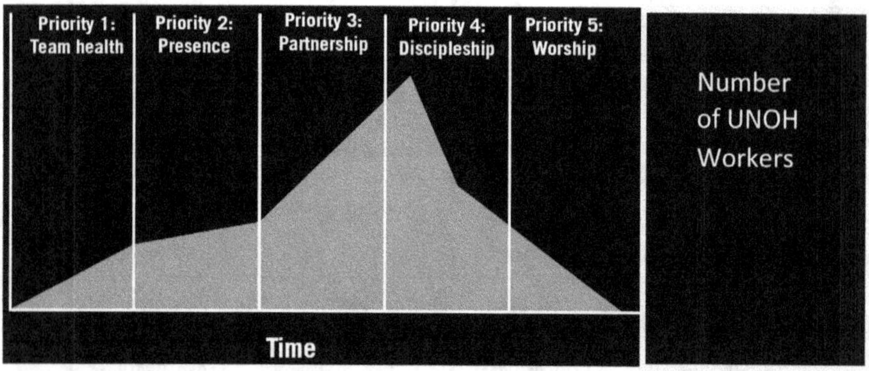

[Chart showing five priority phases over time with Number of UNOH Workers on vertical axis — Priority 1: Team health, Priority 2: Presence, Priority 3: Partnership, Priority 4: Discipleship, Priority 5: Worship. The curve rises from Priority 1, peaks at Priority 3/4, and declines through Priority 5.]

Source: Barker, 2004[16]

In the 70 Rye example, the team started with just Anji and me. Over time, as more partnerships developed, we started to see real discipleship take place and needed more workers. The final stage has been the beginnings of more indigenous forms of discipleship, leadership and worship expressions. Advocacy has also become a key role that supports neighbourhood transformation, and our ongoing contact with our friends in 70 Rye has continued.

That a team, not just individuals, worked together to find neighbourhood momentum by the Spirit was important. The discipline of joining the Creator, following Christ and being empowered by the Spirit would not have had the impact it did had only Anji and I just done our own work.

What this case study illustrates is what is possible for teams to do together in neighbourhoods, and the diverse roles workers can play as they share their gifts. The transformation was not final in either of the two stories, as vulnerabilities and unfinished work remain, but the stories nevertheless illustrate the potential for an incarnational approach to slum transformation. Neither were we always conscious of this framework, but in many ways, intuitively by trial and error, we found our way with God together, and were able to overcome some of the barriers we have considered intrinsic to slum neighbourhoods. What we can take from these case studies is not to make them the only way of doing incarnational mission, but to use them to help us see what can happen when workers are inspired and informed by the work of the incarnating God. What is hoped is that this kind of approach can become more focused and used in more diverse ways in Christian responses to slum and squatter neighbourhoods.

These very practical issues will continue to be taken up in the last few chapters. Having considered how the enfleshed hope motif can inform how teams based in slums can work, we will explore how such teams can be relationally present, and what holistic strategies they can employ. If Christianity is to respond creatively to the needs of a new, urban world, particularly amongst the slums of that world, the role of small, adaptive and innovative teams should not be ignored.

We must insist that there is not one team approach that is *the* model or method for incarnational slum transformation because the diversity within slums and the body of Christ makes this impossible. The Incarnating God, however, can guide the required team responses.

Chapter Twelve

An Incarnational Approach to Local and Relational 'Place-Sharing'

An incarnational approach requires presence. This willingness to be relationally and locally available for people—even above program agendas—can be understood as a special Christian contribution to the transformation process in slums. The almost mystical way that Christians can encounter people 'through Jesus' in sacred 'place-sharing' moments is unlike secular development practice. An incarnational approach can help inform both relationships and localities that can be shared together.

Bonhoeffer argued that 'place-sharing' is about relationships 'in and through Christ'.[1] It can be how Christians share their lives with others within a costly relational presence. When an entire slum neighbourhood cries out for action and resolution such 'place-sharing' can be especially important for Christians in slums. Such place-sharing can be informed by an incarnational approach. Seeking to join with the Creator and follow the risen Jesus in the power of the Spirit in slum communities is a desirable goal, but how this can happen in relationships and in whole neighbourhoods needs to be considered.

Place-sharing requires time, focused people and resources in ways that are not often valued in results-orientated organisations, including Christian ones. It is short sighted to neglect place-sharing, however, for local trust and local knowledge are crucial elements in the process of transformation. Fast-paced evangelistic events or relief projects are often experienced like continual waves that crash onto slums with little time for building authentic relationships of trust. In Klong Toey it is not uncommon to see well-meaning church teams drive into our neighborhoods and stand on the corners of our streets handing out gospel tracts, sometimes preaching via loud public address systems at passers-by, only to drive back out to their homes in the suburbs a few hours later. Most of these visitors are not seen again. If they do return it's often months later. Similar phenomena can be seen in the giving out of food and milk powder to neighbours. What message do these quick fire and often ineffective responses give to neighbours about what Christians have to offer their slum neighbourhoods? As opposed to an incarnational theology of slum engagement, such practice assumes that God is absent, that Christians 'bring in' the gospel in a vacuum and that visitor-Christians can be in total control of what happens and when in slums. To vulnerably listen, look and share life long enough to be able to see where God is already at work or what resources the community already has and how Christians can best contribute, is a crucial, but often neglected, approach. The much needed practical ministry of place-sharing, then, is valued and highlighted here—on the basis of an incarnational theology of relational mission—in at least three ways. The three ways can then be applied in a broader sense to an incarnational theology of place.

1.0 Participating in Relationships 'Through' the Spirit of Jesus

The Spirit is ready to empower Christians and use them as channels of hope with the people they know personally. When Christians step out and share their lives with others in Jesus' name, especially 'with the least of these' (Matthew 25:31ff), the Spirit is present to see 'freedom' occur (2 Corinthians 3:17).

For Christians in slum neighbourhoods relationships as shared life between neighbours can be complex, however. There are often power, trust and credibility dynamics to overcome. Without relational integrity Christians can simply use the 'bait of friendship' to hook vulnerable people for their own agendas. These agendas can include making churches bigger, organisations stronger or donors happier. In UNOH we often need to reassure neighbours that, 'The price of our friendship is not your soul'. This says we care about our neighbours as neighbours and not just as a means for us to gain a 'decision for Christ' or whatever else our friendship currency can gain.

Integral relationships with neighbours can allow room for us to demonstrate the costly love of God and also for us to provide real opportunities for neighbours to encounter and follow Jesus. This is pleasing to God, no matter what our neighbours' responses might be. This approach helps ensure the relationships are a safe and authentic place for both parties to share their lives together. Desired outcomes might be for neighbours to know Jesus, for projects to be effective or for churches to be planted, but even if our friends and neighbours don't end up involved in such activities, God is still pleased. As the Gospels make clear, any love given in and through Jesus will not go unrewarded eternally (Matthew 6:4, 10:42, 25:31ff), and so our friendships continue 'expecting nothing in return' (Luke 6:35).

The apostle Paul is unswerving in his assertion that there can be a deep joy found in such sacrificial service when it is viewed through the lens of the cross of Jesus. Paul uses *chairo* or similar ('rejoice' or 'joy') fifteen times in his short, four chapter letter to the Philippians. Even in places like slums, joy is possible if such a cross-formed mindset can be found because it provides meaning to the sacrifice and service required for transformation. To follow Jesus as a pattern is not senseless oppression or slavery, but following the example of the crucified God as others like Paul have done, doing whatever it takes to see the Kingdom come on earth as in heaven. Indeed, as Eldin Villafañe argues, a Christ-formed mindset and practice in the world can be like a parable and sign that both references the cross and also points to it:

> Our 'parabolic actions' are witnesses to the truth before a world that would read our costly service, our costly discipleship, and, with the help of God, understand 'that (we) are a letter of Christ... written not with ink but with the Spirit of the living God' (2 Corinthians 3:3).[2]

This motif of enfleshing hope finds an important focus in the following of the crucified and risen Jesus as a pattern for place-sharing. Building on John de Gruchy's work, which identified three of Bonhoeffer's questions which 'dominated his theological reflections',[3] Andrew Root lines up Langmead's definition as shown in table 11 below.

Table 11: A comparison of Langmead and Bonhoeffer

Langmead's threefold understanding of incarnational mission		Three questions of Bonhoeffer's theology
1. Jesus as a pattern for mission		1. Who is Jesus Christ?
2. Participation in the presence of Jesus		2. Where is Jesus Christ?
3. Joining God's mission of enfleshment		3. What shall we do? (ethics)

Source: Andrew Root, Revisiting Relational Youth Ministry, 2007[4]

Root and Bonhoeffer do not take up the theme of 'joining' in an eschatological sense as we have done. For Root, 'joining' concerns the more practical and ethical issues which he and we will discuss here as place-sharing. The 'who' and 'where' of the crucified and risen Jesus can help inform the following of and participation with the risen Jesus in slums, with the participation and empowerment of disciples of Jesus through the Holy Spirit an important key to place-sharing.

Friendship alone is not enough to see lasting change take place. No-one can be a good enough friend to bring about the kind of transformation that slums require. Bonhoeffer's idea of relational place-sharing 'through Christ', then, has much to offer here. This theme was taken up by Andrew Root in his critique of youth ministries that use relationships as a tool for evangelism. He summarises many Christian mission approaches to relationships, including in slums, when he says: 'Relationships have been used for cultural leverage (getting adolescents to believe or obey) rather than as the concrete location of God's action in the world'.[5] In contrast, Root argues, it is place-sharing—relating with neighbours as friends 'through Jesus'—that can give real opportunities to find and share life together. Though such relationships can be fragile and costly they have great long-term potential for transformation. A key theme in Bonhoeffer's theology is picked up by Root who argues that to 'live as a disciple of the incarnate' One is to be in relationships, 'empowered by the humanity of God' that 'demands action that is responsible for the very humanity of the other. Therefore, to be in relationship is to take full responsibility for the other, standing in his or her place, becoming his or her advocate'.[6] For Root, this kind of relationship is neither enmeshed co-dependence nor a distanced professional stance, but a kind of deep solidarity of lives that can only be found through Jesus Christ. This includes help to empower people to freely make their own decisions in life, including whether or not to choose faith.

A freedom to choose Christian faith in relationship is especially important in cultures where face-saving and obligation are strongly valued. A meeker approach that respects relationships in culture is required. Few have articulated this approach in the Thai culture better than the husband-and-wife team Nantachai and Ubolwan Mejudhon. Both did their PhD theses at Asbury Theological Seminary in Kentucky on the theme of meekness and they now serve in north Bangkok, making frequent ministry trips to north-east Thailand. Ubolwan has observed that meekness is a dominant trait in Thai culture unlike in much of Western Christianity, but similar to Christ:

> The spreading of the gospel suffers when Christians, Christianity and churches are perceived by the Thai as violating the Thai way of meekness in their presentation of the gospel, discipling, and relationships. Such evangelising violates self-identity, grateful relationships, smooth interpersonal relationships, and flexibility and adaptation in Thai culture. Thai converts cannot fit in with their social networks and kinsmen because of their aggressive ways of witnessing influenced by Western methods rooted in a different culture context.[7]

In Klong Toey, for example, it would not be difficult after an event like a camp to go around and personally invite neighbours to become Christians. Only the most anti-social would not feel obligated to say 'Yes' to us after the good time they had had. Of course, there would be a cost to this immediate 'evangelistic result'. Their lack of understanding of what they were committing to, their later lack of respect toward us and our aggressiveness and, not least, their feeling of being set up to be exploited would be hard to overcome in the longer term. The gain of a 'convert' may well be seen by some as worth this cost, but it's hardly good news to the poor received with gladness. Nor can it be helpful long-term. This dynamic can sometimes be overcome and understood when foreigners are involved, but as Ubolwan made clear, it is very difficult for Thais to use the same methods without alienating friends and family.

The attempt to become a valued part of an extended family and friendship network in our host neighbourhoods has been a most difficult challenge, but it has also enabled some of our most meaningful experiences in life. The Spirit can draw people together and a kind of costly sacredness in relationships can result. Some neighbours have indeed come to accept the invitation to follow Jesus, and they have found all kinds of ways to respond to poverty in their neighbourhoods. They freely chose this though, with the knowledge that their relationship with us was secure in its own right. This process respects what the Spirit can do in the midst of relationships over time, and can help address many of the pressures, inequalities and guilty feelings Christians feel in regard to sharing faith in vulnerable relationships.

2.0 Joining with Humility what the Creator-God is Already Doing in Slum Neighbourhood Cultures

The Creator God incarnates and is present in local cultures. This should be cause for much humility for Christians, especially for those who cross cultures to contribute in the transformation process. Along with John 1:14, perhaps the most often-quoted Bible passage supporting an incarnational approach is Philippians 2:1-11. Both texts have as a theme the humility of Christ, a theme that can inspire and inform the way we go about engaging host cultures in slum neighbourhoods. As we have seen this theme is especially taken up by those with anthropological concerns and is also an important expression of how the Redeemer incarnates. The enfleshed hope theological motif differs from what is often put forth anthropologically in the following way: the former maintains that we can't actually be incarnated in the same way that Jesus was and is. For example, no matter how hard I may try I can't actually be a Thai in Klong Toey in the way that Jesus was a Jew in Galilee. The practical action that can be taken in regard to Christ's humility in a neighbourhood culture can take three stances.

First, Christian slum workers can take a stance of humility like Jesus ('following Jesus' pattern') in regard to local cultures. The word for 'humility' used by Paul in the Epistle to the Philippians was a word made up by the early church—*tapeinoo*—to describe the humility which Christ possessed and which should characterise those who seek to do God's will too.[8] It is a costly humility, to do what is right in relationships 'even unto death'. This theme is taken up by Duane Elmer, who tells a parable about a 'kind monkey' who 'saved' a struggling fish. The monkey jumped into the water, swam against the current and pulled the fish up and out of the water to the 'safety' of land. This saving attempt eventually killed the fish. He argues that similar arrogance can be seen in Christians in cross-cultural settings. There are practical ways, though, that such arrogance in regard to other cultures can be combated. These can be summarised as:

Serving: You can't serve someone you do not understand; at best you will serve like the monkey.

Understanding: You cannot understand others until you have learned about, from and with them.

Learning: You can't learn important information from someone until there is trust in the relationship.

Trust: To build trust others must know that you accept and value them as people.

Acceptance: Before you can communicate acceptance, people must experience your openness—your ability to welcome them into your presence.

Openness: Openness with people different from yourself requires that you are willing to step out of your comfort zone to initiate and sustain relationships in a world of cultural differences.[9]

Without the openness that humility requires, other more obvious responses, including appropriate forms of serving, are not possible. Place-sharing—living among a slum neighborhood and sharing life with neighbours—helps to lay a foundation of openness that can build to higher levels of trust and engagement.

Second, from this humility, Christian slum workers can affirm where God is at work in a culture ('joining the Creator'). The Creator God incarnates and is always present, including within the development of local cultures in slums. This stance opens the way for workers to learn, serve and relate with longer term transformation in mind. It would be foolish to ignore the value of meekness in Thai culture, for example. This is not only because ignoring the value of meekness can alienate non-Christians, but also because it misses an opportunity to draw Thai neighbours to the value God places on meekness: 'Blessed are the meek, for they shall inherit the earth' (Matthew 5:2). Meekness is not an ideal which is always upheld in Thai culture, especially in Thai slums, but God has nevertheless made it an important value within Thai culture. So to highlight and go with the grain of this aspect of Thai culture helps build trust and confidence. If Christian workers in slums work againstthe grain of meekness, making big promises as 'outsiders' that never come through, for example, real barriers are created. Place-sharing, sharing life deeply with neighbours within affirming aspects of local culture, can help overcome and undermine these barriers of arrogance.

Third, an approach of humility focuses on the power of the incarnated Spirit to help transform from within cultures ('participating with the empowering of the Spirit'). Humility is a gift that helps us to keep unity of the Spirit with others (Ephesians 4:1-

3). The incarnated Spirit is beyond our own culture and has the power to transform evils from all cultures, including those in slums. Christian workers need to actively participate with the Spirit in that process. Cross-cultural Christian workers can easily become ethnocentric, experienced locally as judges or enforcers of their own values onto the host culture. In humility, however, Christians can give up loyalties to their own cultural values and be empowered to participate in addressing all cultural evils through the Spirit. As ones who are accepted and trusted in a change process, new ways to serve and seek transformation can be found together. There is power and authority for transformation through the Spirit, centred in Christ, that is beyond the power and authority of all cultures. This power, however, can only be accessed in humility, not in triumphalism or loyalty to any one culture.

This kind of humility is not intuitive. Nor is it a virtue easily exhibited under pressure. This is especially the case in the often chaotic and confusing life of a slum neighbourhood. Indeed, the opposites of humility and meekness—arrogance, pride and a closed attitude—can easily become our default position. N. T. Wright contends that with constant practice a habit or virtue can be developed as a characteristic response—that even humility can become a natural response under pressure. These virtues need to be enacted within culture and relationships, but they come from a future hope:

> We urgently need to recapture the New Testament's vision of a genuinely 'good' human life as a life of character formed by *God's promised future*, as a life with that future-shaped character *lived within the ongoing story of God's people*, and, with that, a freshly worked notion of virtue... you don't get that character just by trying. You get it by following Jesus.[10]

To follow, join and participate in the incarnated God's humility, then, is different to simply using Jesus of Nazareth as a method or model to copy. The power to follow comes by way of joining and participating with what Jesus has initiated in his resurrection. Wright says of Jesus:

> He doesn't go about saying, 'This is how it's done; copy me'. He says, 'God's Kingdom is coming; take up your cross and follow me'. We do encounter Jesus' humility and other virtues. But these are not 'examples of how to do it'. They are indications that a new way of being human has been launched upon the world.[11]

This is a crucial Christian virtue to rediscover if missionaries are to shed their colonialist image and attitudes in slums. The humility of Christ is not something to simply work up, but a way in which Christian workers can follow, join and participate with God until it becomes second nature. Christians can offer more than program delivery; they can become people living as Christ intends with neighbours.

3.0 Following Jesus in Empowered Local Leadership

Following the risen Christ through the Spirit can empower people to find new and creative responses to urban poverty. Residents in slums especially need to find the empowerment to lead these responses. For example, almost every slum neighborhood will already have some initiatives worth supporting. A first priority, even with a pioneering team, should be to support those projects and their leaders for Christ is found in them. This does not mean that these leaders 'are' Christ, but rather that Christ can be found in them through relationships. The shared relationships with these local leaders need to have integrity as we have discussed, but in practical terms they can help workers to find worthy partnerships in ways that are almost impossible to find otherwise. Very few community groups refuse residents willing to volunteer their time and effort to their group's cause. This can be the case for new Christian residents in slums, too. If and when new projects are required, Christian workers can then start them out of a felt need seen by those in existing partnership projects rather than as threatening 'competition' from an outside group.

Even before an intentional team relocates to a slum it is possible for the team to pray about and visit the focus neighbourhood, to start to form relationships within it, and then to seek permission and invitation (in formal and informal ways) to serve. To follow protocols and seek permission from existing leadership can make the difference as to whether neighbourhoods will accept the new workers or not. If Christ is present in the leaders of these places, then there is a real opportunity to follow him.

Slums can be tightly networked, delicately balanced, fragile ecosystems. Those Christian workers who can help sustain this living tissue while nudging it toward Kingdom transformation can be an invaluable resource to its very fabric. Bob Linthicum has identified at least four kinds of local leadership that we can engage with.[12] These can be summarised as follows.

> *Power brokers.* The politicians, those who provide representation for the community to those outside the community. To identify these leaders we can ask community members, 'If you had a problem with an organisation outside the community, whose advice and help would you seek to confront them?'.
>
> *Flak catchers.* The gossips, those who provide information around the networks of the community. To identify these leaders we can ask community members, 'If you wanted to find out what is going on around here, who would know?'.
>
> *Gate keepers.* The protectors, those who decide who is 'in' and 'out' of the community. To identify these leaders we can ask community members, 'When a new person joined this community, who helped you to decide whether they were okay or not?'.

Pastoral carers. The nurturers, those who provide the Tender-Loving-Care for the community. To identify these leaders we can ask community members, 'If you had an emergency at one a.m., who would you call for help?'.

These leadership roles can be played by one or more than one person. Sometimes they are formal positions, but often they are not. Christian workers may not get the formal blessing of each of the four local leaders. Yet it is a great advantage if a team can work with the grain of the community leadership rather than against it.

In contrast to rural villages, slum neighbourhoods can be temporary in every way, including in leadership. This can be a challenge because issues like power imbalances, corruption, violence and vested interests can keep a neighbourhood changing, but not always towards being a healthier place in which to live.

4.0 Taking Seriously an Incarnational Theology of Place

Slum and squatter neighbourhoods are a created place. As such, God is present and each local place has a sacredness about it that requires nurture and attention, especially by local Christians. A call to radical 'localness', therefore, should be a part of an incarnational approach if slum transformation is to occur.

This call to the local is not just for slums, as the global factors that are affecting slums are affecting other parts of the world, too. Sociologist Robert Putnam has explored the loss of community and the decline in civil engagement and social capital in America. He identifies four key factors contributing to the decline: pressures on time and money; suburbanisation, commuting and sprawl; electronic entertainment; and generational changes.[13] These factors disproportionately affect poor, urban neighbourhoods, but are a warning to all:

> While... the erosion of social capital and community engagement has affected Grosse Point [a wealthy lake-side area in Detroit] in essentially the same degree as inner-city Detroit, the impact of that development has so far been greater in the inner city, which lacks the cushioning of other forms of capital. The shooting sprees that affected schools in suburban and rural communities as the twentieth century ended are a reminder that as breakdown of community continues in more privileged settings, affluence and education are insufficient to prevent collective tragedy.[14]

These forces of globalised culture affect all people and the local Christian church is no exception. To survive, most churches have needed to become more regional than local. In a fascinating article, Matt Cleaver mused that while the idea of vocation in churches has moved beyond the Christian professional and includes living out faith in all of life, the strength of the newly-accepted model is often lost because of the lack of local connection.[15] As a response to these very real contemporary human challenges, recent times have seen the development of a theology of local places.

Walter Brueggemann is one contributor to the discussion, drawing a distinction between pursuing space and a sense of place. 'Space' is 'empty', 'out there', ready to be 'filled', but 'place' has 'historic meaning', where 'identity', 'vocation' and 'destiny' are envisioned. Place is where:

> Vows have been exchanged, promises have been made, and demands have been issued. Place is indeed a protest against the unpromising pursuit of space. It is a declaration that our humanness cannot be found in escape, detachment, absence of commitment, and undefined freedom.[16]

To view slum and squatter neighbourhood transformation not in terms of 'space' but 'place' has much to offer. It builds on the relating, the humility, the learning and the supporting of previous initiatives, as discussed above, but goes further. Seeing neighbourhoods in their entirety—as sacred places, worth both preserving and improving—can change the way Christians view slums. Slums as the location of relationships need to find a humanness and divinity if transformation is to occur. A number of benefits can accrue from a focus on neighbourhoods as sacred places for Christians to share.

First, the most ancient forms of Christian faith knew well the importance of place for discipleship and mission. John Inge's important work, *A Christian Theology of Place*, picks up this theme as it relates not only to pilgrimages to 'sacred sites', but also attention to neighbourhoods as sacred places which offer 'great nourishment and sustenance'.[17] Jonathan Wilson-Hartgrove argues that 'Our spiritual growth depends on human beings rooting ourselves in a place on earth with other creatures'.[18] He notes that the early church was 'together in one place' as they shared to such a degree that 'no-one was in need' (Acts 2 and 4). This may well have been an unusual moment in Christian history. Thoughts of Christ's imminent return could have been a factor influencing their generosity. The point, however, is not lost. When Christians connect with the incarnating God in real local places together, radical sharing and transformation is possible. Wilson-Hartgrove also cites Anthony, an early church father, who simply said: 'In whatever place you find yourself, do not easily leave it'.[19] Another advised similarly, 'If a trial comes upon you in the place where you live, do not leave that place when the trial comes. Wherever you go, you will find that what you are running from is ahead of you'.[20] We cannot run away from God or from our own selves. Christians can only find themselves in Christ with others when they stop and stay long enough to share their lives.

Second, a focus on local slum neighbourhoods as shared place can also have benefits in church growth terms. This view has been taken up in some recent church growth literature. For example, in reflecting on the early disciples' sense of community, 'that they were in one place' (Acts 2:1), Randy Frazee writes,

> The re-discovery of neighbourhood is the essential application to discovering a common place. It is really the only option. Why? Because it's the only way we can attain the characteristics that produce authentic community, such as spontaneity, availability and frequency.[21]

The early church did not just meet as an occasional regional network of individuals. Rather, it was a daily, all-of-life experience, not possible without the spontaneity, availability and frequency that living near each other provided. Neighbourhood locations may not be the 'only option' as Frazee contends, but they may well be the best possible focus for slum transformations and churches based within them.

Third, Christian presence rooted in a place has very practical, sociological benefits and possibilities too. Robert Putman notes, for example, that positive, stable families who live in poor neighbourhoods can influence whole neighbourhoods. He writes, for example, that:

> Just as neighbourhoods can affect families, so can families affect neighbourhoods. In economists' terms, family social capital has 'positive externalities', spilling out of the home and into the streets... If we think of youthful troublemaking as a communicable disease—a sort of behavioural chicken pox that spreads through high schools and friendship groups—then stable families provide the vaccines that reduce the number of contagious kids capable of infecting others.[22]

When Christians consider what they have to offer in response to urban slum and squatter neighbourhoods, relocation to be present in a particular local place over time should be considered as an option with great potential for bringing about transformation. This is the case not least in slums, which often have little cushioning for the lack of social capital they typically experience. More will be said about building social capital in the next chapter, but here it's enough to say that a real living presence in a place with little social capital can help to bring about transformation.

Fourth, to focus on slum neighbourhoods as place rather than space can also have potential positive economic and environmental impacts. This is a theme taken up, for example, in Wendell Berry's call for self-sufficient neighbourhoods.[23] If communities can grow their own food and work toward economic independence they can then be free to be interdependent with other neighbourhoods, thus reducing the economic and environmental costs of transporting food and other goods. Berry's work often has rural places in mind, but community gardens based on roofs and local cooperatives are just as possible in slums as in rural lands. A fundamental shift from consumer to citizen does need to take place, however, as McKnight and Block make clear.[24] Christians can have particular hope that such shifts toward neighbourhood self-sufficiency are possible if it is understood that the Creator is present, the Spirit can empower, and Jesus can be followed.

How can the incarnational call to place work out in practice? When as UNOH workers we took stock of our first ten years as a movement, we saw that our ideals, values and passions best lent themselves to local neighbourhoods. We would drive around desperately trying to generate a community to empower and disciple, but this quickly wore us out. Taking neighbourhoods seriously helped us to focus our vocation and life together in ways that were sustainable and helped us to go deeper with people.

How our neighbourhoods could become like 'villages centred on Christ' required some initial definitional work, however. First, we defined a neighbourhood as a common area that neighbours can walk around. Since the poor often do not have their own vehicles or need to use them sparsely, it was crucial that we define neighbourhood by the following test: could a neighbour walk to each neighbour's house easily? By this definition the Kelvin Grove neighbourhood in Springvale, Melbourne, was really one whole neighbourhood block. In Bangkok our first neighbourhood focus was really Jet Sip Rye, rather than the whole of Klong Toey.

Second, there were a number of indicators we began to notice when our localities began to become like villages centred on Christ. These included that our neighbours were available to:

Celebrate together: times of birthday parties, weddings and so on;

Commiserate together: times of loss, death and grief;

Have common meals, including Communion, together: times of fellowship around a meal;

Resolve conflict together: times of clarity and learning to live together;

Be there in times of change together: times of getting to know new neighbours and passage of life changes;

Be there in times of crisis together: times of being out of control and banding together;

Share common goods together: time of sharing what we have with others who don't have;

Share common prayers together: time to pray for people as a normal part of life;

Share a common identity from living in a common place together: time to see each neighbour as part of the same village;

Affirm community contributions: times to let leaders lead in their own areas of responsibility and giftedness and celebrate these contributions.[25]

All of these are events that can happen at any time in a neighbourhood. Most can't be scheduled in a busy timetable. Andrews explains the difference between *chronos* time and *kairos* time in community building in a way that can relate especially to slum life. *Chronos* is planned and scheduled time, but we can easily miss, 'the *kairos*, "the moments", when people are more open than closed and we have the opportunities to develop significant relationships with one another'.[26] He warns that 'these *kairos* moments often pass as quickly as they come' and need to be grasped 'otherwise we risk losing the opportunities they present forever'.[27] To seek to be attentive, available and present in neighbourhoods for such sacred place-sharing moments and to support them prayerfully and physically is crucial in the transformation process.

Discerning Jesus through costly relationships of love, mercy and justice with neighbours can sow the seeds for positive future contributions. Such discernment cannot happen without local knowledge, presence, relationships and even permission to join the neighbourhood. To value neighbours and place before projects gives workers a real opportunity to see transformation happen through Jesus and not just through new resources or technology. There can and should be strategic projects and partnerships that Christian workers can join or instigate, and we will discuss these next. Yet without the right team approach and local connections, such projects and partnerships can ride roughshod over what Jesus is already doing. It is too easy to focus on the real deficits and needs in neighbourhoods and fail to take the time to see what God is already doing, to see God's invitation to join, participate and follow the risen Jesus into the transformation process.

Chapter Thirteen

An Incarnational Approach to Urban Poverty Alleviation

How can poverty alleviation strategies in slums be both effective and distinctly Christian? We have argued that a motif of enfleshing hope is not one special strategy, model or methodology but that it should inform these responses. The last two chapters have outlined how intentional teams and local place-sharing need to take priority over the starting of projects or programs if a sense of the incarnational is to have a real opportunity to be experienced. Partnerships and projects should not be neglected, however, as strategies can help see transformation take place through Christ in slums. To join and instigate strategies can help provide focus and momentum in the transformation process. We outline in this chapter various urban poverty alleviation strategies that can be informed and inspired by joining, participating and following the risen Jesus in an incarnational approach.

There have been numerous schemes to describe different kinds of Christian strategic responses to poverty alleviation in recent times. Some writers like Dave Andrews[1] and Frances O'Gorman[2] work from a table of different responses and analogies, outlining one as the most effectual and transformative. Others like Bryant Myers trace a chronological time line of how understandings of development and poverty alleviation have developed over the last fifty years, with the latest response being the most effectual and transformative.[3] Each of these schemes has real value in comparing and contrasting various possible Christian responses to poverty in general and can be applied to slum and squatter neighbourhoods. These strategies and understandings will be drawn upon in this chapter.

What follows is a brief critical survey of a spectrum of six possible strategies in response to poverty in slum and squatter neighbourhoods. How can an incarnational approach make these strategies more transformative than they would be if they were not informed by the enfleshing hope motif? I have tried not to negatively caricature these responses, by setting up 'straw people' to knock down later. Rather, each response is argued to have biblical (and especially Christ-authorised) legitimacy, inspiring historical precedents and offering the potential to help alleviate urban poverty today. As in all strategies, however, there are both strengths and limitations which need to be especially considered in relation to the often vulnerable contexts of slum and squatter neighbourhoods.

I have plotted the six responses on chart 15 below, with the vertical axis representing the personal dimension and the horizontal axis the political dimension. Those responses nearest the top place a stronger emphasis on individual transformation. Those responses closer to the right hand side place a stronger emphasis on collective and social transformation. This does not suggest that the personal and political are opposites, nor does one axis always have priority over the other; all Christian strategic responses to urban poverty have both personal and political dimensions. Even if, for example, a response places very little emphasis on the political dimension in comparison to the emphasis it places on the personal, it can still be recognised as having both emphases on the chart. This diagram, then, is simply a visual way to plot the possible Christian strategic responses to poverty in slums with two dimensions so they can be analysed in relation to an incarnational approach to slum and squatter neighbourhoods.

Chart 15: Urban poverty alleviation strategies that can be informed and inspired by an incarnational motif

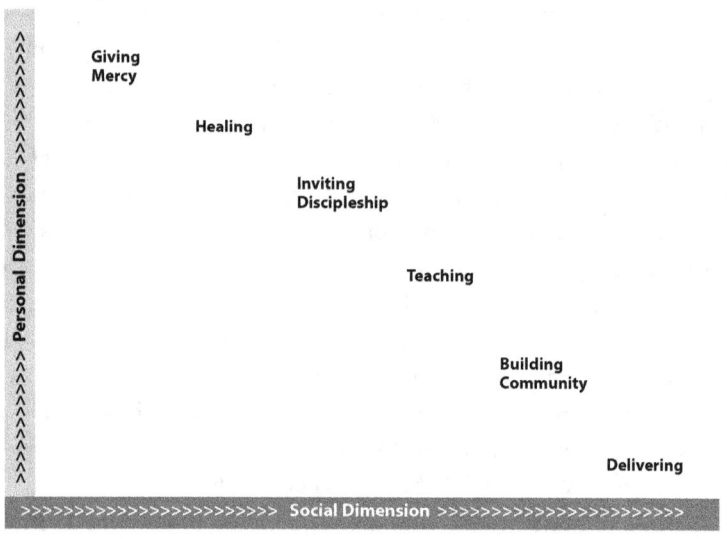

What an incarnational approach can do is enable Christian urban poverty alleviation strategies to be both more personal and more political. To intentionally join the incarnating Creator, follow the incarnating Redeemer and participate for empowerment with the incarnating Spirit can help inspire and inform strategies which would sit in the top right hand corner of chart 16. The *shalom* of God—where relationships between people, place and God are peaceful—can be experienced in seeking such effective and distinctly Christian responses.

There are limitations to what such a diagram can show. It can be difficult to know, for example, where one strategy starts and where another begins. Strategies defined in different ways could be plotted in more than one place. Also, different contexts can quickly move a response around on the grid so that what started as a response with a very strong focus on personal transformation can quickly become a political one. These issues will be discussed as the survey unfolds in relation to the incarnational motif. What is important to note here is that we can start with a strategic response and place it on the chart according to the contemporary ways in which it is used in slums. Incarnational issues and limitations can then be addressed as each of the six responses are explored from left to right of chart 15.

1.0 Incarnational Relief—Giving Mercy

To give mercy is to provide direct relief from misery for people who cannot do it for themselves. It is motivated by a deep sense that a person is suffering needlessly and that direct, practical assistance can help alleviate this. This response of mercy has a rich biblical and Christian tradition. The Hebrew word *hesed* (translated 'mercy' or 'loving kindness') is used over two hundred and forty times in the Hebrew Bible. God's *hesed* is described as being intrinsic to Yahweh's very character and nature (Psalm 116:5). Moved with *hesed*, the Lord helps those who cannot help themselves; examples of this include God's motivation in instigating covenant with Israel, and God's actions to free the Israelites from slavery (Exodus 34:6; Deuteronomy 4:31). Thus, Proverbs 14:31 says, 'He who oppresses the poor reproaches his maker, but he who honours him has mercy on the needy'. *Hesed* is one of the most important terms for Old Testament ethics, drawing on themes of compassion, loving kindness and grace to those in need. As Brueggemann explains, *hesed* is 'rooted in YHWH's own character, reaches beyond the contained community of faith or of ethnicity to those outside that community who, by their very existence, warrant neighborly solidarity'.[4] This includes those vulnerable ones who are refugees (Leviticus 19:34), and widows and orphans (Psalm 68:5).

Jesus' mission can be understood as a mission of mercy, promised by the God of mercy. As John the Baptist's father Zechariah put it, speaking of God's sending of Jesus, 'Thus he has shown the mercy promised to our ancestors, and has remembered his holy covenant' (Luke 1:72). Jesus is a fulfilment of this promise and draws on the ethics of hesed, but goes further than his contemporaries. As the Gospels record, he spent a considerable amount of his ministry 'showing mercy' himself. He touched lepers, fed the hungry masses and met direct needs, motivated by a deep compassion that at times led him to weep over the city (Luke 19:41).

To give mercy was also a core theme and commandment of Jesus' teachings. In the beatitudes, for example, those who are blessed by God are those who show mercy, and they are promised mercy (Matthew 5:7). This is based on the premise that God is merciful and so his children should express the same response to those in need (Matthew 5:7; James 1:27). The famous parable of the Good Samaritan explains that those who are not moved with compassion to show mercy toward a neighbour in need fail to do the will of God (Luke 10:25-37). Lack of mercy to those who are hungry, thirsty, homeless or in jail is an act that, in Jesus' view, has eternal repercussions (Matthew 25:31-46). Mercy, therefore, is not an optional response for Jesus' followers.

The modern poverty alleviation strategy of relief picks up the biblical theme of mercy. World Vision, for example, defines relief as 'the urgent provision of resources to reduce suffering resulting from a natural or man-made disaster… it is by its very nature, immediate, temporary, and prolonged only when self reliance is impossible'.[5] Transformation here is understood as addressing the powerlessness of a person to relieve their own suffering by the means of immediate and direct action. The response of mercy, then, is provided by someone who has the compassion and the power to do something about the suffering of another, and who takes the time to help alleviate and reduce that suffering.

Relief's aim is for a person to accept the help offered them and be freed from suffering, at least temporarily, becoming immediately able to live more humanly in the way God intends for a human to live. This can be considered the most personal and individualistic of the six strategic Christian strategies for urban poverty alleviation because an individual can provide this response for another individual. It is an action by one who has the power to change a situation, offered to another who does not have that same power.

1.1 Relief's limitations in urban slum and squatter neighbourhoods

The strategy of relief, however, has many limitations and weaknesses for transformation in slums. Though relief can be done quickly, the issues of dependency, power and jealousies make relief quite a complex and often unsustainable strategy in slums. This is a common theme in recent community development literature and is why relief is often understood as one of the least helpful responses to urban poverty.[6]

First, giving relief can create dependencies that are ultimately unhelpful for the recipient or sustainable for the giver. It is one thing to offer help in an emergency situation for a limited time, but continual relief places people's daily survival in the hands of others. This does not create freedom to live as God intends, but can end up as another kind of poverty and oppression. Christians with power and compassion in slums who use relief as a strategy face a difficult decision: when do vulnerable people no longer need help; when can they stand on their own? If a slum resident is sick, has no family and cannot work, how will they get food to eat if it is no longer provided?

Responses to such dilemmas are not always helped by the Western, individualised ideal of self-determination. The myth of the rugged, autonomous, self-made person strongly influences how Westerners respond to poverty. 'These people need to help themselves as we have done' is a sentiment Western Christians can often feel. To give food to the hungry is therefore always seen as patronising and undermining the empowerment of individuals, who should be able to do it on their own. Such sentiment does not take into account the help, historical head start and connections from which Westerners have benefited. Most Westerners simply don't see that their position in life has benefited from such intentional forces as colonisation, slavery and monetary systems.

In reality humans cannot survive by themselves for very long. All humans need others. Western ideology is not the most pressing factor for Christians to consider when responding to the needs of slum residents. Indeed, to decide *not* to show mercy to neighbours in need for ideological reasons has spiritual and moral consequences for Christians (Matthew 25:31ff). Where residents have done all they can to help themselves, but there is a lack of compassion from others, there can be unnecessary misery and even death. This is especially the case when fires, floods or other natural disasters overwhelm a slum neighbourhood. Sometimes an inadequate but compassionate response—a symbol of care such as a cup of cold water—can be far better than no response at all.

As we shall see there are other more proactive strategies that take more time and effort than the reactive and limited response of relief. Even in the case where emergency relief is the only possible response, it can often be prepared by a community for their own community ahead of time. That said, even when done in a participatory way relief can be a difficult strategy to maintain over time, and makes it particularly difficult to maintain the long-term dignity and health of recipients. Even good relief should be limited in time and circumstances.

Second, the strategy of relief can undermine the transformation process in slums because local jealousies and threats of corruption can create deep-seated resentment and conflict. Why did one person get help and not another? Why did help stop for me, but continues for my neighbour? If there are limited resources and potentially unlimited needs for food, clothing, shelter and water, tension can arise from decisions about who can and can't receive help. When, for example, twenty pairs of football boots are donated, which of the hundreds of Klong Toey FC's footballers should get them? Questions of who should decide and on what criteria are difficult to resolve without conflict. These dynamics can undermine the sense of trust and community that is so essential for more sophisticated and effective long-term responses to poverty.

Third, power dynamics can undermine the strategy of relief. A kind of distant benevolence can quickly emerge in the relationship between giver and receiver. The questions, 'Who gets to make decisions about who should be helped?' and 'When they no longer need to be helped?' reflect power issues that need to be considered seriously. Duncan teases out this dilemma in *Costly Mission*: a long line of mercy recipients made the Duncans feel like they 'were dispensing life or death through the decisions [they] made' which 'took its toll' on all involved.[7] For the Duncans, resolving this issue meant establishing various local committees to help decide what was most needed where. This helped to relocate power away from the Duncans and to make relief more sustainable.[8] Power was still in the hands of other neighbours, though. To give food, shelter or visitation can instantly help individuals, but fails to address power dynamics and the underlying reasons for power imbalance.

Giving relief as a response to slum and squatter neighbourhoods has real limits as a strategy, but we must also acknowledge that mercy can be a legitimate response for Christians. Giving mercy is a response that draws from biblical and historical sources and has some potential for helping the most desperate in slum and squatter neighbourhoods under certain conditions.

1.2 How can an incarnational approach to mercy and relief help slum transformation?

Can an incarnational approach to relief help and not undermine transformation in slum lives and neighbourhoods? Issues of dependency, power, jealousies and sustainability can be addressed as part of an overall commitment to mercy if workers seek to follow, participate with and join Jesus in relieving suffering. Such a stance can be seen in at least three ways.

First, an incarnational approach to mercy seeks to connect with God's compassion for people. 'God is love' (1 John 4:8) and so there is a wisdom and an empowerment that can only come from God that can help Christians to start with direct needs, but go further both personally and politically. As Marcus Borg points out, *hesed* can be literally translated as 'opening the bowels of compassion', which he explains has rich metaphorical associations with 'compassion is located in a particular part of the body, the loins. In women, this means, of course, in the womb. In men, it is located in the bowels, and explains the otherwise odd biblical expression of bowels being moved with compassion'.[9]

Jean Vanier, founder of the L'Arche communities, argues that the Hebrew word *hesed* actually has two meanings: 'Fidelity and tenderness. In our civilization we can be tender but unfaithful, and faithful without tenderness. The love of God is both tenderness and fidelity. Our world is waiting for communities of tenderness and fidelity. They are coming'.[10] Such an understanding is closer to what following the incarnated God, motivated by costly compassion, can mean. Compassion then can help change power dynamics because of the relational dimension. Fidelity and tenderness with friends calls for solidarity, which in turn calls for direct action and which in turns opens up further committed, even political responses. Without starting with a sense of personal responsibility to act, however, further costly action is undermined. 'We have learnt a bit too late in the day', wrote Bonhoeffer, 'that action springs not from thought, but from a readiness for responsibility'.[11] Relief that is truly merciful requires such a sense of responsibility that even the smallest acts of kindness can help instigate change.

This is why Christianity at its most fundamental calls for love from the heart of God to be shared with the neighbour who is sharing one's place in community. The Hebrew *hesed* is often translated into the New Testament as *eleos* and when translated as 'compassion' instead of 'mercy' it can make familiar passages potentially revolutionary. This can turn the distant and often power loaded term 'mercy' into being 'compassionate as God is compassionate' (Luke 6:36; Matthew 5:48). As Borg argues, this view informs 'the primary quality of a life lived in accord with God... The ethical imperative is to live in accord with God's character'.[12]

In Christian belief God is love and so God requires his people to 'love our neighbour as ourselves', especially those who are suffering. Such love in solidarity is not merely from the heart, but also includes a concern for justice. As José Porfirio Miranda points out, *hesed* goes together with justice (*sedeqah*) and right (*mishpat*) in synonymic parallelism (or hendiadys) in the Hebrew Bible nineteen times.[13] Revolutionary theologians contend that authentic Christian compassion requires a personal and social commitment to love those oppressed as a 'preferential option for the poor'. This invitation to risk our hearts and lives in merciful love by standing in solidarity with those in need is central to Christian faith and practice. Gustavo Gutiérrez argued that such authentic love as this helps us to cross over to God's side of justice.

> Love of neighbour is an essential component of Christian existence. But while I consider my neighbour, the 'near' one, the one I find on my way, the one who comes to me asking for help, my world remains the same... If, on the contrary, I consider my neighbour the one to whom I move... the 'far away' neighbour, in the streets, in farms, factories and mines, then my world changes.[14]

In Christian terms love as mercy from the Creator, Redeemer and Spirit is no easy or romantic requirement in regards to people who are suffering. To apply one of Jesus' most famous teachings on compassion to slum dwellers—the parable of the Good Samaritan (Luke 10:25-37)—is to see neighbours often in need, and to be proactive in sacrificial mercy, doing something about their immediate pain. To have real 'life', Jesus tells a lawyer, we are to 'love God' and 'love our neighbours as ourselves' and this requires being 'the one who shows mercy' (Matthew 22:37-39).

Christianity has a long tradition of appropriate compassion and mercy in significant times of crisis in cities. In fact it is argued by sociologists like Rodney Stark that the rise of early Christianity is at least partly due to compassionate actions by Christian in the face of plagues in urban areas.[15] In the second and third centuries, while pagan leaders were rich enough to escape Roman cities, Christians stayed to risk themselves to nurse those who were sick and dying of various plagues.[16] While initially no more than hundreds in most Roman cities at the end of the first century, over the next two centuries Christians soon became a majority in most cities.[17] How did this happen? Stark argues that because of mercy shown to the sick through nursing and hospitality, urban Christians outlived non-Christians when they were sick and many residents converted to Christianity when they became well. The moral bankruptcy of those who fled, as well as their leaving, gave space for Christians to multiply and become a majority. So we know that costly, compassionate responses to suffering in cities are not only possible for Christians, but have been a defining trait whenever Christianity has been at its most effective. What an incarnational approach to relief in slums can do is ensure that mercy is not just a single transaction but a personal relationship, and not just personal but looking to a social transformation that will change the person's life and context.

Second, an incarnational approach to mercy can address two temptations that face Christians in situations—like slums—that require direct action toward people. Both temptations present danger to power dynamics and sustainability. The first is the temptation of the non-poor to think they are gods. Jayakumar Christian argues that powerful minorities use four methods to 'systematically exclude the poor from access to education, wealth and benefits from the system. They seek to play god in the lives of the poor. They combine to form god-complexes'.[18] Christian identifies these four methods as intentionally seeking to: influence the future of the poor ('eternal tomorrows'); influence multiple areas of life ('all pervasive power'); persuade others that their power is unchallengeable ('immutable power'); and work in conjunction with other powerful people ('a power-pool') to 'play god over the poor, creating god-complexes within poverty relationships'.[19] To enter into God's incarnating work is to help address this by finding a heightened sense of mortality and vulnerability. Perhaps that is why the disciples needed the storm on the lake before they met the demoniac on the other side (Mark 5:1-20).

The second temptation can be seen in the demoniac himself. He is tempted to think he is sub-human and to let others treat him like that. The residents in slums can be so marginalised and treated so badly by those from outside the slum that they begin to internalise this dehumanisation as a reality. Similarly, the man in Mark 5 is considered sub-human by those around him. His dignity is stripped, leaving him with animal-like behaviour, living among the dead and cutting himself with stones. Such are the effects of poverty and oppression that this man is reduced to a kind of animal monster. That is not who he really is; it is what oppression can do to people, especially people living in slums. Just giving the man what he says he wants, however, will not be sufficient for transformation. The internalisation of poverty is a very real challenge in slums. More than by the physical discomfort of living in slums, residents are deeply affected by the consequent diminishing of their humanity and self-identity. Jesus found a way to reach the man, setting him free to help others. In fact, Jesus so completely loved this man back to humanity that he became 'in his right mind' and wanted to join Jesus' apostolic team. Jesus, however, encouraged him to turn his attention to his own region. The man was released to proclaim the good news of the Kingdom in the ten cities of that region (Mark 5:19-20).

An incarnational approach to relief humanises people, including both the 'actor' and the 'respondent'. It can be a direct, immediate and individualised response, despite its limitations. When used as a way to follow, participate with and join with Jesus, such a response can become more transformative in urban slum contexts. An incarnational approach to mercy and relief has some real potential for informing Christian responses to slum and squatter neighbourhoods. This is especially the case for those residents in slums who are severely restricted because of illness, disability or catastrophe and are unable to help themselves. These could include those who are elderly, orphaned, widowed or substantially disabled, or residents in places where there have been disasters such as fires, floods or mudslides. In each of these examples, residents often need the assistance of others if they are to live healthy lives. Many will indeed die unnecessarily if help is withheld. While death is not the end of the story for Christians, finding responses as part of teams and in local place-sharing initiatives can give transformational relationships the best chance of working in slums. Christians can find ways to be dependable in a crisis without creating long-term dependence.

2.0 Incarnational Capacity Building—Healing

Healing, in its broadest sense, addresses issues of disability, disease and discrimination. Healing as a response recognises that not every person begins the race of life at the same starting point. From birth or even during the race of life people are hampered by physical, psychological or social difficulties. Transformation in this case is about building a person's capacity to live more freely as a human being, addressing what disability, disease or discrimination may seek to take from the quality and dignity of a person's life.

While close to giving mercy as a response, healing has a more direct social and political dimension to it. In comparison to giving mercy, healing can require significantly more time, people and social awareness. Also, in terms of power dynamics, this response requires more co-operation than simply receiving. If mercy is about giving a fish, then healing is about building a person's capacity to fish.

People needing healing seem to have a special place in Jesus' heart and ministry. Sight for the blind was a common Messianic sign in Isaiah (29:18, 35:5-6, 42:7-18 and 61:1), and Jesus' announcement that his Messianic ministry was one that would bring 'recovery of sight to the blind' (Luke 4:18) is consistent with this. Perhaps one of the reasons for the prominence of the blind—'blindness' occurs forty-three times in the Gospels—is the severe discrimination and poverty they faced in Jesus' time. If the blind are healed, then no-one will be left behind.

2.1 Healing's limitations in urban slum and squatter neighbourhoods

Healing, however, can be less personal than some of the other strategies we shall consider. Whereas giving mercy in Christian terms is at its best one life reaching out to offer help to another, real healing can be offered as a tonic with little meaningful personal contact. Because more is required on behalf of the one needing healing, and many more people are involved in the response, fewer connections between the individuals involved can be expected.

Healing it its modern form is also most aligned with particular institutions and professionals providing services. Indeed, with the rise of modernism new kinds of specialist Christian communities emerged over two hundred years ago that have understand mission in terms of institution building. In contrast to those in past eras, these Christian organisations focused on Jesus as providing opportunities for the masses. Often, hand in hand with colonisation, Christian workers focused on establishing, building and staffing the many educational, hospital, orphanage, church and other Roman Catholic and Protestant church institutions that began both in the West and in the 'new world'. While many of these mission entities did have common rules, many were established by local bishops or churches to fulfil an institutional need in that diocese. While the groups actually performed remarkably similar roles, Protestants often built their institutions independently, without broader church connections.

Postmodernism has shaken faith in all institutions. The aspiration that modernism had to accomplish great things through institutions and corporations has been challenged. This has had an effect on churches, but also on missional communities which sought change via institutions. Fewer appear willing to give their lives to an institution. People want to keep their options open, rather than give themselves unreservedly to one professional institution. This crisis hit Christendom hard and affects every aspect of a church life built on two centuries of institutions as a primary way to serve. Even generating the willingness to commit to regular local church involvement has become more problematic in recent years. When it comes to long-term, committed healing and capacity building with people, as well as commitment to institutions providing services in vulnerable and often temporary neighbourhoods, the kind of stability that both require can be undermined.

2.2 How can an incarnational approach to healing help slum transformation?

The God who incarnates is also the God who can heal incarnationally through community. The rise of new kinds of committed community out of the decline of previous eras is being ushered in by a small, seemingly insignificant band of faithful believers taking hold of the gospel and running with it. What is important for this section of the study is how an incarnational approach to healing can move beyond simply relying on institutions to do the work of healing for Christians, and how the move to connect through Christ within community and local place-sharing initiatives can help. This is especially important in slums because there is simply little space or available secure land where it is possible to build large institutions like hospitals or schools. More personal, mobile responses to the needs of neighbours are necessary if healing is to occur.

A good example of an incarnational approach to healing is Jesus' healing of blind Bartimaeus, found in both Mark and Luke's Gospels. I have chosen here to use Mark's version because it offers a little more detail (Mark 10:46-52). It is hard for us today to comprehend the depth of misery experienced by Bartimaeus. Not only were there the difficulties of living without sight, but blindness was linked to sin and its judgment by God (John 9:2). Blind people were not allowed to be priests (Leviticus 21:16-20); one of the curses of breaking the covenant with God was blindness (Deuteronomy 28:29; Isaiah 59:1-15); and the blind routinely suffered harassment from all segments of society (Leviticus 19:14; Deuteronomy 27:18). It's not surprising that such assumptions and explanations for suffering kept the blind poor and marginalised, often rejected from families, living outside cities and reduced to begging on roadsides as their only means of financial support. This is where we find Bartimaeus, begging outside of Jericho.

It's not a surprise, then, that the first words we hear spoken by Bartimaeus and other blind people in the Gospels to Jesus is, 'Have mercy on us'. As we see often in the Gospels, Jesus could not resist their cries for help, even though he was often on the way to somewhere else. The way Jesus heals here is instructive, for he heals in a way that empowers and joins with the faith that Bartimaeus brings. The fact that Bartimaeus recognises Jesus as 'the Son of David', that he is one like Solomon who has the power to heal blind people, is only part of what Bartimaeus has going for him. Bartimaeus has faith in Jesus and keeps calling to Jesus despite opposition; he even leaves his only tool for making money, his begging blanket. Jesus then joins with this man's faith: 'What do you want me to do for you?', he asks. This is exactly the same question Jesus had asked the disciples in the previous chapter (Mark 10:36). Where the disciples had wanted to 'sit in places of honour' and were denied, Bartimaeus simply replies, 'I want to see'. Jesus commends his faith and instantly the man can see. Bartimaeus then leaves begging and follows Jesus.

Jesus did physically heal blind people like Bartimaeus, but there was also deep symbolism in this response. While the blind recognised who Jesus was and couldn't keep quiet, the religious and powerful elite did not understand Jesus. His teaching and lifestyle was a threat to them. The irony throughout the Gospels is that the poor and blind are the ones who see, but the powerful are blind. Where Jesus resists the traditions of discrimination in healing blind people, Jesus also draws on traditions of blindness to teach. Those who obey God see reality, while those who resist lack sight. Ched Myers argues that Bartimaeus is Mark's 'archetypal disciple' because he is 'willing to give up everything in order to see, and thereby heals himself (Mark 10:51-52). Mark's Jesus thus redefines faith as the determination to shed denial and face the world as it is, in order to struggle for what could be'.[20] Thus gaining sight becomes a key metaphor of faith in Mark's Gospel.

Personal involvement with physically blind people was a normal part of Jesus' ministry and was understood from early times as part of the healing ministry of the Christian church. Thomas Oden comments on the incarnational nature of these healings and quotes early Christian manuscripts that 'The touch of Jesus was a mystery to the Fathers because it was a touch of the incarnate Lord.'[21] The disadvantage and discrimination experienced by Bartimaeus and others living with disabilities is alive and well today, still needing 'Jesus-responses' to overcome it. The majority of people in Klong Toey, for example, would still consider that those who have a disability deserve it as a result of karma from a previous life or this one.

Healing, capacity building and empowerment can take other forms, too. Institutions and formal organising may be required, but they are not central for this to happen. For over twenty years Crew Duen and the staff of the Klong Toey community centre have sought healing for many. Whether it's through the pre-school, micro-enterprises, recreation, youth work, visitation, welfare, Christmas festivals, English or computer classes, an opportunity is given for Klong Toey residents to live more closely to what God intends. This is not so much a ministry of words, but more a ministry of the Word-made-flesh. Institutions informed by an incarnational motif can be flexible servants, able to help their neighbours use their gifts and respond in their long-term healing process. These kinds of healing, capacity building and empowerment responses are possible in the power of the Spirit.

3.0 Incarnational Evangelism—Inviting Discipleship

Inviting discipleship can help alleviate poverty. It proclaims the good news that another world is possible, one which the current dominant, oppressing socio-cultural condition does not yet recognise. Jesus' evangelistic response invited poor and non-poor alike to be free from oppression and oppressing; to receive repentance and Jesus' faith; and to join, by grace, with Christ in advancing his Kingdom on earth as in heaven. A positive response to this invitation of discipleship results in a new life in Christ for the respondent, and the opportunity to share the good news with those who have not yet experienced the same freedom. The aim of transformation here is that a person will personally receive the authority of Jesus, empowered by the Spirit to live as the Creator-God intends in a fallen, unjust world. It is this life that will be completed when God's justice fully comes and heaven and earth are finally joined together.

Luke records Jesus' inaugural address which identifies Jesus' core mission as 'proclaiming good news to the poor' (Luke 4:18-19). What is this good news that will liberate the poor, which will be a sign of the Kingdom of God's coming? A string of words designed to elicit a *Yes* or *No* is surely not what Jesus had in mind here. It is one thing to promote an ideology or sell a product, but another to introduce a living person able to change lives and transform whole communities. Like the apostle Paul, Christians are called to 'fully preach' the good news of Christ in word, deed and sign (Romans 15:18-19). Making explicit who Christ is, what he has done (and is doing) and how to encounter and follow him is a crucial part of offering this invitation. Only when our words explain our deeds and signs in Christ can good news be really heard and received. As Bonhoeffer wrote, 'Christianity without discipleship is always a Christianity without Jesus Christ'.[22] Such evangelism is especially needed when two out of three slum residents live in places with few neighbours who have experienced the living Christ or the liberating discipleship that is possible for them.

3.1 Evangelism's limitations in urban slum and squatter neighbourhoods

Contemporary understandings of evangelism are not always so engaging of culture and social context. Often understood as a planned event to elicit a 'commitment' to Christ, the radical calling to communal discipleship for the Kingdom is often secondary or not mentioned at all. Even some of the more considered and accepted understandings of evangelism define it as more a task of presentation. For example, the influential 1918 Church of England Report of the Archbishops' Committee states:

> To evangelise is to so present Christ Jesus in the power of the Spirit, that men [and women] shall come to put their trust in God through him, to accept him as their Saviour, and serve him as their King in the fellowship of his Church.[23]

This definition can be understood as trinitarian and for all of life, but it can quickly become primarily about a presentation to enlist new church members. Such an approach can be a serious problem in slums. Residents facing poverty can have their vulnerable circumstances used for abusive proselytism. The giving of rice, entertainment or camps can be used to elicit 'converts', but relationships rarely go further in the transformation process. If evangelism is understood as a presentation isolated from compassionate sharing of life together, such power abuse 'evangelism' can undermine long-term transformation and trust in slums.

For these kinds of reasons, evangelism has not always been understood as having any role to play in poverty alleviation. For example, though some of Australia's largest aid and development organisations are explicitly Christian, it is illegal to use

Australian tax-deductible funds for evangelism or 'activities designed to build up the knowledge and faith of believers including theological training and training in and study of works of religious wisdom such as the Koran, Torah or Bible'.[24] This is not surprising given strict church-state separation laws in Australia, but such stipulations assume that evangelism and discipleship have no role to play in poverty alleviation. The dividing of 'spiritual' and 'physical' work is a rarely challenged religious philosophy in its own right, and given many contemporary understandings and practices of evangelism this is perhaps understandable. For Christians, however, who consider people as enfleshed and spiritual beings made in the image of God in environments with spiritual dimensions, evangelistic responses should not be excluded from a variety of strategies to address urban poverty. Indeed, to intentionally attempt to withdraw Christ from slums, doing only what can be physically touched and seen, is not only impossible from a Christian perspective, but also seeks to withdraw hope which is not visible, but nevertheless very much needed.

3.2 How can an incarnational approach to evangelism help slum transformation?

To invite discipleship should have a greater social dimension than giving mercy and healing in that it invites a greater connection beyond a personal need toward God and towards broader society. Announcing good news, for example, requires a critique of the dominating powers and allegiances if a new way is to be offered; such critique is not usually prominent when giving mercy or healing. Mercy and healing strategies, in general, primarily focus on survival and meeting immediate needs. As I have argued, incarnational approaches do invite all strategic responses to be more personal and social, and this is certainly true when inviting discipleship.

Jesus entrusted his apostolic community with the message that the Kingdom is coming. This was a community tackling the status quo with a message that could cost its members their lives. Proclaiming a public manifesto of good news to the poor in first-century, Roman-occupied Palestine was not a task for the fainthearted. Such actions would inevitably attract the attention of authorities who were already preoccupied with the numerous resistance movements of the time; believers ran the risk of being lumped together with other resistance movements and persecution was inevitable. To be identified as an apprentice of a person like Jesus was dangerous enough, but to openly proclaim his message required even more courage because the implications would be felt firsthand. The early apostolic communities were itinerant not simply to broadcast the message far and wide, but because the messengers were often on the run. To identify, nurture and courageously proclaim the Kingdom's coming then was a core part of the first apostolic community's life together. Real life and hope was offered and those who followed Christ offered both physical and spiritual healing to those 'who have need of a physician' (Matthew 9:12).

'Jim' is an example of evangelistic transformation in slums.[25] A motorbike taxi driver, Jim once had his arm broken in a mafia attack on his family and was unable to work. UNOH worker Rod Sheard was his next door neighbour and moved with Jim and his pregnant wife to another part of the slum outside the syndicate's territory. He would often discuss spiritual things with us and we suggested to Jim to ask, 'God, make yourself real to me'. The few nights after the attack Jim says Jesus came to him in a dream, touched and healed his arm. When Jim woke up he was actually healed and able to go to work. Jim wrote a song that expressed a sense of joy for God's grace in his life that is a constant refrain embedded in Jim's life now.

In late 2008 Jim, Bu and new baby Chip, with their mafia troubles now settled and ready to stretch their spiritual muscles, moved their home back into central Klong Toey. Living next door to other UNOH workers the MacCartney family in the Rom Gow neighbourhood, they had already helped to start a youth group of forty neighbourhood kids. A visit to them now will see their house full of neighbourhood children and young people. The house church Jim helped to start now runs above Second Chance Bangkok and is gaining a spiritual momentum of its own. While Jim and his family still face financial stress with his low-paying courier job, his eyes glow with enthusiasm for life. What contributed to transformation in Jim's life when so many of his slum neighbours have missed out?

Many aspects of the incarnational approach to transformation appear in this one story: Christian neighbourliness; mutual sharing of life; authentic hospitality; openness to grasp opportunities; answered prayer and spiritual conversations; Bible reading with friends; varieties of people and personalities over time; participatory projects and an authentic approach to church. Not least was that Jim was able to meet people who made space in their lives to intentionally join, follow and participate with what God was doing in the slum. This included what God was doing in and through Jim. None of these dimensions would have been possible to experience had they only been done instantly, individually or without risk. Jim's transformation in the Spirit involved lots of small, loving actions though Christ in community—these can create a kind of life-building momentum that is irresistible.

Agnes Liu researched what kind of evangelism transformed factory workers in Hong Kong.[26] She found three key factors that can have real relevance for how change can happen in slums, and all three can be confirmed in Jim's story.

First, there was a change of attitudes toward Christianity. Christianity is often seen as a Western religion, and for the factory workers it was seen as having little relevance to their lives. Similar feelings are often expressed by people in Klong Toey, who start with the belief that to be Thai is to be Buddhist. Many neighbours also report a kind of aggressiveness or even exploitation of their vulnerabilities by Christians, which strengthens the negative stereotype of Christianity. This is reported too by Mejudhon who found that the Thai 'way of meekness' is often 'violated' by Christians.[27] For Jim these attitudes changed over many years through shared life and experiences with Christian neighbours. Fidelity and solidarity helped give credibility among the poor to the viable option of Christian faith. To know that the Creator has not been far from any one of us, has been present from the beginning, suffers with us and invites us to be joined in the new life that is coming, is vital to such transformation.

Second, there was a change in their experience of Christianity. The Hong Kong factory workers began to experience God through answers to prayer and other supernatural encounters. Jim's dream and consequent healing are not unusual occurrences in Klong Toey. Many neighbours report exorcisms, dreams and similar supernatural answers to offerings in the Buddhist temple or to *Mor Duu* (a kind of witch doctor), for example. What was different for Jim was that he attributed his healing to Christ, whom he experienced in a dream. The source of the experience was located in Christ. As we have seen, Christian anthropologists such as Paul Hiebert describe such existential knowledge as 'power encounters',[28] and throughout the Hindu, Buddhist and Muslim worlds these can be the kinds of encounters that can bring about the kind of changes Jim saw. The role of the Spirit incarnated in these experiences and our ability to participate with its empowering work is vital.

Third, there was a change of knowledge and understanding of Christianity. There is a body of knowledge surrounding Christian experience, found in Christian doctrine and the Bible, which is not intuitive. Negative attitudes towards Christianity can often stem from false understandings of Christ. What makes this especially common in places like Klong Toey is that the average Folk Buddhist worldview falsely categories much of Christian doctrine and scripture. John Davis illustrates this point in that even John 3:16 in perfect Thai makes no sense to an average Thai person.[29] For example, the Thai word for God (*Pra Jaow*) can also mean a kind of King. The King in this verse has an attachment, love, which is a *dukka* which causes suffering. The King also wills his Son-heir to be killed and makes anyone who trusts in this King live forever. In the Buddhist worldview, the promise of going around and around in such karmic cycles forever reincarnated is not good news; moreover, it is a kind of punishment for not reaching nirvana.

What Jim experienced, however, was a kind of knowledge that made sense of his experiences and changes in attitude. When Rod helped Jim and a few neighbours to focus on Jesus and seven of his most basic commands,[30] the key was to seek to 'obey all that Jesus commanded' (Matthew 28:20). This committed reflection and action centred on following Christ and created a dynamic knowledge of Christ. This model of discipleship and church planting was proposed by George Patterson in the context of Honduras.[31] It has been adopted by UNOH workers in Australia, Thailand and New Zealand. A disciple of Jesus is simply defined as someone who loves and follows Jesus, and church as a group of people who do this together. Jim's experiences of obeying Jesus personally and with his friends and neighbours helped to build a worldview very different from the one he grew up with. It was a worldview that had the continuity of the Creator, the new experiences of the empowering Sprit, and a focus on the discipleship of Christ. This is a picture of what is possible in incarnational evangelism.

Such an approach can also be seen in the early Methodist movement. John Wesley's evangelism was not just about preaching in a field to 'present' Jesus to working class people. Rather, Wesley would engage people in fields and other places to seek to 'awaken' them with the hope that the 'classes' could work together.[32] The indirect impact of this kind of evangelism on poverty was not insignificant. Wesley charged the early Methodists to cross social barriers to 'constantly visit the poor' despite this not always being 'pleasing to flesh and blood'.[33] As the Methodist movement grew mostly from among the lower classes, more momentum grew in impacting society too.[34] As George Hunter III explains, this included building up local voluntary leadership, local home schools and institutions including 'small interest free loans' to the poor.[35] The Methodists, who were mostly poor to begin with, experienced the kind of 'redemption and lift'[36] and 'Protestant work ethic'[37] that McGavran and Max Weber wrote about. As we saw too in the example of Jim, similar kinds of growth from personal transformation are possible when people encounter Jesus and their lives are profoundly affected. In Jim's case, inviting such discipleship required lots of small, loving actions in community that created a kind of life-building momentum that became irresistible. It also empowered Jim, his family and neighbourhood in ways that would not have been possible if he had not had the opportunity to encounter and follow Christ.

It must be admitted that incarnational evangelism is difficult to isolate from other Christian responses and strategies in poverty alleviation. The Good News offered is broader than just an explicit invitation to discipleship. As we saw with Agnes Liu's research of the evangelistic transformation of factory workers in Hong Kong[38] and the case of Jim, three factors were crucial in finding a different worldview, built on some different knowledge, attitudes and experiences from previously. Much contemporary evangelism is not holistic enough in sharing life to have this kind of impact. Many contemporary poverty alleviation strategies do not go deep enough into the worldviews of those living in poverty and are thus too materialistic. Incarnational evangelism, however, can help workers to understand and address barriers to the long-term transformation of individuals, families, neighbourhoods and societies. It can offer the invitation to discipleship and transformation personally, over time and in community. To explicitly invite discipleship, therefore, requires deep personal and social experiences.

Not every kind of evangelistic strategy is incarnational, but God can still use all kinds of methods to bring about change. Evangelists can, for example, use radio, television and mass rallies that have very little personal connection between the one inviting and the one receiving good news, and we acknowledge that it is possible for God to use these evangelistic strategies for transformation. What we argue here, however, is that incarnational evangelism as a strategy encourages both the social and personal dimensions of engagement and invitation. Inviting people to follow, participate with and join the risen Jesus should become more deeply personal and radically social for both evangelists and would-be disciples. The connections between the inviter and the invited must be 'through Jesus' and not simply in the abstract. Evangelistic responses have not always been understood as needing to inform or transform both personal and broader social relationships and connections, but this is a crucial dimension for distinct and effective Christian responses in slums.

4.0 Incarnational Education—Teaching

Jesus taught and this strategy can help address urban poverty today. Teaching, in this sense, is about creating critical awareness of the causes of poverty, finding Kingdom truths that can replace the dominant myths causing oppression, and learning new ways to live as God intends. The aim of transformation here is for a kind of awakening to occur so that people facing life in slums can see the way the world really is, know what is happening to them and know what is in their power to do about it.

This kind of liberative education is more political than the other responses we have discussed so far. In fact, this kind of teaching can only be liberating if it intentionally addresses the 'why' questions of social injustice. Such a curriculum forces students and teachers alike to deal with society in deeper and more confronting ways than do the other responses considered so far. It is not unrelated to proclaiming, especially in its critique of society's allegiances, but goes deeper because learners have committed to letting go of those allegiances in faith, and are searching to see how far the new way of living can go. Where proclaiming invites commitment, teaching assumes commitment and teases out what this can look like in the disciple's life.

4.1 Education's limitations in urban slum and squatter neighbourhoods

Education is not a cure all for urban poverty. There can sometimes be a sense that if people just know enough that will bring freedom in its own right. The kind of knowledge that empowers and brings about freedom, however, is difficult to mass produce. Individuals and contexts can be so diverse that it is difficult to find a curriculum and teachers to meet all needs, including those in slums.

The limitations of healing ministries within institutional frameworks also apply to educational institutions. Add to this the difficulties educational institutions face in slums because of a lack of adequate space for buildings, a lack funds for sustainability, a lack of recognition by authorities and the transience of both students and teachers. Any attempt at liberative education in slums is therefore a challenge.

The time required for education and the dubious nature of its value after completion can be limiting factors too. With residents often so close to living in survival mode, commitment to an education that has financial and opportunity costs is often not possible. Knowledge, even accredited knowledge, does not necessarily lead to employment and livelihood.

Further, power dynamics between those in power with knowledge and those who need the knowledge can limit educational strategies. Rather than assisting learning, education can quickly become a domesticating and oppressive tool for social control.

4.2 How can an incarnational approach to education help slum transformation?

An incarnational approach to education is rooted in an understanding of the discipleship process. The word *mathetes* ('disciple') occurs 252 times in the Gospels and Acts, and is almost always used to describe those who follow Jesus.[39] The root word *mathano* ('to learn') is used twenty-four times and *didasko* ('teach') is used ninety-five times in the New Testament. Teaching and learning are central dimensions of Jesus' ministry: disciples were to take up and be apprenticed into a new way of life, rather than to learn only in an academic sense. Jesus' teaching in the Sermon on the Mount (Matthew 5-7) and the Sermon on the Plain (Luke 6:17-49) are exemplars of incarnational education. It invites some reflection on ways that Jesus' educational pattern can be followed, joined and participated in.

First, the context is primarily the small apostolic community with whom Jesus shared his life. Jesus did share his teaching ministry more broadly than with the Twelve, but so often focused attention on these apprentice leaders who were living with Jesus and were actively engaged with ministry. This attention to a small group of people is crucial for an incarnational approach to education. Teachers cannot share their lives with a large number of students at once. This is especially the case when teaching in slums, where leaders often fear the education process because of previous bad experiences and require tailored learning processes. In Klong Toey, for example, the local government school often has seventy students to one teacher in a classroom. If the Kingdom coming is as much about what is caught as it is about what is taught, then these kinds of numbers can only undermine the education process and discourage people from learning altogether.

Second, the content of Jesus' teaching about the Kingdom of God was deeply contextualised and personal. Jesus used images, scenes, experiences, sayings and stories that were common to the day, but often gave them a twist to open the eyes of his disciples to what was really happening and what was required of them. Jesus was, in a special way, the embodiment of his teaching about the Kingdom of God. To be near to Jesus is to be near the centre of God's rule. This is not necessarily the same for Christian teachers today. Teachers can clearly teach about Kingdom values, but may not live by them. If teachers are to be involved in incarnational education then they need to stay close to Jesus in a neighbourhood context and find ways to live lives that begin to share what God's Kingdom is like.

Third, Jesus' teaching did not just use a formal lecturing mode, but an integrated action and reflection process. There was often an event, action or conflict and then reflection that caused further questions and actions. The sermons on the mount and the plain almost certainly were composites of teaching from many sessions with Jesus. The experiences of being with Jesus, working with him and engaging with God's truths that emerged from the experiences were not segregated parts of the education and conscientising process. This kind of integrated action-reflection process was taken up Paulo Freire. A Catholic priest working in South America in the 1970s, his book *Pedagogy of the Oppressed* has influenced generations of activist educators.[40] In *Pedagogy of Hope* he argues that such an education process is lost without the tangible inspiration of hope. He writes:

> One of the tasks of the progressive educator, through a serious, correct political analysis, is to unveil opportunities for hope, no matter what the obstacles may be. After all, without hope there is little we can do.[41]

When we consider the kind of education that Jesus engaged in and consider our options for response, there is great potential for transformation.

Community Health and Evangelism (CHE) is a contemporary teaching model that has great potential in urban slums. CHE is used in eighty nations of the world by 325 teams from diverse mission agencies and denominations in over 2,100 villages and neighbourhoods.[42] While well received in rural villages, in recent years CHE practitioners have used seminars to bring people together and have sought to adapt their training model to urban slum neighbourhoods. CHE's Neighbourhood Transformation program is described as a process seeking to empower urban individuals and families to better their lives:

> The intent is to raise up local laypeople as volunteers who will be models and share the physical and spiritual truths they have learned with their neighbours in the home setting. The program is designed to be transferable, multipliable, and ongoing after the training team leaves the area. The desire is to transform cities, neighbourhood by neighbourhood, through the seamless combination of disease prevention, evangelism, and discipleship and community based development, by using local assets and reinstituting neighbour helping neighbour.[43]

Chart 16 below outlines the basic process.

Chart 16: Developing neighbourhood transformation

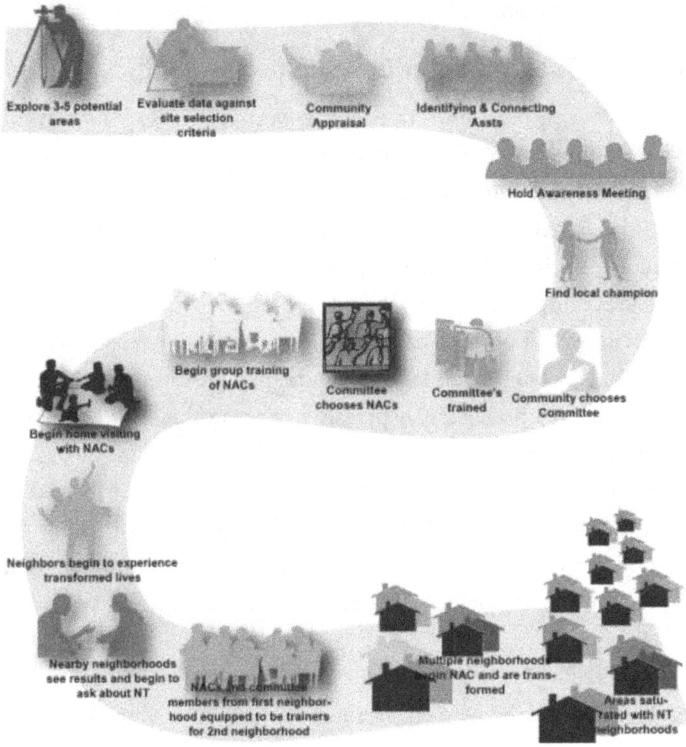

Source: Neighbourhood Transformation[44]

CHE/NT is a flexible but comprehensive training approach that uses the assets neighbourhoods already have. As such it is reproducible and sustainable. There is real potential for this approach to be incarnational and to bring about transformation in slums especially because local leadership is intentionally sought out and empowered. How such an educational process is instigated, as well as how trainers and educational methods connect with the living Christ, is still important, however. Building trust, especially where local churches struggle or are non-existent, is a serious challenge in slums. This is especially the case if the Christian content of the course comes as a surprise to local leaders. Just having a well-thought-out and educationally-sound strategy by itself does not make CHE incarnational. Rolling out programs, even great ones, is not the same as showing the discernment and courage required to follow, join and participate with Christ. That said, as far as educational strategies go, CHE's urban experiments have a lot going for them.

A weakness in teaching ministries generally can often be the distance of power between teacher and students. Compared to other responses we have seen, the power dynamics evident in a teaching strategy represent a positive move in favour of the respondent, but they still reflect a teacher-student hierarchy. An incarnational approach, however, can push these dynamics to becoming more equal, more political, more integral and more personal.

5.0 Incarnational Social Capital Development—Building Community

Building community can help address urban poverty. This is about developing a deep sense of belonging and connectedness with other human beings. The aim of transformation here is to build bridges between people and broader society so that collective work for change in society can be expressed. Whether in small groups, congregations or associations, Christians model particular values and commitments, aspiring to see society improved and to share these values with them.

This response requires far more social and political effort than previous responses. Community building is one of the least individualistic responses a Christian can make to alleviate poverty because it expressly involves others. In terms of power it is far more complex than other responses too. On the one hand it provides less individualised power because those facing poverty are ideally as involved as those pursuing a community building strategy. All can be involved in making decisions at some level. Indeed, a community group can have more power, influence and voice than community builders from outside because it organises and expresses itself collectively.

The Way personified by Jesus with his disciples was able to survive, multiply and thrive among the disciples when Jesus was not with them in the same way as when he was (Acts 4:32-35). There was such sensitivity to God's Spirit in the early church, such a willingness to be learners, that there was not a needy person among them! Such was the way of Jesus and his movement that, in the first flush of enthusiasm, poverty appears to have been eradicated among his followers. The new way Jesus revealed was taken on by his people.

The idea of social capital found in small groups has gained currency in understanding how development and transformation happens. From politicians to activists, the idea that neighbourhoods need to have more than material resources to be healthy has become an accepted norm. Perhaps few have done more to promote this idea than American sociologist Robert Putman. He argues that, 'social capital refers to connections among individuals—social networks and the norms of reciprocity and trustworthiness that arise from them' and that '"social capital" calls attention to the fact that civic virtue is most powerful when embedded in a dense network of reciprocal social relations. A society of many virtues but isolated individuals is not necessarily rich in social capital'.[45] Putnam sees five benefits of social capital for neighbourhoods: the ability to 'resolve collective problems more easily'; 'greasing the wheels that allow communities to advance more smoothly'; 'widening our knowledge of the ways in which our fates our linked'; 'serving as a conduit for helpful information that facilitates achieving our goals'; and 'operating through psychological and biological processes to improve individuals' lives'.[46]

Developing reproducible community-based models that are sensitive to God's leading are essential if lasting change is to occur. This includes the kinds of partnerships formed, the kinds of homes lived in and the kinds of investments made into a community. If a new way to fish can be shown, neighbours can overcome dependence. Responses that don't simply 'give a fish', or even just 'teach how to fish', but rather model new, locally-specific ways to fish that can be taken on by a neighbourhood, are truly transformative.

5.1 Community building's limitations in urban slum and squatter neighbourhoods

The multiplication of small groups in the transformation process has long had advocates in both Christian mission and sociology. Missionaries such as Roland Allen in China,[47] the Church Growth Movement[48] and the emerging-church[49] have all called for church planting movements as the most strategic way to see real transformation happen. David Garrison gives a simple definition of a church planting movement: 'A rapid multiplication of indigenous churches that plant churches that sweep through a people group or population segment'.[50] Given the scale and pace of growth in slums, two-thirds of which are in the 10/40 Window with little Christian presence, such multiplication makes a lot of sense from a purely strategic point of view. As we have seen, however, slum neighbourhoods do not necessarily lend themselves easily to such movements. Dynamics such as 'redemption and lift' (where Christians do well and leave) and high mobility often take emerging church and civil leadership out of neighbourhoods. Momentum for such movements can be undermined before it even has the chance to begin.

5.2 How can an incarnational approach to community building help slum transformation?

The Kingdom of God is 'at hand' because Jesus is present and this has many implications for the kind of community Christians can live out in slums. To follow the cosmic Jesus is to hold to the promise of new community and new creation. Community then, is a sense of belonging that is the fruit of common commitments to this goal. As Bonhoeffer says, 'Everyone enters discipleship alone, but no one remains alone in discipleship'.[51] Jesus' personification of God's will and intention for the world then includes a reconciling of all creation, where all people, groups and systems live like Jesus with others. The importance of a sharing of life centred in following the risen Jesus communally, therefore, cannot be overstated.

Christian slum activists need to personally know *whom* they follow in community. Weak and inadequate reactions to sometime dramatic and immediate needs can easily become a habit unless a deep intimacy and habitual relating with Christ in scripture, silence and solitude with others is cultivated. One of the early and most enduring images from *City of Joy* is Father Stephen trying to find solitude in the slum.[52] He recognises he needs such quiet stillness to be attentive and active in faithfully following Jesus in such an extreme setting. This is a constant theme in the writings of Mother Teresa and Henri Nouwen where 'the fruit of solitude' is not isolation but, counter-intuitively, 'compassion'.[53] So important is this 'furnace of transformation' that it is not only left up to the individual, but embedded into a community based rhythm of life. The Missionaries of Charity's days, for example, are split into three: eight hours for sleep, eight hours for service and eight hours for prayer and renewal. Global culture increasingly values an instant, individualised lifestyle so community living like this can seem limiting and almost legalistic. Bonhoeffer, however defines community in counter-cultural, but deeper terms:

> Christian community means community through Jesus Christ and in Jesus Christ. There is no Christian community that is more than this, and none less than this. Whether it be a brief, single encounter or the daily community of many years, Christian community is solely this. We belong to one another only through and in Jesus Christ. And what does this mean? It means, first, that a Christian needs others for the sake of Christ. It means, second, that a Christian only comes to others through Jesus Christ. It means, third, that from eternity we have been chosen in Jesus Christ, accepted in time, and united for eternity.[54]

Most Christian workers in slums can't intuitively deal with those elements that drive them away from belonging with Jesus with others like this. As Root explains, however, there is tangible hope:

> The resurrected humanity of Christ has crushed the lie that to be human is to be free from God and neighbor. In nearness to Jesus' resurrected humanity we are transformed to live free for God and others, proclaiming in our transformation the future of all creation.[55]

It is no accident that Mark's Gospel has no examples of the singular form 'disciple'—it's always in the plural form—not only because to follow Jesus is impossible by ourselves but because the Kingdom of God is a new communal reality. Those engaging in slum activism, with its external pressures, need this nearness in community more than most.

Jesus did God's will above all else. This is not only a pattern for individual Christian living, in slums or elsewhere, but a pattern inaugurated for the whole cosmos to follow. The confession that 'Jesus is Lord and Saviour' signifies that we are loyal to the One who is putting the whole cosmos to right. We must insist that to follow Jesus in slums is not to seek to be new Messiahs for our neighbours, but to follow the space and power created and opened up by the risen Jesus to God's will on earth as in heaven.

An incarnational approach can also inspire a prophetic approach to local and neighbourhood-based social movements. Church planting movements cannot simply be wished for, but require intentional and sacrificial community-based involvement as well as the cooperation and coordination of instigating workers. John Perkins, for example, suggests that there are three kinds of workers who are especially significant for urban neighbourhood transformation.[56] If slum neighbourhoods are to see Christian movements emerge each of these are especially crucial.

First, there are the *relocators*, those who intentionally move into an area to tie their wellbeing to that of their neighbours. These include the workers we have described as serving in apostolic teams and who are taking place-sharing seriously.

Second, there are the *returners*, those born and raised in the neighbourhood, but who have been able to leave for a better life. No longer trapped by the poverty of their neighbourhood, they choose to return and live in the place they once tried to escape. Arjan Suwat is typical of this kind of worker. After coming to faith, recovering from drug abuse and attending Bible school, he started a church in the North of Thailand. Suwat then had what he describes as a 'Jonah call' to take his young family and share the gospel back in the midst of the slum he grew up in.

Third, there are the *remainers*, those who could have fled the problems of their neighbourhood, but chose to stay and be part of the solution to the problems surrounding them. There are many in Klong Toey who, like our friend Pooh, now have enough money from their small businesses to consider moving out. Yet, for the sake of the gospel and helping others they stay in the neighbourhood with their families.

The last two kinds of workers are perhaps the key to seeing transformative movements happen in slums. Indeed, without their involvement in community building, dependence on relocators or institutions would be bound to form, resulting in a lack of community building momentum.

There is much for Christians to learn in ideas about social capital and movement dynamics. However, an incarnational approach to social capital building must push past a simply collective ideology and ensure that each individual can share their gifts. We saw this kind of transformation through community building when neighbours came together and offered their individual gifts to one other in the 70 Rye neighbourhood. What Christians can offer this process is not just a multiplying of their cells or more individuals like themselves, but a bringing together of people for the glory of God in their location.

6.0 Incarnational Advocacy—Delivering

Advocacy and deliverance from oppression addresses the root causes of poverty at social, systemic and political levels. Transformation here aims to see a more just society, confronting anything that causes the most vulnerable to be exploited or oppressed. It can use advocacy, protest, and changes to laws, policies and political processes as leverage to make life fairer for those facing poverty—to make society healthier.

Jesus gave his first apostolic community authority to cast out demons (Mark 3:15). This supernatural authority to name and deliver evil spirits contributes to disciples' effectiveness as change agents and advocates in the midst of urban poverty and injustice. While the establishment and those with vested interests in the status quo might have said that Jesus' apostolic community was illegitimate and had no real power, Jesus gave his followers God's authority to deliver the most vulnerable from the evil that preys on them—both personal evil and the evil spirituality behind systems. There are demonic principalities and powers that oppress vulnerable people through hidden agendas, systems and structures. To cast out demons is to redeem something or someone from demonic control. The demonic can only pervert. It cannot create. Therefore, everything that oppresses can be redeemed to be what God originally intended. The first mission community did not just declare a message but possessed an authority beyond human powers to bring about transformation.

This is the most explicitly political of the Christian strategies discussed thus far in this chapter. For by confronting injustice there is acknowledgement that people abuse power and energies are focused on changing people and systems who benefit from that oppression. In considering our grid, this response is the most 'social' and can also be the least personal. It is possible, for example, to campaign for the freeing of slaves without personally knowing one. This is a limitation that can helped be addressed by an incarnational approach to advocacy.

Jesus was not afraid to ask the 'Why?' questions. Jesus, empowered by the Spirit, announced the good news to the poor through offering direct relief, healing, inviting discipleship, teaching and community building, but he also went to the socio-spiritual roots of poverty to answer why oppression happens. When Jesus went to the heart of the political and religious life of first century Palestine—the Temple—and turned the tables (Luke 19:45-48) he was making a political statement. Those who profited from the sacrifices-system were outraged, but Jesus stood with those unable to pay for those sacrifices. In response, those who had benefited from the unjust system made sure there would be a price to be paid for asking why the poor are poor. Incarnational theologies point out that God's very nature is justice, and so justice is what is required of God's people. God not only makes a covenant with people, but hears the cries of the oppressed and intervenes with justice, calling his people to be faithful instruments of justice (Isaiah 42:5-7). Miranda points out that in Isaiah 42, 'Yahweh's intervention in our history has only one purpose'. Here it is explicit: 'to serve the cause of justice' and this 'intention of saving from injustice and oppression is the determinant of the entire description which Yahweh makes of himself'.⁵⁷ Miranda further points our attention to the technical Hebrew phrase for social justice as being central to God's character, passion and expectations of people. He notes, for example, that the phrase 'justice and right' or 'right and justice' (*mishpat usedakah*) is used thirty-one times as a hendiadys, in which two words of different meaning are used to signify one complex concept. As in the English use of 'law and order' or 'bed and breakfast', when the Hebrew terms *mishpat* usedakah come together as a hendiadys it has one meaning.⁵⁸ Faithfulness to Yahweh requires joining God in seeking justice for those who are oppressed. Justice simply can't be separated from God's nature.

God's rallies against oppression in all its forms and this is a constant theme in the Hebrew Bible. There are no fewer than nine Hebrew words for our one English word 'oppression' woven throughout the Old Testament.⁵⁹ Because of the slavery of the Hebrews in Egypt and God's concern for their liberation, the revolutionaries argue that such words need deep reflection if we are to understand the nature of urban poverty and the requirements of justice.

God's liberation of the Israelites from oppression by the Egyptians included a promise of freedom and peace. To live in a land flowing with milk and honey was symbolic of a sustainable and joyful life. Poverty and oppression is about a lack of freedom to be able to choose God's *shalom*, to live a meaningful life. For oppressed people to be able to choose *shalom*, justice must be done and this means addressing oppressors.

Why is there so much urban poverty and injustice in the world? Why do so many people lack basic food and access to health today? Why are so many of the poor excluded from worship? Jesus' strategic response in the Temple aimed to bring about freedom for those who were oppressed, and this continues to be an integral part of Jesus' mission today.

The need for justice as freedom to live as God intends is felt by the majority of people living in slums today and provides a serious challenge for Christians responding to urban poverty. It is this understanding of poverty as oppression and injustice that informed Jesus' mission to bring good news to the poor and freedom to the oppressed. To be faithful to Jesus and Christian faith requires responses to the injustice of poor living conditions in slums and the lack of protection from the law on the land occupied by slums. The strategy of 'delivering' or confronting evil requires challenging those who are oppressing the poor and engaging in the long and costly battle to bring them to justice.

6.1 Deliverance's limitations in urban slum and squatter neighbourhoods

Most people resist being labelled an 'oppressor' and the potential of globalisation to make the world a 'flatter' and fairer place has not yet materialised. It may well be too late to revive protected, centralised economies, it might not be too late to try to make globalisation's opportunities work better and more justly for those living in places like urban slums. What may be helpful here is to see oppression and injustice as more than simply an issue of who has the most power. Summarising community development insights from Chambers, Friedman and Christian, Bryant Myers argues that poverty is a kind of breakdown of relationships.[60] God's intended *shalom* for urban slums here is important—a time and place where all relationships work—but also important are complex issues of justice and oppression and how power relates to different individuals, groups and systems today. These social relationships are clearly not working for those living in slums. What matters here is that where Christians put their inherited and developed strength and power affects globalised justice. How can we make our social relationships work?

Choosing political sides and alliances for slum advocacy is fraught with danger. The reputation of many NGOs who sided with either the Red or Yellow shirts in Thai politics in the demonstrations of 2010-11, including those in Klong Toey, is indicative of this. Too often the poor and Christians who stand with them can be used for political gain. That politicians, political parties and movements will increasingly need grassroots slum activists as these populations grow, this does not mean that all political movements can provide what they say they aim to do. Caution is required so that activists are not used by the powers to provide legitimacy or to persuade slum residents to accept unjust terms. Those seeking to be advocates for slum residents can easily get disconnected, even seduced by the powers. There are large, dark and systematic abuses of power that oppress slum residents in very complex ways. Yet these forces use flesh-and-blood people to do their bidding, sometimes manipulating even well-intentioned advocates.

6.2 How can an incarnational approach to deliverance help slum transformation?

Those who seek to offer deliverance from oppression incarnationally must recognise their own involvement in 'the powers' and their own contributions to injustice. Self-understanding of social location is an especially important theme in radical discipleship literature.[61] It is almost impossible for those located at the 'centre' to understand how those at the margins really live. This is because at the centre the system works in ways it simply does not on the margins. It is not uncommon for Western Christians to have trouble understanding the advantages they have started life with, never mind being able to see how they support and benefit from the systems that protect these entitlements. The systems work for them: why not others? Ched Myers picks up this theme when he writes:

> The mechanisms of dominant culture entitlement are so embedded within institutions and practices at every level of society that they are sometimes difficult to

pin down, though they obviously seem more mysterious to the beneficiaries than to the disenfranchised.[62]

There are many Christians at the centre of social systems who have vested interests in keeping the status quo and who would love to be considered 'neutral' to urban injustices. Because they enjoy the fruit of the current social and structural arrangements it is understandable that they don't want to see structural changes in favour of those on the margins. Why inflict on oneself the suffering or lessening of privileges that seeking such change may entail? Besides, such is the view from the 'top' that most really can't see that these systems are not working for the vast majority of marginalised people. It is far easier and safer in a busy and hectic life to keep eyes closed—to keep separate from those affected by social failure—than to seek to be a relevant factor in addressing it incarnationally. As pointed out above, Jesus had a lot to say about those with power at the centre being blind, but those on the edge being able to receive healing and truly see.

In specific regard to the crisis of slums, why would Christians seek to be relevant if it could require significant loss of time, money, status and security? Just to change squatter land rights, for example, would at least require far higher salaries for blue-collar workers, leading to dearer goods and services, and therefore a higher cost of living for those at the centre. Why seek to be relevant if the personal costs of change could be so high? The answer is that such relevance is intimately linked with faithfulness to Christ. The very credibility of those who follow Jesus is at stake. If the real suffering of the urban majority is not taken seriously, then the Christian's relevance as humans and as people of faith is lost. As the sub-title of one of Sobrino's recent books puts it, there's *No salvation outside the poor*.[63] Christian advocacy inspired by the incarnational motif has a rich tradition of people who have voluntarily put their own immediate welfare aside to be faithful to God in the face of oppressive contexts. The revolutionary theologians point to those Christian witnesses who have stood, and are still standing, for justice and life in the midst of oppression and death. As mentioned above, the Greek word for 'witness' also means 'martyr'. The cost of incarnational advocacy is raised as the numbers of those living in urban poverty rise each day.

Addressing the structural powers that keep slum residents oppressed is complex. There are dark forces at work in the masses of homes, undermining God's will in peoples' lives, causing poverty and vulnerability. When we pray for God's *shalom* and will to be done in our neighbourhood as in heaven, we know it will require a miracle. Yet this is exactly the kind of work the Spirit does and wants us to do. Indeed, it is the Spirit who empowers and flows through those who are close enough to advocate and stand in the gap.

What exactly to advocate for and with whom are not easy questions to answer in a slum context. Politically speaking, slums are avoided by governments where possible, with few levels of government eager to take up their responsibilities in the same way as in other neighbourhoods. An advocacy tool that is helpful here is *Adaptive Approaches to Urban Slums: A multimedia sourcebook on adaptive and proactive strategies*. Developed by the World Bank and full of case studies and interviews, it outlines in over nine hours of modular multimedia content on a CD-ROM the kind of advocacy that is possible with and for slum residents. It is particularly helpful regarding the complex issue of land tenure, certainly one of the key issues that define the slum challenge. It argues, for example, that there are only really four long-term options in responding to the underlying land tenure issues faced by slums. These are:

1. Forced evictions: Simply bulldozing slum neighbourhoods in eradication programs.

2. Clearance and relocation: Reclaiming land occupied by slums, but moving residents to a new neighbourhood.

3. Clearance and on-site development: Evacuation of residents and then rebuilding planned neighbourhoods on the existing site before residents return.

4. Upgrading in place: Residents staying while their neighbourhood is rebuilt and housing tenure secured.[64]

In general terms the least preferred option is the first. The most preferred option is the last, because it causes the least disruption to residents' lives and squatter land claims are less disputed. However, this is not always possible and a much larger city-wide housing strategy may be required. As the World Bank explains, in the period between 2000 and 2030 urban areas in the developing world will triple or grow by 'the same amount of built-up urban area as the entire existing urban world had done up to the year 2000. The magnitude and rate of this urban transition is unprecedented'.[65] To prepare for this future there is a need for city development strategies that can address issues such as 'economic development, good governance, municipal finance, urban environment, job creation and poverty reduction', but can also 'have a considered impact on the ability of cities to manage the needs of the urban poor living in slums. Within the broader scope of city development strategies, a focused inquiry into low-cost shelter options for the poor will require understanding and assessing the dimension of demand for land and housing'.[66] For such large scale planning to occur there would need to be high level political imagination, strategy and will, combined with grassroots neighbourhood movements. An intentional push from the edges and a concerted pull from the centre would be required to engage such a big agenda as preparing a city for its future. Without such planning and policy, vested interests would choose what is most convenient to them. That the World Bank notes that there are five million forced evacuations happening each year and that these are 'a brutal blow to vulnerable people'⁶⁷ indicates that the least preferred strategy toward slums is often the most convenient for the relevant powers .

Christian advocacy needs to be informed both by Christ and by consultative analysis of the larger planning strategy. In a sense, the most obvious incarnational approach is to be on the side of those facing the actual housing crisis. There is a role for well-trained and creative Christians, however, who can seek to develop fair plans and policies in cities, taking into account several interests for a just and workable solution. It is not enough for Christians to simply call for justice; we must help shape it.

Advocacy with and for slum residents can be informed, inspired and invited by the God who incarnates. Incarnational approaches to confronting injustices are not disconnected from real people, real laws and the real challenges faced by slum and squatter neighbourhoods. Risks and vulnerabilities cannot be avoided. The way an advocate can stay grounded is to know and invest personally in what is happening by joining, participating and following Jesus in actual slums, not from a distance or only in theory.

Summary

What has been outlined here is not an exhaustive list but a sample of strategies that can help the transformation process in slum and squatter neighbourhoods, arguing that they can have their best chance of being truly Christian and transformative if they are invited, inspired and informed by the risen Christ in an incarnational approach. There is a great deal of thoughtfulness, prayer and courage required to follow, join and participate with the God who incarnates in these ways. There is also no guarantee of success. If taken seriously, however, an incarnational approach can help Christians discern faithful, relevant and hope-inducing responses in the face of great personal, neighbourhood and political vulnerabilities.

Final Challenge: Should I stay or should I go now?

Those of us with enough power to read and write books like this are faced with unique challenges in this new urban world. A crucial one is this: how do I know if it's time to relocate somewhere new or to dig deep and persevere where I am? As an urban missionary for over twenty years I know how much is at stake. It pains me to see so many Christian workers either hang on to an assignment for far too long, wringing the life out of a community, stopping others to step up and grow. It is also possible, however, to withdraw prematurely and miss out on what was possible in that neighbourhood or community, creating distrust and a sense of being used. How can we know the difference between transitioning too early or leaving it too late? How can we multiply ourselves, but go deep in life with others? I have transitioned a few times now and helped many others to do this too, so here is what I have found helpful.

Do you have a niggle?

A move with our family to a slum in the Majority World started with what I could only describe as a 'niggle in my spirit'. Like a tugging on the end of our fishing line that we shouldn't ignore, first we needed to explore an unusual discontent in our then roles with Urban Neighbours Of Hope (UNOH) in our then mission in the multicultural neighbourhood of Melbourne, Australia. As we talked with the team and prayed we realised we needed to be released to explore a longing for Majority World ministry. This was something Anji and I had kept in our hearts since we first met as teenagers not long after separately standing up at a Tony Campolo sermon, willing to go anywhere for the cause of Christ. Identifying this niggle needed attention and was not a decision to leave Melbourne, but a request for the freedom to explore possibilities and return with recommendations. Actually, the first time this prompting happened was in 1997. UNOH had just come through a traumatic first founding 5 years and had now stabilised. However, when we were released to explore our next steps we returned from an exploratory trip to Vietnam and recommitted to Melbourne for another five years. As we discussed this with our community we all realised we needed to stay and adjust our roles, though still aware of this sense of call to the Majority World was still on our hearts. This first niggle was about the need to change some focuses in our roles for the next season of our lives and that of a growing organisation. A rule of thumb can be if you are responsible for work that is over 50% outside of your gifting and passion then perhaps change is needed. Every-one needs to do difficult work in a fallen world, but if it gets over a certain tipping point the stress of the role shouldn't last for too long.

It can be easy to try to ignore and suppress these niggles or conversely act too hastily upon them. A prompting is not a fool-proof 'Word from the Lord', but something to explore prayerfully with a few confidants who are both affected by our decisions and concerned for our long term well-being. This niggle can happen when our role needs to change, but also often happen when we least expect it. It was actually the latter which helped us move to Bangkok as you will see.

Do you have confirmation?
For a successful transition those who invest the most in us and our ministry need to be respected and involved in the decision to transition. By 1999 our roles in UNOH had been adjusted and we saw our ministries in Melbourne begin to blossom. As part of our recommitment to Melbourne, we planned to work in an orphanage on a 3 month sabbatical to Vietnam. At the last minute, however, our visa request was rejected. One of my friends was working at the Australian Embassy in Bangkok and said, 'You'll love Bangkok! There's great slums here!' He was right and our time in Klong Toey slum, Bangkok, for those 3 months was a real joy. Because we loved our roles and ministry in Melbourne, we naturally thought some-one else from UNOH could go to Bangkok. 'God loves you and Ash has a wonderful plan for your life' is a common joke. It was not until a stop-over trip to Klong Toey, Bangkok a year later that an overwhelming sense of 'I was home' came over me. Of course, it is one thing having ideas one thousand miles from home. Flying back to Melbourne my stomach was knotted thinking of the right time to talk with Anji. I couldn't even wait until the end of the trip home from the airport. When our van pulled up out the front of our flat I said, "Anji, I had this amazing experience in Bangkok. I think we should go and start a UNOH team there within two years." Then held my breath.

"You're joking!" Anji said, as tears began to well up in her eyes. "I have been trying to give up that dream but it wouldn't go away!"

After talking over the idea of starting a new UNOH team in Bangkok with the team and key stakeholders in our ministry (local people, Churches of Christ leaders, then UNOH board) we worked out the consequences and made a decision after a three-month discernment process. We all believed God was calling us to go, if a few things came off. A key one was connecting with the Church of Christ in Thailand (CCT) who had a community centre in Klong Toey. John Gilmore, UNOH's chair, knew the then General Secretary of CCT, Dr Sint, and through him a way was made for the Churches of Christ in Thailand and UNOH's governing body the Churches of Christ in Victoria and Tasmania to enter into a covenant together and for us to live and serve in Klong Toey with them. Before we knew it, our support was raised from churches and individuals from around Australia and we were headed for Bangkok. It took 18 months from that initial niggle of feeling to finding what we needed to see happen to be released to pursue this in March 2002.

Anji and I with our then 5 year old daughter Amy, stepped out in faith knowing we needed others confirming our call, but not how much. This became so apparent in the first six month of living in Klong Toey, which were so traumatic. Living in a slum of 80,000 mostly Buddhist people in 2 square kilometres in a home the size of four double beds was hard enough, but Dengue fever four times, dysentery, floods, trouble with language learning, all tested our resolve as our lives adjusted to the harsh conditions. At one point as I went in and out of consciousness in hospital I thought I was going to die. I could only go back to that old hymn 'I surrender all' and rest in the sense that we all believed as best as we knew that our family were to follow this call 'come what may'. In the end that hospital visit was hemorrhagic Dengue fever (and not a virus in my heart as was thought) and our lives did eventually adjust. I don't think we could have got through that if we thought this was just our own whims. Our calling is not our own. We are part of the Body of Christ and its important that those who have a stake in our current ministry and will host us in a potential new one can feel like they can discern and confirm with us our next steps.

Does your current community have good momentum?

I can still remember our farewell dinner in Melbourne in March 2002. We crowded into a Vietnamese restaurant around the corner from our Springvale Mission Centre with over a hundred people from the local area to say our goodbyes. One by one someone from one of the communities we served – Aboriginal, East Timorese, Rainbow, Pacific Islanders, Kelvin Grove - got up and presented us with farewells that we shall never forget. The UNOH team did an appropriate rendition of the song and dance sequence at the end of the movie Shrek, and Amy and some of her friends from the street danced to 'These are the best days' by Nikki Webster. Amy also did a Samoan dance with her friends Vince and Junior in full Samoan costume, which was a highlight for me. It seemed to symbolise her early years built on experiencing the good in a broad range of cultures. This was the last of a marathon of farewells all around the country since we had first sensed God calling to Bangkok over two years ago. While all were overwhelming, this last supper was the most emotional.

At his last supper Jesus was able to summon words so profound and insightful about what was going on that we still use them each week to remember his farewell. Yet, there Anji and I were, overwhelmed by a much smaller farewell, and all we could get out sounded like cheap clichés. How do you respond when some-one looks into your eyes and says, 'You've helped me get a life. I'll never forget what you've done for me?' I can remember praying at the end of the night, 'Lord, let our hearts continue to be one as we go to Bangkok.' In a real way we are just at the tip of an iceberg in this Bangkok adventure as the friendship, support and prayers go with us. St. Paul once wrote, "Because there is one bread, we who are many are one body, for we all partake of the one bread." (1 Cor. 10:17). As the night closed we felt gratitude at being part of this one bread both in Melbourne and Bangkok that went beyond mere words.

It felt like we were at our own funeral as the different neighbours and communities eulogused how God had impacted their lives through us. Had we left prematurely in 1997 we would have missed this special moment and what it represented in the lives of those there that night. Had we stayed we could well have stifled their growth. By far the best time to transition is when things are on the up and light is shining. The worst time to make a decision about endings is when things are down and dark. We just can't be sure in the darkness if it is a knee-jerk reaction. I know momentum is not always possible, but it is certainly preferable for real hope to be established so that we can go, grow and multiply beyond us.

Can you finish well?

Sometimes we experience endings faster than we expect them. On the 18th August, 2009, I was sitting at my desk at the Klong Toey Community centre when wild wind, thunder claps and thick sheets of rain suddenly descended upon us. Tree branches cracked and fell down on the dark road outside. Then the electricity went out. I started for home once the rain eased a bit to see if our house was flooded again. It wasn't, but as I walked down our small lane-way I could see thick black smoke, bellowing up into the moving sky. Anji called on the phone, sopping wet, taking shelter under a bridge with the kids on her motor-scooter but heard about the fire. 'Get the dog, rabbit and hamsters, maybe your computer too. We don't have much else, so get out of there'. The fire was still about 100 metres away, but it was close to a LP Gas shop. I went to see if we could help, but with literally thousands of people running in all directions, some with their hands full with plastic baskets of clothes, others with old TVs and some even small fridges, it was simply chaos. The first red fire-ute arrived with a few teenagers hanging off the back, they didn't have enough water or power or long enough hose to get down the narrow soi to the homes on fire. The fire, meanwhile, edged closer to the LPG store. Soon the real fire trucks arrived and quickly extinguished the fire. Though some of our neediest neighbours lost five homes, amazingly no-one was seriously injured and few belongings burnt.

Then I saw Rod. Three concrete power poles were literally broken in half from trees coming down on the corner of our main 70 Rye street. Rod's ute was right in the middle of them. No damage done was done as the poles and trees fell around the blue ute and only the wires and leaves landed on it! The electric company guys came in their orange trucks and within hours started to replace the concrete poles and take stray branches out of thin, corrugated iron roofs.

With the immediate danger of fire and gale force winds gone, there was a tangible sense of relief as well as the smoke in the air. Since the electricity was still off throughout our neighbourhood, neighbours spontaneously gathered together in our common court-yard. I bought some pizza and as we ate told stories of close escapes and rumours of motorbikes flying in the air. There was the kind of nervous laugher of survivors, but it didn't take long for discussions to turn back to normal life, like football again. 'What will Man U do without Ronaldo?' By midnight the electricity was back on in 70 Rye and life continued on as if nothing happened.

Out of the blue the next day (18th August) the option of a new home in a new, poorer neighbourhood suddenly appeared from no-where. We had been praying about a move. Our 70 Rye neighourhood now had a strong church with growing leaders at Ta Rua based in the old Mafia mansion at the end of our street. Christian neighbours were now running micro-enterprises themselves like Poos 'Helping Hands' cooking school and Bla with Klong Toey Handicrafts. When we first arrived in April 1st, 2002 none of this was there. Also, we realised our two kids Aiden (then 6) and Amy (then 12) had started to need more space, and as we just committed to Bangkok for another 7 years we also realized we needed new grassroots challenges.

So while as missionaries we always aimed to be like scaffolding that could be removed from 70 Rye to allow an indigenous Christian movement emerge, the storm and fire seemed to confirm to us that Christian hope was now firmly established. Despite what the elements threw at our neighbourhood, together they could not only survive, but adapt and respond together for a better future without us needing to live there. While the new home was only moved 500 metres away to the Lock 4 neighbourhood, the hope that was found together in 70 Rye will stay there with key neighbours as well as go with us to the new area. We had an ending that would enable us to be released to start again. After much prayer, discussion and building work we moved into our 'renovator's delight' in Lock 4, Klong Toey on October 20th, 2009 where we live to this day. Promptings, confirmations, momentum and finishing well had happened again. It was time to go begin again and follow Jesus into a new place.

SLUM LIFE RISING

PERSONAL AND GROUP QUESTIONS:

1. What have been your best and worst experiences in teams? What were crucial insights from these experiences that could relate to teams in slum ministry? What roles can preparation and spiritual formation play in helping new workers get started and transition into new roles and places?

2. How important has a sense of belonging with neighbours and place been to you? What has helped and hindered community building in places that could relate to slum transformations?

3. If poverty is about oppression, then Christian responses to urban poverty require empowerment and freedom-creating opportunities. Why then, are transitions by those with inherited power so important for those with little inherited power in places like slums? How can you give away more of your inherited power, to enable more freedom in slums?

4. As we come to the close of this book, what will your response to slums be? If you couldn't fail what would you love to do with slum residents for the glory of God? Can you identify some short term and long term challenges that can help you address your responsibilities in a new urban world?

Conclusion

We have sought to address the challenge to Christian mission posed by the rapid rise of urban slum and squatter neighbourhoods in the Two-thirds World. To give some much needed focus a practical-theology methodology was used, asking four guiding questions posed by Osmer: What is happening? Why is it happening? What ought to be happening? How can this be done? To help evaluate what was developed, a criterion for Good News was also proposed and Klong Toey slum was used as a way of earthing our theories. Evaluating these questions can help inform our conclusion.

1.0 Practical Theology Questions

First, we found that the rapid rise of urbanisation in general and slums in particular poses a serious challenge to Christian faith and mission. The very nature of these fast growing, changing and often temporary neighbourhoods mired in urban poverty can undermine many contemporary Christian development and church growth strategies, as such strategies often require stable environments with institutional approaches. That almost 100,000 new slum residents are now added to these neighbourhoods each day—neighbourhoods which are already 1.2 billion people strong—heightens the significance of the crisis. What is especially problematic for Christianity is that two out of three of these residents, over 700 million people, are located geographically in the 10/40 Window where Christians are least present. The relevance and faithfulness of Christianity in a new urban world is at stake, requiring urgent and focused attention by Christians.

Second, a critical survey was undertaken of a variety of incarnational missiologies in relation to slums. These missiologies have become popular given the real struggles faced by institutionally based approaches in terms of conditions, locations and the adaptability required to respond effectively in slums. The survey considered a number of positions on a continuum depicting how the metaphor of enfleshment could be applied in slums. It was concluded that it is theologically and practically justifiable to use enfleshing metaphors, but that not all uses are helpful or even possible in slums. The theological and practical strengths and limitations of several of these missiologies in regard to slums were identified and explored. Why Christianity is struggling in slums is at least in part due to the need to find appropriate theological frameworks, including incarnational approaches, to slum transformation.

Third, what ought to be an incarnational approach of Christians toward slum transformation was proposed. Rather than incarnational mission understood as one particular model, method or value, it is possible to hold a view of incarnational mission which utilises a trinitarian motif of enfleshing hope. This approach built on Langmead's three-part definition of incarnational mission. We can conclude that joining the incarnating Creator, following the incarnating Redeemer and participating for empowerment with the incarnating Spirit can bring about important eschatological and deeply practical promises for slum transformation. Such an approach is not without cost to Christians, but the despair, the demonic and the deaths that cause so much misery in slums can ultimately be transformed through joining, following and participating with the incarnating God.

Fourth, how this approach can be applied was explored with special reference to Klong Toey. The enfleshing hope motif can inspire deeper, more personal as well as more radical social change than if this motif was not used to inform slum responses. While further, comparative field-based research is required, it is concluded that the motif of enfleshing hope has the potential to inform and invite distinctive and effective Christian responses to the challenge of slums. This can be especially seen in the way this approach can assist in developing more transformative Christian teams, local place-sharing and poverty alleviation strategies in slums.

2.0 Criteria for Good News

It can also be concluded that the motif of enfleshing hope is consistent with what is required for a distinctly Christian theology of mission in slums. As was noted in the introduction, a criterion can be identified to determine whether this is Good News or not, and from this criterion conclusions can be drawn.

First, is this Good News true to biblical concerns and established Christian traditions? The key themes of hope, Trinity and incarnation find a biblical basis in both the Old and New Testaments. This is especially seen in God's incarnating work in creation, covenants, the Christ Event and the Advocate's empowering. God's concern for discipleship and justice within an eschatological framework for slums is especially significant. These are important Christian themes historically, as well as being significant for recently influential Christian theologians such as Bonhoeffer, Moltmann and N. T. Wright, as well as liberation and revivalist theologians. Indeed it would be hard to imagine Christian faith and mission without some understanding of hope, Trinity, discipleship and incarnation.

Second, can this Good News address the real concerns and challenges faced by slum dwellers? The nature of slums and their cost was especially identified in the way despair, the demonic and death cause misery for residents. The motif of enfleshing hope can help inform, inspire and invite holistic responses that can directly and indirectly address such suffering.

Third, can this Good News lead to transformative action? The motif of enfleshing hope is designed to help provide a framework for transformative action. This can especially be seen in the ways that such a motif can help address challenges to teams, local place-sharing and poverty alleviation strategies.

Fourth, is this Good News intelligible and coherent enough to understand? It must be acknowledged that identifying each person of the Trinity, exploring how they enflesh hope, and investigating what Christians can do in response in slums, is a process with its own mystery and complexity. Though my original research aimed to be at a doctorate level, it is hoped that at a grassroots level the motif of enfleshing hope can be comprehended in slums through this book.

Slum Life Rising was birthed out of sense of being overwhelmed. This sense grew more intense as the scale, speed and complexity of suffering faced by multitudes of slum residents emerged from the research, but also in my neighbours' lives. As the focus turned to the incarnating God, however, an urgent and creative invitation right into the eye of a perfect storm of poverty also emerged. Active faith in such a God can be Good News for all: those living in slums and those benefiting from them. Transformation is possible in slums through the incarnating God of hope. I pray that *Slum Life Rising* helps generate in Christians a courageous sense of responsibility to focus our best resources on this phenomenon shaping our common future. As Abraham Heschel reminds us, 'Few are guilty, but all are responsible'.[1]

Preface

1. The Lausanne Committee for World Evangelization, 'How Were the Various Issues Chosen?' www.lausanne.org/Brix?pageID=13895 (accessed January 23, 2007).
2. The Lausanne Committee for World Evangelization, 'The 2004 Forum for World Evangelization,' www.lausanne.org/Brix?pageID=12897 and '2004 Forum Frequently Asked Questions,' www.lausanne.org/Brix?pageID=14228 (accessed January 22, 2007).
3. See www.unoh.org for more details about Urban Neighbours Of Hope.
4. Robert McAfee Brown, *Liberation Theology: An introduction* (Westminster: John Knox Press, 1993), 35-36.
5. Jo Beall and Sean Fox, *Cities and Development* (New York: Routledge, 2009), Kindle loc. 421-48.
6. The Lausanne Committee for World Evangelization, *Lausanne Occasional Paper Number 35: Towards the transformation of cities/regions*. http://www.lausanne.org/documents/2004forum/LOP37_IG8.pdf (accessed August 10, 2010). 38.
7. While I initially argued for a separate sub-group for slums I ended up working on the 'Diverse-city' section and became its principal writer and scribe. See 'Diverse-city' in section five of The Lausanne Committee for World Evangelization, *Lausanne Occasional Paper Number 35*. 24-32. It quickly became obvious, however, that this section was a big enough topic in its own right; it was clearly not able to give much attention at all to slums.
8. United Nations Human Settlements Program. *The Challenge of Slums: Global report on human settlements 2003*, (London: Earthscan, 2003).
9. The Lausanne Committee for World Evangelization, *Lausanne Occasional Paper Number 35*. 38-41.
10. The Lausanne Committee for World Evangelization, *A Call to Develop Christ-like Leaders*, http://community.gospelcom.net/lcwe/assets/LOP41_IG12.pdf (accessed January 23, 2007), 38-39.
11. Chris Sugden, 'Jesus Christ: Saviour and Liberator', in *Sharing the Good News with the Poor*, ed. Bruce Nicholls and Beulah R. Woods (Bangalore: Baker, 1996), 86.
12. Ashley Barker, *Make Poverty Personal: The Bible's call to end oppression* (Melbourne: UNOH Pubs, 2006). It was short-listed for Australian Christian Book of the Year 2006 and then also went on to be published by Baker Publishing as Ash Barker, *Make Poverty Personal: Taking the poor as seriously as the Bible does* (Grand Rapids: Baker, 2009).
13. Ross Langmead, *The Word Made Flesh: Towards an incarnational missiology* (Lanham: University Press of America, 2004).

Introduction

1. United Nations, *World Urbanization Prospects—The 2009 Revision*, (New York: United Nations, 2010), 2.

2. UN, *World Urbanization Prospects—The 2009 Revision*, 2.
3. Population Reference Bureau, 'Human Population: Urbanization', www.prb.org/Educators/TeachersGuides/HumanPopulation/Urbanization.aspx (accessed February 2, 2010).
4. Jo Beall and Sean Fox, *Cities and Development: Routledge Perspectives on Development* (New York: Routledge, 2009), Kindle loc. 421-48.
5. UN, World Urbanization Prospects—The 2009 Revision, 2.
6. UN, *World Urban Population Prospects – The 2009 Revision*, 1.
7. UN-Habitat, *State of the World's Cities 2006/7* (London: Earthscan, 2006), 19. It must be acknowledged, however, that there is an inherent unreliability with informal housing figures in the Two-thirds World.
8. UN-Habitat, *The Challenge of Slums: Global Report on Human Settlements 2003* (London: Earthscan, 2003), xxiv. David Barrett, 'Status of Global Mission, 2009, in the Context of 20th and 21st Centuries', http://ockenga.gordonconwell.edu/ockenga/globalchristianity/resources.php (accessed May 30, 2011).
9. Matt Rosenberg, 'Current World Population: Current world population and world population growth since the year one', http://geography.about.com/od/obtainpopulationdata/a/worldpopulation.htm (accessed February 2, 2010).
10. UN-Habitat, *Challenge of Slums*, iv.
11. UN-Habitat, *Challenge of Slums*, xxiv.
12. Rosenberg, 'Current World Population.'
13. UN-Habitat, 'The Challenge', www.unhabitat.org/content.asp?typeid=19&catid=10&cid=928 (accessed August 11, 2010).
14. Alex Kirby, 'Slum Growth "Shames the World"', www.news.bbc.co.uk/2/hi/science/nature/3161812.stm (accessed February 2, 2010).
15. UN-Habitat, *Challenge of Slums*, 12.
16. United Nations Development Programme, 'Goal Seven: Ensure environmental sustainability', *Millennium Development Goals*, http://www.undp.org/mdg/goal7.shtml (accessed August 9, 2010).
17. J. C. Carrasco, 'Transformation', in *Dictionary of Mission Theology: Evangelical foundations*, ed. John Corrie (Nottingham: InterVarsity Press, 2007), 393.
18. The Free Dictionary, http://www.thefreedictionary.com/incarnate (accessed August 10, 2010), s. v. 'Incarnate'.
19. Langmead, *The Word Made Flesh: Towards an incarnational missiology* (Lanham: University Press of America, 2004), 8.
20. UN-Habitat, *Challenge of Slums*, iv.
21. [21] UN-Habitat, *Challenge of Slums*, iv.
22. [22] UN-Habitat, 'The Challenge'.
23. [23] UN-Habitat, *The Recife Declaration: Habitat II—1996*, http://ww2.unhabitat.org/programmes/ifup/documents/rde.rtf, (accessed January 29, 2007), 9.
24. United Nations, *World Urbanization Prospects*, 13.
25. UN-Habitat, *Challenge of Slums*, iv.
26. UN-Habitat, *State of the World's Cities 2006/7*, 34.
27. UN-Habitat, 'The Challenge'.
28. Robert Neuwirth, *Shadow Cities: A billion squatters, a new urban world* (London: Routledge, 2005), 67-70.
29. Neuwirth, *Shadow Cities*, 241-250.
30. UN-Habitat, *Challenge of Slums*, 5.
31. See, American Bible Society, *The Poverty and Justice Bible—CEV* (New York: American Bible Society, 2009), which highlights in orange these '2,000 verses that reveal God's heart for the

poor and oppressed'.

32. Ignacio Ellacuria and Jon Sobrino, eds., *Mysterium Liberationis: Fundamental concepts of liberation theology* (Maryknoll: Orbis, 1993).
33. See David Bosch, *Transforming Mission: Paradigm shifts in theology of mission* (Maryknoll: Orbis, 1991), 432-446. See also more conservative voices like Rick Warren, Billy Graham and John Stott advocating for the Make Poverty History Campaign in, Rick Warren, 'The One Campaign: An advocacy letter from Rick Warren', Beliefnet, http://www.beliefnet.com/story/168/story_16821_1.html (accessed January 29, 2007).
34. Richard Robert Osmer, *Practical Theology: An introduction* (Cambridge, UK: Eerdmans, 2008), Kindle loc. 86-97.
35. Osmer, *Practical Theology*, Kindle loc. 35-49.

Chapter 1

1. For more information on Urban Neighbours Of Hope see www.unoh.org.
2. For a fuller account of our first year in Klong Toey see Ashley Barker, *Finding Life: Reflections from a Bangkok slum* (Melbourne: UNOH Publishing, 2003).
3. Ry is a traditional land measurement like an acre, but much smaller.
4. Sidney Goldstein, *The Demography of Bangkok: A case study in differentials between big city and rural populations* (Bangkok: Chulalongkorn University, 1972), 38-39.
5. Marc Askew, *Bangkok: Place, practice and representation* (London: Routledge, 2002), 153.
6. Richard Swift, 'Lease on life', *New Internationalist*, Jan/Feb (2006): 10.
7. Askew, *Bangkok*, 152.
8. Eugene Peterson, in his Foreword to Eric Jacobsen, *Sidewalks in the Kingdom: New urbanism and the Christian faith* (Grand Rapids: Brazos, 2003), Kindle loc. 29-42.
9. The full title of the city is actually Krungthep mahanaknhorn amon ratanakosin mahintrara ayuthaya mahadilok popnoppararat ratchanthani burirom ubonomratchaniwet mahasathan amonpiman avatansathit sakkathattiiya witsanukamprasit. 'Krungthep' is the shortened name, used by the majority of Thais.
10. Sopon Pornchokchai, 'Global Report on Human Settlements 2003 City Report Bangkok', www.thaiappraisal.org/pdfNew/HABITAT1new.pdf (accessed March 13, 2010), 4.
11. National Statistical Office Thailand, 'Population and Housing Census 2000', www.web.nso.go.th/pop2000/prelim_e.htm (accessed August 16, 2010).
12. Asian Development Bank, 'Urban Sector and Strategy and Operations', www.adb.org/Documents/Supplementary-Appendixes/SST-REG-2006-03/SES-USSO-SupplementaryAppendix.pdf (accessed August 16, 2010).
13. United Nations, 'World Urbanization Prospects: The 2009 revision population database', http://esa.un.org/unpd/wup/unup/p2k0data.asp (accessed August 16, 2010).
14. UN, 'World Urbanization Prospects – 2009', but there are scholars predicting that Thailand may be urbanized to a degree as high as 70% by 2025, e.g., Ulla Haapala, 'Urbanization and Water: The stages of development in Latin America, South-East Asia and West Africa', (Master's Thesis, Helsinki University of Technology, 2002). This would put Bangkok's population at over 50 million by 2025.
15. United Nations, 'World Urbanization Prospects: The 2009 revision population database', http://esa.un.org/unup/p2k0data.asp (accessed August 22, 2010).
16. United Nations, 'World Urbanization Prospects: The 2009 revision population database', http://esa.un.org/UNPP/p2k0data.asp (accessed August 16, 2010).
17. Again, figures projecting Thailand's 2025 urbanization at 70%, and Bangkok's population at over 50 million, come from scholars like Haapala, 'Urbanization and Water'. These figures can be contrasted with more conservative figures in United Nations, 'World Urbanization Prospects: The 2009 revision population database', http://esa.un.org/unpd/wup/unup/p2k0data.asp (accessed August 16, 2010).

18. Pornchokchai, 'Global Report', 14.
19. UN-Habitat, *Challenge of Slums*, 201-202.
20. Sopon Pornchokchai, 'Council Member Biography,' http://www.glgroup.com/Council-Member/Sopon-Pornchokchai-184101.html (accessed March 15, 2010).
21. Pornchokchai, 'Global Report', 14.
22. Pornchokchai, 'Global Report', 11.
23. Pornchokchai, 'Global Report'; National Statistical Office Thailand.
24. [24] Urban Poor Asia, 'The Poor in Bangkok City', http://www.achr.net/th_overview.htm (accessed August 22, 2010).
25. Pornchokchai, 'Global Report', 7.
26. Pornchokchai, 'Global Report'; National Statistical Office Thailand.
27. United Nations, 'Slum Populations as Percentage of Urban', http://data.un.org/Data.aspx?d=MDG&f=seriesRowID:710#f_9 (accessed August 22, 2010).
28. Office for the Registrar General of India, 'Census of India 2001, Slum Population in Million Plus Cities, 2001', http://censusindia.gov.in/Tables_Published/Admin_Units/Admin_links/slum1_m_plus.html (accessed August 23, 2010).
29. [2]Mark Kramer, *Dispossessed: Life in our world's urban slums* (Maryknoll: Orbis, 2006), 126.
30. Bryan Tinlin, Urban poor and Public Policies in Thailand: An assessment of the State's implementation of slum relocation and upgrading in Klong Toey district, Bangkok (Toronto: York University Department of Geography, 1999), 25-30, cited in Kramer, Dispossessed, 126.
31. Duang Prateep Foundation, 'Monthly News for December 2002', http://web.sfc.keio.ac.jp/~thiesmey/dpf200212.htm (accessed August 22, 2010).
32. Hernando de Soto, *The Mystery of Capital* (London: Black Swan, 2001), 33.
33. Kamol Sukin, 'Asbestos can cause cancer but 'it's cheap': Official sees 'no reason' for more expensive substitutes', *The Nation*, http://www.nationmultimedia.com/2006/05/14/headlines/headlines_30003982.php (accessed January 15, 2007).
34. UN-Habitat, State of the World's Cities 2006/7, 58.
35. Barker, *Finding Life*, 59.
36. UNICEF, 'Conditions for Children in Urban Areas', in *Quest for Hope in the Slum Community*, ed. Scott Bessenecker (Waynesboro: Authentic, 2005), 207.
37. Now Public, 'More Fires in Bangkok's Shanty Town', http://www.nowpublic.com/environment/more-fires-bangkok-shanty-town (accessed August 22, 2010).
38. Now Public, 'More Fires in Bangkok's Shanty Town', http://www.nowpublic.com/environment/more-fires-bangkok-shanty-town (accessed August 22, 2010).
39. UN-Habitat, *Challenge of Slums*, 11.
40. UN-Habitat, *State of the World's Cities 2006/7*, 70.
41. UN-Habitat, *State of the World's Cities 2006/7*, 68.
42. UNICEF, 'Conditions for Children in Urban Areas', 207.
43. UN-Habitat, Challenge of Slums, 40.
44. Mike Davis, *Planet of Slums* (London: Verso, 2006), 137.
45. UN-Habitat, *State of the World's Cities 2006/7*, 105.
46. UN-Habitat, *State of the World's Cities 2006/7*, 84.
47. Davis, *Planet of Slums*, 137.
48. UN-Habitat, *State of the World's Cities 2006/7*, 108.
49. Cited in Davis, *Planet of Slums*, 142.
50. UN-Habitat, *State of the World's Cities 2006/7*, 109.
51. Neuwirth, *Shadow Cities*.
52. For more examples of these kinds of challenges, read my experiences from our first year in Klong Toey in Barker, *Finding Life*.

53. Human Rights Watch, 'Thailand: Not Enough Graves: The war on drugs, HIV/AIDS, and violations of human rights', http://www.unhcr.org/refworld/type,COUNTRYREP,HRW,THA,41 2efec42,0.html (accessed, August 22, 2010).
54. Karl Taro Greenfeld, 'Need for Speed', *Time Magazine*, March 4, 2001, http://www.time.com/time/magazine/article/0,9171,100581,00.html (accessed August 22, 2010).
55. UN-Habitat, *Challenge of Slums*, 69.
56. UN-Habitat, *State of the World's Cities 2006/7*, 122.
57. UN-Habitat, *State of the World's Cities 2006/7*, 122.
58. UN-Habitat, *State of the World's Cities 2006/7*, 120.
59. UN-Habitat, *State of the World's Cities 2006/7*, 122.
60. See chart for comparisons between urban, rural, urban non-slum and urban slum net enrolment rates in eighteen countries in UN-Habitat, *State of the World's Cities 2006/7*, 122.
61. Davis, *Planet of Slums*, 128.
62. Davis, *Planet of Slums*, 129.
63. Oscar Lewis, 'The Culture of Poverty' in *Urban Life: Readings in the anthropology of the city*, 4th ed., eds. George Gmelch and Walter P. Zenner (Long Grove: Waveland Press, 2002), 271.
64. Lewis, 'The Culture of Poverty', 272-274.
65. Lewis, 'The Culture of Poverty', 274.
66. Barker, *Finding Life*, 139-143.
67. Lewis, 'The Culture of Poverty', 274.
68. Martin Visser, *Conversion Growth of Protestant Churches in Thailand* (Zoetermeer, the Netherlands: Uitgeverij Boekencentrum, 2008), 61.
69. Visser, *Conversion Growth of Protestant Churches in Thailand*, 91.
70. David Chaney, 'Statistics by Country by Catholic Population', *The Hierarchy of the Catholic Church: Current and Historical Information About its Bishops and Dioceses*, http://www.catholic-hierarchy.org/country/sc1.html (accessed January 6, 2010).
71. The 2000 Thai census figures have the total Christian population at 438,600 in Thailand, and 64,400 in Bangkok. National Statistical Office Thailand, 'Population by religion and sex: 2000', http://web.nso.go.th/pop2000/table/eadv_tab3.pdf (accessed January 6, 2010).
72. The AGC has Thailand's Christian population in 2010 at 849,000 or 1.3%. Todd Johnson and Kenneth Ross, eds., *Atlas of Global Christianity* (Edinburgh: University Press, 2009), 149.
73. Operation World has the number of Christians in Thailand at 749,532 (1.10%), with Evangelicals making up 307,305 (0.5%). Operation World, 'Thailand', http://www.operationworld.org/country/thai/owtext.html (accessed January 6, 2010).
74. Visser, Conversion Growth of Protestant Churches in Thailand. 183.
75. Visser, Conversion Growth of Protestant Churches in Thailand, 77.
76. Visser, Conversion Growth of Protestant Churches in Thailand , 77.
77. Barker, *Finding Life*, 147-150.
78. St Stephen's society was started in Hong Kong by Jackie Pullinger. For more information see Kalana Vineyard Christian Church's website, http://www.kelownavineyard.com/index.cfm?i=31 42&mid=22&smgroupid=11557 (accessed January 6, 2010).
79. Mercy Centre website, http://www.mercycentre.org/ (accessed August 23, 2010).
80. Frank Mann, 'Priest Saves Souls, Lives in Thailand's Slaughterhouse', *The Queens Gazette*, November 12, 2008, http://www.qgazette.com/news/2008-11-12/features/033.html (accessed August 23, 2010).
81. Askew, *Bangkok*, 140.
82. Mercy Centre website, 'George W. Bush to Visit Bangkok Slum Children', http://mercycentre.org/index.php?option=com_content&view=article&id=118%3Ageorge-w-bush-to-visit-bangkok-slum-children&catid=2%3Aarticles-about-the-mercy-centre&Itemid=27&lang=en (accessed June 28, 2010).
83. Askew, *Bangkok*, 140.

84. These teach basic literacy and numeracy, preparing children aged roughly 3 to 7 for mainstream schooling. In 2008 at least 9 of these were run by specifically Christian organizations.
85. Viv Grigg, *Cry of the Urban Poor* (Monrovia; MARC, 1992), 98.
86. This was an unpolished list of Bangkok churches from Visser's research.
87. Grigg, Cry of the Urban Poor, 95.
88. Peterson, 'Foreword', Kindle loc. 29-42.

Chapter 2
1. UN-Habitat, Challenge of Slums, 9-10.
2. Neuwirth, *Shadow Cities,* 16.
3. 'Cities with slums' is the name given to some UN sponsored programs. See, for example, UN-Habitat, 'A cities without slums program in Morocco set to achieve slum free targets by 2010', http://www.unhabitat.org/content.asp?cid=2668&catid=491&typeid=3&subMenuId=0&AllContent=1 (accessed August 23, 2010).
4. UN-Habitat, *Challenge of Slums*, vi.
5. UN-Habitat, *Challenge of Slums*, iii.
6. UN-Habitat, *Challenge of Slums*, 10-11.
7. UN-Habitat, *Challenge of Slums*, 11.
8. For example, Scott Bessenecker (ed), *Quest for Hope in the Slum Community: A global urban reader* (Waynesboro: Authentic, 2005).
9. See, one of four categories of such neighbourhoods in Colombo, Sri Lanka is 'shanties'. Cited in UN-Habitat, *Challenge of Slums,* 208.
10. Katy Salmon, 'Nairobi's "Flying Toilets": Tip of an Iceberg', *Terra Villa*, http://ipsnews.net/riomas10/2608_3.shtml (accessed January 7, 2010).
11. Mike Davis, *Planet of Slums* (London: Verso, 2006), 137.
12. Davis, *Planet of Slums*, 21.
13. UN-Habitat, Challenge of Slums, 9.
14. Friedrich Engels, "The Conditions of Working Class England", cited in Davis, *Planet of Slums,* 138.
15. Davis, *Planet of Slums*, 11. The Charles Dickens quote is from 'A December Vision', 1850.
16. Davis, *Planet of Slums*, 21.
17. UN-Habitat, Challenge of Slums, 9.
18. UN-Habitat, Challenge of Slums, 9.
19. UN-Habitat, Challenge of Slums, 10.
20. UN-Habitat, *Challenge of Slums,*11-12.
21. UN-Habitat, *Challenge of Slums*, 11.
22. UN-Habitat, *Challenge of Slums*, 12.
23. UN-Habitat, Challenge of Slums, 12.
24. UN-Habitat, *Challenge of Slums*, 12.
25. UN-Habitat, *Challenge of Slums*, 12-13.
26. UN-Habitat, *Challenge of Slums*, 12-13.
27. Used by, for example, Neuwirth, *Shadow Cities*.
28. For example, see Jorge E Hardoy and David Satterthwaite, 'The Legal and Illegal City' in *Squatter Citizen: Life in the urban third world* (London: Earthscan, 1989), 12-36.
29. For example, Hernando de Soto, *The Mystery of Capital* (London: Black Swan, 2001), 33.
30. Neuwirth, *Shadow Cities,* 180.
31. C. R. Whittaker, *Land, City and Trade in the Roman Empire* (Brookfield: Ashgate, 1993), cited in Neuwirth, *Shadow Cities*, 181.

32. Neuwirth, *Shadow Cities*, 303-304.
33. Neuwirth, *Shadow Cities*, 182.
34. de Soto, The Mystery of Capital, 108.
35. de Soto, *The Mystery of Capital*, 109-113.
36. Neuwirth, *Shadow Cities*, 8.
37. Neuwirth, *Shadow Cities*, 8.
38. UN-Habitat, Challenge of Slums, 196.
39. Jonathan Rigg, *Southeast Asia: A region in transition*, (London: Routledge, 1991), 143.
40. Sopon Pornchokchai, 'Global Report on Human Settlements 2003 City Report: Bangkok', http://www.thaiappraisal.org/pdfNew/HABITAT1new.pdf (accessed June 27, 2011), 29.
41. Neuwirth, *Shadow Cities*, 25-176.
42. Richard Swift, 'Welcome to Squatter Town', *New Internationalist*, Jan/Feb 2006, 2, http://www.newint.org/features/2006/01/01/introduction/, (accessed February 6, 2007). This edition did include an article by Neuwirth which may have influenced the editorial.
43. Hari Srinivas, 'Urban Squatters and Slums', http://www.gdrc.org/uem/squatters/squatters.html (accessed January 15, 2007).
44. Srinivas, 'Urban Squatters and Slums'.
45. For example, Swift, 'Welcome to Squatter Town', 2.
46. For example, United Nations Human Settlements Program or UN-Habitat.
47. For example, Bessenecker, Quest for Hope in the Slum Community.
48. Davis, *Planet of Slums*, 30-31.
49. UN-Habitat, *Challenge of Slums*, 212-213.
50. Davis, *Planet of Slums*, 33-34.
51. Davis, *Planet of Slums*, 28.
52. UN-Habitat, Challenge of Slums, 12.
53. Steward Brand, 'City Planet', http://www.scribd.com/doc/6575294/Stewart-Brand-City-Planet (accessed January 7, 2010), 4.
54. Brand, 'City Planet', 4.
55. Brand, 'City Planet', 4.
56. David Satterthwaite, 'The Scale of Urban Change Worldwide 1950-2000 and its Underpinnings', http://www.odi.org.uk/speeches/horizons_nov06/8Nov/URBAN%20CHANGE%202005%20-%20David%20Satterthwaite%20paper.pdf (accessed February 1, 2007), 11.
57. Hardoy and Satterthwaite, *Squatter Citizen*, 242.
58. David Satterthwaite, 'The Transition to a Predominantly Urban World', http://pubs.iied.org/pdfs/10550IIED.pdf (accessed January 7, 2010), 29.
59. Neuwirth, *Shadow Cities*, 91.
60. Hardoy and Satterthwaite, *Squatter Citizen*, 21.
61. Neuwirth, *Shadow Cities*, 92.
62. Neuwirth, *Shadow Cities*, 92.
63. UN-Habitat, Challenge of Slums, 219.
64. UN-Habitat, Challenge of Slums, 219.
65. Brand, 'City Planet', 5.
66. Satterthwaite, 'The Transition to a Predominantly Urban World', 26.
67. United States Senate, 'S. Doc. 105-24: The United States Senate Committee on Agriculture, Nutrition, and Forestry 1825-1998', http://www.access.gpo.gov/congress/senate/sen_agriculture/ch5.html (accessed January 13, 2007).
68. Jeffrey Sachs, The End of Poverty: How can we make it happen in our lifetime (London: Penguin, 2005), 36.
69. Sachs, The End of Poverty, 36.

70. Davis, *Planet of Slums*, 70-94.
71. Jeffrey Sachs, 'Foreword', UN Millennium Project Taskforce on Improving the Lives of Slum Dwellers, *A Home in the City* (London: Earthscan, 2005), iii.
72. Satterthwaite, 'The Transition to a Predominantly Urban World', 25.
73. Davis, Planet of Slums, 48.
74. Davis, Planet of Slums, 48.
75. UNHCR, 'Refugee Figures', http://www.unhcr.org/pages/49c3646c1d.html (accessed June 28, 2011)
76. Central Intelligence Agency, 'World Fact Book', https://www.cia.gov/cia/publications/factbook/geos/xx.html (accessed January 13, 2007).
77. Satterthwaite, 'The Transition to a Predominantly Urban World', 9.
78. Davis, Planet of Slums, 135.
79. Satterthwaite, 'The Transition to a Predominantly Urban World', 28.
80. Dennis Gray, 'Bangkok Has That Sinking Feeling', *Associated Press*, October 20, 2007, http://www.wildsingapore.com/news/20070910/071020-3.htm (accessed January 10, 2010).
81. Associated Press, 'Rising Seas Threaten 21 Mega-Cities', October 21, 2007, http://www.wildsingapore.com/news/20070910/071020-3.htm (accessed January 10, 2010).
82. Robert Kunzig, 'Seven Billion', *National Geographic*, January, 2011, 63.
83. Anna Tibaijuka, 'Cities Without Slums', *Our Planet,* United Nations Environment Programme January 16, 2005, http://www.unep.org/ourplanet/imgversn/161/tibaijuka.html (accessed on January 14, 2011).

Chapter 3

1. Todd Johnson, November 27, 2010, personal email message to author used with permission.
2. Rodney Stark, *The Rise of Christianity: How the obscure, marginal Jesus movement became the dominant religious force in the Western world in a few centuries* (San Francisco: HarperCollins, 1996), 73-94.
3. Stark, *The Rise of Christianity*, 91-93.
4. David Barrett and Todd Johnson, 'Status of Global Mission, 2004, in Context of 20th and 21st Centuries', *International Bulletin of Missionary Research* 28 no. 1 (2004): 25.
5. Barrett and Johnson, 'Status of Global Mission 2004'.
6. Todd M. Johnson and Kenneth R. Ross, *Atlas of Global Christianity* (Edinburgh: Edinburgh University Press, 2009), 238.
7. David Barrett and Todd Johnson, 'Status of Global Mission, 2010, in Context of 20th and 21st Centuries', IBMR 34:1, http://www.gordonconwell.edu/sites/default/files/IBMR2010.pdf (accessed September 6, 2010).
8. Barrett and Johnson, 'Status of Global Mission 2010'.
9. Barrett and Johnson, 'Status of Global Mission 2010'.
10. Johnson and Ross, Atlas of Global Christianity, 242-243.
11. Johnson and Ross, Atlas of Global Christianity, .238-239.
12. Johnson and Ross, Atlas of Global Christianity, 238.
13. Johnson and Ross, *Atlas of Global Christianity*, 238-239.
14. United Nations, 'World Urbanization Prospects: The 2007 revision population database', http://esa.un.org/unup/ (accessed September 6, 2010).
15. Johnson and Ross, Atlas of Global Christianity, 57.
16. The Joshua Project, 'What is the 10/40 Window?', http://www.joshuaproject.net/10-40-window.php (accessed December 20, 2010).
17. Luis Bush, 'What is the 10/40 Window?' http://www.tumi.org/migration/images/stories/pdf/lga/docs/WHATIS10.pdf (accessed September 8, 2010).

18. Bush, 'What is the 10/40 Window?'
19. Bush, 'What is the 10/40 Window?'
20. P. H. Liotta and James F. Miskel, 'The "Mega-Eights": Urban Leviathans and international instability', Foreign Policy Research Institute, http://www.fpri.org/enotes/201002.liottamiskel.megaeights.html (accessed September 8, 2010).
21. Johnson and Ross, Atlas of Global Christianity, 136.
22. Johnson and Ross, Atlas of Global Christianity, 140.
23. UN-Habitat, *Challenge of Slums*, xxv-xxvii.
24. The Global Education Project, 'Earth: A graphic look at the state of the world', http://www.theglobaleducationproject.org/earth/human-conditions.php (accessed June 29, 2011).
25. Johnson and Ross, *Atlas of Global Christianity*, 208-209.
26. Government of India, 'Census of India 2001 (Provisional) Slum Population in Million Plus Cities (Municipal Corporations)', http://censusindia.gov.in/Tables_Published/Admin_Units/Admin_links/slum1_m_plus.html (accessed September 10, 2010).
27. Johnson and Ross, Atlas of Global Christianity, 246.
28. One World, 'Dhaka's Slum Population Doubles in a Decade', http://us.oneworld.net/node/133390 (accessed December 21, 2010).
29. Johnson and Ross, *Atlas of Global Christianity*, 246.
30. Daily Times, 'Pakistan's Urban Population To Equal Rural by 2030: UNFPA', http://www.dailytimes.com.pk/default.asp?page=2007%5C06%5C28%5Cstory_28-6-2007_pg7_9 (accessed December 21, 2010).
31. Johnson and Ross, *Atlas of Global Christianity*, 246.
32. Johnson and Ross, Atlas of Global Christianity, 246.
33. Johnson and Ross, *Atlas of Global Christianity*, 246.
34. Viv Grigg, 'Where Are the Churches of the Poor?' *Urban Leaders*, http://www.urbanleaders.org/weburbpoor/04Context(CX)/Global%20Movements/where%20are%20the%20churches%20of%20the%20poor/Churches%20of%20the%20poor.htm (accessed January 11, 2011).
35. Grigg, 'Where are the Churches Of The Poor?'.
36. Earth Observatory, 'Dakar, Senegal', http://earthobservatory.nasa.gov/IOTD/view.php?id=8886 (accessed January 10, 2011).
37. Johnson and Ross, *Atlas of Global Christianity*, 244.
38. Jeremy Page, 'Indian Slum Population Doubles in Two Decades', *The Sunday Times*, http://www.timesonline.co.uk/tol/news/world/asia/article1805596.ece (accessed December 21, 2010).
39. Johnson and Ross, *Atlas of Global Christianity*, 246.
40. UN-Habitat, State of the World's Cities 2006/7, 72.
41. Johnson and Ross, *Atlas of Global Christianity*, 136.
42. Johnson and Ross, *Atlas of Global Christianity*, 140.
43. Jeremy Page, 'Indian Slum Population Doubles In Two Decades'.
44. See, Harvie Conn and Manuel Ortiz, *Urban Ministry: The Kingdom, the city and the people of God* (Downers Grove: InterVarsity Press, 2001).
45. See, for example, Ray Bakke and Jim Hart, *The Urban Christian: Effective ministry in today's urban world* (Downers Grove: InterVarsity Press, 1987).
46. See, Robert Linthicum, *City of God, City of Satan* (Grand Rapids: Zondervan, 1991).
47. See, Colin Marchant, *Signs of the City* (London: Hodder and Stoughton, 1985).
48. Jacques Ellul, *The Meaning Of The City* (Grand Rapids: Eerdmans, 1970).
49. Harvey Cox, *The Secular City: Secularization and urbanization in theological perspective* (London: SCM Press, 1966).
50. Ray Bakke, *A Theology As Big As The City* (Downers Grove: InterVarsity Press, 1997).

51. Roger Greenway and Timothy Monsma, *Cities: Missions' new frontier* (Grand Rapids: Baker, 2000), 68.
52. Viv Grigg, cited in Geneva Sector Intelligence, *Urban Slums Worldwide* (unpublished, 2004): 1.
53. Viv Grigg, *Cry of the Urban Poor* (Monvrovia: MARC,1992), 95.
54. Geneva Sector Intelligence, *Urban Slums Worldwide*, 22.
55. Geneva Sector Intelligence, *Urban Slums Worldwide*, 22.
56. Geneva Sector Intelligence, *Urban Slums Worldwide*, 22.
57. Geneva Sector Intelligence, *Urban Slums Worldwide*, 22-23.
58. Grigg, 'Where Are the Churches of the Poor?'.
59. Johnson and Ross, Atlas of Global Christianity, 260.
60. Johnson and Ross, Atlas of Global Christianity, 261.
61. Johnson and Ross, *Atlas of Global Christianity*, 260-261 (original chart). This summary version of the chart comes from David Barrett, 'Sending and Receiving Missionaries by UN Region', *International Bulletin of Missionary Research* 34 no. 1 (2010): 29–36, http://www.internationalbulletin.org/system/files/2010-01-030-scatter.html (accessed January 10, 2011).
62. World Convention, 'National Profiles: USA', http://www.worldconvention.org/country.php?c=US (accessed December 22, 2010).
63. Doug Priest, November 11, 2010, personal email message to author used with permission.
64. David Kupp, 'Urban Issues: Discussion Papers', http://www.transformational-development.org/Ministry/TransDev2.nsf/webmaindocs/094A3B847DCC22F4852570A4005626B6?OpenDocument (accessed June 29, 2011). These figures are derived by adding up costings from 669 of WV's projects in 2004 which were identified as urban in general and 'slums' specifically in 'So, Where Are Those Urban Programmes?' Discussion Paper #4 Transformational Development News 2005 Jul 22; Vol. 3(3): 6-7. These figures were published in WV's 2004 budget, in World Vision International, '2004 Annual Review', http://www.wvi.org/wvi/wviweb.nsf/webmaindocs/1C72CA5128025B288825737C00756949?OpenDocument (accessed January 8, 2010). For the full Excel sheet and notes about urban projects, see Kupp, 'So, Where Are Those Urban Programmes?'
65. World Vision, '2004 Annual Review'.
66. See, Tetsunao Yamori, Bryant Myers and Kenneth Luscombe, eds., *Serving with the Urban Poor* (Monrovia: MARC, 1998). For a fuller treatment of Urban Advance and WV's struggles with urban development see David Kupp, 'World Vision's Urban History and Theology', http://www.transformational-development.org/Ministry/TransDev2.nsf/A6748A23BB21C3F08825725700707E73/$file/Urban%20R&D%20Report%20-%20Chapter%206%20(Draft)%20-%20Jan%209,%202007.pdf (accessed January 10, 2011).
67. The Urban Working Group, 'The Keys to the City: Finding New Doorways to Urban Transformation—A Report and Recommendations', (Draft: 2007), http://www.transformational-development.org/Ministry/TransDev2.nsf/A6748A23BB21C3F08825725700707E73/$file/Urban%20R&D%20Report%20-%20Summary%20(Draft)%20-%20Jan%209,%202007.pdf (accessed January 8, 2010).
68. The Urban Working Group, 'The Keys to the City'.
69. One World Vision survey comparing sponsored children in urban and rural areas found that over four years the percentage child drop-out rates were significantly higher in urban areas each year in each region: David Kupp, 'Urban Child Sponsorship and Fundraising', 5, http://www.transformational-development.org/Ministry/TransDev2.nsf/A6748A23BB21C3F08825725700707E73/$file/Urban%20R&D%20Report%20-%20Chapter%209%20(Draft)%20-%20Jan%2010,%202007.pdf (accessed January 11, 2011).
70. See, for example, World Vision's work in rural Peru with children: World Vision, 'Putting Children First in the Highlands of Peru', http://www.worldvision.com.au/Issues/Transforming_Lives___Child_Sponsorship/WhatIsOurResponse/Putting_children_first_in_the_highlands_of_Pe.aspx (accessed December 22, 2010).
71. David Kupp, 'Playing "Catch Up" with the City: How are other international agencies responding to urban poverty?', World Vision International, http://www.transformational-development.org/Ministry/TransDev2.nsf/094A3B847DCC22F4852570A4005626B6/$file/

Urban%20Issues%207%20-%20Playing%20Catch-Up%20With%20the%20City.pdf (accessed January 8, 2011).
72. Australian Government, 'Statistical Summary 2008–2009: Australia's International Aid Program', http://www.ausaid.gov.au/publications/green-book/AusAID%20Statistical%20 Summary%202008-09.pdf (accessed January 21, 2011).
73. Jenny Beechey (TEAR Australia Project Accountability Officer), January 21, 2011, personal email message to author used with permission.
74. Howard Culbertson, '10/40 Window: Do you need to be stirred into action?' *Southern Nazarene University*, http://home.snu.edu/~hculbert/1040.htm#abc (accessed July 11, 2011).
75. World Christian News, 'Statistics: The 21st century world', *World Christian News*, issue 24; *Population Reference Bureau, Data Sheet 2002* http://home.snu.edu/~hculbert/world.htm (accessed December 22, 2010).
76. World Christian News, 'Statistics: The 21st century world'.
77. Steve Corbett and Brian Fikkert, *When Helping Hurts: How to alleviate poverty without hurting the poor and yourself* (Chicago: Moody, 2009), Kindle loc. 2316-29.
78. World Christian News, 'Statistics: The 21st century world'.
79. Mike Davis, 'Planet of Slums', *New Left Review*, March-April, 2004, 26, http://newleftreview.org/A2496 (accessed January 10, 2011).
80. Government of India, 'Census of India 2001'.
81. Viv Grigg, September 7, 2010, personal email message to author used with permission.
82. Grigg, personal email used with permission.
83. Daniel H. Levines, 'Assessing the Impact of Liberation Theology in Latin America', *The Review of Politics* Vol. 50 No 2, 1988, http://www.jstor.org/pss/1407649 (accessed June 27, 2011).
84. Rachelle Dragani, 'Mother Teresa (1910-1997)', *Time Magazine*, November 19, 2010.
85. Christine Bodewes, *Parish Transformation in Urban Slums: Voices of Kibera, Kenya* (Nairobi: Pauline Publications, 2006).
86. Exodus Kutoka, 'Network of Catholic Parishes Working in Slums (Informal Settlements) Nairobi, Kenya', http://www.kutokanet.com/network/Brochure_KutokaNetwork.pdf (accessed December 21, 2010).
87. See, Greg Barrett, *The Gospel of Father Joe* (San Francisco: Jossey-Bass, 2008).
88. See, Jane Sutton, 'Telling It on a Mountain', http://www.urbana.org/articles?RecordId=343%20 (accessed December 21, 2010).
89. Paul Pierson, *The Dynamics of Christian Mission: History through a missiological perspective* (Pasadena: William Carey Library, 2009), Kindle loc. 8412-16.
90. Scott Bessenecker, October 22, 2010, personal email to author used with permission.
91. Scott Bessenecker, personal email used with permission.
92. Ash Barker, 'Epilogue: Challenges and Possibilities for a New Generation of Mission Workers', *Living Mission: The vision and voices of new friars*, ed. Scott Bessenecker (Downers Grove: InterVarsity Press, 2010), 156-166.
93. See Urban Leadership Foundation, 'Encarnação Alliance of Urban Poor Movement Leaders', http://www.urbanleaders.org/encarnacao2_joomla/ (accessed January 10, 2010).
94. Viv Grigg, personal email used with permission.

Chapter 4

1. Osmer, *Practical Theology*, Kindle loc. 86-97.
2. My first year in Klong Toey, including this story, is told in Ashley Barker, *Finding Life: Reflections from a Bangkok slum* (Melbourne: Go Alliance, 2003), 52-63.
3. January to August 2010. Bangkok Post, 'WHO Warns Dengue Fever is on the Rise', *Bangkok Post* (Bangkok), September 13, 2010, http://www.bangkokpost.com/news/local/195921/who-warns-dengue-fever-is-on-the-rise (accessed September 13, 2010).
4. See, for example, John Livingston Nevius, *The Planting and Development of Missionary Churches* (Handcock: Monadnock Press, 2003). This book was originally published by Presbyterian Press,

Shanghai in 1886.
5. See, for example, Roland Allen, *Missionary Methods: St Pauls or ours?* (Grand Rapids: Eerdmans, 1968).
6. Donald McGavran, *Understanding Church Growth* (Grand Rapids: Eerdmans, 1980), 375-376.
7. See, for example, George Barna, *Marketing the Church: What they never taught you about church growth* (Colarado Springs: Navpress, 1988).
8. Eddie Gibbs, *Emerging Churches: Creating Christian community in postmodern cultures* (Grand Rapids: Baker, 2005). Gibbs has been on the Fuller faculty since 1982 and is the senior professor of Church Growth at Fuller Seminary.
9. See, for example, the use of the National Church Life Survey in Australia. NCLS Research, 'National Church Life Survey', http://www.ncls.org.au/ (accessed January 13, 2010).
10. McGavran, Understanding Church Growth, 250.
11. McGavran, Understanding Church Growth, 251.
12. McGavran, Understanding Church Growth, 254-256.
13. McGavran, Understanding Church Growth, 295-313.
14. McGavran, Understanding Church Growth, 19-22.
15. McGavran, Understanding Church Growth, 332.
16. See, Sachs, The End of Poverty.
17. David Bornstein, How to Change the World: Social entrepreneurs and the power of new ideas (Oxford, UK: Oxford University Press, 2004), 4.
18. William Easterly, The White Man's Burden: Why the West's efforts to aid the rest have done so much ill and so little good (London: Penguin, 2006), 4.
19. Robert Linthicum, Empowering the Poor: Community organizing among the city's rag, tag and bobtail (Monrovia: MARC, 1999).
20. Bryant Myers, Walking with the Poor: Principles and practices of transformational development (Maryknoll: Orbis, 1999).
21. Jayakumar Christian, God of the Empty-Handed: Poverty, power and the Kingdom of God (Monrovia: MARC, 1999).
22. See, Easterly, *The White Man's Burden*; Graham Handcock, *Lords of Poverty* (London: Macmillan, 1989); and Leonard Frank, 'The Development Game', *The Post-Development Reader* (London: Zed Books, 1997). A whole edition of *New Internationalist* was dedicated to the critique of BINGOs (Big International Non-Government Organizations) in 2005, with the feature article being: David Ransom, 'The Big Charity Bonanza', *New Internationalist*, no. 383 (2005), http://www.newint.org/features/2005/10/01/keynote/ (accessed January 13, 2011).
23. Thomas W. Dichter, Despite Good Intentions: Why development assistance to the third world has failed (Boston: University of Massachusetts Press, 2003).
24. See, the *Live Eight* concert in 2005 and Michael Cress, 'Can Rockers and Religious Leaders End Poverty?', *Belief Net*, http://www.beliefnet.com/News/2005/07/Can-Rockers-And-Religious-Leaders-End-Poverty.aspx (accessed January 13, 2011).
25. Easterly, The White Man's Burden, 3-4.
26. Easterly, The White Man's Burden, 4.
27. Dichter, Despite Good Intentions, 2.
28. David Barrett, Peter Crossing and Todd Johnson, 'Status of Global Mission, 2010, in Context of 20th and 21st Centuries', *International Bulletin of Missionary Research* (2010): 29-36, http://www.internationalbulletin.org/system/files/2010-01-029-johnson.html (accessed January 13, 2010).
29. Dichter, Despite Good Intentions, 1.
30. See, for example, Dichter, *Despite Good Intentions*, 128-150.
31. Dichter, Despite Good Intentions, 156.
32. Gary Brock from Christian Missionary Fellowship, personal correspondence with author used with permission.

33. Urban Advance, *Belo Horizonte* (World Vision, unpublished).
34. Urban Advance, *Belo Horizonte*, 3.
35. Urban Advance, *Belo Horizonte*, 4.
36. Urban Advance, *Belo Horizonte*, 4.
37. Dichter, Despite Good Intentions, 68.
38. The five worst disasters impacting on cities in terms of numbers of people killed between 2000-2010 were: 1) South Asian tsunami (2004)—226,408 deaths, 2) Haiti earthquake (2010)—222,570 deaths, 3) Cyclone Nargis, Myanmar (2008)—138,366 deaths, 4) Sichuan earthquake, China (2008)—87,476 deaths, and 5) Kashmir earthquake, Pakistan (2005)—73,338 deaths. International Federation of Red Cross and Red Crescent Societies, 'World Disasters Report 2010 – Focus on Urban Risk', http://www.ifrc.org/Docs/pubs/disasters/wdr2010/WDR2010-full.pdf (accessed January 13, 2010).
39. Dischter, *Despite Good Intentions*, 257-263.
40. David Kupp, 'Urban Child Sponsorship and Fundraising'.
41. See the report: Social Development and Services Unit, *History and Work of Klong Toey Community Centre* (Bangkok: Church of Christ in Thailand, unpublished), 1.
42. Dichter, Despite Good Intentions, 28.
43. Dichter, Despite Good Intentions, 30.
44. Dichter, Despite Good Intentions, 30.
45. Paul Collier, The Bottom Billion: Why the poorest countries are failing and what can be done about it. (Oxford, UK: Oxford University Press, 2007).
46. Dichter, Despite Good Intentions, 132.
47. Dichter, Despite Good Intentions, 132.
48. Dichter, Despite Good Intentions, 132.
49. Marc Askew, *Bangkok: Place, practice and representation* (London: Routledge, 2002), 149-150.
50. Dichter, Despite Good Intentions, 66.
51. See, James Blackburn, Robert Chambers and John Gaventa, 'Mainstreaming Participation in Development—OED Working Paper Series', World Bank, no. 10: 9, http://lnweb90.worldbank.org/oed/oeddoclib.nsf/DocUNIDViewForJavaSearch/1D8EC8BB36C8C76E85256977007257C1/$file/Mnstream.pdf (accessed June 29, 2011).
52. Askew, *Bangkok*, 148.
53. Bangkok Post, 'Taksin Promises End to Slums in Three Years', *Bangkok Post*, October 5, 2005, http://www.orientexpat.com/forum/4107-thaksin-promises-end-to-slums-in-three-years/ (accessed June 29, 2011).
54. Anan Paengnoy, 'Task of Building 100,000 Units a Year "Tough for NHA"', *The Nation*, http://www.nationmultimedia.com/2006/09/04/national/national_30012712.php (accessed January 15, 2007).
55. Bangkok Post, 'Ban Mankong: From slum upgrade to social uplift', *Bangkok Post*, February 2, 2010, http://www.bangkokpost.com/news/investigation/32500/ban-mankong-from-slum-upgrading-to-social-upliftment (accessed March 10, 2010).
56. UN Taskforce Improving the Lives of Slum-Dwellers, *A Home in the City* (London: Earthscan, 2005), 10.
57. Corbett and Fikkert, *When Helping Hurts*. Kindle loc. 2327-35.
58. See, Alan Hirsch, *The Forgotten Ways: Reactivating the missional church* (Grand Rapids: Brazos, 2006), 127-148.
59. See, Scott Bessenecker, *New Friars: The emerging movement serving the world's poor* (Downers Grove, USA: InterVarsity Press, 2006), 74-84.
60. See, Jon Sobrino, Christianity at the Crossroads: A Latin American approach (Maryknoll: Obis, 1984), 124.
61. See, Darrell Guder, *Be My Witnesses* (Grand Rapids: Eerdmans, 1985), 18-34; and John Stott, *Christian Mission in the Modern World* (London: Falcon, 1975), 22-25.

62. Langmead, *The Word Made Flesh*, 61-214.
63. Not her real name. For a fuller discussion of 'Lek's' story see Barker, 'Epilogue', *Living Mission*, 157-159.
64. See, Jonathan Bonk, Missions and Money: Affluence as a missionary problem... Revisited (Maryknoll: Orbis, 2006).
65. Brian Houston, You Need More Money: God's amazing financial plan for your life (Sydney: Maximised Leadership, 1999). 1-3.
66. Bonk, *Missions and Money*, 95.
67. Michael Duncan, *Costly Mission: Following Christ into the slums* (Monrovia: MARC, 1996), 34-36.
68. Ronald Sider, *Rich Christians in an Age of Hunger* (London: Hodder and Stoughton, 1990), 3-45.
69. Bonk, *Missions and Money*, 51-156.
70. Michael Duncan, *The Incarnational Approach: The Journey Series, No 2* (Christchurch, New Zealand: Servants to Asia's Urban Poor, 1991), 3.
71. Ken Baker, 'The Incarnational Model: Perception of deception?' *Evangelical Missions Quarterly*, January 2002, 16-24.
72. Duncan, *Costly Mission*, 74-75.
73. Bessenecker, Quest for Hope in the Slum Community, 7.
74. Grigg, Cry of the Urban Poor, 126.
75. Baker, 'The Incarnational Model', 54.
76. Langmead, The Word Made Flesh, 48.
77. Janet Martin Soskice, *Metaphor and Religious Language* (Oxford: Clarendon, 1985), 15.
78. Suzanne Langer, *Philosophy in a New Key* (New York: Mentor, 1948), 114.
79. Langmead, The Word Made Flesh, 37.
80. John Hayes, *Sub-merge: Living Deep in a Shallow World* (Ventura: Regal, 2006), 114-120.

Chapter 5

1. See Fung's email discussions with Langmead, which were one catalyst for Langmead, *The Word Made Flesh*, 4.
2. See, Andreas J. Köstenberger, *The Missions of Jesus and the Disciples According to the Fourth Gospel* (Grand Rapids: Eerdmans, 1998), 213-217.
3. See, for example, David Hesselgrave, *Paradigms in Conflict: 10 key questions in Christian missions today* (Grand Rapids: Kregal, 2005), 141-165.
4. See Baker, 'The Incarnational Model', 16-24.
5. Tim Chester, 'Why I Don't Believe in Incarnational Mission', *Reformed Spirituality and Missional Church*, http://timchester.wordpress.com/2008/07/19/why-i-dont-believe-in-incarnational-mission/ (accessed February 4, 2011).
6. Wolfgang Simson, *The Starfish Manifesto* (Antioch: Asteroidea Books, 2009), Kindle loc. 6875-78.
7. Simson, *The Starfish Manifesto*, Kindle loc. 6954-56.
8. Hesselgrave, *Paradigms in Conflict*, 145 and 162.
9. Hesselgrave, *Paradigms in Conflict*, 148-149.
10. Hesselgrave, Paradigms in Conflict, 144.
11. Hesselgrave, *Paradigms in Conflict*, 146.
12. Stott, *Christian Mission in the Modern World*, 32, cited in Hesselgrave, *Paradigms in Conflict*, 146-147.
13. Hesselgrave, *Paradigms in Conflict*, 155.
14. See Barker, *Finding Life*, 97-99.

15. Köstenberger, *The Missions of Jesus and the Disciples*, 13 and 213-217.
16. Köstenberger, *The Missions of Jesus and the Disciples*, 215.
17. Hesselgrave, 'Incarnationalism and representationalism', 153.
18. Hesselgrave, *Paradigms in Conflict*, 152.
19. Irenaeus, 'Irenaeus against Heresies', *Ante-Nicene Fathers*, Book IV, Chapter VII, cited in Diana Butler Bass, *A People's History of Christianity* (New York: HarperCollins, 2009), Kindle loc. 614-16.
20. Jürgen Moltmann, *God in Creation: An ecological doctrine of creation* (London: SCM, 1985), 245-246.
21. See Thorwald Lorenzen, *Resurrection and Discipleship: Interpretive models, biblical reflections, theological consequences* (Maryknoll: Orbis, 1996), 244.
22. Langmead, *The Word Made Flesh*, 61-91.
23. N. T. Wright, Surprised by Hope: Rethinking heaven, the resurrection and the mission of the church (New York: HarperOne, 2008), 93-106.
24. The events are well recorded in books like Linda Polman, *We Did Nothing* (London: Penguin Viking, 2003) and films like *Hotel Rwanda*.
25. Brian McLaren, *Everything Must Change: Jesus, global crises and a revolution of hope* (Nashville: Thomas Nelson, 2007), 22.
26. Dietrich Bonhoeffer, *The Cost of Discipleship* (Suffolk: SCM, 2003), 3.
27. Christian, *God of the Empty Handed*. 121-125.
28. See, for example, Chris Green, 'The Incarnation and Mission', in *The Word Became Flesh: Evangelicals and the Incarnation*, ed. David Peterson (Carlisle: Paternoster Press, 2003), 81-101.
29. Tim Chester, 'Why I Don't Believe in Incarnational Mission'.
30. Cited in Langmead, *The Word Made Flesh*, 4.
31. Langmead, *The Word Made Flesh*, 220-221.
32. Timothy C. Morgan, 'Purpose Driven in Rwanda: Rick Warren's sweeping plan to defeat poverty', *Christianity Today*, http://www.christianitytoday.com/ct/2005/october/17.32.html?start=2 (accessed February 8, 2011).
33. Langmead, *The Word Made Flesh*, 220-222.

Chapter 6

1. John Perkins, *With Justice For All: A strategy for community development* (Ventura: Regal Books, 1982), 88.
2. Hayes, *Sub-merge*, 116.
3. Dave Andrews, *Compassionate Community Work: An introductory course for Christians* (Carlisle: Piquant, 2006), 31-32.
4. Langmead, *The Word Made Flesh*, 219-220.
5. Stott, *Christian Mission in the Modern World*, 23.
6. Langmead, *The Word Made Flesh*, 219-228.
7. See, Harold S Bender, *The Anabaptist Vision* (Scottdale: Herald, 1944), 11-16; John Howard Yoder, *The Politics of Jesus: Vicit agnus noster* (Grand Rapids: Eerdmans, 1994), 115-127; Stuart Murray, *The Naked Anabaptist: Bare essentials of a radical faith* (Scottdale: Herald, 2010), 117-134; David Augsburger, *Dissident Discipleship: A spirituality of self-surrender, love of God and love of neighbour* (Grand Rapids: Brazos, 2006), 171-188.
8. See, Orlando Costas, Christ Outside the Gate: Mission beyond Christendom (Maryknoll: Orbis, 1982); Vinay Samuel and Albert Hauser, eds., Proclaiming Christ in Christ's Way: Studies in integral evangelism (Oxford: Regnum, 1989); Athol Gill, Life on the Road: The Gospel basis for a messianic lifestyle (Homebush West: Lancer, 1989); Duncan, Costly Mission.
9. Leonardo Boff, Jesus Christ Liberator: A critical Christology for our time (Maryknoll: Orbis, 1986); Jon Sobrino, The Principle of Mercy: Taking the crucified people from the cross

(Maryknoll: Orbis, 1992); Gustavo Gutiérrez, We Drink From Our Own Wells: A spiritual journey of a people (Maryknoll: Orbis, 1984).

10. Langmead, *The Word Made Flesh*, 61-141.
11. Eugene H Peterson, *The Message: The Bible in contemporary language* (Colorado Springs: NavPress, 2007).
12. Gerhard Kittel and Gerhard Friedrich, eds., *Theological Dictionary of the New Testament*, abridged ed., translated by Geoffrey W Bromiley. (Grand Rapids: Eerdmans, 1985), 1040.
13. Andrews, *Compassionate Community Work*, 31-32.
14. Dorothy Harris, 'Incarnation as a Journey in Relocation' in *Sharing the Good News with the Poor*, eds. Bruce J. Nicholls and Beulah R. Woods (Grand Rapids: Baker, 1996), 175.
15. Perkins, *With Justice for All*, 88.
16. Michael Duncan, *Mission: The Incarnational approach, The Journey Series 2* (Christchurch, New Zealand: Servants to Asia's Urban Poor, 1991), 3.
17. Duncan, *Mission*, 13.
18. Rob O'Callaghan, 'What do we mean by "Incarnational Methodology?"', *The Cry* Vol.10:3, 2004, 6-8.
19. Sudhakar Mondithoka, 'Incarnation', *Dictionary of Mission Theology*, 178.
20. Michael Frost and Alan Hirsch, *The Shaping of Things to Come: Innovation and mission for the 21st century church* (Peabody, MA: Hendrickson, 2003), 41.
21. Frost and Hirsch, *The Shaping of Things to Come*, 37-38.
22. Frost and Hirsch, *The Shaping of Things to Come*, 38.
23. Anthony J. Gittins, Gifts and Strangers: Meeting the challenge of inculturation (New York: Paulist, 1989).
24. Cited without source Project 1516, 'Famous Quotes about Christian Missions' http://www.project1615.org/quotes.htm (accessed September 17, 2010).
25. O'Callaghan, 'What do we Mean by "Incarnational Methodology?"'
26. Judith E. Lingenfelter and Sherwood G. Lingenfelter, *Teaching Cross-culturally: An incarnational model for learning and teaching* (Grand Rapids: Baker, 2007), 22.
27. SEDOS, 'Agenda for Future Planning, Study, and Research in Mission: Agenda for the SEDOS Research Seminar on the Future of Mission, Rome, March 1981', in *Trends in Mission: Toward the third millennium. Essays in celebration of twenty-five years of SEDOS*, eds. William Jenkinson and Helen O'Sullivan (Maryknoll: Orbis, 1991), 29, 404.
28. J. Todd Billings, 'Incarnational Ministry and the Unique, Incarnate Christ', http://contendearnestly.blogspot.com/2010/03/incarnational-ministry-and-unique.html (accessed June 15, 2010).
29. Billings, 'Incarnational Ministry and the Unique, Incarnate Christ'.
30. Langmead, *The Word Made Flesh*, 55.
31. Andrew Root, Revisiting Relational Youth Ministry: From a strategy of influence to a theology of incarnation, (Downers Grove: IVP Books, 2007).
32. Root, *Revisiting Relational Youth Ministry*, 50-53.
33. Root, *Revisiting Relational Youth Ministry*, 52-53.
34. Root, *Revisiting Relational Youth Ministry*, 53.
35. Root, *Revisiting Relational Youth Ministry*, 62-80.
36. Root, Revisiting Relational Youth Ministry, 83.
37. See, for example, Hirsch, *The Forgotten Ways*, 190-216; Simson, *The Starfish Manifesto;* and Steve Addison, *Movements that Change the World* (Smyrna: Missional Press, 2009).
38. Grigg, *Cry of the Urban Poor*, 163.
39. Grigg, *Cry of the Urban Poor*, 218.
40. Grigg, *Cry of the Urban Poor*, 217.

41. Viv Grigg, 'Sorry! The Frontier Moved' in *Planting and Growing Urban Churches*, ed. Harvie Conn (Grand Rapids: Baker, 1997), 159.
42. Roger S. Greenway, 'Eighteen Barrels and Two Big Crates: How and why our "stuff" gets in the way of our witness', Mission Frontiers, March/April (1992), http://www.missionfrontiers.org/1992/0304/ma925.htm (accessed June 2, 2008).
43. See, Ronald J. Sider, *Rich Christians in an Age of Hunger: Moving from affluence to generosity* (Nashville: Thomas Nelson, 2005).
44. Bonk, Missions and Money, 95.
45. Bonk, *Missions and Money*, 95.
46. Bonk, *Missions and Money*, 96.
47. Bonk, *Missions and Money*, 61-64.
48. Hayes, *Sub-merge*, 115.
49. Hayes, *Sub-merge*, 120.
50. Hayes, *Sub-merge*, 113.
51. Johann Adam Mohler, *Symbolism; or, Exposition of the Doctrinal Differences Between Catholics and Protestants as Evidenced by Their Symbolic Writings* (New York: E Dunigan, 1844), 333.
52. Vatican, 'The Catechism of the Catholic Church', Part 1, Chapter 2, Section 3, #9.2.1, para. 790, http://www.vatican.va/archive/ccc_css/archive/catechism/p123a9p2.htm (accessed September 16, 2010).
53. Witness Lee, 'The History of the Local Churches', http://www.local-church-history.org/local-church-2-aspects-b.htm (accessed June 16, 2010).
54. Rick Warren, *The Purpose Driven Life* (Grand Rapids: Zondervan, 2002), 132.
55. Frost and Hirsch, *The Shaping of Things to Come*, 41.
56. Robert D Putnam, Bowling Alone: The collapse and revival of American community (New York: Touchstone, 2000), 213.
57. Jude Tiersma, 'What Does it Mean to Be Incarnational When We Are Not the Messiah?' In *God So Loves the City: Seeking a theology for urban mission*, eds. Charles Van Engen and Jude Tiersma (Monrovia: MARC, 1994), 7–25.

Chapter 7

1. Richard Foster, *Streams of Living Water: Celebrating the great traditions of Christian faith* (San Francisco: Harper SanFrancisco, 2001), 260-261.
2. Foster, *Streams of Living Water*, 263.
3. Foster, *Streams of Living Water*, 236.
4. Foster, *Streams of Living Water*, 272.
5. Foster, *Streams of Living Water*, 272.
6. Mother Teresa, *Heart of Joy* (Ann Arbor: Servant Books, 1987), 32.
7. Dominique Lapierre, *City of Joy* (New York: Warner Books, 1992).
8. Foster, *Streams of Living Water*, 267.
9. Foster, *Streams of Living Water*, 268.
10. Langmead, *The Word Made Flesh*, 55.
11. Darrell Guder, *The Incarnation and the Church's Witness* (Eugene: Wipf & Stock, 1999), xii.
12. Guder, *The Incarnation and the Church's Witness*, xii.
13. Bosch, *Transforming Mission*, 512.
14. Bosch, *Transforming Mission*, 512-513.
15. Bosch, *Transforming Mission*, 512-518.
16. Bosch, *Transforming Mission*, 518.
17. Bessenecker, *Living Mission*, 9.

18. Bessenecker, *The New Friars*, Kindle loc. 1182-94.
19. Bessenecker, *The New Friars*, Kindle loc. 1182-94.
20. Hayes, *Sub-merge*, 120.
21. Tom Pratt, 'Serving Slums', *Momentum*, January/February 2007, 42.
22. Barker, 'Epilogue' in Bessenecker (ed), *Living Mission*, 156-166.
23. John Hick (ed), *The Myth of God Incarnate* (London: SCM Press, 1977).
24. Walter Wink, *The Human Being: Jesus and the enigma of the Son of Man* (Minneapolis: Fortress, 2002), 201.
25. Wink, *The Human Being*, 201.
26. Marcus Borg and N. T. Wright, *The Meaning of Jesus: Two visions* (New York: HarperOne, 2007), 147-148.
27. Guder, *The Incarnation and the Church's Witness*, xiii.

Chapter 8

1. Langmead, *The Word Made Flesh*, 20.
2. Moltmann, *God in Creation*, Kindle loc. 320-21.
3. Wright, *Surprised by Hope*, Kindle loc. 3367-69.
4. Dietrich Bonhoeffer, *Creation and Fall: Dietrich Bonhoeffer Works Volume 3* (Minneapolis: Fortress Press, 2004), Kindle loc. 693-714.
5. Moltmann, *God in Creation*, Kindle loc. 1179-85.
6. Moltmann, *God in Creation*, Kindle loc. 321-40.
7. Wright, *Surprised by Hope*, Kindle loc. 1706-09.
8. Langmead, *The Word Made Flesh*, 21.
9. Langmead, *The Word Made Flesh*, 21.
10. See, Wright, *Surprised by Hope*, 93-108.
11. James Orr, 'Hope', in *International Standard Encyclopaedia of the Bible* (Grand Rapids: Eerdmans, 1915), http://www.bible-history.com/isbe/H/HOPE/ (accessed September 20, 2011).
12. Wright, *Surprised by Hope*, 102.
13. John McKnight and Peter Brock, *The Abundant Community: Awakening the power of families and neighbourhoods* (San Francisco: Berrett-Koehler, 2010), Kindle loc.189-223.
14. McKnight and Brock, *The Abundant Community*, Kindle loc. 224-233.
15. Adam and Eve's mandate to be 'fruitful', 'multiply' and 'steward' creation (Genesis 1:28); Noah as a new representative of creation after the flood (Genesis 8 and 9) and the tower of Babel (Genesis 11:1-9).
16. Walter Brueggemann, *Reverberations of Faith: A theological handbook of Old Testament themes* (Louisville: Westminster John Knox Press, 2002), 37.
17. Brueggemann, *Reverberations of Faith*, 37.
18. Christopher J. H. Wright, *The Mission of God: Unlocking the Bible's grand narrative* (Downers Grove: InterVarsity, 2006), 28.
19. Borg and Wright, *The Meaning of Jesus*, 166.
20. Wright, *Surprised by Hope*, 230.
21. Stephen J. Pope, ed., *Hope and Solidarity: Jon Sobrino's challenge to Christian theology* (Maryknoll: Orbis, 2008).
22. Vera Ivanise Bombonatto. 'The Commitment to Taking the Poor Down from the Cross', in *Getting the Poor Down from the Cross: Christology of liberation*, ed. José María Vigil (Cyberspace: International Theological Commission of the Ecumenical Association of Third World Theologians, 2007), http://www.servicioskoinonia.org/LibrosDigitales/LDK/EATWOTGettingThePoorDownFull.pdf (accessed January 12, 2011), 41.
23. Jürgen Moltmann, *Theology of Hope: On the ground and the implications of a Christian eschatology* (Minneapolis: Fortress Press, 1993), Kindle loc. 154-63.
24. Jürgen Moltmann, *A Broad Place: An autobiography* (Minneapolis: Fortress Press, 2008), Kindle

loc. 1334-41.
25. Moltmann, *A Broad Place*, Kindle loc. 1319-26.
26. Wright, *Surprised by Hope*, Kindle loc. 741-45.
27. Wright, *Surprised by Hope*, Kindle loc. 3298-3311.

Chapter 9

1. Langmead, *The Word Made Flesh*, 219-220.
2. Langmead, *The Word Made Flesh*, 49-52.
3. See especially John 1 and 1 John 3 and 4.
4. See, Romans 7 and 8.
5. Langmead, *The Word Made Flesh*, 25.
6. Borg and Wright, *The Meaning of Jesus*, 150.
7. *TDNT, abridged*, 178.
8. The first sign was that Jesus turned water to wine (John 2:1-12); second, Jesus healed the man by the pool in Bethesda (John 5:1-29); third, Jesus healed the centurion's servant (John 4:46-54); fourth, Jesus fed the five thousand in the wilderness (John 6:1-15); fifth, Jesus healed the man born blind (John 9); sixth, Jesus raised Lazarus from the dead (John 11:1-44).
9. N. T. Wright, *Following Jesus: Biblical reflections on discipleship* (Grand Rapids: Eerdmans, 1994), 40.
10. Jean Vanier, *Drawn into the Mystery of Jesus through the Gospel of John* (Toronto: Novalis, 2004), 355.
11. New Advent, 'Eutychianism', *Catholic Encyclopaedia*, http://www.newadvent.org/cathen/05633a.htm (accessed September 22, 2010).
12. Millard J. Erickson, *The Word Made Flesh: A contemporary incarnational Christology* (Grand Rapids: Baker, 1991), 65.
13. Langmead's seven understandings of the Incarnation are summarized below. He considers positions six and seven to be 'non-incarnational'.

    1. Jesus had two natures, in the 'substance' terms for the Chalcedonian formulation.

    2. Jesus is the only divine incarnation, absolute and final, a revelation 'qualitatively' superior to all others.

    3. Jesus is God's fully given self-gift. The revelation is 'quantitatively' superior to all others, and Jesus is fully God and fully human.

    4. Christ pre-existed in some divine form, e.g., the Logos.

    5. Jesus Christ was fully human, and His divinity consists in His total transparency and obedience to the Spirit of God.

    6. God was involved in Jesus' life in a special and powerful way. Jesus' exceptional relationship with God has universal significance.

    7. God is involved in human life, e.g., being present in time and history, being 'God with us'. This is claimed by all Christian theologies, and is more an incarnational theology than an incarnational christology.

    Langmead, *The Word Made Flesh*, 30-31.
14. Hans Kung, *On Being a Christian* (New York: Doubleday, 1976), 410.
15. Langmead, *The Word Made Flesh*, 18-19.
16. Langmead, *The Word Made Flesh*, 18.
17. Bosch, *Transforming Mission*, 512-518.
18. Langmead, *The Word Made Flesh*, 19.
19. Jürgen Moltmann, *The Crucified God: The cross of Christ as the foundation and criticism of Christian theology* (London: SCM, 1974), Kindle loc. 811-14.
20. Jon Sobrino, 'Epilogue', in *Getting the poor down from the cross: Christology of liberation*, ed. José María Vigil (n.p.: Ecumenical Association of Third World Theologians, 2007), 309, http://

www.servicioskoinonia.org/LibrosDigitales/LDK/EATWOTGettingThePoorDownFull.pdf (accessed July 12, 2011).
21. Wright, *Surprised by Hope*, 234.
22. Thomas Merton, *New Seeds of Contemplation* (New York: New Directions, 1972), 1.
23. Merton, *New Seeds of Contemplation*, 3.
24. Wes Howard Brook and Anthony Gwyther, *Unveiling Empire: Reading Revelation then and now* (Maryknoll: Orbis, 1999), 231.
25. Myers, *Walking with the Poor*, 86.
26. Ash Barker, 'Community Building is Not for the Faint-hearted', *Finding Life* (September 2010): 2.
27. Cited by Javier Jiménez Limón, 'Suffering, Death, Cross and Martyrdom', in *Mysterium Liberationis: Fundamental concepts of liberation theology*, eds. Ignacio Ellacuría and Jon Sobrino (Maryknoll: Orbis, 1993), 715.
28. Todd M. Johnson, David B. Barrett and Peter F. Crossing, 'Status of Global Mission, 2011, in Context of the 20th and 21st Centuries', *International Bulletin of Missionary Research* (January 2011), 29.

Chapter 10

1. Langmead, *The Word Made Flesh*, 44.
2. Langmead, *The Word Made Flesh*, 45.
3. Langmead, *The Wold Made Flesh*, 220.
4. For an insightful contemporary discussion about this controversy see Jürgen Moltmann, *The Trinity and the Kingdom of God: The doctrine of God* (London: SCM, 1993), 178-180.
5. First Council of Constantinople (381AD).
6. Langmead, *The Word Made Flesh*, 143.
7. Langmead, *The Word Made Flesh*, 144.
8. See, for example, Jürgen Moltmann, 'Preface', in *The Spirit of the World: Emerging Pentecostal theologies in global contexts*, ed. Veli-Matti Kärkkäinen (Grand Rapids: Eerdmans, 2009), viii-xii.
9. Langmead, *The Word Made Flesh*, 94-116.
10. Though from a Reformed church background, Charles Ringma was influenced by the Charismatic movement in Australia and started the Pentecostal drug rehabilitation and drop-in ministry Teen Challenge in Australia after visiting David Wilkerson in the USA. See Charles Ringma, *Catch the Wind* (Sunderland: Albatross, 1996). Both Michael Duncan and Viv Grigg were influenced by the Charismatic renewal movement in New Zealand. See Mick Duncan, 'Gifts in the City' in *Following Fire: How the Spirit leads us to fight injustice*, ed. Cheryl Catford (Melbourne: UNOH, 2008), 240-246 and Viv Grigg, *Companion to the Poor* (Waynesborough: Authentic Media, 2004).
11. See, for example, the diverse typologies of Pentecostal and Charismatic streams in Stanley M Burgess and Eduard M van der Mass, eds., *The New International Dictionary of Pentecostal and Charismatic Movements* (Grand Rapids: Zondervan, 2002).
12. See, for example, the social influence and emphasis of the Spirit with Revivalists such as John Wesley, Jonathan Edwards, Barton Stone and Charles Finney.
13. Douglas Peterson, 'Pentecostals: Who are they?' in *Mission as Transformation: A theology of the whole Gospel*, eds. Vinay Samuel and Chris Sugden (Oxford: Regnum, 1999), 78.
14. Frank Macchi, 'Baptized in the Spirit: Towards a global theology of Spirit baptism' in *The Spirit of the World: Emerging Pentecostal theologies in global contexts*, ed. Veli-Matti Kärkkäinen (Grand Rapids: Eerdmans, 2009), 4.
15. See, for example, how Pentecostalism has primarily been a movement of the poor in Koo Dong Yun, 'Pentecostalism from Below: Minjung liberation and Asian Pentecostal theology' in *The Spirit of the World: Emerging Pentecostal theologies in global contexts*, ed. Veli-Matti Kärkkäinen (Grand Rapids: Eerdmans, 2009), 89-114.

16. Johnson, Barrett and Crossing, 'Status of Global Mission, 2011', 29.
17. Johnson and Ross, *Atlas of Global Christianity*, 102.
18. Johnson and Ross, *Atlas of Global Christianity*, 102-103.
19. Johnson and Ross, *Atlas of Global Christianity*, 102.
20. Yun, 'Pentecostalism from Below', 89-114.
21. Johnson and Ross, *Atlas of Global Christianity*, 140.
22. Johnson and Ross, *Atlas of Global Christianity*, 247.
23. Moltmann, 'Preface', xviii.
24. See, for example, articles in Veli-Matti Kärkkäinen, ed., *The Spirit of the World* and the Brussels Statement, 'Pentecostal Mission and Social Concern' in *Mission as Transformation: A theology of the whole Gospel*, ed. Vinay Samuel and Chris Sugden (Oxford: Regnum, 1999), 112-117.
25. Langmead, *The Word Made Flesh*, 94.
26. Moltmann, 'Preface', ii-iii.
27. Moltmann, *A Broad Place*, Kindle loc.1245.
28. Moltmann, *A Broad Place*, Kindle loc.1425.
29. Moltmann, 'Preface', ix-xii.
30. See, for example, Moltmann's lectures at the 'Society for Pentecostal Studies and the Wesleyan Theological Society, 2008'. MP3s of his lectures, including 'Sighs, Signs, and Significance: A theological hermeneutic of nature' can be downloaded from http://www.andyrowell.net/andy_rowell/duke-divinity-school/page/2/ (accessed March 14, 2010).
31. See, for example, Jürgen Moltmann, 'A Response to My Pentecostal Dialogue Partners', *Journal of Pentecostal Theology* 4 (1994).
32. Moltmann, 'Preface', x.
33. See, Murray Dempster, 'A Theology of the Kingdom: A Pentecostal contribution', in *Mission as Transformation*, 50.
34. Brueggemann, *Reverberations of Faith*, 199.
35. Jürgen Moltmann, *The Source of Life: The Holy Spirit and the theology of life* (Minneapolis: Fortress Press, 1997), 19.
36. Macchia, 'Baptized in the Spirit', 4.
37. Macchia, 'Baptized in the Spirit', 5.
38. *TDNT, abridged*, 840.
39. Macchia, 'Baptized in the Spirit', 4.
40. Duncan, 'Gifts in the City', 241.
41. Yun, 'Pentecostalism From Below', 94.
42. Charles F. Parham, 'Free-Love', *The Apostolic Faith* 1, no. 10 (1912): 4-5, cited in *The Spirit of the World*, 50.
43. Wonsuk Ma, 'When the Poor are Fired Up: The role of pneumatology in Pentecostal/Charismatic mission' in *The Spirit of the World*, 51.
44. Murray Dempster, 'The Church's Moral Witness: A study of glossolalia in Luke's theology of Acts', *Paraclete* 23 (1989): 1-7.
45. Thomas Cahill, *How the Irish Saved Civilization: The untold story of Ireland's role from the fall of Rome to the rise of medieval Europe* (London: Doubleday, 1995), 105.
46. Diane Severance, 'Herrnhut Revival: A Golden Summer' in *Christian History*, www.christianity.com/ChurchHistory/11630208/ (accessed March 15, 2010).
47. See Daniel R. Jennings, *The Supernatural Occurrences of Charles G. Finney* (Oklahoma City: SEAN Multimedia, 2009) and Daniel R. Jennings, *The Supernatural Occurrences of John Wesley* (Oklahoma City: SEAN Multimedia, 2005).
48. Ma, 'When the Poor are Fired Up', 44-46.
49. Timothy C. Tennent, *Theology in the Context of World Christianity: How the global church is*

influencing the way we think about and discuss theology (Grand Rapids: Zondervan, 2007), 164.

50. Douglas Peterson, 'A Moral Imagination: Pentecostals and social concern in Latin America', in *The Spirit of the World: Emerging Pentecostal theologies in global contexts*, ed. Veli-Matti Kärkkäinen (Grand Rapids: Eerdmans, 2009), 56-57.
51. Tetsunao Yamamori and Donald E. Miller, *Global Pentecostalism: The new face of Christian social engagement* (Berkeley: University of California Press, 2007), Kindle loc. 32-55.
52. See, Jürgen Moltmann, *The Coming of God: Christian eschatology* (Minneapolis: Fortress Press, 2004), 257-322.
53. Moltmann, *God in Creation*, 100.
54. For example, Stibbe has trouble with what he perceives in Moltmann's work to be the lack of transcendence of God. See Mark W. G. Stibbe, 'A British Appraisal', *Journal of Pentecostal Theology* 4 (1994): 12.
55. Sean William Anthony, 'The Holistic Pneumatology of Jürgen Moltmann: A Pentecostal examination', http://xanthicus.tripod.com/moltmann.html (accessed March 15, 2011).
56. Langmead, *The Word Made Flesh*, 144.
57. Root, *Revisiting Relational Youth Ministry*, 104-107.
58. Isaiah 47:9-14; Jeremiah 51:8-9.
59. Revelation 18:14.
60. Ellul, *The Meaning of the City*, 57.
61. Aubrey Johnson, *The Vitality of the Individual in the Thought of Ancient Israel* (Cardiff: University of Wales Press, 1964), 30-32.
62. Moltmann, *The Source of Life*, 31.
63. Walter Brueggemann, cited at the Emergent Convention, Atlanta, Georgia, September 16, 2004. In Len Hjalmarson, 'Another Look at Certainty', *Next Reformation*, http://nextreformation.com/wp-admin/general/certainty.htm (accessed March 15, 2011).
64. Ellul, *The Meaning of the City*, 57.
65. See, for example, the idea of our current time as battles between V-Day and D-Day in Oscar Cullman, 'Eschatology and Missions in the New Testament', in *The Theology of Christian Missions*, ed. Gerald Anderson (Nashville: Abingdon Press, 1961), 42-54.
66. See, for example, spiritual warfare novels like those by Frank Peretti, *This Present Darkness* (Westchester: Crossway, 1986).
67. Thomas McAlpine, *Facing the Powers: What are the options?* (Monrovia: MARC, 1991).
68. Paul Hiebert, 'Spiritual Warfare and Worldview', in *Global Missiology for the 21st Century: The Iguassu dialogue*, ed. William Taylor (Grand Rapids: Baker Academic, 2000), 174-176.
69. McAlpine, *Facing the Powers*, 67.
70. *TDNT, abridged*, 1135.

Chapter 11

1. Jenni M. Craig, *Servants Among The Poor* (Manila: OMF Literature, 1998), 182.
2. Steve Mosher, *God's Power, Jesus' Faith and World Mission: A study in Romans* (Scottdale: Herald Press, 1996), 17.
3. Michael Duncan, 'An Exodus Community' (unpublished paper): 1, cited in Craig, *Servants Among the Poor*, 182.
4. Dietrich Bonhoeffer, *Life Together* (London: SCM Press, 2002), 15.
5. Ralph D. Winter, 'The Two Structures of God's Redemptive Mission', in *Perspectives on the World Christian Movement: A reader*, eds. Ralph D. Winter and Steven C. Hawthorne, 4th ed (Pasadena, CA: William Carey Library, 2009), 249.
6. Ralph Winter, 'Protestant Mission Societies: The American experience', *Missiology*, 7, no. 2 (April 1979): 139-178.
7. Patricia Wittberg, *The Rise and Fall of Catholic Religious Orders: A social movement perspective*

(New York: State University of New York Press, 1994).
8. See Ashley Barker, *Collective Witness: A theology and praxis for a missionary order* (Melbourne: UNOH, 2000).
9. Barker, *Surrender All*, 127-180.
10. Duncan, *Costly Mission*, 9.
11. Gerald Arbuckle, *From Chaos to Mission: Refounding religious life formation* (Homebush: St Pauls, 1996), 102.
12. Arnold van Gennep, *Anthropology and Ethnography: The rites of passage* (London: Routledge, 2004 (1960)).
13. Adapted from Ash Barker, 'Hope That Can Even Be Found in Storms and Fire', *Finding Life* (September 2009), 1.
14. *Jon Haley, 'Seeing the Big Picture: A unified theory of our task', Evangelical Missions Quarterly 32, no. 4 (1996): 424-429.*
15. *Haley, 'Seeing the Big Picture'. 424.*
16. Barker, *Surrender All*, 186.

Chapter 12

1. Dietrich Bonhoeffer, *Ethics* (Minneapolis: Fortress Press, 2005), 221.
2. Eldin Villafañe, *Beyond Cheap Grace: A call to radical discipleship, incarnation, and justice* (Grand Rapids: Eerdmans, 2006), 15.
3. John de Gruchy, *Bonhoeffer and South Africa: Theology in dialogue* (Grand Rapids: Eerdmans, 1984), 20.
4. Root, *Revisiting Relational Youth Ministry*, 83.
5. Root, *Revisiting Relational Youth Ministry*, 78.
6. Root, *Revisiting Relational Youth Ministry*, 126.
7. Ubolwan Mejudhon, *The Way of Meekness: Being Christian and Thai in the Thai way* (Asbury Theological Seminary: PhD dissertation, unpublished, 1997), 6.
8. See Kenneth Wuest, *Studies in the Vocabulary of the Greek New Testament* (Grand Rapids: Eerdmans, 1945), 100-105.
9. Duane Elmer, *Cross-Cultural Servanthood: Serving the world in Christlike humility* (Downers Grove: IVP, 2006), 38.
10. N. T. Wright, *After You Believe: Why Christian character matters* (New York: HarperOne, 2010), 57. Italics follow Wright's use.
11. Wright, *After You Believe*, 127.
12. Linthicum, *Empowering the Poor*, 31.
13. Putnam, *Bowling Alone*, 283.
14. Putman, *Bowling Alone*, 318.
15. Matt Cleaver, 'A Theology of Geography: Locality and proximity', blog at *Matt Cleaver: Youth Ministry Reimagined*, http://mattcleaver.com/2008/10/22/a-theology-of-geography-locality-and-proximity (accessed December 10, 2010).
16. Walter Brueggemann, *The Land: Place as gift, promise and challenge in biblical faith* (Minneapolis: Fortress, 2002), 4.
17. John Inge, *A Christian Theology of Place: Explorations in practical, pastoral and empirical theology* (Aldershot: Ashgate Publishing, 2003), 137.
18. Jonathan Wilson-Hartgrove, *The Wisdom of Stability: Rooting faith in a mobile culture* (Brewster: Paraclete Press, 2010), 4.
19. Wilson-Hartgrove, *The Wisdom of Stability*, 35.
20. Wilson-Hartgrove, *The Wisdom of Stability*, 35.
21. Randy Frazee, *The Connecting Church: Beyond small groups to authentic community* (Grand

Rapids: Zondervan, 2001), 158.
22. Putnam, *Bowling Alone*, 314.
23. Wendell Berry, *The Art of Commonplace: The agrarian essays of Wendell Berry* (Berkeley: Counterpoint, 2002).
24. McKnight and Block, *The Abundant Community*, Kindle loc. 260-261.
25. Ash Barker, 'Finding Life in Neighbourhood Transformations' (unpublished discussion paper, 2003): 4-5.
26. Andrews, *Compassionate Community Work*, 116.
27. Andrews, *Compassionate Community Work*, 116.

Chapter 13

1. Andrews, *Compassionate Community Work*, 40-45.
2. Frances O'Gorman, *Charity and Change: From bandaid to beacon* (Melbourne: World Vision Australia, 1992), 3-74.
3. Myers, *Walking With the Poor*, 94-110.
4. Brueggemann, *Reverberations of Faith*, 126.
5. Douglas E. Millham, 'Training for Relief and Development', in *Christian Relief and Development: Developing workers for effective ministry*, ed. Edgar J. Elliston (London: Word Publishing, 1989), 257.
6. See, for example, O'Gorman, *Charity and Change*, 10-13; Myers, *Walking with the Poor*, 96-98; Andrews, *Compassionate Community Work*, 40-45.
7. Duncan, *Costly Mission*, 34.
8. Duncan, *Costly Mission*, 35-44.
9. Marcus Borg, *Jesus: Uncovering the life, teachings and relevance of a religious revolutionary* (New York: Harper Collins, 2006), 183.
10. Jean Vanier, *Community and Growth* (London: St Paul Publications, 1989), 63.
11. Dietrich Bonhoeffer, *Letters and Papers from Prison* (New York: Touchstone, 1997), 298.
12. Borg, *Jesus*, 175.
13. José Porfirio Miranda, *Marx and the Bible: A critique of the philosophy of oppression* (Maryknoll: Orbis, 1974), 47. The references are: Jeremiah 9:23; Isaiah 16:5; Micah 6:8; Hosea 2:21-22, 6:6, 10:12, 12:7; Zechariah 7:9; Psalm 25:9-10, 33:5, 36:6-7, 36:11, 40:11, 85:11, 88:12-13, 89:15, 98:2-3, 103:17, 119:62-64.
14. Gustavo Gutiérrez, *A Theology of Liberation* (Maryknoll: Orbis, 1973), 204-205.
15. Stark, *The Rise of Christianity*, 73-94.
16. Stark, *The Rise of Christianity*, 76-82.
17. Stark, *The Rise of Christianity*, 129-145.
18. Christian, *God of the Empty-handed*, 121.
19. Christian, *God of the Empty-handed*, 121-122.
20. Ched Myers, *Who Will Roll Away the Stone? Discipleship queries for First World Christians* (Maryknoll: Orbis, 1997), 46.
21. Thomas C. Oden, *The Good Works Reader* (Grand Rapids: Eerdmans, 2007), 180-181, citing Opus Imperfectum in Matthaem, Homily 36, Matthew 20:33-34.
22. Dietrich Bonhoeffer, *Discipleship: Dietrich Bonheoffer Works, Vol. 4* (Minneapolis: Fortress Press, 2001), 59.
23. Cited in Richard Peace, 'Evangelism', in *Dictionary of Mission Theology: Evangelical Foundations*, ed. John Corrie (Downers Grove: InterVarsity Press, 2007), 116.
24. Australian Government, 'Tax Deductibility—Overseas Aid Gift Deduction Scheme', AUS-Aid, http://www.ausaid.gov.au/ngos/tax.cfm (accessed April 22, 2011).
25. Ash Barker, 'Key Challenge: How to rebuild lives and communities', *Finding Life* (January 2010), 1.

26. Agnes Liu, 'Training the Poor for Ministry to the Poor', *Evangelical Review of Theology* 18, no. 2 (April 1994): 167-172.
27. Mejudhon, *The Way of Meekness*, 126-209.
28. Hiebert, 'Spiritual Warfare and Worldview', 174-76.
29. John Davis, *Poles Apart? Contextualizing the gospel in Asia* (Bangalore: Theological Book Trust, 1998), 2-3.
30. Those chosen were: 'Repent and believe' (Mark 1:15), 'Be baptised and live it' (Matthew 28:18-20), 'Love God and neighbour in a practical way' (Matthew 22:37-40), 'Celebrate the Lord's supper' (Luke 22:17-20), Pray (Matthew 6:5-15), 'Give generously' (Matthew 6:19-21) and 'Disciple others' (Matthew 18-20).
31. See, for example, George Patterson, 'The Spontaneous Multiplication of Churches' in *Perspectives on the World Christian Movement*, eds. Ralph D. Winter and Steven C. Hawthorne, 2nd ed. (Pasadena: William Carey Library, 1992), D76-94.
32. Wesley, *Works*, Vol. 13, 71.
33. Wesley, *Works*, Vol. 12, 302.
34. For an early exploration of this theme see, D. D. Thompson, *John Wesley as a Social Reformer* (New York: Eaton and Mains, 1896).
35. George G. Hunter III, *To Spread the Power: Church growth in the Wesleyan spirit* (Nashville: Abingdon Press, 1987), 132.
36. McGavran, *Understanding Church Growth*, 295-313.
37. Max Weber, *The Protestant Ethic and the Spirit of Capitalism* (New York: Charles Scribner's Sons, 1950), 139-143.
38. Liu, 'Training the Poor for Ministry to the Poor', 167-172.
39. Matthew 71 times, Mark 42 times, Luke 37 times, John 74 times and Acts 28 times.
40. Paulo Freire, *The Pedagogy of the Oppressed* (New York: Seabury, 1970).
41. Paulo Freire, *Pedagogy of Hope: Reliving pedagogy of the oppressed* (London: Continuum, 1994), 3.
42. Neighbourhood Transformation, 'About CNT', www.neighborhoodtransformation.net/about.php (accessed March 15, 2011).
43. Neighbourhood Transformation, 'Urban CHE Overview', www.neighborhoodtransformation.net (accessed December 15, 2010), 1.
44. Neighbourhood Transformation, 'Urban CHE overview', 8-9.
45. Putnam, *Bowling Alone*, 19.
46. Putnam, *Bowling Alone*, 288-289.
47. See, Roland Allen, *The Spontaneous Expansion of the Church and the Causes Which Hinder It* (Grand Rapids: Eerdmans, 1963 (1927)).
48. See, McGavran, *Understanding Church Growth*.
49. See, Hirsch, *The Forgotten Ways*.
50. David Garrison, *Church Planting Movements: How God is redeeming a lost world* (Midlothian: Wigtake, 2005), 21.
51. Bonhoeffer, *Discipleship*, 99.
52. Lapierre, *The City of Joy*, 67.
53. See, Mother Teresa, *A Simple Path* (New York: Random House, 1995), 3-38 and Henri Nouwen, *The Way of the Heart: Desert spirituality and contemporary ministry* (New York: Seabury Press, 1983), 17-40.
54. Dietrich Bonhoeffer, *Life Together and Prayerbook of the Bible* (Minneapolis: Fortress Press, 2005), Kindle loc. 412-22.
55. Root, *Revisiting Relational Youth Work*, Kindle loc. 961-69.
56. John Perkins, *With Justice For All*, 60-101.

57. Miranda, *Marx and the Bible*, 78.
58. Miranda, *Marx and the Bible*, 94.
59. Elsa Tamez, *Bible of the Oppressed* (Eugene: Wipf and Stock, 2006).
60. Myers, *Walking With the Poor*, 86.
61. See for example, Walter Wink, *The Powers That Be: Theology for a New Millennium* (New York: Doubleday, 1999).
62. Myers, *Who Will Roll Away the Stone?* 16.
63. Jon Sobrino, *The Eye of the Needle: No salvation outside the poor: A prophetic-utopian essay* (Maryknoll: Orbis, 2008).
64. Barjor Mehta and Arish Dastur (eds), *Adaptive Approaches to Urban Slums: A multimedia sourcebook on adaptive and proactive strategies* (Washington: World Bank, 2008), CD-ROM, presentation slide 26.
65. Mehta and Dastur, *Adaptive Approaches to Urban Slums*, 30.
66. Mehta and Dastur, *Adaptive Approaches to Urban Slums*, 30-31.
67. Mehta and Dastur, *Adaptive Approaches to Urban Slums'*, 28.

Conclusion

1. Abraham Joshua Heschel, *The Prophets* (New York: Harper Collins, 1962), 19.

Bibliography

Addison, Steve. *Movements That Change the World*. Smyrna: Missional Press, 2009.

Agyeman, Julian. *Sustainable Communities and the Challenge of Environmental Justice*. New York: New York University Press, 2005.

Aldrich, Brian C., and R. S. Sandhu. *Housing the Urban Poor: Policy and Practice in Developing Countries*. London: Zed Books, 1995.

Alinsky, Saul D. *Rules for Radicals: A Practical Primer for Realistic Radicals*. New York: Vintage Books, 1971.

Allen, Roland. *Missionary Methods: St Paul's or Ours?* Grand Rapids: Eerdmans, 1968.

———. *The Spontaneous Expansion of the Church and the Causes Which Hinder It*. Grand Rapids: Eerdmans, 1963.

Amador, J. D. H. 'The Word Made Flesh: Epistemology, Ontology and Postmodern Rhetorics.' In *Rhetorical Analysis of Scripture*, edited by Stanley E. Porter and Thomas H. Olbricht, 53-65. Sheffield: Sheffield Academic Press, 1997.

American Bible Society. *The Poverty and Justice Bible - CEV*. New York: American Bible Society, 2009.

Anderson, Gerald, ed. *The Theology of Christian Missions*. Nashville: Abingdon Press, 1961.

Andrews, Dave. *Compassionate Community Work: An Introductory Course for Christians*. Carlisle: Piquant, 2006.

Angel, Shlomo. *Land Tenure for the Urban Poor*. Bangkok: Human Settlements Division Asian Institute of Technology, 1982.

Angel, Shlomo, and Sopon Pornchokchai. 'Bangkok Slum Lands: Policy Implications of Recent Findings.' *Cities*, May 1989, 136-47.

Anthony, William. 'The Holistic Pneumatology of Jürgen Moltmann: A Pentecostal Examination', *Xanthicus*. http://xanthicus.tripod.com/moltmann.html. Accessed March 15, 2011.

Arbuckle, Gerald. *From Chaos to Mission: Refounding Religious Life Formation*. Homebush: St Pauls, 1996.

Arias, Mortimer. *Announcing the Reign of God: Evangelization and the Subversive Memory of Jesus*. Lima: Academic Renewal Press, 1984.

Arnold, Eberhard. *Salt and Light: Living the Sermon on the Mount*. Farmington: Plough Publishing House, 2007.

Asian Development Bank. 'Urban Sector and Strategy and Operations.' *Asian Development Bank*. www.adb.org/Documents/Supplementary-Appendixes/SST-REG-2006-03/SES-USSO-SupplementaryAppendix.pdf. Accessed July 11, 2011.

Askew, Marc. *Bangkok: Place, Practice and Representation*. London: Routledge, 2002.

Associated Press. 'Rising Seas Threaten 21 Mega-Cities.' *Associated Press*. http://www.wildsingapore.com/news/20070910/071020-3.htm. Accessed June 28, 2011.

Augsburger, David. *Dissident Discipleship: A Spirituality of Self-Surrender, Love of God and Love of Neighbour*. Grand Rapids: Brazos, 2006.

Australian Government. 'Tax Deductibility—Overseas Aid Gift Deduction Scheme.' *AusAID*. http://www.ausaid.gov.au/ngos/tax.cfm. Accessed June 30, 2011.

Australian Government. 'Statistical Summary 2008-2009: Australia's International Aid Program.' *AusAID*. http://www.ausaid.gov.au/publications/green-book/AusAID%20Statistical%20Summary%202008-09.pdf. Accessed June 29, 2011.

Auyero, Javier, and Debora Alejandra Swistun. *Flammable: Environmental Suffering in an Argentine Shantytown*. Oxford: Oxford University Press, 2009.

Azevedo, Marcello. *Vocation for Mission: The Challenge of Religious Life Today*. New York: Paulist Press, 1988.

Baker, Ken. 'The Incarnational Model: Perception of Deception?' *Evangelical Missions Quarterly*, January 2002, 16-24.

Bakke, Raymond J. 'Apostle to the City: To Urban Expert Ray Bakke, Cities Are the Laboratory of God's Mission in the World, Not a Problem to Be Solved.' *Christianity Today* 41 (1997): 36-40.

———. 'The Challenge of World Urbanization to Mission Strategy: Perspectives on Demographic Realities.' *Urban Mission* 4 (1986): 6-17.

———. 'Overcoming the Real Barriers to Urban Evangelization.' In, *Urban Mission*, edited by John Kyle, 71-78. Downers Grove: InterVarsity Press, 1988.

———. *A Theology as Big as the City*. Downers Grove: InterVarsity Press, 1997.

———. 'Urban Evangelization: A Lausanne Strategy since 1980.' *International Bulletin of Missionary Research* 8 (1984): 149-54.

Bakke, Raymond J., and Jim Hart. *The Urban Christian: Effective Ministry in Today's World*. Downers Grove: InterVarsity Press, 1987.

Banerjee, Abhijit, and Easter Duflo. *Poor Economics: A Radical Rethinking of the Way to Fight Poverty*. New York: PublicAffairs, 2011.

Bangkok Post. 'Ban Mankong: From Slum Upgrade to Social Uplift.' *Bangkok Post*. http://www.bangkokpost.com/news/investigation/32500/ban-mankong-from-slum-upgrading-to-social-upliftment. Accessed June 29, 2011.

———. 'Taksin Promises End to Slums in Three Years.' *Bangkok Post*. http://www.orientexpat.com/forum/4107-thaksin-promises-end-to-slums-in-three-years. Accessed June 29, 2011.

———. 'WHO Warns Dengue Fever Is on the Rise.' *Bangkok Post*. http://www.bangkokpost.com/news/local/195921/who-warns-dengue-fever-is-on-the-rise. Accessed June 29, 2011.

Barclay, Oliver R., and Chris Sugden. 'Biblical Social Ethics in a Mixed Society.' *Evangelical Quarterly* 62 (1990): 5-18.

Barker, Ashley. *Collective Witness: A Theology and Praxis for a Missionary Order*. Melbourne: UNOH, 2000.

———. *Finding Life: Reflections from a Bangkok Slum*. Melbourne: Go Alliance, 2003.

Barker, Ash. 'Community Building Is Not for the Faint-Hearted.' *Finding Life*, September, 2010, 2.

———. 'Finding Life in Neighbourhood Transformations.' Melbourne: UNOH, 2003.

———. 'Hope That Can Even Be Found in Storms and Fire.' *Finding Life* September, (2009).

———. 'Key Challenge: How to Rebuild Lives and Communities.' *Finding Life* January, (2010): 1.

———. *Make Poverty Personal: Taking the Poor as Seriously as the Bible Does*. Grand Rapids: Baker, 2009.

———. *Make Poverty Personal: The Bible's Call to End Oppression*. Melbourne: UNOH, 2006.

———. *Surrender All: A Call to Sub-Merge with Christ*. Melbourne: UNOH, 2005.

Barna, George. *Marketing the Church: What They Never Taught You About Church Growth*. Colorado Springs: Navpress, 1988.

Barns, Ian. 'Another City: Theology and the Ecology of Urban Life.' *St Mark's Review* 181 (2000): 3-11.

Baron, Lloyd I. Z. *Land and Squatter Communities: A Strategic Relationship*. Vancouver: Centre for Human Settlements, the University of British Columbia, 1982.

Barrett, David. 'Sending and Receiving Missionaries by UN Region.' *International Bulletin of Missionary Research* 34 no. 1 (2010): 29-36.

———. 'Status of Global Mission, 2009, in the Context of 20th and 21st Centuries.' *Gordon Conwell Theological Seminary.* http://ockenga.gordonconwell.edu/ockenga/globalchristianity/resources. php. Accessed July 11, 2011.

_____. 'Silver and Gold Have I None: Church of the Poor or Church of the Rich.' *International Bulletin of Missionary Research* 7 no. 4 (1983): 146-51.

Barrett, David, and Todd Johnson. 'Status of Global Mission, 2004, in Context of 20th and 21st Centuries.' *International Bulletin of Missionary Research* 28 no. 1 (2004).

———. 'Status of Global Mission, 2010, in Context of 20th and 21st Centuries.' *International Bulletin of Missionary Research* 34 no. 1 (2010).

Barrett, David and Peter Crossing and Todd Johnson, 'Status of Global Mission, 2010, in Context of 20th and 21st Centuries', *International Bulletin of Missionary Research* (2010): 29-36. http://www.internationalbulletin.org/system/files/2010-01-029-johnson.html. Accessed January 13, 2010.

Barrett, Greg. *The Gospel of Father Joe*. San Francisco: Jossey-Bass, 2008.

Bascom, Tim. 'God in the Slums.' *The Other Side* Vol 37 no. 2 (2001).

Beal, Jo, and Sean Fox. *Cities and Development*. New York: Routledge, 2009.

Beechey, Jenny. jenny@tear.og. 'Results of Tear slum inquiry' Private e-mail message to Ash Barker ashbarker@unoh.org. January 21, 2011.

Beliefnet. 'The One Campaign: An Advocacy Letter from Rick Warren.' *Beliefnet.* http://www.beliefnet.com/story/168/story_16821_1.html. Accessed July 11, 2011.

Bellamy, John, Alan Black, Keith Castle, Philip Hughes, and Peter Kaldor. *Why People Don't Go to Church*. Adelaide: Open Book, 2002.

Bellingham, George Robert. 'A Biblical Approach to Social Transformation', Doctor of Ministry Thesis-Project, Eastern Baptist Theological Seminary, 1987.

Belshaw, Deryke, Robert Calderisi, and Chris Sugden. *Faith in Development: Partnership between the World Bank and the Churches of Africa*. Washington, DC: World Bank, 2001.

Bender, Harold S. *The Anabaptist Vision*. Scottdale: Herald, 1944.

Berner, Erhard. *Defending a Place in the City: Localities and the Struggle for Urban Land in Metro Manila*. Quezon City: Ateneo de Manila University Press, 1997.

Berry, Wendell. *The Art of Commonplace: The Agrarian Essays of Wendell Berry*. Berkeley: Counterpoint, 2002.

Bessenecker, Scott, ed. *Living Mission: The Vision and Voices of New Friars*. Downers Grove: InterVarsity Press, 2010.

———. *New Friars: The Emerging Movement Serving the World's Poor*. Downers Grove: InterVarsity, 2006.

———. sbessenecker@intervarsity.org. 'PhD help', Private e-mail to Ash Barker, ashbarker@unoh.org. October 22, 2010.

———, ed. *Quest for Hope in the Slum Community: Global Urban Reader*. Waynesboro: Authentic, 2005.

Billings, Todd J. 'Incarnational Ministry and the Unique, Incarnate Christ.' *Contend Earnestly.* http://contendearnestly.blogspot.com/2010/03/incarnational-ministry-and-unique.html. Accessed June 30, 2011.

Bittlinger, Arnold. *The Church Is Charismatic*. Geneva: World Council of Churches, 1981.

Black, Maggie. *The No-Nonsense Guide to International Development*. Oxford: New Internationalist, 2009.

Blackburn, James, Robert Chambers, and John Gaventa. 'Mainstreaming Participation in Development—OED Working Paper Series.' *World Bank.* http://lnweb90.worldbank.org/oed/oeddoclib.nsf/DocUNIDViewForJavaSearch/1D8EC8BB36C8C76E85256977007257C1/$file/Mnstream.pdf. Accessed June 29, 2011.

Bloesch, Donald G. *Jesus Christ: Savior and Lord*. Downers Grove: InterVarsity Press, 1997.

Bloom, David E., and Tarun Khanna. 'The Urban Revolution.' *Finance and Development* 44, no. 3 (September 2007).

Bodewes, Christine. *Parish Transformation in Urban Slums*. Nairobi: Pauline Publications, 2006.

Boff, Leonardo. *Jesus Christ Liberator: A Critical Christology for Our Time*. Maryknoll: Orbis, 1986.

Bombonatoo, Vera Ivanise. 'The Commitment to Taking the Poor Down from the Cross.' In *Getting the Poor Down from the Cross: Christology of Liberation*, edited by Jose Vigil. Cyberspace: International Theological Commission of the Ecumenical Association of Third World Theologians, 2007.

Bonhoeffer, Dietrich. *Communion of Saints*. New York: Harper and Row, 1963.

———. *The Cost of Discipleship*. London: SCM Press, 2003.

———. *Creation and Fall: Dietrich Bonhoeffer Works, Volume 3*. Edited by Wayne Whitson Floyd, Jr. Minneapolis: Fortress Press, 2004.

———. *Discipleship: Dietrich Bonheoffer Works, Volume 4*. Edited by Wayne Witson Floyd, Jr. Minneapolis: Fortress Press, 2001.

———. *Ethics*. New York: Touchstone, 1995.

———. *Ethics*. Minneapolis: Fortress Press, 2005.

———. *God Is in the Manger: Reflections on Advent and Christmas*. Louisville: Westminster John Knox Press, 2010.

———. *Letters and Papers from Prison*. New York: Touchstone, 1997.

———. *Life Together*. London: SCM Press, 2002.

———. *Life Together and Prayerbook of the Bible: Dietrich Bonhoeffer Works, Volume 5*. Edited by Wayne Whitson Floyd, Jr. Minneapolis: Fortress Press, 2005.

———. *Wondrously Sheltered*. Minneapolis: Augsburg, 2006.

———. *The Cost of Discipleship*. Suffolk: SCM, 2003.

Bonk, Jonathan. *Missions and Money: Affluence as a Missionary Problem... Revisited*. Maryknoll: Orbis, 2006.

Boonyabancha, Somsook. 'Baan Mankong: Going to Scale with "Slum" and Squatter Upgrading in Thailand.' *Environment and Urbanization* 17, no. 1 (2005): 21-46.

———. 'Causes and Effects of Slum Eviction in Bangkok.' In *Land for Housing the Poor*, edited by S. Angel. Singapore: Select Books, 1983.

Borg, Marcus J. *Jesus: Uncovering the Life, Teachings and Relevance of a Religious Revolutionary*. London: St Paul Publications, 2006.

Borg, Marcus J., and Dominic Crossan. *The First Christmas: What the Gospels Really Teach About Jesus' Birth*. London: HarperCollins, 2007.

Borg, Marcus J., and N. T Wright. *The Meaning of Jesus: Two Visions*. New York: HarperOne, 1999.

Bornstein, David. *How to Change the World: Social Entrepreneurs and the Power of New Ideas*. Oxford: Oxford University Press, 2004.

Bosch, David. *Transforming Mission: Paradigm Shifts in Theology of Mission*. Maryknoll: Orbis, 1991.

Bowen, Roger. *... So I Send You: A Study Guide to Mission*. London: SPCK, 1996.

Bowers, Joyce M., ed. *Raising Resilient MKs: Resources for Caregivers, Parents, and Teachers*. Colorado Springs: Association of Christian Schools International, 1998.

Boyd, Gregory A. *Seeing Is Believing: Experience Jesus through Imaginative Prayer*. Grand Rapids: Baker, 2004.

Boyle, Gregory. *Tattoos on the Heart: The Power of Boundless Compassion*. New York: Simon and Schuster, 2010.

Bradshaw, Bruce. *Change across Cultures: A Narrative Approach to Social Transformation*. Grand Rapids: Baker, 2002.

Brafman, Ori, and Rod A. Beckstrom. *The Starfish and the Spider: The Unstoppable Power of Leaderless Organisations*. New York: The Penguin Group, 2007.

Brand, Steward. 'City Planet.' *Scribd*. http://www.scribd.com/doc/6575294/Stewart-Brand-City-Planet. Accessed July 11, 2011.

Bressan, Luigi. *A Meeting of Worlds: The Interaction of Christian Missionaries and Thai Culture*. Bangkok: Assumption University Press, 2000.

Brook, Wes Howard. *Becoming Children of God: John's Gospel and Radical Discipleship*. Maryknoll: Orbis, 1994.
Brook, Wes Howard, and Anthony Gwyther. *Unveiling Empire: Reading Revelation Then and Now*. Maryknoll: Orbis, 1999.
Brook, Wes Howard, and Sharon H. Ringe, eds. *The New Testament—Introducing the Way of Discipleship*. Maryknoll: Orbis, 2002.
Brown, Robert McAfee. *Liberation Theology: An Introduction*. Westminster: John Knox Press, 1993.
Brueggemann, Walter. *The Land: Place as Gift, Promise and Challenge in Biblical Faith*. Minneapolis: Fortress Press, 2002.
———. *Old Testament Theology: An Introduction*. Nashville: Abingdon Press, 2008.
———. *Power, Providence and Personality: Biblical Insight into Life and Ministry*. Louisville: Westminster John Knox Press, 1990.
———. *The Prophetic Imagination*. Minneapolis: Fortress Press, 1978.
———. *Reverberations of Faith: A Theological Handbook of Old Testament Themes*. Louisville: Westminster John Knox Press, 2002.
———. *An Unsettling God: The Heart of the Hebrew Bible*. Minneapolis: Fortress Press, 2009.
Brugmann, Jeb. *Welcome to the Urban Revolution: How Cities Are Changing the World*. New York: Bloomsbury Press, 2009.
Burgess, Stanley M, and Eduard van der Mass, eds. *The New International Dictionary of Pentecostal and Charismatic Movements*. Grand Rapids: Zondervan, 2002.
Bush, Luis. 'What Is the 10/40 Window?' *The Urban Ministry Institute*. http://www.tumi.org/migration/images/stories/pdf/lga/docs/WHATIS10.pdf. Accessed June 29, 2011.
Butler-Bass, Diana. *A People's History of Christianity*. New York: HarperCollins, 2009.
Cahill, Thomas. *How the Irish Saved Civilization: The Untold Story of Ireland's Role from the Fall of Rome to the Rise of Medieval Europe*. London: Doubleday, 1995.
Cairncross, Sandy, Jorge Enrique Hardoy, and David Satterthwaite. *The Poor Die Young: Housing and Health in Third World Cities*. London: Earthscan, 1990.
Camp, Lee C. *Mere Discipleship: Radical Christianity in a Rebellious World*. Grand Rapids: Brazos Press, 2008.
Carrasco, J. C. 'Transformation.' In *Dictionary of Mission Theology: Evangelical Foundations*, edited by John Corrie, 393-95. Nottingham: InterVarsity Press, 2007.
Carter, Craig A. *The Politics of the Cross: The Theology and Social Ethics of John Howard Yoder*. Grand Rapids: Brazos, 2001.
Carter, Warren. *Matthew and the Margins: A Socio-political and Religious Reading*. Maryknoll: Orbis, 2001.
Casey, Michael. *Fully Human, Fully Divine: An Interactive Christology*. Mulgrave: John Garratt Publishing, 2004.
Catford, Cheryl, ed. *Following Fire: How the Spirit Leads Us to Fight Injustice*. Melbourne: UNOH, 2008.
Central Intelligence Agency. 'World Fact Book.' *Central Intelligence Agency*. https://www.cia.gov/cia/publications/factbook/geos/xx.htm. Accessed June 28, 2011.
Cerillo, Augustus, Jr. 'Pentecostals and the City.' In *Called and Empowered: Global Mission in Pentecostal Perspective*, edited by Murray Dempster, Byron Klaus, and Douglas Petersen. 98-104. Peabody: Hendrickson, 1991.
Chaney, David. 'Statistics by Country by Catholic Population.' http://www.catholic-hierarchy.org/country/sc1.html. Accessed July 11, 2011.
Chester, Tim. 'Why I Don't Believe in Incarnational Mission.' *Reformed Spirituality and Missional Church* http://timchester.wordpress.com/2008/07/19/why-i-dont-believe-in-incarnational-mission. Accessed July 11, 2011.
Chia, Roland. *Hope for the World: The Christian Vision*. Leicester: Inter-Varsity Press, 2006.

Choguill, Charles L. *New Communities for Urban Squatters: Lessons from the Plan That Failed in Dhaka, Bangladesh*. New York: Plenum, 1987.

Chomsky, Noam. *Media Control: The Spectacular Achievements of Propaganda*. New York: Seven Stories Press, 2002.

Christian, Jayakumar. *God of the Empty-Handed: Poverty, Power and the Kingdom of God*. Monrovia: MARC, 1999.

Claerbaut, David. *Urban Ministry in a New Millennium*. Waynesboro: Authentic, 2005.

Claiborne, Shane. *The Irresistible Revolution: Living as an Ordinary Radical*. Grand Rapids: Zondervan, 2006.

Claiborne, Shane, and Jonathan Wilson-Hartgrove. *Becoming the Answer to Our Prayers: Prayer for Ordinary Radicals*. Downers Grove: IVP Books, 2008.

Clark, David. *Germs, Genes and Civilisation: How Epidemics Shaped Who Are Today*. Upper Saddle River: FT Press, 2010.

Cleaver, Matt. 'A Theology of Geography: Locality and Proximity.' *Matt Cleaver: Youth Ministry Reimagined*. http://mattcleaver.com/2008/10/22/a-theology-of-geography-locality-and-proximity. Accessed December 10, 2010.

Clinton, Bill. *Giving: How Each of Us Can Change the World*. New York: Alfred A. Knopf, 2007.

Cohen, Barney. 'Urban Growth in Developing Countries: A Review of Current Trends and a Caution Regarding Existing Forecasts.' *World Development* 32 no. 1 (2004): 23-51.

Coleman, Simon. *The Globalisation of Charismatic Christianity: Spreading the Gospel of Prosperity*. Cambridge: Cambridge University Press, 2000.

Collier, Paul. *The Bottom Billion: Why the Poorest Countries Are Failing and What Can Be Done About It*. Oxford: Oxford University Press, 2007.

Collins, James C., and Jerry I. Porras. *Built to Last: Successful Habits of Visionary Companies*. New York: HarperCollins, 2002.

Conn, Harvie M. *Planting and Growing Urban Churches: From Dream to Reality*. Grand Rapids: Baker, 1997.

Conn, Harvie M., and Manuel Ortiz. *Urban Ministry: The Kingdom, the City and the People of God*. Downers Grove: InterVarsity Press, 2001.

Corbett, Steve, and Brian Fikkert. *When Helping Hurts: How to Alleviate Poverty without Hurting the Poor and Yourself*. Chicago: Moody, 2009.

Corrie, John, ed. *Dictionary of Mission Theology: Evangelical Foundations*. Nottingham: InterVarsity Press, 2007.

Costas, Orlando. *Christ Outside the Gate: Mission Beyond Christendom*. Maryknoll: Orbis, 1982.

Costello, Tim, and Rod Yule, eds. *Another Way to Love*. Brunswick East: World Vision/Acorn Press, 2009.

Cox, Harvey. *Fire from Heaven: The Rise of Pentecostal Spirituality and the Reshaping of Religion in the 21st Century*. Cambridge: Da Capa Press, 1995.

──── . *The Future of Faith*. London: HarperCollins, 2009.

──── . *The Secular City: Secularization and Urbanization in Theological Perspective*. London: SCM Press, 1966.

Coyle, Stephen. *Sustainable and Resilient Communities: A Comprehensive Action Plan for Towns, Cities and Regions*. Hoboken: John Wiley and Sons, 2011.

Craig, Jenni M. *Servants among the Poor*. Manila: OMF Literature, 1998.

Cress, Michael. 'Can Rockers and Religious Leaders End Poverty?' *BeliefNet* http://www.beliefnet.com/News/2005/07/Can-Rockers-And-Religious-Leaders-End-Poverty.aspx. Accessed January 13, 2011.

Culbertson, Howard. '10/40 Window: Do you need to be stirred into action?' *Southern Nazarene University* http://home.snu.edu/~hculbert/1040.htm#abc. Accessed July 11, 2011.

Cullmann, Oscar. 'Eschatology and Missions in the New Testament.' In *The Theology of Christian Missions*, edited by Gerald Anderson, 42-54. Nashville: Abingdon Press, 1961.

Cunningham, Loren. *Is That Really You God?* Lincoln: Chosen Books, 2001.

Daily Times. 'Pakistan's Urban Population to Equal Rural by 2030: UNFPA.' *Daily Times* June 28, 2007 http://www.dailytimes.com.pk/default.asp?page=2007%5C06%5C28%5Cstory_28-6-2007_pg7_9. Accessed December 21, 2010.

Davey, Andrew. *Urban Christianity and the Global Order: Theological Resources for an Urban Future.* Peabody: Hendrickson, 2002.

Davis, John. *Poles Apart? Contextualizing the Gospel in Asia.* Bangalore: Theological Book Trust, 1998.

Davis, Mike. *Planet of Slums*. London: Verso, 2006.

———. 'Planet of Slums: Urban Involution and the Informal Proletariat.' *New Left Review* 26 (2004). http://newleftreview.org/A2496 Accessed January 10, 2011.

D'Costa, Gavin. 'The Christian Trinity: Paradigm for Pluralism?' In *Pluralism and the Religions. The Theological and Political Dimensions*, edited by John D'Arcy. 22-39. London: Cassell, 1998.

de Gruchy, John W. *Bonhoeffer and South Africa: Theology in Dialogue.* Grand Rapids: Eerdmans, 1984.

———, ed. *The Cambridge Companion to Dietrich Bonhoeffer.* Cambridge: Cambridge University Press, 1999.

De Silva, Lynn A., and Aloysius Pieris. 'The Buddhist and Christian Attitudes to the Problem of Poverty: The 3rd Congress of Asian Monks, Kandy, Ag 1980.' *Dialogue* no. 7 (1980): 97-121.

de Soto, Hernando. *The Other Path: Economic Answers to Terrorism.* New York: Basic Books, 1989.

———. *The Mystery of Capital: Why Capitalism Triumphs in the West and Fails Everywhere Else.* London: Black Swan, 2001.

Dean, Judith M., Julie Schaffner, and Stephen L. S. Smith, eds. *Attacking Poverty in the Developing World: Christian Practitioners and Academics in Collaboration.* Waynesboro: Authentic, 2005.

Dempster, Murray. 'The Church's Moral Witness: A Study of Glossolalia in Luke's Theology of Acts.' *Paraclete* 23 (1989): 1-7.

Dennis, James S. *Christian Missions and Social Progress: A Sociological Study of Foreign Missions.* New York: Flemming H. Revell Company, 1897.

Dennison, Jack. *City Reaching: On the Road to Community Transformation.* Pasadena: William Carey Library, 1999.

Dichter, Thomas W. *Despite Good Intentions: Why Development Assistance to the Third World Has Failed.* Boston: University of Massachusetts Press, 2003.

Dictionary, The Free. 'Incarnate.' *The Free Dictionary* http://www.thefreedictionary.com/incarnate Accessed August 10, 2010.

Dorr, Donald. *Option for the Poor: Catholic Social Teaching.* Blackburn: CollinsDove, 1992.

Dragani, Rachelle. 'Mother Teresa (1910-1997).' *Time Magazine*. November 19, 2010.

Dramm, Sabine. *Dietrich Bonhoeffer and the Resistance.* Minneapolis: Fortress Press, 2009.

D'Souza, Shalini, and Arundhuti Roy Choudhury. *Community and Communal Consciousness: Communication Network in Delhi Slums.* New Delhi, India: ISI Pr, 1995.

D'Souza, Victor S. 'Religious Minorities in India : A Demographic Analysis.' *Social Action* 33 no. 4 (1983): 365-85.

du Plessis, Jean. 'The Growing Problem of Forced Evictions and the Crucial Importance of Community-Based, Locally Appropriate Alternatives.' *Environment and Urbanization* 17 (2005): 123-34.

Duang Prateep Foundation. 'Monthly News for December 2002.' *Duang Prateep Foundation* http://web.sfc.keio.ac.jp/~thiesmey/dpf200212.htm. Accessed August 22, 2010.

Duncan, Michael. *Costly Mission: Following Christ into the Slums.* Monrovia: MARC, 1996.

———. *Costly Mission: Following Jesus into Neighbourhoods Facing Poverty.* Melbourne: UNOH, 2007.

———. 'The God of the Enemy.' *Stimulus* 2 (1994): 3-5.

———. 'Gifts in the City' in *Following Fire: How the Spirit Leads Us to Fight Injustice,* edited by Cheryl Catford, 240-46. Melbourne: UNOH, 2008.

———. *Mission: The Incarnational Approach: The Journey Series, No 2*. Christchurch: Servants to Asia's Urban Poor, 1991.

———. *A Journey in Development*. Vol. 3, Bridge Series. Melbourne: World Vision Australia, 1990.

———. 'A Journey in the Slums of Asia.' *Transformation* 10 (1993): 23-26.

———. 'Serving Christ in the Slums.' *Evangelical Missions Quarterly* 25 no. 1 (1989): 6-15.

———. 'Spiritual Gifts for Community Building in the Urban Slums.' *Evangelical Review of Theology* 22 (1998): 176-81.

———. 'Thinkers at the Coalface.' *Stimulus* 2 (1994): 13-16.

———. *Who Stands Fast? Discipleship in Difficult Places*. Melbourne: UNOH, 2005.

Dwyer, D. J. *People and Housing in Third World Cities: Perspectives on the Problem of Spontaneous Settlements*. London: Longman, 1975.

Earth Observatory. 'Dakar, Senegal.' *Earth Observatory* http://earthobservatory.nasa.gov/IOTD/view.php?id=8886. Accessed January 10, 2011.

Easterbrook, Gregg. *The Progress Paradox*. New York: Random House, 2003.

Easterly, William. *The White Man's Burden: Why the West's Efforts to Aid the Rest Have Done So Much Ill and So Little Good*. London: Penguin, 2006.

Ellacuria, Ignacio and Jon Sobrino, eds. *Mysterium Liberationis: Fundamental Concepts of Liberation Theology*. Maryknoll: Orbis, 1993.

Elliston, Edgar J. *Christian Relief and Development: Developing Workers for Effective Ministry*. London: Word Publishing, 1989.

Ellul, Jacques. *The Meaning of the City*. Grand Rapids: Eerdmans, 1997.

———. *The Politics of God and the Politics of Man*. Grand Rapids: Eerdmans, 1972.

———. *The Technological Society*. New York: Vintage Books, 1964.

Ellul, Jacques, and Willem H. Vanderburg. *On Freedom, Love and Power*. Toronto: University of Toronto Press, 2010.

Elmer, Duane. *Cross-Cultural Servanthood: Serving the World in Christlike Humility*. Downers Grove: IVP, 2006.

Engels, Friedrich. *The Conditions of Working Class England*. Moscow: Institute of Marxism-Leninism, 1969.

Engels, James F., and William A. Dyrness. *Changing the Mind of Missions: Where Have We Gone Wrong?* Downers Grove: InterVarsity Press, 2000.

Erickson, Brad, ed. *Call to Action: Handbook for Ecology, Peace and Justice*. San Francisco: Sierra Club Books, 1990.

Erickson, Millard J. *The Word Became Flesh: A Contemporary Incarnational Christology*. Grand Rapids: Baker, 1991.

Exodus Kutoka. 'Network of Catholic Parishes Working in Slums (Informal Settlements) Nairobi, Kenya.' *Exodus Kutoka Network: Catholic Parishes Network in Informal Settlements, Nairobi-Kenya* http://www.kutokanet.com/network/Brochure_KutokaNetwork.pdf. Accessed December 21, 2010.

Ferm, Deane WIlliam, ed. *Third World Liberation Theologies*. Maryknoll: Orbis, 1990.

Flemming, Dean. *Contextualization in the New Testament: Patterns for Theology and Mission*. Downers Grove: InterVarsity Press, 2005.

Foster, Richard. *Streams of Living Water: Celebrating the Great Traditions of Christian Faith*. San Francisco: Harper SanFrancisco, 2001.

Frank, Leonard. 'The Development Game.' In *The Post-Development Reader*, edited by Majid Rahnema and Victoria Bawtree. 263-73. New York: Zed Books, 1997.

Franke, John R. *The Character of Theology: A Postconservative Evangelical Approach*. Grand Rapids: Baker Academic, 2005.

Frazee, Randy. *The Connecting Church: Beyond Small Groups to Authentic Community*. Grand Rapids: Zondervan, 2001.

Freire, Paulo. *Pedagogy of Hope: Reliving Pedagogy of the Oppressed*. London: Continuum, 1994.

———. *The Pedagogy of the Oppressed*. New York: Seabury, 1970.

Friedl, John, and Noel J. Chrisman. *City Ways: A Selective Reader in Urban Anthropology*. New York: Crowell, 1975.

Friedman, Thomas. *The World Is Flat: The Globalized World in the Twenty-First Century*. London: Penguin Books.

Frost, Michael. *Exiles: Living Missionally in a Post-Christian Culture*. Peabody: Hendrickson, 2006.

———. *Seeing God in the Ordinary: A Theology of the Everyday*. Peabody: Hendrickson, 2000.

Frost, Michael, and Alan Hirsch. *The Shaping of Things to Come: Innovation and Mission for the 21st Century*. Peabody: Hendrickson, 2003.

Fuchs, Josef. *Christian Morality: The Word Becomes Flesh*. Washington, DC: Georgetown University Press, 1987.

Fung, Raymond. 'The Kingdom of God as Strategy for Mission.' *International Review of Mission* 68 (1979): 102-08.

Gandal, Keith. *The Virtues of the Vicious: Jacob Riis, Stephen Crane, and the Spectacle of the Slum*. New York: Oxford University Press, 1997.

Gans, Herbert J. 'The Ending of Urban Poverty.' *Social Progress* 53 (1962): 27-32.

Garrison, David. *Church Planting Movements*. Richmond: Office of Overseas Operations, International Mission Board of the Southern Baptist Convention, 1999.

———. *Church Planting Movements: How God Is Redeeming a Lost World*. Midlothian: Wigtake, 2005.

Garvin, Alexander. 'The City of Tomorrow.' *World Order* 21 no. 3 (1987): 25-44.

———. 'We Can Solve Urban Problems.' *World Order* 17 no. 2 (1982): 31-42.

Gaskell, S. Martin. *Slums*. Leicester: Leicester University Press, 1990.

Geneva Sector Intelligence. 'Urban Slums Worldwide.' Unpublished, 2004.

Gibbs, Eddie. *Emerging Churches: Creating Christian Community in Postmodern Cultures*. Grand Rapids: Baker, 2005.

Gill, Athol. *Life on the Road: The Gospel Basis for a Messianic Lifestyle*. Homebush West: Lancer, 1989.

Gittins, Anthony J. *Gifts and Strangers: Meeting the Challenge of Inculturation*. New York: Paulist, 1989.

Gladwell, Malcolm. *Outliers: The Story of Success*. New York: Little, Brown and Company, 2008.

Glaeser, Edward. *Triumph of the City. How Our Greatest Invention Makes Us Richer, Smarter, Greener, Healthier and Happier*. New York: Penguin, 2011.

Goldstein, Sidney. *The Demography of Bangkok: A Case Study in Differentials between Big City and Rural Populations*. Bangkok: Chulalongkorn University, 1972.

Gonzalez, Justo. *Faith and Wealth: A History of Early Christian Ideas on the Origin, Significance and Use of Money*. West Broadway: Wipf and Stock, 1990.

Gordon, Wayne L. *Real Hope in Chicago: The Incredible Story of How the Gospel Is Transforming a Chicago Neighborhood*. Grand Rapids: Zondervan, 1995.

Gorman, Michael J. *Cruciformity: Paul's Narrative Spirituality of the Cross*. Grand Rapids: Eerdmans, 2001.

Goudzwaard, Bob. *Capitalism and Progress: A Diagnosis of Western Society*. Grand Rapids: Eerdmans, 1997.

Gray, Dennis. 'Bangkok Has That Sinking Feeling.' *Wild Singapore*. September 10, 2007. http://www.wildsingapore.com/news/20070910/071020-3.htm. Accessed January 10, 2010.

Green, Chris. 'The Incarnation and Mission.' In *The Word Became Flesh: Evangelicals and the Incarnation*, edited by David Peterson, 81-101. Carlisle: Paternoster Press, 2003.

Green, Laurie. *Urban Ministry and the Kingdom of God*. London: SPCK, 2003.

Greenfield, Karl Taro. 'Need for Speed.' *Time Magazine*, http://www.time.com/time/magazine/article/0,9171,100581,00.html. Accessed March 4, 2010.

Greenway, Roger S. 'Eighteen Barrels and Two Big Crates: How and Why Our "Stuff" Gets in the Way of Our Witness.' *Mission Frontiers* March/April 1992.

Greenway, Roger S., and Timothy M Monsma. *Cities: Missions' New Frontiers*. Grand Rapids: Baker, 2000.
Greer, Peter, and Phil Smith. *The Poor Will Be Glad*. Grand Rapids: Zondervan, 2009.
Grenz, Stanley J. . *Created for Community: Connecting Christian Belief with Christian Living*. Grand Rapids: Baker Academic, 2005.
Griffin, Emilie, and Douglas V. Steere, eds. *Quaker Spirituality: Selected Writings*. San Francisco: HarperSanFrancisco, 2005.
Grigg, Viv. *Companion to the Poor: Christ in the Urban Slums*. Rev ed. Monrovia: MARC, 1990.
———. *Cry of the Urban Poor*. Monrovia: MARC, 1992.
———. 'Intercessors and Cosmic Urban Spiritual Warfare.' *International Journal of Frontier Missions* 10 no. 4 (1993): 195-200.
———. 'The Lostness of Urban Squatters: Is There Any Hope?' *Evangelical Review of Theology* 15:1 (1991): 51-61.
———. vgrigg@apu.edu. 'Number of churches among the poor.' Private e-mail message to Ash Barker ashbarker@unoh.org. September 7, 2010.
———. 'Sorry! The Frontier Moved.' In *Planting and Growing Urban Churches*, edited by Harvie M. Conn, 12-25. Grand Rapids: Baker, 1987.
———. 'Squatters: The Most Responsive Unreached Bloc.' *Urban Mission* 6 (1989): 41-50.
———. 'Where Are the Churches of the Poor?' *Urban Leaders* http://www.urbanleaders.org/weburbpoor/04Context(CX)/Global%20Movements/where%20are%20the%20churches%20of%20the%20poor/Churches%20of%20the%20poor.htm. Accessed January 11, 2009.
Guder, Darrell. *Be My Witnesses*. Grand Rapids: Eerdmans, 1985.
———. *The Continuing Conversion of the Church*. Grand Rapids: Eerdmans, 2000.
———. *The Incarnation and the Church's Witness*. Eugene: Wipf and Stock, 1999.
———, ed. *Missional Church: A Vision for the Sending of the Church in North America*. Grand Rapids: Eerdmans, 1998.
Gutiérrez, Gustavo. *A Theology of Liberation*. Maryknoll: Orbis, 1973.
———. *We Drink from Our Own Wells: A Spiritual Journey of a People*. Maryknoll: Orbis, 1984.
Haapala, Ulla. 'Urbanization and Water: The Stages of Development in Latin America, South-East Asia and West Africa.' Master's Thesis, Helsinki: Helsinki University of Technology, 2002.
Haley, Jon. 'Seeing the Big Picture: A Unified Theory of Our Task.' *Evangelical Missions Quarterly* 32 no. 4 (1996): 424-9.
Halter, Hugh, and Matt Smay. *The Tangible Kingdom: Creating Incarnational Community—the Posture and Practices of the Ancient Church Now*. San Francisco: Jossey-Bass, 2008.
Hamdi, Nabeel. *Small Change: About the Art of Practice and the Limits of Planning in Cities*. London: Earthscan, 2004.
Hamilton, Clive. *Growth Fetish*. Crows Nest: Allen and Unwin, 2003.
Handcock, Graham. *Lords of Poverty*. London: Macmillan, 1989.
Hardoy, Jorge Enrique, Sandy Cairncross, and David Satterthwaite. *The Poor Die Young: Housing and Health in the Third World*. London: Earthscan, 1989.
Hardoy, Jorge E., Diana Mitlin, and David Satterthwaite. *Environmental Problems in an Urbanizing World: Finding Solutions for Cities in Africa, Asia and Latin America*. New ed. London: Earthscan, 2001.
———. *Environmental Problems in an Urbanizing World: Finding Solutions in Africa, Asia and Latin America*. Updated, expanded ed. London: Earthscan,, 2000.
———. *Environmental Problems in Third World Cities*. London: Earthscan, 1992.
Hardoy, Jorge E., and David Satterthwaite. *Shelter: Need and Response. Housing, Land and Settlement Policies in Seventeen Third World Nations*. Chichester: Wiley, 1981.
———. *Small and Intermediate Urban Centres: Their Role in Regional and National Development in the Third World*. London: Hodder & Stoughton and the International Institute for Environment and Development, 1986.

Hardoy, Jorge Enrique, and David Satterthwaite. *Squatter Citizen: Life in the Urban Third World*. London: Earthscan, 1989.
Harris, Dorothy. 'Incarnation as a Journey in Relocation.' In *Sharing the Good News with the Poor*, edited by Bruce J. Nicholls and Beulah R. Woods, 175-88. Grand Rapids: Baker, 1996.
———. 'Incarnation as Relocation among the Poor.' *Evangelical Review of Theology* 18 (1994): 117-27.
Hasan, Arif, Sheela Patel, and Alfred W. Satterthwaite. 'How to Meet the Millennium Development Goals (MDGs) in Urban Areas.' *Environment and Urbanization* 17, no. 3 (2005): 2-22.
Hata, Tatsuya. *Bangkok in the Balance: Bangkok's 'Slum Angel' and the Bloody Events of May 1992*. Bangkok: Duang Prateep Foundation, 1996.
Hauerwas, Stanley, and Jean Vanier. *Living Gently in a Violent World: The Prophetic Witness of Weakness*. Downers Grove: InterVarsity Press, 2008.
Hayes, John. *Sub-Merge: Living Deep in a Shallow World*. Ventura: Regal, 2006.
Haynes, Stephen R. *The Bonhoeffer Phenomenon: Portraits of a Protestant Saint*. Minneapolis: Fortress Press, 2004.
Heschel, Abraham Joshua. *The Prophets*. New York: Harper Collins, 1962.
Hesselgrave, David. *Paradigms in Conflict: 10 Key Questions in Christian Missions Today*. Grand Rapids: Kregal, 2005.
Heurtz, Christopher. *Simple Spirituality: Learning to See God in a Broken World*. Downers Grove: InterVarsity Press, 2008.
Heuertz, Christopher, and Christine Pohl. *Friendship at the Margins: Discovering Mutuality in Service and Mission*. Downers Grove: InterVarsity Press, 2010.
Hick, John, ed. *The Myth of God Incarnate*. London: SCM Press, 1977.
Hiebert, Paul. *The Gospel in Human Contexts: Anthropological Explorations for Contemporary Missions*. Grand Rapids: Baker, 2009.
———. 'Spiritual Warfare and Worldview.' In *Global Missiology for the 21st Century: The Iguassu Dialogue*, edited by William Taylor, 163-78. Grand Rapids: Baker Academic, 2000.
Hirsch, Alan. *The Forgotten Ways: Reactivating the Missional Church*. Grand Rapids: Brazos, 2006.
Hjalmarson, Len. 'Another Look at Certainty.' *Next Reformation* http://nextreformation.com/wp-admin/general/certainty.htm. Accessed March 15, 2011.
Hogan, Brian. *There's a Sheep in My Bathtub: Birth of a Mongolian Church Planting Movement*. Bayside: Asteroidea Books, 2008.
Hollyday, Joyce. 'The Word Become Flesh: A Short Story for Christmas.' In *Constructive Christian Theology in the Worldwide Church*, edited by William Barr, 382-86. Grand Rapids: Eerdmans, 1997.
Holt, Simon. *God Next Door: Spirituality and Mission in the Neighbourhood*. Brunswick East: Acorn Press, 2007.
Hopkins, Stephen, Bill Bosworth, and Brad Lennon. 'Urban People in Poverty: Towards an Alternative Model of Ministry.' In *Justice as Mission*, edited by Terry Brown and Christopher Lind, 153-61. Burlington: Trinity Press, 1985.
Hostetler, Virginia A. 'Faith in a Favela: Why Two North Americans Chose to Live in a Brazilian Slum.' *Other Side* (1983): 24-27.
Houston, Brian. *You Need More Money: God's Amazing Financial Plan for Your Life*. Sydney: Maximised Leadership, 1999.
Howell, Richard. *Transformation in Action*. Bangkok: 2004 Lausanne Forum for World Evangelization, 2004.
Hughes, Dewi. *God of the Poor: A Biblical Vision of God's Present Rule*. Milton Keynes: Authentic, 1998.
Human Rights Watch. 'Thailand—Not Enough Graves: The War on Drugs, HIV/AIDS, and Violations of Human Rights.' *Human Rights Watch* 16, no. 8 (June 2004), http://www.hrw.org/sites/default/files/reports/thailand0704.pdf. Accessed August 17, 2011.
Hunter, George, III. *To Spread the Power: Church Growth in the Wesleyan Spirit*. Nashville: Abingdon Press, 1987.

Igel, Barbara, and Asian Institute of Technology. Human Settlements Division. *The Economy of Survival in the Slums of Bangkok*, HSD Research Report: No. 27. Bangkok: Division of Human Settlement Development Asian Institute of Technology, 1992.

India, Government of. 'Census of India 2001 (Provisional) Slum Population in Million Plus Cities (Municipal Corporations).' *Census India* http://censusindia.gov.in/Tables_Published/Admin_Units/Admin_links/slum1_m_plus.html. Accessed September 10, 2010.

Inge, John. *A Christian Theology of Place: Explorations in Practical, Pastoral and Empirical Theology*. Aldershot: Ashgate, 2003.

International Federation of Red Cross and Red Crescent Societies. 'World Disasters Report 2010—Focus on Urban Risk.' *International Federation of Red Cross*, http://www.ifrc.org/Docs/pubs/disasters/wdr2010/WDR2010-full.pdf. Accessed January 20, 2010.

Inverson, Eric T. 'Reimaging Relocation: Can Christians Walk with the Poor without Leaving Their Neighborhood?' *Prism* March/April (2007).

Irvin, Dale T. 'The Church, the Urban, and the Global: Mission in an Age of Global Cities.' *International Bulletin of Missionary Research* 33, no. 4 (2009): 177-81.

Jack, Kristin, ed. *The Sound of Worlds Colliding: Stories from Servants among the Poor*. Phnom Penh: Servants to Asia's Urban Poor, 2008.

Jacobsen, Eric. *Sidewalks in the Kingdom: New Urbanism and the Christian Faith*. Grand Rapids: Brazos, 2003.

Jennings, Daniel. *The Supernatural Occurrences of Charles G. Finney*. Oklahoma City: SEAN, 2009.

Jennings, Daniel R. . *The Supernatural Occurrences of John Wesley*. Oklahoma City: SEAN, 2005.

Johnson, Aubrey. *The Vitality of the Individual in the Thought of Ancient Israel*. Cardiff: University of Wales, 1964.

Johnson, Kelly. *The Fear of Beggars: Stewardship and Poverty in Christian Ethics*. Grand Rapids: Eerdmans, 2007.

Johnson, Luke Timothy. *Living Jesus: Learning the Hearth of the Gospel*. San Francisco: HarperCollins, 1999.

Johnson, Todd. tjohnson@gordonconwell.edu. 'Ash and the PhD saga!' Private e-mail message to Ash Barker ashbarker@unoh.org. November 27 2010.

Johnson, Todd, and Kenneth Ross, eds. *Atlas of Global Christianity*. Edinburgh: Edinburgh University Press, 2009.

Johnson, Todd, and David B. Barrett and Peter F. Crossing. 'Status of Global Mission, 2011, in Context of the 20th and 21st Centuries', *International Bulletin of Missionary Research* January 2011, 29.

Jones, E. Stanley. *Christ of the Indian Road*. London: Hodder and Stoughton, 1925.

———. *A Song of Ascents*. Nashville: Abingdon Press, 1968.

Kagawa, Toyohiko. *Christ and Japan*. New York: Friendship Press, 1934.

Kalana Vineyard Christian Church. *Kalana Vineyard Church*. http://www.kelownavineyard.com/index.cfm?i=3142&mid=22&smgroupid=11557. Accessed January 6, 2010.

Kaldor, Peter, John Bellamy, Sandra Moore, Ruth Powell, Keith Castle, and Merilyn Correy. *Mission under the Microscope: Keys to Effective and Sustainable Mission*. Adelaide: Open Book Publishers, 1995.

Kanagaraj, Key J. *The Gospel of John: A Commentary with Elements of Comparison to Indian Religious Thoughts and Cultural Practices*. Secunderabad: OM Books, 2005.

Kärkkäinen, Veli-Matti, ed. *The Spirit of the World: Emerging Pentecostal Theologies in Global Contexts*. Grand Rapids: Eerdmans, 2009.

Karlan, Dean, and Jacob Appel. *More Than Good Intentions: How a New Economics Is Helping to Solve Global Poverty*. New York: Penguin, 2011.

Kelly, Geffrey B, and Nelson F. Burton. *The Cost of Moral Leadership: The Spirituality of Dietrich Bonhoeffer*. Grand Rapids: Eerdmans, 2003.

Kierkegaard, Soren. *Training in Christianity*. New York: Random House, 2004.

Kirby, Alex. 'Slum Growth "Shames the World."' *BBC*. October 6, 2003. http://news.bbc.co.uk/2/hi/science/nature/3161812.stm. Accessed February 2, 2010.

Kittel, Gerhard. 'Skene.' In *Theological Dictionary of the New Testament, Abridged*, edited by Gerhard Kittel and John Friedrich. 1040-44. Grand Rapids: Eerdmans, 1985.

Köstenberger, Andreas J. *The Missions of Jesus and the Disciples According to the Fourth Gospel*. Grand Rapids: Eerdmans, 1998.

Kotkin, Joel. *The City: A Global History*. New York: Modern Library, 2005.

Koyama, Kosuke. *Water Buffalo Theology*. Maryknoll: Orbis, 1974.

Kraft, Charles. *Anthropology for Christian Witness*. Maryknoll: Orbis, 2006.

―――. *Christianity in Culture: A Study in Dynamic Biblical Theologizing in Cross-Cultural Perspective*. Maryknoll: Orbis, 1981.

―――. *Confronting Powerless Christianity: Evangelicals and the Missing Dimension*. Grand Rapids: Chosen Books, 2002.

―――. *I Give You Authority: Practicing the Authority Jesus Gave Us*. Grand Rapids: Chosen Books, 1997.

Krakauer, Jon. *Three Cups of Deceit*. San Francisco: Byliner, 2011.

Kramer, Mark. *Dispossessed: Life in Our World's Urban Slums*. Maryknoll: Orbis, 2006.

Kraybill, Donald B., and Carl F. Bowman. *On the Backroad to Heaven: Old Order Hutterites, Mennonites, Amish and Brethren*. Baltimore: John Hopkins University Press, 2001.

Küng, Hans. *Global Responsibility: In Search of a New World Ethic*. London: SCM, 1990.

―――. *On Being a Christian*. New York: Doubleday, 1976.

Kunzig, Robert. 'Seven Billion.' *National Geographic* 219, no. 1 (2011): 32-69.

Kupp, David. 'Playing "Catch up" with the City: How Are Other International Agencies Responding to Urban Poverty?' *Transformational Development*. http://www.transformational-development.org/Ministry/TransDev2.nsf/094A3B847DCC22F4852570A4005626B6/$file/Urban%20Issues%207%20-%20Playing%20Catch-Up%20With%20the%20City.pdf. Accessed January 11, 2011.

―――. 'So, Where Are Those Urban Programmes?' *Discussion Paper #4 Transformational Development News* 2005 July 22: Vol. 3. http://www.transformational-development.org/Ministry/TransDev2.nsf/webmaindocs/094A3B847DCC22F4852570A4005626B6?OpenDocument. Accessed January 11, 2011.

―――. 'Urban Child Sponsorship and Fundraising.' *Transformational Development*. http://www.transformational-development.org/Ministry/TransDev2.nsf/A6748A23BB21C3F0882572570 0707E73/$file/Urban%20R&D%20Report%20-%20Chapter%209%20(Draft)%20-%20Jan%2010,%202007.pdf. Accessed January 11, 2011.

―――. 'Urban Issues Discussion Papers.' *Transformational Development*. http://www.transformational-development.org/Ministry/TransDev2.nsf/webmaindocs/094A3B847DCC22F4852570A400562 6B6?OpenDocument. Accessed January 11, 2011.

―――. 'World Vision's Urban History and Theology.' *Transformational Development*. http://www.transformational-development.org/Ministry/TransDev2.nsf/A6748A23BB21C3F0882572570070 7E73/$file/Urban%20R&D%20Report%20-%20Chapter%206%20(Draft)%20-%20Jan%209,%20 2007.pdf. Accessed January 11, 2011.

Kyle, John E. *Urban Mission: God's Concern for the City*. Downers Grove: InterVarsity Press, 1988.

Langer, Suzanne. *Philosophy in a New Key*. New York: Mentor, 1948.

Langmead, Ross. *The Word Made Flesh: Towards an Incarnational Missiology*. Lanham: University Press of America, 2004.

Lapierre, Dominique. *The City of Joy*. New York: Warner Books, 1992.

Lappe, Frances Moore, Joseph Collins, and Peter Rosset. *World Hunger: Twelve Myths*. New York: Grove Press, 1998.

Lash, Nicholas. *Theology for Pilgrims*. London: Darton, Long and Todd, 2008.

Lausanne Committee for World Evangelisation. 'The 2004 Forum for World Evangelization.' *The Lausanne Movement*. www.lausanne.org/Brix?pageID=12897. Accessed January 27, 2007.

―――. 'A Call to Develop Christ-Like Leaders.' *Community Gospel* http://community.gospelcom.net/lcwe/assets/LOP41_IG12.pdf. Accessed January 23, 2007.

———. 'How Were the Various Issues Chosen?' *The Lausanne Movement*. www.lausanne.org/Brix?pageID=13895. Accessed January 23, 2007.

———. 'Lausanne Occasional Paper Number 35: Towards the Transformation of Cities/Regions.' *The Lausanne Movement*. www.lausanne.org/documents/2004forum/LOP37_IG8.pdf Accessed August 10, 2010.

Lee, Witness. 'The History of the Local Churches.' *Local Church History* http://www.local-church-history.org/local-church-2-aspects-b.htm. Accessed June 16, 2010.

Leffel, Gregory P. *Faith Seeking Action: Mission Social Movements and the Church in Motion*. Lanham: The Scarecrow Press, 2007.

Levines, Daniel H. 'Assessing the Impact of Liberation Theology in Latin America.' *The Review of Politics* Vol. 50 no. 2 (1988): 241-63.

Lewis, Oscar. 'The Culture of Poverty.' In *Urban Life: Readings in the Anthropology of the City*. 4th Edition. Edited by George Gmelch and Walter P. Zenner. 175-84. Long Grove: Waveland Press, 2002:.

Lingenfelter, Judith E., and Sherwood G. Lingenfelter. *Teaching Cross-Culturally: An Incarnational Model for Learning and Teaching*. Grand Rapids: Baker, 2007.

Linthicum, Robert. *Building a People of Power: Equipping Churches to Transform Their Communities*. Waynesboro: Authentic, 2005.

———. *City of God, City of Satan*. Grand Rapids: Zondervan, 1991.

———. *Empowering the Poor: Community Organizing among the City's Rag, Tag and Bobtail*. Monrovia: MARC, 1999.

Liotta, P. H., and James F. Miskel. 'The "Mega-Eights": Urban Leviathans and International Instability.' *The Foreign Policy Research Institute*. http://www.fpri.org/enotes/201002.liottamiskel.megaeights.html. Accessed September 8, 2010.

Liu, Agnes. 'Training the Poor for Ministry to the Poor.' *Evangelical Review of Theology* 18, no. 2 (1994): 167-72.

Lloyd, Peter Cutt. *Slums of Hope? Shanty Towns of the Third World*. Manchester: Manchester University Press, 1979.

Lorenzen, Thorwald. *Resurrection and Discipleship: Interpretive Models, Biblical Reflections, Theological Consequences*. Maryknoll: Orbis, 1996.

Lowery, Joseph E. *Singing the Lord's Song in a Strange Land*. Nashville: Abingdon Press, 2011.

Lupton, Robert D. *Renewing the City: Reflections on Community Development and Urban Renewal*. Downers Grove: InterVarsity Press, 2005.

Ma, Wonsuk, 'When the Poor are Fired Up: Pneumatology in Pentecostal/Charismatic Missio.' In *The Spirit of the World: Emerging Pentecostal Theologies in Global Contexts*. Edited by Veli-Matti Kärkkäinen, 40-52. Grand Rapids: Eerdmans, 2009.

MacKendrick, Karmen. 'The Word Made Flesh: The Embodiment of Christ in the Fourth Gospel.' In *Explorations in Contemporary Continental Philosophy of Religion*, 105-14. Amsterdam; New York: Rodopi, 2003.

Macchia, Frank D. 'Baptised in the Spirit: Towards a Global Theology of Spirit Baptism.' In *The Spirit of the World: Emerging Pentecostal Theologies in Global Contexts*. Edited by Veli-Matti Kärkkäinen, 3-20. Grand Rapids: Eerdmans, 2009.

Maier, Joe. *The Slaughterhouse: True Stories from Bangkok's Klong Toey Slum*. Bangkok: Post Books, 2002.

Mallison, John. *Mentoring to Develop Disciples and Leaders*. Adelaide: Open Book Publishers, 1998.

Mann, Frank. 'Priest Save Souls, Lives in Thailand's Slaughterhouse.' *The Queens Gazette* November 12, 2008. http://www.qgazette.com/news/2008-11-12/features/033.html. Accessed August 23, 2010.

Marchant, Colin. *Signs of the City*. London: Hodder and Stoughton, 1985.

Marris, Peter. *The Meaning of Slums and Patterns of Change*. Comparative Urbanization Studies. Los Angeles: School of Architecture and Urban Planning University of California, 1978.

Marsh, Charles, and John Perkins. *Welcoming Justice: God's Movement toward Beloved Community*. Downers Grove: InterVarsity Press, 2009.

Matthews, John W. *Anxious Souls Will Ask? The Christ-Centred Spirituality of Dietrich Bonhoeffer*. Grand Rapids: Eerdmans, 2005.

McAlpine, Thomas. *Facing the Powers: What Are the Options?* Monrovia: MARC, 1991.

McDonnell, Thomas, ed. *A Thomas Merton Reader*. New York: DoubleDay, 1996.

McGavran, Donald. *Understanding Church Growth*. Grand Rapids: Eerdmans, 1980.

McGrath, Alister. *Incarnation*. Minneapolis: Fortress Press, 2006.

McKnight, John, and Peter Brock. *The Abundant Community: Awakening the Power of Families and Neighbourhoods*. San Francisco: Berrett-Koehler, 2010.

McLaren, Brian. *Everything Must Change: Jesus, Global Crises and a Revolution of Hope*. Nashville: Thomas Nelson, 2007.

McMinn, Lisa Graham, and Megan Anna Neff. *Walking Gently on the Earth*. Downers Grove: InterVarsity Press, 2010.

Meeks, Wayne A. *The First Urban Christians: The Social World of the Apostle Paul*. New Haven: Yale University Press, 2003.

Mehta, Barjor Mehta, and Arish Dastur. *Adaptive Approaches to Urban Slums: A Multimedia Sourcebook for Adaptive and Proactive Strategies*. Washington DC: World Bank, 2008.

Mehta, Suketu. *Maxium City: Bombay Lost and Found*. London: Headline Book Publishing, 2004.

Mejudhon, Ubolwan. 'The Way of Meekness: Being Christian and Thai in the Thai Way.' PhD Thesis, Wilmore: Asbury Theological Seminary, 1997.

Mercy Centre. 'George W. Bush to Visit Bangkok Slum Children.' *Mercy Centre*. http://mercycentre.org/index.php?option=com_content&view=article&id=118%3Ageorge-w-bush-to-visit-bangkok-slum-children&catid=2%3Aarticles-about-the-mercy-centre&Itemid=27&lang=en. Accessed June 28, 2010.

———. *Mercy Centre* http://www.mercycentre.org. Accessed August 23, 2010.

Merton, Thomas. *The Inner Experience: Notes on Contemplation*. San Francisco: HarperCollins, 2002.

———. *New Seeds of Contemplation*. New York: New Directions, 1972.

Micklethwait, John, and Adrian Woolridge. *God Is Back: How the Global Revival of Faith Is Changing the World*. New York: The Penguin Press, 2009.

Millham, Douglas E. 'Training for Relief and Development.' In *Christian Relief and Development: Developing Workers for Effective Ministry*, edited by Edgar J Elliston, 261-67. London: Word Publishing, 1989.

Millspaugh, Martin, and Gurney Breckenfeld. *The Human Side of Urban Renewal: A Study of the Attitude Changes Produced by Neighbourhood Rehabilitation*. New York: Ives Washburn, 1960.

Milne, Bruce. *The Message of Heaven and Hell*. Downers Grove: InterVarsity Press, 2002.

Miranda, José Porfirio. *Marx and the Bible: A Critique of the Philosophy of Oppression*. Maryknoll: Orbis, 1974.

Mitlin, Diana, and David Satterthwaite. *Empowering Squatter Citizen: Local Government, Civil Society and Urban Poverty Reduction*. London: Earthscan, 2004.

Möhler, Johann Adam. *Symbolism; or, Exposition of the Doctrinal Differences between Catholics and Protestants as Evidenced by Their Symbolic Writings*. New York: E Dunigan, 1844.

Molnar, Paul D. *Incarnation and Resurrection: Toward a Contemporary Understanding*. Grand Rapids: Eerdmans, 2007.

Moltmann, Jürgen. *A Broad Place: An Autobiography*. Minneapolis: Fortress Press, 2008.

———. *The Coming of God: Christian Eschatology*. Minneapolis: Fortress Press, 2004.

———. *The Crucified God: The Cross of Christ as the Foundation and Criticism of Christian Theology*. New York: Harper and Row, 1974.

———. *Experiences of God*. Minneapolis: Fortress Press, 2007.

———. *The Future of Creation: Collected Essays*. Minneapolis: Fortress Press, 2007.

———. *God in Creation: A New Theology of Creation and the Spirit of God*. Minneapolis: Fortress Press, 1993.

———. *God in Creation: An Ecological Doctrine of Creation*. London: SCM, 1985.
———. *In the End—the Beginning: The Life of Hope*. Minneapolis: Fortress Press, 2004.
———. *Jesus Christ for Today's World*. London: SCM, 1994.
———. *On Human Dignity: Political Theology and Ethics*. Minneapolis: Fortress Press, 2007.
———. *The Passion for Life: A Messianic Lifestyle*. Minneapolis: Fortress Press, 2007.
———. *Pilgrimage of Love: Moltmann on the Trinity and Christian Life*. Oxford: Oxford University Press, 2005.
———. 'A Response to My Pentecostal Dialogue Partners.' *Journal of Pentecostal Theology* 4 (1994): 59-70.
———. 'Sighs, Signs, and Significance: A Theological Hermeneutic of Nature.' *Andy Rowell* http://www.andyrowell.net/andy_rowell/duke-divinity-school/page/2/ Accessed March 14, 2010.
———. *The Source of Life: The Holy Spirit and the Theology of Life*. Minneapolis: Fortress Press, 1997.
———. *The Spirit of Life: A Universal Affirmation*. Minneapolis: Fortress Press, 2001.
———. *Theology of Hope: On the Ground and Implications of a Christian Eschatology*. Minneapolis: Fortress Press, 1993.
———. *The Trinity and the Kingdom: The Doctrine of God*. Minneapolis: Fortress Press, 1993.
———. *The Way of Jesus Christ*. Minneapolis: Fortress Press, 1993.
———. 'Preface.' In *The Spirit of the World: Emerging Pentecostal Theologies in Global Contexts*. Edited by Veli-Matti Kärkkäinen, vii-xii. Grand Rapids: Eerdmans, 2009.
Mondithoka, S. 'Incarnation.' In *Dictionary of Mission Theology: Evangelical foundations*, edited by John Corrie, 177-81. Nottingham: Inter-Varsity Press, 2007.
Monsma, Steve. *Healing for a Broken World: Christian Perspectives on Public Policy*. Wheaton: Crossway Books, 2008.
Moore, Steve. *Who Is My Neighbor? Being a Good Samaritan in a Connected World*. Colorado Springs: NavPress, 2010.
Moreau, A. Scott, Harold Netland, and Charles Van Engen, eds. *Evangelical Dictionary of World Mission*. Grand Rapids: Baker, 2000.
Morell, Susan, and David L. Morell. *Six Slums in Bangkok: Problems of Life and Options for Action, a Report Prepared for UNICEF*. Bangkok: United Nations Children's Fund, 1972.
Morgan, Timothy C. 'Purpose Driven in Rwanda: Rick Warren's Sweeping Plan to Defeat Poverty.' *Christianity Today* October 17, 2005. http://www.christianitytoday.com/ct/2005/october/17.32.html?start=2. Accessed February 11, 2011.
Mosher, Steve. *God's Power, Jesus' Faith and World Mission: A Study in Romans*. Scottdale: Herald Press, 1996.
Mulder, Niels. *Inside Thai Society: Religion, Everyday Life, Change*. Chiang Mai: Silkworm Books, 2000.
Müller-Fahrenholz, Geiko. *The Kingdom and the Power: The Theology of Jürgen Moltmann*. Minneapolis: Fortress Press, 2001.
Murray, Stuart. *The Naked Anabaptist: Bare Essentials of a Radical Faith*. Scottdale: Herald, 2010.
Myers, Bryant. *Walking with the Poor: Principles and Practices of Transformational Development*. Maryknoll: Orbis, 1999.
Myers, Ched. *Binding the Strong Man: A Political Reading of Mark's Story of Jesus*. Maryknoll: Orbis, 1988.
———. *Who Will Roll Away the Stone? Discipleship Queries for First World Christians*. Maryknoll: Orbis, 1997.
Myers, Ched, Marie Dennis, Joseph Nangle, Cynthia Moe-Lobeda, and Stuart Taylor. *Say to This Mountain: Mark's Story of Discipleship*. Maryknoll: Orbis, 2003.
National Statistical Office Thailand. 'Population and Housing Census 2000.' www.web.nso.go.th/pop2000/prelim_e.htm. Accessed January 6, 2010.
———. 'Population by Religion and Sex: 2000.' http://web.nso.go.th/pop2000/table/eadv_tab3.pdf. Accessed January 6, 2010.

NCLS Research. *National Church Life Survey*. http://www.ncls.org.au/. Accessed January 13, 2010.

Neighborhood Transformation. 'About CNT.' *Neighborhood Transformation*. www.neighborhoodtransformation.net/about.php. Accessed March 15, 2011.

———. 'Urban CHE Overview.' *Neighborhood Transformation*. www.neighborhoodtransformation.net. Accessed December 15, 2010.

Neill, Stephen *Christian Faith and Other Faiths*. Downers Grove: InterVarsity Press, 1984.

Neuwirth, Robert. *Shadow Cities: A Billion Squatters, a New Urban World*. New York: Routledge, 2005.

Nevius, John Livingston. *The Planting and Development of Missionary Churches*. Hancock: Monadnock, 2003 (1886).

New Advent. 'Eutychianism.' *New Advent*. http://www.newadvent.org/cathen/05633a.htm. Accessed August 17, 2011.

Newbigin, Lesslie. *Foolishness to the Greeks: The Gospel and Western Culture*. Grand Rapids: Eerdmans, 1999.

———. *The Gospel in a Pluralist Society*. Geneva: WCC Publications, 1989.

———. *Living Hope in a Changing World*. London: Alpha International, 2003.

———. *The Open Secret*. Grand Rapids: Eerdmans, 1983.

———. *Proper Confidence: Faith, Doubt and Certainty in Christian Discipleship*. Grand Rapids: Eerdmans, 1995.

———. *Signs Amid the Rubble: The Purposes of God in Human History*. Grand Rapids: Eerdmans, 2003.

———. *A Word in Season: Perspective on Christian World Mission*. Grand Rapids: Eerdmans, 1994.

Nicholls, Bruce J. 'Sharing Good News with the Poor.' *Evangelical Review of Theology* 18, (1994): 99-192.

Niebuhr, Reinhold. *Moral Man and Immoral Society: A Study in Ethics and Politics*. London: Continuum, 2005 (1960).

Norridge, Mark. 'Incarnational Mission.' *Community Church Northampton*. http://www.ccn-online.org.uk/Downloads/Incarnational%20Mission.pdf Accessed August 17, 2011.

Nouwen, Henri. *Encounters with Merton: Spiritual Reflections*. New York: Crossroad, 1991.

———. *In the Name of Jesus: Reflections on Christian Leadership*. New York: Crossroad, 2002.

———. *Life of the Beloved and Our Greatest Gift*. London: Hodder and Stoughton, 2002.

———. *Reaching Out: The Three Movements of the Spiritual Life*. New York: Doubleday, 1986.

———. *The Road to Peace*. Maryknoll: Orbis, 1999.

———. *The Way of the Heart: Desert Spirituality and Contemporary Ministry*. New York: Seabury Press, 1983

Nussbaun, Stan, ed. *The Congregational Contribution to the Battle with HIV/Aids at the Community Level*. Oxford: Oxford Centre for Mission Studies, 2005.

O'Callaghan, Rob. 'What Do We Mean by "Incarnational Methodology?"' *The Cry* 10, no. 3 (2004): 6-8.

Oden, Thomas. *The Good Works Reader*. Grand Rapids: Eerdmans, 2007.

O'Gorman, Frances. *Charity and Change: From Bandaid to Beacon*. Melbourne: World Vision Australia, 1992.

One World. 'Dhaka's Slum Population Doubles in a Decade.' *One World*. http://us.oneworld.net/node/133390. Accessed December 21, 2010.

Operation World. 'Thailand.' *Operation World*. http://www.operationworld.org/country/thai/owtext.html. Accessed January 6, 2010.

Orr, James. 'Hope.' In *International Standard Encyclopaedia of the Bible*, edited by James Orr. Grand Rapids: Eerdmans, 1915.

Ortiz, Manuel, and Susan S. Baker. *The Urban Face of Mission: Ministering the Gospel in a Diverse and Changing World*. Phillipsburg: R Publishing, 2002.

Osmer, Richard Robert. *Practical Theology: An Introduction*. Cambridge, UK: Eerdmans, 2008.

Padilla, René. *Transforming Church and Mission*. Bangkok: 2004 Lausanne Forum for World Evangelization, 2004.

Padilla, René, and Lindy Scott. *Terrorism and the War in Iraq*. Buenos Aires: Kairos, 2004.

Paengnoy, Anan. 'Task of Building 100,000 Units a Year "Tough for NHA."' *The Nation*, September 4, 2006. http://www.nationmultimedia.com/2006/09/04/national/national_30012712.php. Accessed January 15, 2007.

Page, Jeremy. 'Indian Slum Population Doubles in Two Decades.' *The Sunday Times*, May 18, 2007. http://www.timesonline.co.uk/tol/news/world/asia/article1805596.ece. Accessed August 17, 2011.

Palmer, Parker. *The Active Life: A Spirituality of Work, Creativity and Caring*. San Francisco: Jossey-Bass, 1990.

———. *The Courage to Teach: Exploring the Inner Landscape of a Teacher's Life*. San Francisco: Jossey-Bass, 1998.

———. *A Hidden Wholeness: The Journey toward an Undivided Life*. San Francisco: Jossey-Bass, 2004.

———. *Let Your Life Speak: Listening for the Voice of Vocation*. San Francisco: Jossey-Bass, 2000.

Pascale, Richard T., Mark Willemann, and Linda Gioja. *Surfing on the Edge of Chaos: The Laws of Nature and New Laws of Business*. New York: Three Rivers Press, 2000.

Patterson, George. 'The Spontaneous Multiplication of Churches.' In *Perspectives on the World Christian Movement: A Reader*, edited by Ralph D Winter and Steven C Hawthorne, 2nd ed., D76-94. Pasadena: William Carey Library, 1992.

Peck, M. Scott. *People of the Lie: The Hope for Healing Human Evil*. London: Arrow Books, 1990.

Penalosa, Enrique. 'Why Cities Must Build Equality.' *Urban World* December-January, (2009): 8-11.

Peretti, Frank. *This Present Darkness*. Westchester: Crossway, 1986.Perkins, John. *With Justice for All: A Strategy for Community Development*. Ventura: Regal Books, 2007 (1982).

Peterson, Douglas, 'A Moral Imagination: Pentecostals and social concern in Latin America'. In *The Spirit of the World: Emerging Pentecostal theologies in global contexts*. Edited by Veli-Matti Kärkkäinen, 53-66. Grand Rapids: Eerdmans, 2009.

Peterson, Eugene. *Living the Resurrection: The Risen Christ in Everyday Life*. Colorado Springs: NavPress, 2006.

———. *The Message: The Bible in Contemporary Language*. Colorado Springs: NavPress, 2007.

Pidwell, Harold. *A Gentle Bunyip: The Athol Gill Story*. West Lakes: Seaview Press, 2007.

Pierson, Paul. *The Dynamics of Christian Mission: History through a Missiological Perspective*. Pasadena: William Carey Library, 2009.

Pixley, Jorge, and Clodovis Boff. *The Bible, the Church and the Poor*. Tunbridge Wells: Burns and Oates, 1989.

Pohl, Christine. *Making Room: Recovering Hospitality as a Christian Tradition*. Grand Rapids: Eerdmans, 1999.

Polman, Linda. *We Did Nothing*. London: Penguin Viking, 2003.

Pope, Stephen J., ed. *Hope and Solidarity: Jon Sobrino's Challenge to Christian Theology*. Maryknoll: Orbis, 2008.

Popplestone, Gerry. 'More Fires in Bangkok's Shanty Town.' *Now Public*. http://www.nowpublic.com/environment/more-fires-bangkok-shanty-town. Accessed August 22, 2010.

Population Reference Bureau. 'Human Population: Urbanisation.' *Population Reference Bureau*. ww.prb.org/Educators/TeachersGuides/HumanPopulation/Urbanization.aspx. Accessed February 2, 2010.

Pornchokchai, Sopon. 'Council Member Biography.' *GL Group*. http://www.glgroup.com/Council-Member/Sopon-Pornchokchai-184101.html. Accessed March 15, 2010.

———. 'Global Report on Human Settlements 2003 City Report Bangkok.' *UN-Habitat*. www.thaiappraisal.org/pdfNew/HABITAT1new.pdf. Accessed March 13, 2010.

Portes, Alejandro. *Social Capital: Its Origins and Applications in a Modern Sociology*. Princeton: Princeton University, 1998.

Prahalad, C. K. *The Fortune at the Bottom of the Pyramid: Eradicating Poverty through Profits*. Upper Saddle River: Wharton School Publishing, 2006.

Pratt, Tom. 'Serving Slums: Has the Mission Community Largely Ignored the Most Important Demographic Shift of the Past 100 Years?' *Momentum* January/February 2007, 41-43.

Priest, Doug. DougPriest@cmfi.org. 'Mission Among the Urban Poor Stats.' Private e-mail to Ash Barker ashbarker@unoh.org. November 11, 2010.

Project 1516. 'Famous Quotes About Christian Missions.' *Project 1516*. http://www.project1615.org/quotes.htm. Accessed September 17, 2010.

Pulikottil, Paulson. 'One God, One Spirit, Two Memories: A Postcolonial Reading of the Encounter Between Western Pentecostalism and Native Pentecostalism in Kerala.' In *The Spirit of the World: Emerging Pentecostal Theologies in Global Contexts*. Edited by Veli-Matti Kärkkäinen, 69-88. Grand Rapids: Eerdmans, 2009.

Pullinger, Jackie. *Chasing the Dragon*. London: Hodder and Stoughton, 2001.

Putnam, Robert D. *American Grace: How Religion Divides and Unites Us*. New York: Simon and Schuster, 2010.

———. *Bowling Alone: The Collapse and Revival of American Community*. New York: Simon and Schuster, 2000.

Putnam, Robert D., Lewis M. Feldstein, and Don Cohen. *Better Together: Restoring the American Community*. New York: Simon and Schuster, 2003.

Rainer, Thom S., and Jess W. Rainer. *The Millennials: Connecting to America's Largest Generation*. Nashville: B and H Publishing Group, 2011.

Ransom, David. 'The Big Charity Bonanza.' *New Internationalist* no. 383 (October 2005).

Ratanachaichan, Nutta. 'Ban Mankong: From Slum Upgrading to Social Upliftment.' *Bangkok Post* http://www.bangkokpost.com/news/investigation/32500/ban-mankong-from-slum-upgrading-to-social-upliftment. Accessed August 22, 2010.

Rauschenbusch, Walter, and Paul Rauschenbusch. *Christianity and the Social Crisis in the 21st Century*. New York: HarperOne, 2007.

Rawls, John. *A Theory of Justice*. Cambridge: The Belknap Press of Harvard University Press 1999.

Reese, Robert. *Roots and Remedies of the Dependency Syndrome in World Missions*. Pasadena: William Carey Library, 2010.

Rigg, Jonathan. *Southeast Asia: A Region in Transition*. London: Routledge, 1991.

Riis, Jacob A. *The Battle with the Slum*. London: Macmillan, 1902.

Ringma, Charles. *Catch the Wind*. Sunderland: Albatross, 1996.

———. *Seek the Silences with Thomas Merton: Reflections on Identity, Community and Transformative Action*. Vancouver: Regent College Publishing, 2003.

Rivera-Pagan, Luis N. 'The Word Became Flesh: Incarnation, Gospel, and Culture in Latin America.' In *Hope and Justice for All in the Americas*, edited by Oscar Bolioli, 52-69. New York: Friendship Press, 1998.

Robertson, Edward Stanley. *The State and the Slums*. London: Liberty and Property Defence League, 1884.

Robinson, Stuart. *Mosques and Miracles: Revealing Islam and God's Grace*. Upper Mount Gravatt: CityHarvest Publications 2003.

Rohr, Richard. *Adam's Return: The Five Promises of Male Initiation*. New York: Crossroad, 2004.

Rommen, Edward. 'Last Things: The Eschatological Dimensions of the Church.' *International Bulletin of Missionary Research* 33 no. 3 (2009): 115-18.

Root, Andrew. *Revisiting Relational Youth Ministry: From a Strategy of Influence to a Theology of Incarnation*. Downers Grove: InterVarsity Press, 2007.

Rosenberg, Matt. 'Current World Population: Current World Population and World Population Growth since the Year One.' *Geography*. http://geography.about.com/bio/Matt-Rosenberg-268.htm. Accessed February 2, 2010.

Ross, Kenneth. *Following Jesus and Fighting HIV/AIDS*. Edinburgh: Saint Andrews Press, 2002.

Sachs, Jeffery. *Common Wealth: Economics for a Crowded Planet*. London: Allen Lane, 2008.

―――. *The End of Poverty: How We Can Make It Happen in Our Lifetime*. London: Penguin, 2005.

Sachs, Wolfgang, ed. *Global Ecology: A New Arena of Political Conflict*. London: Zed Books, 1995.

Salmon, Katy. 'Nairobi's "Flying Toilets": Tip of an Iceberg.' *Terra Villa*. http://ipsnews.net/riomas10/2608_3.shtml. Accessed January 7, 2010.

Samuel, Vinay, and Albert Hauser, eds. *Proclaiming Christ in Christ's Way: Studies in Integral Evangelism*. Oxford: Regnum, 1989.

Samuel, Vinay, and Chris Sugden, eds.. *The Church in Response to Human Need*. Grand Rapids: Eerdmans, 1987.

―――. 'Evangelism and Development.' In *New Frontiers in Mission*, edited by Patrick Sookhdeo, 115-24. Exeter: Paternoster, 1987.

―――. 'Evangelism and Social Responsibility: A Biblical Study on Priorities.' In *In Word and Deed*, edited by Bruce J. Nichols, 189-214. Grand Rapids: Eerdmans, 1986.

―――, eds. *Evangelism and the Poor*. Oxford: Regnum, 1987.

―――. *Evangelism and the Poor: A Third World Study Guide*. Bangalore: Asian Trading Corporation, 1983.

―――. 'God's Intention for the World.' In *Church in Response to Human Need*, edited by Vinay Samuel and Chris Sugden, 128-60. Grand Rapids: Eerdmans, 1987.

―――. 'God's Intention for the World: Tension between Eschatology and History.' In *Church in Response to Human Need*, edited by Vinay Samuel and Chris Sugden, 179-230. Grand Rapids: Eerdmans, 1987.

―――. 'A Just and Responsible Lifestyle: An Old Testament Perspective.' In *Lifestyle in the Eighties*, edited by Ron Sider, 42-53. Philadelphia: Westminster Press, 1982.

―――, eds. *Mission as Transformation: A Theology of the Whole Gospel*. Oxford: Regnum, 1999.

―――, eds. *Sharing Jesus in the Two Thirds World: Evangelical Christologies from the Contexts of Poverty, Powerlessness and Religious Pluralism*. Grand Rapids: Eerdmans, 1983.

Sanchez-Jankowski, Martin. *Cracks in the Pavement: Social Change and Resilience in Poor Neighbourhoods*. Berkeley: University of California Press, 2008.

Sarin, Madhu. *Policies Towards Urban Slums: Slums and Squatter Settlements in the Escap Region: Case Studies of Seven Cities*. New York: United Nations, 1980.

Satterthwaite, David, ed. *The Earthscan Reader in Sustainable Cities*. London: Earthscan, 1999.

―――. *The Environment for Children: Understanding and Acting on the Environmental Hazards That Threaten Children and Their Parents*. London: Earthscan, 1996.

―――. 'The Scale of Urban Change Worldwide 1950-2000 and Its Underpinnings.' *Overseas Development Institute*. http://www.odi.org.uk/speeches/horizons_nov06/8Nov/URBAN%20CHANGE%202005%20-%20David%20Satterthwaite%20paper.pdf. Accessed February 1, 2007.

―――. 'The Transition to a Predominately Urban World.' *International Institute for Environment and Development*. http://pubs.iied.org/pdfs/10550IIED.pdf. Accessed January 7, 2010.

Satterthwaite, David and Jorge E Hardoy. *Squatter Citizen: Life in the Urban Third World* London: Earthscan, 1989.

Saunders, Doug. *Arrival City: How the Largest Migration in History Is Reshaping Our World*. New York: Pantheon Books, 2010.

Savant-Mohit, Radhika. 'Security of Tenure and the Way Forward: The Case of Samakee Pattana, Bangkok.' *Habitat International* 28 (2003): 301-16.

Sayers, Mark. *The Trouble with Paris: Following Jesus in a World of Plastic Promises*. Nashville: Thomas Nelson, 2008.

Schaller, Lyle E. *The Change Agent*. Nashville: Abingdon Press, 1972.

Schlingensiepen, Ferdinand. *Dietrich Bonhoeffer 1906-1945: Martyr, Thinker, Man of Resistance*. London: T and T Clark, 2010.

Schut, Michael, ed. *Simpler Living, Compassionate Life: A Christian Perspective*. Denver: Living the Good News, 2003.

Seamands, Stephen. *Ministry in the Image of God: The Trinitarian Shape of Christian Ministry*. Downers Grove: InterVarsity Press, 2005.

SEDOS. 'Agenda for Future Planning, Study, and Research in Mission: Agenda for the SEDOS Research Seminar on the Future of Mission, Rome, March 1981.' In *Trends in Mission: Toward the Third Millennium. Essays in Celebration of Twenty-Five Years of SEDOS*, edited by William Jenkins and Helen O'Sullivan, 399-414. Maryknoll: Orbis, 1991.

Segovia, Fernando F., and Mary Ann Tolbert, eds. *Reading from This Place: Social Location and Biblical Interpretation in Global Perspective*. Minneapolis: Fortress Press, 1995.

Sen, Amartya. *Development as Freedom*. New York: Anchor Books, 1999.

Sender, Ursula. 'Charismatic Renewal and the Slums of Latin America.' In *Church Is Charismatic*, edited by Arnold Bittlinger, 189-92. Geneva, Switzerland: World Council of Churches, 1981.

Severance, Diane. 'Herrnhut Revival: A Golden Summer.' *Christian History*. www.christianity.com/ChurchHistory/11630208. Accessed March 15, 2010.

Shearer, Murray Brian. 'Catalyst for Change or Empty Exchange? Evaluating the Impact of Short Term Home-Stays in Manila Squatter Communities on Participating New Zealanders.' Master of Philosophy in Development Studies. Auckland: Massey University, 2005.

Sheldon, Charles Monroe. *In His Steps*. Peabody: Hendrickson, 2004.

Shelly, Rubel, and Randall Harris. *The 2nd Incarnation: A Theology for the 21st Century Church*. Abilene: Hillcrest Publishing, 2001.

Shin, Hong-Sik *Principles of Church Planting as Illustrated in the Thai Theravada Buddhist Context*. Bangkok: Kanok Bannasan (OMF Publishers), 1989.

Sider, Ronald. *One-Sided Christianity? Uniting the Church to Heal a Lost and Broken World*. Grand Rapids: Zondervan, 1993.

———. *Rich Christians in an Age of Hunger*. London: Hodder and Stoughton, 1990.

———. *Rich Christians in an Age of Hunger: Moving from Affluence to Generosity*. Nashville: Thomas Nelson, 2005.

Simson, Wolfgang. *Houses That Change the World: The Return of the House Churches*. Waynesboro: Authentic, 1998.

———. *The Starfish Manifesto*. Antioch: Asteroidea Books, 2009.

Sine, Tom. *The Mustard Seed Conspiracy: You Can Make a Difference in Tomorrow's Troubled World*. Waco: Word Books, 1981.

Singer, Peter. *The Life You Can Save: Acting Now to End World Poverty*. New York: Random House, 2009.

Slane, Craig. *Bonhoeffer as Martyr: Social Responsibility and Modern Christian Commitment*. Grand Rapids: Brazos Press, 2004.

Slater, Josephine Berry. 'Naked Cities: Struggle in the Global Slums.' *Mute: Culture and Politics After the Net* 2, no. 3 (2006): 1-2.

Slaughter, Mike. *Change the World: Recovering the Message and Mission of Jesus*. Nashville: Abingdon Press, 2010.

Smith, Alex. *Siamese Gold: A History of the Church Growth in Thailand*. Bangkok: Kanok Bannasan (OMF Publishers), 2004.

Smyth, Bernard T. *Paul: Mystic and Missionary*. Maryknoll: Orbis, 1980.

Sobrino, Jon and Ignacio Ellacuria, ed. *Mysterium Liberationis: Fundamental Concepts of Liberation Theology*. Maryknoll: Orbis, 1993.

Sobrino, Jon. *Christianity at the Crossroads: A Latin American Approach*. Maryknoll: Orbis, 1984.

———. *The Eye of the Needle: No Salvation Outside the Poor; a Prophetic Essay*. Maryknoll: Orbis, 2008.

———. *The Principle of Mercy: Taking the Crucified People from the Cross*. Maryknoll: Orbis, 1992.

———. 'Epilogue.' In *Getting the Poor Down From the Cross: Christology of Liberation*, edited by José María Vigil, 305-15. Cyberspace: Ecumenical Association of Third World Theologians, 2007. http://www.servicioskoinonia.org/LibrosDigitales/LDK/EATWOTGettingThePoorDownFull.pdf. Accessed July 12, 2011.

Social Development and Services Unit. 'History and Work of Klong Toey Community Centre.' Unpublished. Bangkok: Church of Christ in Thailand, 2005.

Sofield, Loughlan, Rosine Hammett, and Carroll Juliano. *Building Community: Christian, Caring, Vital.* Notre Dame: Ave Maria Press, 1998.

Soskice, Janet Martin. *Metaphor and Religious Language.* Oxford: Clarendon, 1985.

Speakman, Danielle. *Nothing but a Thief: The Street and Her Children.* Tonbridge: Sovereign Word, 2002.

Spence, Michael, Patricia Clarke Annez, and Robert M. Buckley, eds. *Urbanization and Growth: Commission on Growth and Development.* Washington: The World Bank, 2009.

Srinivas, Hari. 'Urban Squatters and Slums.' *Global Development Research Center.* http://www.gdrc.org/uem/squatters/squatters.html. Accessed January 15, 2007.

Stark, Rodney. *Cities of God: The Real Story of How Christianity Became an Urban Movement and Conquered Rome.* San Francisco: HarperCollins, 2006.

–––. *The Rise of Christianity: How the Obscure, Marginal Jesus Movement Became the Dominant Religious Force of the Western World in a Few Centuries.* San Francisco: HarperCollins, 1996.

Stewart, Robert B., ed. *The Resurrection of Jesus: John Dominic Crossan and N. T. Wright in Dialogue.* Minneapolis: Fortress Press, 2006.

Stibbe, Mark W. G. 'A British Appraisal.' *Journal of Pentecostal Theology* 4 (1994): 12.

Stott, John. *Christian Mission in the Modern World.* London: Falcon, 1975.

–––. *The Radical Disciple.* Nottingham: InterVarsity Press, 2010.

Sugden, Chris. 'Jesus Christ: Saviour and Liberator.' In *Sharing the Good News with the Poor*, edited by Bruce J. Nicholls and Beulah R. Woods. 86-94. Bangalore: Barker, 1996.

–––. 'The Land and the Environment in the Purposes of God: A Biblical Reflection with Special Reference to Romans 8:18-30.' *Transformation* 13 (1996): 8-9.

–––. 'Partnership.' *Transformation* 14 (1997): 28-29.

–––. *Seeking the Asian Face of Jesus: The Practice and Theology of Christian Social Witness in Indonesia and India, 1974-1996.* Oxford: Regnum Books, 1997.

–––. 'What Is Good About Good News to the Poor.' In *AD2000 and Beyond*, edited by Vinay Samuel and Chris Sugden, 56-81. Oxford: Regnum Bks, 1991.

Sugden, Chris, and David J. Bosch. 'From Partnership to Marriage: Consultation on the Relationship between Evangelism and Social Responsibility (CRESR).' *Missionalia* 10, no.2 (1982): 75-77.

Sukin, Kamol. 'Asbestos Can Cause Cancer but "It's Cheap": Official Sees "No Reason" for More Expensive Substitutes. *The Nation.* May 14, 2006. http://www.nationmultimedia.com/2006/05/14/headlines/headlines_30003982.php. Accessed January 15, 2007.

Sutter, K., and S. Sutter. *Keys to Church Planting Movements.* McKinleyville: Asteroidea Books, 2006.

Sutton, Jane. 'Telling It on a Mountain.' *Urbana: Intervarsity's Student Mission Conference.* http://www.urbana.org/articles?RecordId=343%20. Accessed December 21, 2010.

Swift, Richard. 'Lease on Life.' *New Internationalist* January/February 2006.

–––. 'Welcome to Squatter Town.' *New Internationalist* January/February 2006. http://www.newint.org/features/2006/01/01/introduction. Accessed February 6, 2007.

Taleb, Nassim Nicholas. *The Black Swan: The Impact of the Highly Improbable.* London: Penguin, 2007.

Taylor, John V. *The Go between God: The Holy Spirit and the Christian Mission.* New York: Oxford University Press, 1972.

Taylor, William, ed. *Global Missiology for the 21st Century: The Iguassu Dialogue.* Grand Rapids: Baker Academic, 2000.

Tennent, Timothy. *Theology in the Context of World Christianity: How the Global Church Is Influencing the Way We Think About and Discuss Theology.* Grand Rapids: Zondervan, 2007.

Teresa, Mother. *Heart of Joy.* Ann Arbor: Servant Books, 1987.

–––. *A Simple Path.* New York: Random House, 1995.

Teresa, Mother, and Brian Kolodiejchuk. *Come Be My Light: The Private Writings of the 'Saint of Calcutta'.* New York: Doubleday, 2007.

The Global Education Project. 'Earth: A Graphic Look at the State of the World.' *The Global Education Project*. http://www.theglobaleducationproject.org/earth/human-conditions.php. Accessed June 29, 2010.

The Joshua Project. 'What Is the 10/40 Window?' *The Joshua Project*. http://www.joshuaproject.net/10-40-window.php. Accessed December 20, 2010.

The Urban Working Group. 'The Keys to the City: Finding New Doorways to Urban Transformation - a Report and Recommendations (Draft: 2007).' *Transformational Development*. http://www.transformational-development.org/Ministry/TransDev2.nsf/A6748A23BB21C3F08825725700 707E73/$file/Urban%20R&D%20Report%20-%20Summary%20(Draft)%20-%20Jan%209,%20 2007.pdf. Accessed January 8, 2010.

Thompson, D. D. *John Wesley as a Social Reformer*. New York: Eaton and Mains, 1896.

Tibaijuka, Anna. 'Cities without Slums.' *United Nations Environment Programme*. http://www.unep.org/ourplanet/imgversn/161/tibaijuka.html. Accessed January 14, 2011.

Tiersma, Jude. 'What Does It Mean to Be Incarnational When We Are Not the Messiah?' In *God So Loves the City: Seeking a Theology for Urban Mission*, edited by Charles Van Engen and Jude Tiersma, 7-25. Monrovia: MARC, 1994.

Tinlin, Bryan. *Urban Poor and Public Policies in Thailand: An Assessment of the State's Implementation of Slum Relocation and Upgrading in Klong Toey District, Bangkok*. Toronto: York University Department of Geography, 1999.

Tolstoy, Leo. *Divine and Human and Other Stories*. London: Hodder and Stoughton, 2001.

Tooley, James. *The Beautiful Tree: A Personal Journey into How the World's Poorest People Are Educating Themselves*. Washington: Cato Institute, 2009.

Townsend, Craig. 'In Whose Interest? A Critical Approach to South East Asia's Urban Transportation Dynamics.' Doctor of Philosophy thesis. Perth: Murdoch University, 2003.

Tutu, Desmond. *No Future without Forgiveness*. London: Rider Books, 1999.

UN Habitat. 'The Challenge.' *UN-Habitat*. http://www.unhabitat.org/content.asp?typeid=19&catid=10&cid=928. Accessed August 11, 2010.

———. *The Challenge of Slums: Global Report on Human Settlements, 2003*. London: Earthscan, 2003.

———. 'A Cities without Slums Program in Morocco Set to Achieve Slum Free Targets by 2010.' *UN-Habitat*. http://www.unhabitat.org/content.asp?cid=2668&catid=491&typeid=3&subMenuId=0 &AllContent=1. Accessed August 23, 2010.

———. *Community Development Fund in Thailand: A Tool for Poverty Reduction and Affordable Housing*. Nairobi: UN-Habitat, 2009.

———. 'Fourth Session of the World Urban Forum Launched in Beijing.' *UN-Habitat* http://www.unhabitat.org/content.asp?cid=5675&catid=5&typeid=6&subMenuId=0. Accessed May 16, 2011.

———. *Housing Finance Mechanisms in Thailand*. Nairobi: UN-Habitat, 2008.

———. 'The Recife Declaration: Habitat II - 1996.' *UN-Habitat*. http://ww2.unhabitat.org/programmes/ifup/documents/rde.rtf. Accessed July 29, 2007.

———. *Slum Dwellers Could Double by 2030: Millennium Development Goal Could Fall Short*. Nairobi: UN-Habitat, 2007.

———. *State of the World's Cities 2006/2007*. London: Earthscan, 2006.

———. *State of the World's Cities 2008/2009: Harmonious Cities*. London: Earthscan, 2008.

———. *Survey of Slum and Squatter Settlements*. Dublin: Tycooly International Publications, 1982.

UNHCR. 'Refugee Figures.' *United Nations High Commission for Refugees*. http://www.unhcr.org/pages/49c3646c1d.htm. Accessed June 28, 2011.

UNICEF. 'Conditions for Children in Urban Areas.' In *Quest for Hope in the Slum Community*, edited by Scott Bessenecker, 197-218. Milton Keynes: Authentic Books, 2005.

United Nations. 'Slum Populations as Percentage of Urban.' *United Nation.s* http://data.un.org/Data.aspx?d=MDG&f=seriesRowID:710#f_9. Accessed August 22, 2010.

———. *World Urbanization Prospects—the 2009 Revision*. New York: United Nations, 2010.

———. 'World Urbanization Prospects: The 2007 Revision Population Database.' *United Nations.* http://esa.un.org/unup. Accessed September 6, 2010.

———. *World Urbanization Prospects: The 2009 Revision.* New York: United Nations, 2009.

United Nations Development Programme. 'Goal Seven: Ensure Environmental Sustainability.' *United Nations* http://www.undp.org/mdg/goal7.shtml. Accessed August 9, 2010.

United States Senate. 'S. Doc. 105-24: The United States Senate Committee on Agriculture, Nutrition, and Forestry 1825-1998.' *Access.* http://www.access.gpo.gov/congress/senate/sen_agriculture/ch5.html. Accessed January 13, 2007.

UN Millennium Project Taskforce. *A Home in the City.* London: Earthscan, 2005.

Urban Neighbours of Hope, www.unoh.org.

UN Taskforce Improving the Lives of Slum Dwellers. *A Home in the City.* London: Earthscan, 2005.

Urban Advance. 'Belo Horizonte.' *World Vision.* Unpublished.

Urban Leadership Foundation. 'Encarnação Alliance of Urban Poor Movement Leaders.' *Urban Leaders.* http://www.urbanleaders.org/encarnacao2_joomla. Accessed January 10, 2010.

Urban Poor Asia. 'The Poor in Bangkok City.' *Asian Coalition for Housing Rights.* http://www.achr.net/th_overview.htm. Accessed August 22, 2010.

Usavagovitwong, Nattawut, and Prayong Posriprasert. 'Urban Poor Housing Development on Bangkok's Waterfront: Securing Tenure, Supporting Community Processes.' *Environment and Urbanization* 18 no. 2 (2006): 523-36.

Valeri, Mark, and Douglas A. Hicks, eds. *Global Neighbors: Christian Faith and the Moral Obligation in Today's Economy.* Grand Rapids: Eerdmans, 2008.

Van Engen, Charles. *God's Missionary People: Rethinking the Purpose of the Local Church.* Grand Rapids: Baker, 2001.

Van Engen, Charles, and Jude Tiersma, eds. *God So Loves the City: Seeking a Theology for Urban Mission.* Monrovia: MARC, 1994.

van Gennep, Arnold. *Anthropology and Ethnography: The Rites of Passage.* London: Routledge, 2004 (1960).

Vanier, Jean. *Becoming Human.* London: Darton, Longman and Todd, 2003.

———. *Community and Growth.* London: St Pauls Publications, 1989.

———. *Drawn into the Mystery of Jesus through the Gospel of John.* Toronto: Novalis, 2004.

Vatican. 'The Catechism of the Catholic Church.' *Vatican* http://www.vatican.va/archive/ccc_css/archive/catechism/p123a9p2.htm. Accessed August 18, 2011.

Villafañe, Eldin. *Beyond Cheap Grace: A Call to Radical Discipleship, Incarnation, and Justice.* Grand Rapids: Eerdmans, 2006.

Viratkapan, Vichai. 'Slum Relocation Projects in Bangkok: What Has Contributed to Their Success or Failure?' *Habitat International* 30 (2006): 157-74.

Visser, Martin. *Conversion Growth of Protestant Churches in Thailand.* Zoetermeer, Netherlands: Uitgeverij Boekencentrum, 2008.

Volf, Miroslav. *Exclusion and Embrace: A Theological Exploration of Identity, Otherness and Reconciliation.* Nashville: Abingdon Press, 1996.

———. *Free of Charge: Giving and Forgiving in a Culture Stripped of Grace.* Grand Rapids: Zondervan, 2005.

Wagner, C. Peter. *Church Growth and the Whole Gospel: A Biblical Mandate.* Bromley: MARC Europe, 1981.

Wainwright, Geoffrey. *Lesslie Newbigin: A Theological Life.* Oxford: Oxford University Press, 2000.

Warren, Rick. 'The One Campaign: An Advocacy Letter from Rick Warren.' *BeliefNet.* http://www.beliefnet.com/story/168/story_16821_1.html. Accessed January 29, 2007.

———. *The Purpose Driven Life.* Grand Rapids: Zondervan, 2002.

Weber, Max. *The Protestant Ethic and the Spirit of Capitalism.* New York: Charles Scribner's Sons, 1950.

Webster, Douglas. 'Affordable Housing Delivery in Thailand: A Contextual Assessment.' *GH Bank Housing Journal* 2009: 72-82.
Weerasingha, Tissa. *The Cross and the Bo Tree: Communicating the Gospel to Buddhists*. Taichung: Asia Theological Association, 1989.
Westcott, Brooke Foss. *Gospel of the Resurrection: Thoughts on Its Relation to Reason and History*. London: MacMillan and Co, 1866.
———. *The Incarnation and Common Life*. London: MacMillan and Co, 1908.
Williams, Iso. *The Receptive Ear: Communicating Biblical Truths in Thai World Views*. Columbia: Columbia International University, 1995.
Williams, Rowan. *Silence and Honey Cakes: The Wisdom of the Desert*. Oxford: Lion Hudson, 2003.
Wilson-Hartgrove, Jonathan. *God's Economy: Redefining Health and Wealth Gospel*. Grand Rapids: Zondervan, 2009.
———. *The Wisdom of Stability: Rooting Faith in a Mobile Culture*. Brewster: Paraclete Press, 2010.
Wimber, John. *Power Evangelism: Signs and Wonders Today*. London: Hodder and Stoughton, 1986.
Wink, Walter. *The Human Being: Jesus and the Enigma of the Son of Man*. Minneapolis: Fortress Press, 2002.
———. *The Powers That Be: Theology for a New Millennium*. New York: Doubleday, 1999.
Winslow, Lance. *Action Plan for the Nairobi Slums*. Nairobi: World Think Tank, 2007.
Winter, Ralph D. 'Protestant Mission Societies: The American Experience.' *Missiology* 7 no. 2 (1979): 139-178.
Winter, Ralph D. 'The Two Structures of God's Redemptive Mission.' In *Perspectives on the World Christian Movement: A Reader*, edited by Ralph D Winter and Steven C Hawthorne, 244-53. Pasadena: William Carey Library, 2009.
Wittberg, Patricia. *The Rise and Fall of Catholic Religious Orders: A Social Movement Perspective*. New York: State University of New York Press, 1994.
World Christian News. 'Statistics: The 21st Century World.' *World Christian News*. http://home.snu.edu/~hculbert/world.htm. Accessed December 22, 2010.
World Convention. 'National Profiles: USA.' *World Convention*. http://www.worldconvention.org/country.php?c=US. Accessed December 22, 2010.
World Vision International. '2004 Annual Review.' *World Vision International* http://www.wvi.org/wvi/wviweb.nsf/webmaindocs/1C72CA5128025B288825737C00756949?OpenDocument. Accessed January 8, 2010.
———. 'Putting Children First in the Highlands of Peru', *World Vision Australia*. http://www.worldvision.com.au/Issues/Transforming_Lives___Child_Sponsorship/WhatIsOurResponse/Putting_children_first_in_the_highlands_of_Pe.aspx. Accessed December 22, 2010.
Worldwatch Institute. *Vital Signs 2006-2007: The Trends That Are Shaping Our Future*. New York: W. W. Norton and Company, 2007.
Wright, Christopher J. H. *The Mission of God: Unlocking the Bible's Grand Narrative*. Downers Grove: InterVarsity, 2006.
———. *Old Testament Ethics for the People of God*. Leicester: InterVarsity, 2004.
———. *Salvation Belongs to Our God*. Nottingham: InterVarsity, 2008.
———. *The Uniqueness of Jesus*. London: Monarch Books, 2001.
Wright, N. T. *After You Believe: Why Christian Character Matters*. New York: HarperOne, 2010.
———. *The Climax of the Covenant: Christ and the Law in Pauline Theology*. Minneapolis: Fortress Press, 1993.
———. *The Crown and the Fire: Meditations on the Cross and the Life of the Spirit*. Grand Rapids: Eerdmans, 1992.
———. *Following Jesus: Biblical Reflections on Discipleship*. Grand Rapids: Eerdmans, 1994.
———. *Jesus and the Victory of God: Christian Origins and the Question of God, Volume Two*. Minneapolis: Fortress Press, 1996.

———. *The New Testament and the People of God: Christian Origins and the Question of God, Volume One*. London: SPCK, 1993.

———. *Paul in Fresh Perspective*. Minneapolis: Fortress Press, 2005.

———. *The Resurrection of the Son of God: Christian Origins and the Question of God, Volume Three*. Minneapolis: Fortress Press, 2003.

———. *Simply Christian*. London: SPCK, 2006.

———. *Small Faith, Great God: Biblical Faith for Today's Christians*. Downers Grove: InterVarsity Press, 2010.

———. *Surprised by Hope: Rethinking Heaven, the Resurrection, and the Mission of the Church*. New York: HarperOne, 2008.

Wuest, Kenneth. *Studies in the Vocabulary of the Greek New Testament*. Grand Rapids: Eerdmans, 1945.

Yamamori, Tetsunao, and Kim-Kwong Chan. *Witnesses to Power: Stories of God's Quiet Work in a Changing China*. Waynesboro: Authentic, 2000.

Yamamori, Tetsunao, and Donald Miller. *Global Pentecostalism: The New Face of Christian Social Engagement* London: University of California, 2007.

Yamamori, Tetsunao, Bryant Myers, and Kenneth Luscombe, eds. *Serving with the Urban Poor*. Monrovia: MARC, 1998.

Yoder, John Howard. *The Politics of Jesus: Vicit Agnus Noster*. 2nd ed. Grand Rapids: Eerdmans, 1994.

Yoder, John Howard, Theodore J. Koontz, and Andy Alexis-Baker. *Christian Attitudes to War, Peace and Revolution*. Grand Rapids: Brazos, 2009.

Yong, Amos. 'From Azusa Street to the Bo Tree and Back: Strange Babblings and Interreligious Interpretations in Pentecostal Encounter with Buddhism.' In *The Spirit of the World: Emerging Pentecostal Theologies in Global Contexts*. Edited by Veli-Matti Kärkkäinen, 203-226. Grand Rapids: Eerdmans, 2009.

Yohannan, K. P. *Revolution in World Missions*. Carrollton: Gospel For Asia, 2004.

Yun, Koo Dong. 'Pentecostalism from Below: Minjung Liberation and Asian Pentecostal Theology.' In *The Spirit of the World: Emerging Pentecostal Theologies in Global Contexts*. Edited by Veli-Matti Kärkkäinen, 89-114. Grand Rapids: Eerdmans, 2009.

Yunus, Muhammad. *Banker to the Poor: The Story of the Grameen Bank*. London: Aurum Press, 2003.

———. *Creating a World without Poverty: Social Business and the Future of Capitalism*. New York: PublicAffairs, 2007.

Zahniser, A. H. Mathias. *Symbol and Ceremony: Making Disciples Across Cultures*. Monrovia: MARC, 1997.

Zdero, Rad, ed. *Nexus: The World House Church Movement Reader*. Pasadena: William Carey Library, 2007.

Zimmermann, Wolf-Dieter, and Ronald Gregor Smith, eds. *I Knew Dietrich Bonhoeffer*. New York: Fontana Books, 1973.

www.ingramcontent.com/pod-product-compliance
Lightning Source LLC
Chambersburg PA
CBHW070127080526
44586CB00015B/1588